The United States and the Vietnam War

Significant Scholarly Articles

Series Editor

Walter L. Hixson
University of Akron

A Garland Series

Series Contents

The Lessons and Legacies of the Vietnam War

Edited with introductions by

Walter L. Hixson
University of Akron

GARLAND PUBLISHING, INC.
A MEMBER OF THE TAYLOR & FRANCIS GROUP
New York & London
2000

Library of Congress Cataloging-in-Publication Data

The lessons and legacies of the Vietnam War / edited with introductions by Walter L. Hixson

p. cm. — (The United States and the Vietnam War. Significant scholarly articles ; 5)

Includes bibliographical references.

ISBN 0-8153-3535-0 (alk. paper) — ISBN 0-8153-3530-X (6 v. set)

1. Vietnamese Conflict, 1961–1975—United States. 2. Vietnamese Conflict, 1961–1975—Influence. 3. Vietnamese Conflict, 1961–1975—Veterans—United States. 4. United States—History—1969– I. Hixson, Walter L. II. Series.

DS558.L45 2000
959.704'3373—dc21 00-030857

Printed on acid-free, 250-year-life paper
Manufactured in the United States of America

5000113307

UH
University of
Hertfordshire

WITHDRAWN

Contents

Series Introduction

These six volumes focus on the history and legacies of the Vietnam War on the basis of the best scholarly articles. The six volumes analyze, respectively, the origins of the Indochina wars; military strategy; the role of prominent individuals; the antiwar movement; the lessons of Vietnam; and representations of the war in popular culture. A brief introduction accompanies each volume.

The six volumes address most of the key issues pertaining to the history of the Indochina conflict. The articles, culled from journals published over a span of nearly 50 years, reflect the divergent interpretations of more than 100 authors. The brief narrative history that appears in each volume provides context and a ready resource for the reader. Taken as whole, the series offers a comprehensive source for students, specialists, and the interested public.

* * * * * *

The United States and the Vietnam War: A Brief Narrative History

The war in Southeast Asia, which claimed millions of Asian and American casualties and left the United States deeply divided, was inextricably linked to the Cold War. Indeed, the Vietnam War, engulfing all of Indochina (comprising Vietnam, Laos, and Cambodia), was the most violent and sustained conflict of the Cold War era.

European colonialism lay at the root of the Vietnam conflict. France established its control over Vietnam in the mid-nineteeth century in a quest for profits and world influence. Resistance evolved until Vietnamese nationalists, led by Ho Chi Minh, pressed for independence in the aftermath of World War I (1914–1918). While France clung to its empire, Ho embraced Marxism-Leninism and built a determined following. Ho's organization, the Vietminh, prepared to assume power after the Second World War, which had left France greatly weakened. Partly based on a racist contempt for the Vietnamese, however, French officials still believed they could reassert control over Indochina.

THE FIRST INDOCHINA WAR (1946–54)

War erupted in 1946 and lasted until Vietnam defeated France at the battle of Dienbienphu in 1954. In the settlement at Geneva ending the First Indochina War, France agreed to withdraw. Ho, supported by the Soviet Union and the People's Republic of China, held power over North Vietnam. The diplomats in Geneva agreed that there would be elections in 1956 to reunify Vietnam as an independent nation. The Cold War, however, intervened. The United States did not sign the Geneva Accords and, though it pledged not to disrupt them, in fact proceeded to undermine the planned elections. Encouraged by Washington, a mandarin elite and former monk, Ngo Dinh Diem, proclaimed the existence of an independent government based in Saigon, "South Vietnam."

The United States, which had funneled millions of dollars into the French war effort, now pledged millions more to Diem's government. Beginning in the late 1950s, a revolutionary movement, the National Liberation Front (NLF) — indigenous to South Vietnam but supported by Ho — launched a guerrilla war against the Saigon regime. Diem's government could overcome neither the rebels nor its own internal enemies. Plagued by the NLF guerrillas, sectarian violence, and his own ineptitude, Diem fell in a U.S.-sanctioned military coup in November 1963. President John F. Kennedy, himself assassinated only three weeks after Diem's murder by the South Vietnamese army, left a legacy of 16,700 U.S. advisors in the country and a commitment to contain communism in Southeast Asia.

JOHNSON TAKES COMMAND

Lyndon Johnson, Kennedy's successor, had no intention of abandoning the effort in Southeast Asia. Johnson recalled how the fallout from the "loss" of China in 1949 had destroyed fellow Democrat Harry S. Truman's presidency. He vowed that no nation would fall to communism on his watch. Yet a succession of military leaders failed to establish a stable government in Saigon. The NLF, meanwhile, continued to gain momentum. Not all of the southern Vietnamese revolutionaries were communists, to be sure, but they opposed the Saigon government as a puppet regime of the United States — a continuation of foreign control that Vietnam had been struggling to overcome since the establishment of French colonialism.

As the southern insurgency gained more and more ground in South Vietnam, Johnson decided that only direct U.S. military intervention could reverse a deteriorating situation that threatened to confront him with the dreaded charge of losing a country to communism. Johnson, who had been awaiting an opportunity to gain broader congressional authority to wage war against the southern insurgents, achieved his aim by misrepresenting a naval clash in the Gulf of Tonkin in August 1964. The subsequent Tonkin Gulf Resolution, passed by both houses of Congress with only two dissenting votes in the Senate, gave Johnson a blank check to take any and all actions he deemed necessary to defend the United States against "aggression." The President immediately launched retaliatory bombing raids against North Vietnam. The southern insurgency, backed by Ho's government in Hanoi, stepped up its resistance in the South and branded the United States the aggressor. The war was on.

In February 1965, using a guerrilla sapper attack on a U.S. base in Pleiku as a pretext to implement a planned escalation, Johnson ordered more retaliatory air strikes that eventually became Rolling Thunder, a regular campaign of aerial bombardment. Soon bombs rained not only on Vietnam, but on guerrilla sanctuaries and supply lines, as well as other communist forces, in neighboring Laos and Cambodia. Both of those nations found themselves sucked into the vortex of war. Washington was fighting an increasingly unlimited "limited war" in Indochina.

THE DEPLOYMENT OF COMBAT TROOPS

U.S. national security elites concluded that the NLF and North Vietnam would abandon their efforts under the weight of the enormous number of casualties that could be inflicted by U.S. firepower. Hence Johnson authorized U.S. combat troops to embark on "search and destroy" missions aimed at finding the guerrillas and killing them. Under this strategy, gauging success depended on the number of enemy dead bodies that could be amassed. In less than a year the United States had dramatically Americanized the Vietnam conflict. Extrication years later would prove to be a far more wrenching ordeal than the original escalation.

For years the United States pummeled Indochina with a total tonnage of bombs that exceeded that expended by all belligerents in all theaters of World War II. Washington also employed Agent Orange and other defoliants — later determined to have caused cancer in thousands of U.S. troops and countless villagers — in an effort to remove natural vegetation which provided the southern rebels with cover. In the face of punishing U.S. military power, the determined Vietnamese continued their struggle and even executed a surprise uprising, the Tet Offensive of January 1968, in an effort to win the war. Launched simultaneously in hundreds of hamlets, towns, and cities across South Vietnam, Tet failed to achieve its ultimate objective of igniting a collapse of the Saigon government. Massive U.S. military might eventually put down the offensive, which caused widespread destruction in an increasingly ugly and inconclusive war. The NLF infrastructure suffered heavy losses, though increasing numbers of North Vietnamese regular army troops entered the southern mountains and jungles to replace them.

It had long since been clear that U.S. bombing could not bring an end to the war. Millions of Americans had erupted in protest, especially in the wake of Tet when the press published reports that Johnson was considering sending 200,000 additional troops to Vietnam. Already more than half a million Americans were fighting in Indochina, with more every year coming home in body bags. The war was proving not only divisive, but alarmingly expensive as well. While the fighting and bombing continued, a defeated LBJ scaled back U.S. involvement, opened neogitations, and abandoned his own plans to seek reelection.

NIXON'S STRATEGY OF EXTRICATION

Most Americans wanted out of Vietnam but did not want to lose a war to a communist government backed by China and the Soviet Union. Richard Nixon, elected President in 1968, promised to achieve an honorable settlement. Nixon began systematically to withdraw U.S. troops, but he authorized the most intense bombing campaign in history while seeking a negotiated settlement.

The antiwar movement, restrained in Nixon's first year, exploded anew in the spring of 1970 when Nixon announced that U.S. troops would fight in Cambodia. At Kent State University in northeast Ohio, National Guard units stunned the nation by opening fire on protesters, killing four students. America was coming apart over the Vietnam War.

Nixon and his chief foreign policy aide, Henry A. Kissinger, finally negotiated a peace settlement in Paris in January 1973. U.S. prisoners of war, some of whom had been detained for almost a decade, returned home, but North Vietnamese troops were allowed to stay in place in South Vietnam. In reality, the Paris agreement offered no solution to the conflict, only an opportunity for America to get out. The Saigon government, headed by Nguyen Van Thieu, bitterly opposed the agreement, fearing accurately that the U.S. pullout would lead to its own rapid demise.

THE COLLAPSE OF SOUTH VIETNAM

That is precisely what happened. Sickened by the long, divisive, and indecisive war, most Americans did not even want to hear the word Vietnam spoken again after the Paris agreement. Congress turned sharply against the war, repealing the Tonkin Gulf Resolution in 1971, cutting off money for bombing, and in 1973 passing the War Powers Act, legislation limiting the President's ability to make war without eventual direct congressional authorization.

With the Nixon administration destroyed by the Watergate scandal, a series of illegalities that forced the President to resign in August 1974, no U.S. response materialized to the final offensive launched by North Vietnam in 1975. North Vietnamese forces steamrolled through cities and the countryside on the way to Saigon, which they captured in April. The South Vietnamese regime, the Achilles heel of the American war effort, collapsed in a heap. Millions of South Vietnamese frantically left the country for the next several years. Many of these "boat people" perished in rickety craft on the high seas or fell prey to pirates. Others languished in refugee camps throughout Southeast Asia. The United States admitted millions of Vietnamese, Cambodians, and Laotian mountain dwellers who had supported U.S. efforts.

While the Hanoi government did not launch a bloodbath, the fanatical communists who took over Cambodia, the Khmer Rouge, engaged in genocide against their own people, killing as many as three million. The communists assumed power in Laos as well, but no other Southeast Asian states adopted communist governments. The much-feared domino effect never transpired. In fact, the communist states turned on one another. By 1969 the Soviet and Chinese communist regimes were on the brink of war — with each other. Ten years later, the communist governments of Vietnam and China fought in a brief but bloody conflict over a Vietnamese attack into Cambodia against the Khmer Rouge.

The consensus in the United States was that the Vietnam War had been a colossal mistake. More than 58,000 Americans, most of them very young men, died in Indochina. Hundreds of thousands more returned home with physical or psychological wounds. The nation as a whole struggled for decades to recover from a foreign policy debacle that, however tragic, had flowed logically from U.S. Cold War perceptions. As for Indochina itself, with millions dead and maimed and ideological divisions still rife, generations would be required to recover from one of the twentieth century's longest and bloodiest wars.

Volume Introduction

The Vietnam War generated controversy long after the guns went silent in Southeast Asia. At first, a consensus emerged that the war had been a tragic "mistake" in U.S. foreign policy. But with the revival of the Cold War under President Ronald W. Reagan — who proclaimed that the Vietnam conflict had been a "noble cause" — revisionists began to reinterpret the history and meaning of the war. As a new conflict emerged in Central America, some argued that the lesson of Vietnam was to avoid direct involvement in such struggles, while others insisted that the United States could not afford to be paralyzed by a "Vietnam syndrome," which equated military intervention with failure.

Among the additional lessons and legacies of the war was its impact on the men who fought in Vietnam. For complex reasons, explored by authors in this volume, powerful myths about Vietnam veterans emerged in postwar American culture.

While the Vietnam War was, of course, a product of American foreign policy, the conflict had a profound impact on domestic life. Not only did the antiwar movement convulse U.S. society, but the war had a dramatic economic impact as well. In "The Economic Crisis of 1968 and the Waning of the 'American Century,'" Robert M. Collins analyzes the devastating economic consequences of Lyndon Johnson's efforts to have boths "guns and butter": domestic prosperity and a foreign war simultaneously.

If one lesson of the war was its high cost in economic terms, another was the danger of investing so heavily in a client whose culture the United States understood poorly. In "People's Quite Apart," George C. Herring examines the gulf that divided Americans and their clients in Saigon, men who came to resent American heavy-handedness yet proved helpless against their adversaries when the Americans finally pulled out of Vietnam.

The overwhelming majority of Americans expressed relief when the last U.S. forces departed under terms of the 1973 Paris Agreement. After the fall of Saigon in April 1975, there was little witch-hunting at home. Americans were sick of Vietnam and most agreed the war had been a tragic mistake.

That view began to change in the late 1970s, however, as President Jimmy Carter, who had condemned the nation's "inordinate fear of communism," found himself embroiled in foreign policy crises in Iran and with the Soviet invasion of Afghanistan. Ronald Reagan swamped Carter in a 1980 presidential campaign based in part on a call for renewed commitment to waging the Cold War and offering no apologies for Vietnam. Reagan's triumph reflected a wave of revisionism, or rethinking of the war as a just cause that had been lost only because of a lack of the will to win.

In "The 'Vietnam Syndrome' and American Foreign Policy," George C. Herring, a leading expert on the Vietnam conflict, calls attention to a debate ignited by Reagan and his first Secretary of State, Alexander Haig. Both argued that the Vietnam War had been a just cause rather than a mistake and that defeat in Vietnam had been self-inflicted. Moreover, the Reagan foreign policy team reignited the Cold War on several fronts, arguing that the Carter administration had been weak and even paralyzed in its handling of foreign policy as a result of the previous failure in Vietnam. This paralysis was the much-feared malaise known as the "Vietnam syndrome.

One of the first theaters of action in the Reagan Cold War revival was Central America. The battle in El Salvador and Nicaragua between leftists and rightists in the early 1980s set off a debate in the United States over the proper lessons of Vietnam. In "Historical Memory and Illusive Victories," Thomas G. Paterson averred that the Reagan administration was making the same mistakes in Central America as Washington had made in Vietnam by exaggerating the external communist threat while paying insufficient attention to local forces in the essentially civil conflicts in El Salvador and Nicaragua.

In "The Last War, the Next War, and the New Revisionists," Walter LaFeber analyzes the "remarkable rewriting of the Vietnam War's history." By shifting the blame for failure in Vietnam from the national security establishment to the antiwar movement, LaFeber charges, the new revisionists were attempting to remove restraints that might have been imposed by the Vietnam experience in the path of military intervention abroad, and most immediately in Central America.

To many, the dangers of an "imperial presidency" and a runaway "national security state" were among the lessons and legacies of Vietnam. Kenneth E. Sharpe argues in his article, however, that the phenomenon remained a powerful force despite the Vietnam experience. As the crisis in Central America in the 1980s demonstrated, U.S. foreign policy continued to reflect the pervasive influence of "a hard-to-control national security apparatus dedicated to maintaining U.S. hegemony and largely unchallenged by the post-Vietnam reforms."

Similarly, Kenneth S. Zagacki's article on presidential rhetoric after Vietnam reveals that the war had little impact on foreign policy discourse. Post-Vietnam presidential rhetoric reflected little evidence of introspection or of challenging some of the myths which had led to U.S. intervention. Depicting Vietnam as an aberration, presidents reasserted foundational myths and ideology that made future military conflicts more likely.

In "The Stab-in-the-Back Legend and the Vietnam War," Jeffrey P. Kimball analyzes the Reagan-era wave of Vietnam revisionism, especially the notion that the United States lost the Indochina war at home. Such "ersatz history" ignores the real reasons for American failure in Vietnam, argues Kimball, as part of a campaign to pursue an agenda of vilification of the antiwar movement, civilian control over the military, Democratic presidents, Congress, leftists, liberals, and the press.

In an article recalling his own experience in Vietnam, journalist Charles Mohr rejects the revisionist theme that negative media reporting undermined the U.S. war effort in Vietnam. Mohr admits that errors occurred, especially in reporting on the 1968 Tet Offensive, but that overall coverage of the conflict was sound. He concludes that journalists in a free society cannot be expected to embrace uncritically the official government version of events.

Oscar Patterson III's research suggests that television news coverage of the Vietnam War was not typically inflammatory and hence likely to turn the public against the conflict. Rather, a few atypical but undeniably sensational television events — such as a Buddhist monk immolating himself in 1963, or the street execution of a Vietcong suspect in 1968 — established the false perception that television covered the war in such a way as to promote public revulsion.

Clarence R. Wyatt's article on newspaper reporting on the war found no substantiation for charges of a powerful and antagonistic press challenging U.S. policy in Vietnam. Rather than being monolithic, newspaper coverage differed substantially and often supported the official U.S. government position on the war, as the government and military were able to exert influence by controling reporters' access to combat areas and to the flow of information.

After the war, the press did little for many years to combat one of the most enduring and irrational myths to come out of the Vietnam War: that U.S. prisoners of war were still being held in Southeast Asia years after the conflict. H. Bruce Franklin's article shatters the myth, first perpetrated by the Nixon administration. Hollywood producers soon discovered the profits inherent in films such as Missing in Action, which focused on heroic missions to free prisoners from a capitivity which, in reality, did not exist.

Films and literature also tended to perpetuate the stereotype that, because Vietnam was an unpopular war, returning Vietnam veterans suffered more than the veterans of previous wars. In "The Myth of the Troubled and Scorned Vietnam Veteran," Eric Dean argues that the experiences of returning Vietnam soliders actually were typical of the veterans of previous conflicts. Moreover, although the war was a shattering experience for many, Vietnam veterans enjoyed greater access to benefits than veterans of other wars and adjusted quite well, comparatively and on the whole, to civilian life. Along the same lines, James B. Jacobs and Dennis McNamara show in "Vietnam Veterans and the Agent Orange Controversy" how Vietnam veterans mobilized as a powerful political and legal lobby in an age of rights-conscious assertiveness.

Like Eric Dean, Gaines M. Foster adopts a comparative perspective, drawing parallels in this case between the United States and the post-Civil War American South. While the Vietnam War and the Civil War were quite distinct, one a foreign and the other an internecine conflict, both postwar societies grappled with similar issues: how to receive defeated veterans, how to reconcile former enemies, and how to come to grips with defeat.

The lessons, legacies, lives of veterans, and other issues continue to emerge as the Vietnam War remains a compelling subject for historians, journalists, and political scientists. In "Vietnam Reconsidered," Robert Divine shows how historical interpretation goes through cycles of change before a synthesis of initial and revisionist views emerges.

With respect to the Vietnam War, Divine finds some exceptions but in the end what emerged was a synthesis interpreting the war as neither evil nor justified, but as a great national tragedy.

In an even more in-depth analysis of the historical literature, or historiography, Gary R. Hess also concludes that a more complete understanding of the war is emerging. Conspiracy theories and "if only" this-and-such-had-been-done arguments have little lasting appeal, Hess argues. He adds that the Vietnamese side of the picture needs much greater development for a more complete history of the war.

In his analytical review article on three important books on Vietnam published in the mid-1980s, George C. Herring, the dean of Vietnam historians, identifies key interpretive issues on the history of the war. He also raises the major questions that have yet to be answered and offers an agenda for future historical research.

The Lessons and Legacies of the Vietnam War

The Economic Crisis of 1968 and the Waning of the "American Century"

ROBERT M. COLLINS

IN EARLY 1968, THE MOST SERIOUS ECONOMIC CRISIS since the Great Depression shook the Western world. The disruption exposed a variety of economic ills plaguing the U.S. and world economies, some of recent vintage but others with roots that reached back a decade or more. The problems, both long-term and short-run, were tightly intertwined, and they culminated in March in a speculative run on gold that *Time* magazine called "the largest gold rush in history, a frenetic speculative stampede that . . . threatened the Western world."[1]

Among policymakers in Washington, the mood was appropriately tense. "Everybody was just petrified," recalled Undersecretary of the Treasury Joseph W. Barr. "It was a hair-raising period in which we literally had to watch the gold markets day by day and hour by hour." At the National Security Council, Edward Fried, a specialist in international monetary affairs, feared "that this was not something that was any longer under control." President Lyndon B. Johnson's national security adviser, Walt W. Rostow, briefed the president on the stakes "at a most important moment in postwar history": a misstep, he wrote, "could set in motion a financial and trade crisis which would undo much that we have achieved in these fields in the past twenty years and endanger the prosperity and security of the Western world."[2]

It is one of the more intriguing features of the history of the 1960s that, despite its drama and apparent significance, the economic crisis of 1968 has been so completely lost to sight. Its eclipse began almost immediately. The basic issues involved in the crisis—the balance of payments, the gold exchange standard, international monetary affairs and the regime that administered them—were complex, and their esoteric nature was, to much of the public, both intimidating and incomprehensible. When *Time* ran a cover story on the crisis, it noted apologetically that "such subjects are often considered too complicated to have wide reader

I gratefully acknowledge the financial support of the University of Missouri Research Council (1993) and the Lyndon B. Johnson Foundation (1994) in the preparation of this essay. I am indebted to the All-UC Group in Economic History at the University of California (especially Michael Bernstein, Stephen Haber, Richard Musgrave, and Ed Perkins) for the opportunity to try out the basic ideas of the essay in a most congenial professional setting. Thanks also to Bruce Schulman and the other *AHR* referees for their incisive comments and helpful criticism.

[1] *Time* (March 22, 1968): 24.

[2] Joseph W. Barr Oral History Memoir (hereafter, OHM; all such references are to written transcripts), Tape 2, p. 8, Lyndon B. Johnson Presidential Library, Austin, Texas (hereafter, LBJL); Edward Fried OHM, p. 19, LBJL; Walt Rostow to LBJ, memo, March 15, 1968, National Security File, Memos to the President (Rostow), Box 31, LBJL.

appeal."[3] More important, the economic crisis was simply overwhelmed in the popular mind by the other events that gave the momentous year 1968 its particular historical resonance—the seizure of the U.S.S. *Pueblo*, the Tet Offensive, the New Hampshire primary and Johnson's withdrawal from the presidential campaign, Martin Luther King, Jr.'s assassination and the racial unrest that followed, Robert Kennedy's murder, campus rebellions, including the dramatic shutting down of New York's Columbia University, the Poor People's March on Washington, the presidential nominating conventions in Miami and Chicago, and the most violent fighting of the entire Vietnam War.

Thus overwhelmed at the time, the economic crisis of 1968 has since been similarly overshadowed in both popular and scholarly reconstructions of the 1960s. *Time*'s twentieth-anniversary retrospective on what it called the annus mirabilis of 1968 failed even to include the March crisis on its two-page time line.[4] The scholarly literature on the 1960s continues the omission. Studies that focus tightly on the year 1968 generally slight the gold crisis, and broad synthetic studies of the era often omit the economic turmoil of 1968 entirely.[5] Similarly, most economic histories pay little attention to the events of 1968.[6] The gap exists even in the excellent specialized scholarship that chronicles the rise and fall of the Bretton Woods

[3] *Time* (March 29, 1968): 13.

[4] *Time* (January 11, 1988): 16–27.

[5] Studies focusing on 1968 include David Caute, *The Year of the Barricades: A Journey through 1968* (New York, 1988); Charles Kaiser, *1968 in America: Music, Politics, Chaos, Counterculture, and the Shaping of a Generation* (New York, 1988); and Robert V. Daniels, *Year of the Heroic Guerrilla: World Revolution and Counterrevolution in 1968* (New York, 1989). Broad studies of the 1960s include William L. O'Neill, *Coming Apart: An Informal History of America in the 1960s* (Chicago, 1971); Godfrey Hodgson, *America in Our Time* (Garden City, N.Y., 1976); Allen Matusow, *The Unraveling of America: A History of Liberalism in the 1960s* (New York, 1984); Todd Gitlin, *The Sixties: Years of Hope, Days of Rage* (New York, 1987); Kim McQuaid, *The Anxious Years: America in the Vietnam-Watergate Era* (New York, 1989); John Morton Blum, *Years of Discord: American Politics and Society, 1961–1974* (New York, 1991); and David Farber, *The Age of Great Dreams: America in the 1960s* (New York, 1994).

Lyndon Baines Johnson, *The Vantage Point: Perspectives of the Presidency, 1963–1969* (New York, 1971), devotes considerable attention to the crisis of 1968 and its antecedents, but the credibility gap that compromised LBJ's presidency seems to have dogged him into history as well. In general, scholars have failed to follow his lead. A significant exception is Irwin Unger and Debi Unger, *Turning Point, 1968* (New York, 1988), reissued as *America in the 1960s* (St. James, N.Y., 1993), which gives perceptive attention to the 1968 gold crisis. Irving Bernstein, *Guns or Butter: The Presidency of Lyndon Johnson* (New York, 1996), published when the present essay was in press, provides a splendid account of tax policy but neglects the several other dimensions and the policy consequences of the 1968 developments.

[6] See, for example, Robert Aaron Gordon, *Economic Instability and Growth: The American Record* (New York, 1974); Herbert Stein, *Presidential Economics: The Making of Economic Policy from Roosevelt to Reagan and Beyond* (New York, 1984); Bernard D. Nossiter, *Fat Years and Lean: The American Economy since Roosevelt* (New York, 1990); Tom Kemp, *The Climax of Capitalism: The US Economy in the Twentieth Century* (London, 1990); and Joseph Finkelstein, *The American Economy: From the Great Crash to the Third Industrial Revolution* (Arlington Heights, Ill., 1991). A recent journalistic exception is Hobart Rowen, *Self-Inflicted Wounds: From LBJ's Guns and Butter to Reagan's Voodoo Economics* (New York, 1994), 3–39. There are, additionally, two first-rate essays on economic policy in the Johnson years, but neither focuses on the crisis of 1968. However, both have informed the present article in important ways and remain essential starting points for any consideration of the political economy of the 1960s. See Donald F. Kettl, "The Economic Education of Lyndon Johnson: Guns, Butter, and Taxes," in *The Johnson Years*, Volume 2: *Vietnam, the Environment, and Science*, Robert A. Divine, ed. (Lawrence, Kan., 1987), 54–78; and Burton I. Kaufman, "Foreign Aid and the Balance-of-Payments Problem: Vietnam and Johnson's Foreign Economic Policy," in Divine, *Johnson Years*, 2: 79–109. The process of economic policymaking in the Johnson administration is described well in James E. Anderson and Jared E. Hazelton, *Managing Macroeconomic Policy: The Johnson Presidency* (Austin, Tex., 1986).

international monetary regime. In these studies, the problem is relative neglect rather than complete omission, with the 1968 crisis serving mainly as a prelude to the suspension of dollar convertibility in 1971 and the institution of a new regime of floating exchange rates in 1973, and a not terribly significant prelude at that.[7]

The present essay seeks to return the 1968 economic crisis to the historiographical discussion of that pivotal year and the era surrounding it. It is important to do so for several reasons. First, the episode serves as a frame through which we can view with unusual clarity the interplay of forces that determined the shape of the national and world political economy, as the postwar economic regime and the economic golden age it had engendered in the United States came to a close. The crisis marked the beginning of the end of America's postwar economic boom and the initial recasting of the postwar order to accommodate an emergent, more troubled economic reality. To analyze the crisis is to begin to understand how and why that transition occurred.

Second and equally important, the crisis figured significantly in the most important political and public-policy decisions of the time. The ideology driving the Kennedy and Johnson presidencies was an amalgam of growth economics and government activism both at home and abroad that I have elsewhere labeled "growth liberalism."[8] Growth liberalism sought to update the nation's still potent reform tradition for the era of affluence, influence, and optimism well captured in Henry Luce's prescient conceit, the "American Century." But, by the late 1960s, growth liberalism's combination of growth-inducing tax cuts, an escalating war in Vietnam, and increased social spending at home had overstrained economic institutions and capabilities. The economic crisis of 1968 provided irrefutable proof of that strain and figured prominently in the decisions to cap U.S. escalation in Vietnam and rein in the Great Society initiatives at the top of LBJ's presidential agenda. Those decisions—and the problems that elicited them—left growth liberalism in disarray and the American Century in retreat.

Finally and most broadly, to illuminate these events and developments, their interconnections, and their consequences is to assert the significance of political economy for an understanding of the 1960s. At a time when the record of the 1960s is understood largely in terms of political protest and cultural rebellion, and when both political and economic history are more generally overshadowed by other scholarly approaches, it may be salutary to reaffirm that in history, as in the present, political economy still matters.

[7] Alfred E. Eckes, Jr., *A Search for Solvency: Bretton Woods and the International Monetary System, 1941–1971* (Austin, Tex., 1975); Fred L. Block, *The Origins of International Economic Disorder: A Study of United States International Monetary Policy from World War II to the Present* (Berkeley, Calif., 1977); David P. Calleo, *The Imperious Economy* (Cambridge, Mass., 1982); John S. Odell, *U.S. International Monetary Policy: Markets, Power, and Ideas as Sources of Change* (Princeton, N.J., 1982); and Joanne Gowa, *Closing the Gold Window: Domestic Politics and the End of Bretton Woods* (Ithaca, N.Y., 1983). The specialized study that devotes the closest attention to the "great gold rush of 1967–1968" is Robert Solomon, *The International Monetary System, 1945–1981*, updated edn. (New York, 1982). Solomon participated in much that he analyzes in his capacity as an official at the Federal Reserve Board. His treatment focuses tightly (and penetratingly) on the systemic aspects of the crisis, with less attention than the present essay to the domestic political context and consequences of events.

[8] Robert M. Collins, "Growth Liberalism in the Sixties: Great Societies at Home and Grand Designs Abroad," in *The Sixties: From Memory to History*, David Farber, ed. (Chapel Hill, N.C., 1994), 11–44.

THE ECONOMIC CRISIS OF 1968 was dramatic but essentially no surprise. What made the crisis so daunting, and so difficult to resolve, was not its suddenness but rather the way it tied together a number of serious problems that fed off one another in a perverse synergy. The most deeply rooted such problem concerned the United States' chronic balance-of-payments deficit.

The immediate context for the balance-of-payments difficulty extended back in time to the gathering of seven hundred delegates at the Mount Washington Hotel in Bretton Woods, New Hampshire, in 1944. The Bretton Woods conference created the International Monetary Fund (IMF) and the World Bank, erecting on that foundation a new monetary system that would order the world economy for over a quarter-century. The Bretton Woods regime outlawed discriminatory currency practices and exchange restrictions and established pegged exchange rates. In practice, the U.S. dollar was pegged to gold at $35 an ounce, and all other IMF members then pegged their currencies to the dollar. The United States committed itself to exchange gold for dollars at the rate of $35 per ounce upon the demand of foreign governments; the other IMF members agreed to keep their currencies from deviating from their respective dollar parities by more than 1 percent in either direction. The IMF administered an international fund to provide short-term credit for the financing of balance-of-payments deficits, with the understanding that fundamental (that is, large and chronic) deficits might legitimately occasion a change in par value. The overall result of the Bretton Woods innovations was a system based on two major forms of international money—gold and foreign exchange, mostly U.S. dollars and British sterling.[9]

The United States began to suffer chronic balance-of-payments deficits early on under the new order, as four years of surpluses (1946–49) gave way in 1950 to a string of deficits that ran into the 1960s (with the exception of 1957, when the unusual impact of the Suez Crisis helped generate a surplus).[10] At first, the U.S. deficits seemed benign, since they were relatively small and appeared to have the salutary effect of pumping dollars into an international economy troubled since the end of World War II by a shortage of dollars, the currency needed by the rest of the world for the purchase of U.S. goods for postwar reconstruction. But, by the end of the 1950s, the deficits began to appear more ominous to technicians, academics, and policymakers alike as they grew in size.

Basic social, political, and economic trends contributed to the growth of the U.S. balance-of-payments deficit. The maturation of America's own consumer culture made tourism an industry, and spending by American tourists abroad contributed increasingly to the payments deficit. The Cold War occasioned higher expenditures for foreign aid and heavy overseas military deployments. The economic resurgence of Europe and, to a lesser extent at this point, Japan increased both American imports from these areas and the outflow of capital, as overseas investment

[9] Introductions to the Bretton Woods regime include Eckes, *Search for Solvency*, chap. 6; Odell, *U.S. International Monetary Policy*, 80–88; Solomon, *International Monetary System*, chap. 2; and Michael D. Bordo, "The Bretton Woods International Monetary System: A Historical Overview," in *A Retrospective on the Bretton Woods System: Lessons for International Monetary Reform*, Bordo and Barry Eichengreen, eds. (Chicago, 1993), 3–85.

[10] Alvin H. Hansen, *The Postwar American Economy: Performance and Problems* (New York, 1964), 74–75.

opportunities became more appealing. President John F. Kennedy expressed the problem succinctly in early 1961: "The surplus of our exports over our imports, while substantial, has not been large enough to cover our expenditures for United States military establishments abroad, for capital invested abroad by private American businesses and for government economic assistance and loan programs."[11] By the early 1960s, the feared dollar shortage had become a dollar glut.

The dollar glut highlighted several tensions inherent in America's de facto role as central banker for the world under the Bretton Woods regime. First, the system came to depend on the outflow of dollars generated by U.S. balance-of-payments deficits to provide the increased liquidity needed to finance expanding world trade. But those same chronic deficits made foreign governments and central banks increasingly reluctant to hold more of the dollars cascading overseas, and by 1959 other nations had begun to ask the U.S. Treasury to convert their dollar holdings into gold. Hence, ending U.S. payments deficits threatened a world liquidity shortage; continuing them risked a hemorrhaging of the U.S. gold stock.[12] Second, the United States found itself beset by the conflicting demands of international monetary stability on the one hand and domestic economic well-being on the other. A classic remedy for chronic balance-of-payments deficits is deliberately to restrain the domestic economy in order to bring the nation's international account into equilibrium. President Dwight D. Eisenhower made that sacrifice for the sake of the international monetary system when he engineered a large budget surplus and thereby induced a mild recession in 1960, chiefly to "help reassure other nations as to America's ability to pay her debts and lessen their desire to convert their dollars into gold."[13] The commitment of the Democratic administrations of the 1960s to economic growth, full employment, and government activism foreclosed this option, however. Thus the ascendancy of growth liberalism increased the likelihood that the inherent conflict between international responsibilities and domestic aspirations would result in a serious crisis, as it did in 1968.

President Kennedy worked hard to reconcile domestic economic growth with international monetary stability. Within two weeks of his inauguration, he proposed a balance-of-payments program that included both rhetoric and action. The substantive measures were a mixed bag. The administration asked America's European allies to shoulder more of the burden of the Cold War by increasing their own foreign-aid expenditures and purchasing military equipment in the United States. The federal government sought to promote American exports in a number of ways, including tying them to U.S. loans to underdeveloped countries. It increased short-term interest rates to attract and hold volatile capital and restricted foreign borrowing from the American capital market. The administration also placed new, lower limits on the amount of goods American tourists could bring

[11] U.S., President, *Public Papers of the Presidents of the United States* (Washington, D.C., 1962), John F. Kennedy, 1961, 58.

[12] This tension is often referred to as Triffin's dilemma, after the Yale economist Robert Triffin, who gave the problem its classic formulation. See Triffin, *Gold and the Dollar Crisis: The Future of Convertibility* (New Haven, Conn., 1960).

[13] Dwight D. Eisenhower, *The White House Years*, Volume 2: *Waging Peace, 1956–1961* (Garden City, N.Y., 1965), 460, n. 7.

home duty-free. None of the initiatives was earth shattering, but in combination they brought some improvement.[14]

Lyndon B. Johnson built on JFK's initiatives by introducing voluntary programs designed to limit direct investment overseas and further reduce bank lending and by continuing to try to cut military expenditures abroad. "These things worked reasonably well," in the judgment of LBJ's undersecretary of the treasury for monetary affairs, Frederick Deming, "but [then] Viet Nam came along."[15] Deming was right on both counts: by 1965, the balance-of-payments deficit measured on a liquidity basis had been reduced to $1.3 billion from its 1960 high of $3.9 billion; but the onset in 1965 of all-out fighting in Vietnam quickly negated such progress. The cost of maintaining U.S. forces in Southeast Asia added substantially to foreign payments, and the inflation unleashed by the war fueled a dramatic increase in imports. By 1967, the balance-of-payments deficit was again running at the level of 1960, nearly $4 billion.[16]

The Vietnam War, then, constituted the second source of the economic crisis of 1968. It aggravated the balance-of-payments problem and sparked off a round of inflation that twisted the economy out of shape, with consequences that would still be felt decades later. "There's no dimension of the American economy in the last three-and-a-half years," asserted LBJ's last chairman of the Council of Economic Advisers (CEA) in 1969, "which hasn't been touched by Viet Nam; Viet Nam changed the entire budget posture. It took all the elbow room away."[17]

Put simply, federal spending for the Vietnam War and the Great Society domestic agenda overheated the U.S. economy, which was already enjoying an expansion spurred by the impact of the 1964 tax cut. In the fourth quarter of 1965, the gross national product rose by the largest amount in U.S. history. The rate of inflation (as measured in consumer prices) that had averaged 1.3 percent per year for the period 1961–1965 increased to 2.9 percent in 1966, fell back to 2.3 percent for the first half of 1967, and then shot up to 3.8 percent for the second half of 1967 and 4.4 percent for the first four months of 1968.[18]

By the end of 1965, the danger of a serious inflation had become clear, if not entirely unmistakable. In December, the Federal Reserve Board reacted by hiking the discount rate—the rate that banks pay on loans from the system—in order to apply some braking pressure to the economy. Later that month, Gardner Ackley, chair of the CEA, wrote to Johnson, "The only conclusion I can reach is that an increase of individual and corporate income tax rates should be planned, whatever the FY 1967 budget may be (within the limits we have heard discussed) . . . From

[14] On the Kennedy program, see Hansen, *Postwar American Economy*, 76–77; Amy Elisabeth Davis, "Politics of Prosperity: The Kennedy Presidency and Economic Policy" (Ph.D. dissertation, Columbia University, 1988), 186–210, 384–428; and Robert V. Roosa, *The Dollar and World Liquidity* (New York, 1967), 3–39.

[15] Frederick Deming OHM, Tape 2, p. 7, LBJL.

[16] U.S. Department of the Treasury, *Maintaining the Strength of the U.S. Dollar in a Strong Free World Economy* (Washington, D.C., 1968), 9, 47.

[17] Arthur Okun OHM, Tape 2, p. 4, LBJL.

[18] The statistics are from Arthur Okun, Cabinet Meeting Minutes, May 29, 1968, Cabinet Papers, Box 13, LBJL.

an economic standpoint, it needs to be done as soon as possible."[19] The timing of Ackley's assessment, one of the first intimations that the Keynesian growth liberalism of the 1960s was stretching the U.S. economy dangerously thin, was unintentionally ironic, for on December 31 *Time* magazine put John Maynard Keynes on its cover, the first time a person no longer living had been so honored. Achieving a unique mark of popular acclaim, the Keynesian creed had already begun its long retreat into disrepute.

At first, Johnson resisted calling for a major tax increase. He sought instead to pursue a policy of guns and butter funded by the growth that the new economics had already unleashed. Not until August 1967—more than a year and a half after Ackley had advised LBJ of the compelling need for a tax increase—did the administration present a concrete plan for a temporary 10 percent surcharge on both corporate and individual income taxes to deal with what Johnson now called "the hard and inescapable facts."[20]

Just why the administration dawdled has been a matter of considerable speculation and debate. In his published memoirs, Johnson defended his foot-dragging on the tax front by emphasizing the lack of support for a tax increase in Congress, the business community, organized labor, or his own Cabinet. The CEA's Arthur Okun recalled, "Anybody who wanted to slow things down was a killjoy." In 1966 and 1967, both the *New York Times* and the *Washington Post* opposed a major tax increase. As late as January 1968, a Gallup poll found 79 percent of the public opposed to raising taxes.[21] Ackley has since contended that Johnson's political pessimism was both genuine and determinative:

> I have no question that he [LBJ] was convinced that a tax increase was needed, badly needed, right at the beginning of 1966; and that if he didn't get it, the economy really was going to go to hell and all kinds of problems . . . And he was also convinced that he couldn't get a tax increase if he tried. I'm sure also, that he wasn't really very enthusiastic about trying, but I really think he was convinced that he couldn't get it, no matter how hard he tried, and that an attempt to get it would do more harm than good.[22]

The difficulty of the task did not, however, fully explain LBJ's reluctance to fight for a tax hike. There is little doubt that Johnson realized the seriousness of the problem. But he was playing for the highest of stakes: the fate of his Great Society. To force the issue of a tax hike would allow critics of the Vietnam War to savage the administration; it would also encourage conservatives to demand that the Great

[19] Gardner Ackley to Johnson, memo, December 27, 1965, White House Central Files, Confidential File, FI 4, LBJL.

[20] U.S., President, *Public Papers of the Presidents of the United States* (Washington, D.C., 1968), Lyndon B. Johnson, 1967, 2: 733. For a good discussion of LBJ's efforts in 1966 to control inflation without a tax hike, see Joseph A. Califano, Jr., *The Triumph and Tragedy of Lyndon Johnson: The White House Years* (New York, 1991), 137–48. Regarding the struggle to develop a tax program, see Harvey C. Mansfield, Sr., *Illustrations of Presidential Management: Johnson's Cost Reduction and Tax Increase Campaigns* (Austin, Tex., 1988); Henry Fowler OHM, Tape 3, p. 9, LBJL; and "Chronology of President Johnson's Tax Proposals, 1965–66," Aides Files, Joseph Califano, Box 54, LBJL.

[21] Johnson, *Vantage Point*, chap. 19; Arthur M. Okun, *The Political Economy of Prosperity* (Washington, D.C., 1970), 71. On the important role played by the chief economic editorialists of the *New York Times* and *Washington Post*, see Walter Heller OHM, Tape 2, pp. 47–48, LBJL. The Gallup poll is in the *New York Times*, January 24, 1968.

[22] Gardner Ackley OHM, Tape 1, p. 32, LBJL.

Society programs be cut back lest they interfere with the financing of the war. So Johnson hesitated on taxes and fudged on the cost of the war. His judgment was partially validated when his long-delayed tax bill, introduced in August 1967, was immediately bottled up in Congress by those who wished to make the administration trim its domestic spending.

Having hesitated on the tax issue for a disastrously long time, Johnson now found himself stymied by the determination of Representative Wilbur Mills, the Democratic chairman of the House Ways and Means Committee, to exact cuts in domestic spending as the price for congressional action on the administration's tax proposal. It was a clash of legislative titans. Mills had entered Congress in 1939, and by the mid-1960s was perhaps the most powerful figure on Capitol Hill.[23] Mills saw Johnson as a wastrel, a spender of the New Deal stripe: "I thought I knew the President well enough to know that if we gave him ten billion dollars more money to spend, that he would spend it if we didn't tie his hands to where he couldn't spend it."[24] The issue was, Mills believed, a fundamental one. To increase taxes without simultaneously cutting expenditures would "have a serious long-range impact upon the direction of our economy." He feared that the president's path "would mean bigger and bigger government with a smaller and smaller range of freedom of activity for the private sector."[25]

Mills's critique was more than the reflexive howl of a powerful but provincial fiscal conservative. Indeed, behind his insistence on spending cuts as the price for a tax increase lay a sophisticated attempt to decouple the defining elements of growth liberalism, to separate growth economics from liberal activism. Mills believed he had been burned by the Kennedy-Johnson tax cut of 1964, which he had ultimately come to support as an application of Andrew Mellon's free-enterprise tax policy of the late 1920s—tax reduction that would produce economic growth by unleashing the productive power of the private sector.[26] To Mills's dismay, the Eighty-ninth Congress in 1965 and 1966 had passed a host of Great Society initiatives, and expenditures had "taken off like the Apollo spaceship . . . to . . . the Moon." Instead of constraining federal activism, the 1964 tax cut had underwritten an unprecedented expansion of governmental programs. The heating up of the Vietnam War had exacerbated the problem, and Mills excoriated LBJ's guns-and-butter policy: "I just do not believe," he observed, "that when we are in a war that is costing us $25 to $30 billion a year we can carry on as usual at home."[27]

For Mills, the heart of the matter was the overreach of growth liberalism. "Like you," he wrote to a constituent in October 1967, "I have raised the same questions of whether . . . this country is strong enough to be able to police every corner of the world, fight limited wars, attempt to raise the living standards of the peoples of the

[23] See, for example, "Our Congressmen—Who Is Best? Who Is Worst?" *Pageant Magazine* (November 1964): 6–14; and Julius Duscha, "The Most Important Man on Capitol Hill Today," *New York Times Magazine*, February 25, 1968.

[24] Wilbur Mills OHM, Tape 1, p. 38, LBJL. See also p. 21 for similar sentiments.

[25] Wilbur Mills, speech, "Expenditures and Taxes in the Context of Today's Problems," November 20, 1967, Cabinet Papers, Box 11, LBJL.

[26] Duscha, "Most Important Man on Capitol Hill Today," 72.

[27] Wilbur Mills, speech, "Some International and Domestic Aspects of Tax and Expenditure Policy," December 3, 1968; Wilbur Mills, speech at Hazen, Arkansas, March 15, 1968, both in Box 420, Wilbur Mills Papers, Hendrix College, Conway, Arkansas.

underdeveloped areas of the world, satisfy our needs of our people at home and go to the moon all at the same time without the creation of unstable deficits."[28] Consequently, Mills fought Johnson not only to cut current expenditures but also to influence the future by cutting both the old and new obligational authority that constituted the pipeline for future spending.[29]

Mills brought to his side a majority of the Ways and Means Committee, which in October 1967 voted 20 to 5 to table Johnson's 10 percent surcharge proposal temporarily. LBJ's budget director, Charles L. Schultze, had confidently predicted to the president that Mills and his committee were playing "chicken" in an "eyeball-to-eyeball" confrontation with the administration, and that Mills would blink first.[30] But the chairman's gaze proved pitiless as the sun, and the Vietnam inflation worsened dramatically in the last quarter of 1967. By exacerbating the chronic balance-of-payments problem and fueling a dangerous inflation, the Vietnam War worked a double whammy on the U.S. economy. In doing so, the war also weakened the U.S. dollar. That weakness emerged dramatically in the last months of 1967 to challenge policymakers on yet another front.

The assault on the dollar was the third and most immediate of the sources that in their interaction caused the economic crisis of 1968.[31] Ironically, the assault was ignited by the travails of another currency, the British pound. The pound had been weak and vulnerable to raids by speculators through much of the 1960s. In Frederick Deming's words, "You've got a major confidence crisis in sterling about every fall on the fall, so to speak, and there was in '64, '65, '66, and then it culminated in '67."[32] When the pressure against sterling crested in mid-November 1967, Deming, the treasury undersecretary for monetary affairs, was already in Paris for regularly scheduled meetings with senior treasury and central bank officials of the major industrial powers (the so-called Group of Ten), and he led an effort to mobilize multilateral support for the pound.[33] But the attempt failed, and on November 17 the British ambassador informed Johnson that the British would on the following day announce a 14.3 percent devaluation.

The British devaluation touched off a frenzy in the gold market. Treasury Secretary Henry Fowler had earlier warned Johnson that one result of devaluation would be "that the gold market would come under very great pressure—and might

[28] Wilbur Mills to B. Freeland, October 19, 1967, Box 509, Mills Papers.

[29] Wilbur Mills, "Statement . . . on the Necessity for Establishing Controls over the Future Course of Federal Spending," October 6, 1967, Box 425, Mills Papers; and Mills to H. Hodge, June 25, 1968, Box 509, Mills Papers.

[30] Charles L. Schultze to Johnson, memo, September 16, 1967, Aides Files, Califano, Box 54, LBJL.

[31] The discussion that follows draws heavily on "The Gold Crisis, Nov. 1967–March 1968," undated manuscript, and "Gold Crisis—1967: Chronology and Annotated Index of Documents," undated manuscript, both in National Security File, National Security Council History (hereafter, NSCH), Box 53, LBJL.

[32] Frederick Deming OHM, Tape 2, p. 18, LBJL. A high-level British perspective on the 1967 sterling devaluation episode is found in Harold Wilson, *A Personal Record: The Labour Government, 1964–1970* (Boston, 1971), chap. 23.

[33] The Group of Ten was created in 1961 to enlarge the lending resources of the International Monetary Fund. Its members—the United States, Britain, Germany, France, Italy, the Netherlands, Belgium, Sweden, Canada, and Japan—agreed to provide additional money to the IMF and to communicate together regarding developments in the international monetary system.

explode."[34] Demand for gold was already strong because of the uncertainty generated by the summer's Six Day War in the Middle East, because industrial use was rising faster than new production, and because the Soviets had refused in both 1966 and 1967 to sell gold on the world market.[35] The chronic weakness of the pound caused further movement away from paper money into gold, and Britain's devaluation provided the final spark that caused the gold market to explode just as Fowler had feared. The so-called gold pool—formed in 1961 by the United States and eight other countries to sell gold when the demand was too great or buy gold when the supply was too great in order to keep its price in the London gold market close to the official $35 per ounce—intervened to stabilize the gold market and from November 20 through 27 incurred losses of $641 million (of which the U.S. share was 59 percent).[36]

The devaluation of sterling and the financial unrest that followed sent tremors of fear through the U.S. economic establishment. Alfred Hayes, president of the Federal Reserve Bank of New York, worried that the gold pool was at the point of disintegrating.[37] Fed chairman William McChesney Martin, Jr., observed, "It is the first time in all my 16 years with the Fed that I have seen all the important bankers and directors agree that we face a crisis ahead." "The real question," Fowler told the Cabinet, "is can we keep confidence in the dollar. The answer affects all the world."[38]

The United States responded to the British devaluation and its aftermath with a three-pronged defense of the dollar. First, the president made clear the American commitment to keep the price of gold at $35 an ounce. Second, the administration worked to get other nations to agree to maintain their existing exchange rates in order to prevent a chain reaction of competitive currency realignments. Third, Secretary Fowler called on the bipartisan leadership to build confidence in the dollar: "No single act could more effectively restore and maintain confidence in the dollar, and shore up our balance of payments position—both short and long term—than the passage of an expenditure reduction and tax increase package at this Session of Congress." "Markets don't wait," he added pointedly.[39]

[34] Henry Fowler to Johnson, memo, November 12, 1967, National Security File, NSCH, Box 53, LBJL.

[35] Fowler to Johnson, memo, November 13, 1967, National Security File, NSCH, Box 53, LBJL.

[36] Ackley to Johnson, memo, November 27, 1967, National Security File, NSCH, Box 53, LBJL. The gold pool has been described by one of the policymakers who helped create it as "a little bit like a cartel, but in the interests of the world monetary system." For more on the arrangement, see Robert Roosa OHM, Tape 1, pp. 23–26, LBJL.

[37] "Memorandum of Conversation: Highlights of Meeting of Deming Group with Secretary Fowler on Gold Policy," November 24, 1967, National Security File, NSCH, Box 53, LBJL. Deming, however, flew to Frankfurt and on November 26 negotiated a renewed agreement among the seven remaining members of the gold pool (Belgium, Germany, Italy, the Netherlands, Switzerland, Britain, and the United States—France, an original member, had dropped out earlier in 1967) to maintain a firm line on the gold price in London. See Ackley to Johnson, memo, November 27, 1967, National Security File, NSCH, Box 53, LBJL.

[38] Cabinet Meeting Minutes, November 20, 1967, Cabinet Papers, Box 11, LBJL. For similar sentiments, see E. Ernest Goldstein OHM, Tape 3, p. 2, LBJL.

[39] Press release, "Statement by the President," November 18, 1967, National Security File, NSCH, Box 53, LBJL. The overall strategy and Fowler's quoted remarks are from "Notes on the President's Meeting with Bipartisan Leadership," November 20, 1967, Meeting Notes File, Box 2, LBJL. See also "Notes on the President's Meeting with the Leadership," November 19, 1967, Meeting Notes File, Box 2, LBJL.

Fowler's remarks underscore how intertwined the problems of the balance of payments, the Vietnam War, and the strength of the dollar had become by the end of 1967. The war and the administration's apparent inability to get the tax hike needed to dampen domestic demand heightened international concern about the U.S. balance of payments, and that concern in turn weakened the dollar by encouraging heavy sales of dollars and purchases of gold in the international market. It was this terrible interlocking combination of problems that became the stuff of the economic crisis of 1968.

THE INTERNATIONAL MONETARY SYSTEM recovered from the British devaluation episode, but it quickly fell prey to further shocks. The week of December 4–8 saw the return of relative calm to the gold market, as the determination of the gold pool countries to hold the line "down to the last bar [of gold]" temporarily stanched their losses and resulted in a net gain for the week of $9 million. In the next week (December 11–15), gold pool losses rocketed back up to $548 million, and Rostow notified the president that "the gold market has come to a boil again." Once again, the gold pool wavered under the pressure. Later, Hubert Ansiaux of the Belgian central bank told William McChesney Martin that "we [the Belgian, German, Italian, Dutch, and Swiss members of the gold pool] were strongly of the opinion until yesterday night [December 14] ... to recommend that we should stop our intervention in the London market." But the gold pool partners agreed to soldier on, provided the United States make public a new program for dealing with the balance-of-payments deficit.[40]

On New Year's Day, 1968, Johnson announced a new balance-of-payments program that strengthened existing initiatives in the areas of loans, investment, and trade and called on Americans to limit overseas travel and spending.[41] The initial public response was strongly positive, and a week after the announcement Ackley reported "widespread optimism that speculation in gold should be substantially halted." "But," he added, "in fact, the gold market could flare up over anything."[42] Indeed, Johnson's plan of action soon confronted new realities that threatened to tie the threads of the balance of payments, Vietnam, and the vulnerable dollar into a knot beyond undoing.

The bad news seemed endless. On the payments front, the latest statistics were grim. The Council of Economic Advisers had informed the president in late December 1967 that the fourth-quarter outflow had been nearly $2 billion, threatening "to turn the year into a disaster" by creating a deficit that "may

[40] "Gold Pool Activity," attachment I to "The Gold Crisis, Nov. 1967–March 1968," manuscript, n.d.; Rostow to Johnson, memo, December 12, 1967; and summary of telephone call, Hubert Ansiaux to William McChesney Martin, Friday, December 15, 1967, all in National Security File, NSCH, Box 53, LBJL. See also Rostow to Johnson, December 15, 1967, National Security File, NSCH, Box 53, LBJL.

[41] U.S., President, *Public Papers*, Johnson, 1968–69, 1: 8–13; "The Balance of Payments Program of New Year's Day, 1968," manuscript, n.d., and "The President's Balance of Payments Message of January 1, 1968: Chronology and Annotated Documents," both in National Security File, NSCH, Box 54, LBJL; and Frederick Deming OHM, Tape 2, pp. 8–16.

[42] Ackley to Johnson, memo, January 6, 1968, National Security File, NSCH, Box 54, LBJL.

challenge 1960's unhappy record of $3.9 billion."[43] The economic fallout from Vietnam was equally troubling. Inflation worsened, with consumer prices rising 0.3 percent in January—the fourth straight monthly increase of that magnitude—and the wholesale price index up 0.4 percent in January and 0.6 percent in February. "Price increases," warned the Bureau of Labor Statistics, "are becoming more pervasive throughout the economy."[44] Moreover, the surprise Tet Offensive at the end of January raised the distinct possibility that even more U.S. troops would be committed to the struggle, with any such commitment likely necessitating calling up the reserves and a general mobilization for war. Meanwhile, the administration began to despair over passage of its tax surcharge proposal, with one official describing the attitude in the House as "one of almost anarchistic willingness to pull down the temple around their ears on the grounds that our budgetary expenditures are out of control."[45] The tax-hike difficulty was all the more vexing because, as Rostow acknowledged, "it has become a symbol in Europe of what the U.S. itself is willing to do."[46]

On the dollar and gold front, still other problems frustrated the administration's New Year's plan. American efforts to calm the gold market continued to be hampered by the failure of new gold production to meet the liquidity requirements of the expanding world economy. The leveling off of new gold production, rising industrial use, and heavy speculative demand combined to draw down the total monetary gold stock; at the same time, the increasing hesitancy of other nations to hold reserves in dollars made it impossible to depend on that reserve currency to meet the world's expanding liquidity needs. The end result of this liquidity crunch was greater pressure on the dollar, as speculators increasingly bet that the United States (and the rest of the world) would be forced to raise the price of gold to provide a one-time addition to liquidity.[47] A second problem vexing U.S. policy-makers and intensifying the risk of crisis involved the legal requirement that the United States allocate sufficient gold reserves to "cover" 25 percent of the nation's domestic note issue (essentially, the paper money in circulation). This amounted to approximately $10 billion of the nation's gold supply that could not legally be used to fulfill the commitment to dollar convertibility.[48] Attempts were under way to remedy both problems, liquidity and the gold cover, but in the first months of 1968 they had not yet come to fruition, and that fact added to the economic volatility of the moment.

The crisis suddenly came to a head in March. "The gold market broke out again last week," Fowler told the president on March 4. "After a few weeks of quiet, gold pool losses last week came to $123 million, including $88 million on Friday. Today losses were $53 million. We face the prospect of increasingly heavy sales during the rest of the week." On Friday, March 8, Rostow reported that the gold pool had that

[43] Ackley to Johnson, memo, December 21, 1967. See also "Minutes of the Cabinet Committee on Balance of Payments," December 21, 1967, both in National Security File, NSCH, Box 54, LBJL.

[44] *New York Times*, March 1, 1968.

[45] Rostow to Johnson, March 14, 1968, National Security File, NSCH, Box 53, LBJL.

[46] Rostow to Johnson, January 23, 1968, National Security File, NSCH, Box 53, LBJL.

[47] Ernest Goldstein to Johnson, memo, January 24, 1968, National Security File, NSCH, Box 54, LBJL; and Rostow to Johnson, memo, February 14, 1968, National Security File, NSCH, Box 53, LBJL.

[48] "The Gold Crisis," National Security File, NSCH, Box 53, LBJL; Joseph Barr OHM, Tape 2, pp. 9-10, LBJL; and Frederick Deming OHM, Tape 2, pp. 30–34, LBJL.

day suffered its third largest loss ever, $179 million.[49] The speculative spiral was out of control. McGeorge Bundy had once quipped that "only the greedy, the frightened, country folk and the Frenchmen love gold"—if true, then it was those groups who now dictated events. On Tuesday, March 12, Rostow told the president, "My own feeling is that the moment of truth is close upon us."[50]

On Wednesday, March 13, losses for the day totaled approximately $200 million, and Federal Reserve chairman Martin called his European counterparts to alert them that the United States might seek to close the gold markets.[51] The administration postponed action so that Congress would have time to pass the pending gold-cover legislation; Thursday, March 14—which Fowler later called "one of the most hectic days of my life"—became the day of decision. As LBJ met twice with his economic advisers, losses for the day reached nearly $400 million. After much debate, the administration, fearful that another day's losses might run to $1 billion, asked the British to shut down the London gold market on Friday and invited the central bankers of the gold pool countries to Washington for an emergency meeting over the weekend. When it proved impossible to reach some of the foreign officials by phone, Secretary of State Dean Rusk instructed the duty officers at embassies and consulates across Europe to contact them "at once, waking them if necessary." Rusk closed with a flourish, "You must track down these men at all costs."[52] The melodramatic tone was fitting.

HAVING PREVAILED ON THE BANK OF ENGLAND to close the London gold market and having invited to Washington the governors of the central banks of the gold pool nations, Johnson quickly sought to drive home the message that the price of gold would be held. In a March 15 telegram to West Germany's chancellor Kurt Kiesinger, LBJ observed, with a certain populist vengeance, "The speculators are banking on an increase in the official price of gold. They are wrong."[53] The United States had blinked, unwilling to play the game "to the last bar," but it also refused to give the speculators what they wanted—devaluation. The alternative was to shore up the Bretton Woods system, and that the administration proceeded to do.

The crisis atmosphere of March 1968 produced several immediate changes that, together, returned the international monetary system to working order. The first of these was the implementation of a "two-tier system" for gold transactions. The so-called Washington Communique issued at the end of the weekend meetings made it clear that the gold market would henceforth be separated into an official market, where monetary gold for central banking purposes would be governed by

[49] Fowler to Johnson, memo, March 4, 1968; and Rostow to Johnson, memo, March 8, 1968, both in National Security File, NSCH, Box 53, LBJL.

[50] McGeorge Bundy quoted in "The Dollar Is Not as Bad as Gold," *Time* (January 12, 1968): 16; Rostow to Johnson, memo, March 12, 1968, Diary Backup, Box 92, LBJL.

[51] The discussion that follows relies heavily on "The Gold Crisis," National Security File, NSCH, Box 53, LBJL.

[52] Henry Fowler OHM, Tape 1, p. 33, LBJL; Dean Rusk to American Consul, Frankfurt, and others, telegram, March 15, 1968, National Security File, NSCH, Box 53, LBJL.

[53] Johnson to Kurt Kiesinger, telegram, March 15, 1968, National Security File, NSCH, Box 53, LBJL. The administration's rationale for opposing any increase in the official price of gold is found in T. Page Nelson to Hunt, February 16, 1968, Henry Fowler Papers, Box 83, LBJL.

dollar-gold convertibility at $35 an ounce, and a private market, where gold for industrial and speculative purposes would be governed by the basic laws of supply and demand.[54] As one Zurich banker put it, "The central bankers are saying to the speculators: 'Take it to the dentist.'"[55] In effect, the central bankers were also saying that in the future they would meet their reserve and liquidity needs through a new kind of "paper" international reserve asset rather than through buying more gold. The concept behind the two-tier system was not newly minted at the March 1968 conference; Guido Carli of the Bank of Italy had advanced the idea back in November 1967. But two things had changed in the interim. The plans for the new "paper gold" reserve asset, on which any two-tiered arrangement would rely, were now much further advanced. And, as Arthur Okun has contended, the experience of the crisis itself had an important effect: "I don't think we could have gotten the other countries onboard if we had opted for . . . [the two-tier system] earlier. They had bled a little, and they knew that some accommodations had to be made. They wanted to stop their losses of gold . . . and they became very enthusiastic about this."[56]

A second immediate change to which the March crisis contributed mightily was the removal of the American gold cover. The Washington Communique noted specifically and approvingly that the removal of the gold cover "makes the whole of the gold stock of the nation available for defending the value of the dollar." This, too, was a change long discussed. As early as 1961, President Kennedy had been advised to seek repeal of the gold-cover commitment, but he feared that any such proposal by him would be wrapped around his neck politically as "Democratic funny-money finagling."[57] Resistance to the suggested change centered on the fact that the gold cover dated back to the creation of the Federal Reserve system and so enjoyed the imprimatur of both time and financial probity.

Johnson asked Congress to remove the cover in his State of the Union address on January 17, 1968, but winning congressional approval proved difficult, and again the March crisis played a role. Treasury Undersecretary Joseph Barr recalled that on the day the Senate voted on the measure, at the peak of the gold crisis, Senate majority leader Mike Mansfield (Democrat-Montana) called to report that he was no longer sure he had the votes. "So Fowler and I and Bill Martin . . . sat down with the leadership on both sides . . . explained to them that the crisis was getting worse and worse, and that if we did not pass that bill that day, we might be forced to renege the next day on our promise to deliver gold." Finally, at 7:30 in the evening, the Senate approved the repeal of the gold cover by a 39–37 vote. In the future, all of the nation's gold stock would be placed behind its commitment to maintain the price of gold and value of the dollar.[58]

The third immediate result of the March crisis was a renewed and strengthened

[54] "Communique," March 17, 1968, National Security File, NSCH, Box 53, LBJL. See also the discussion in Solomon, *International Monetary System*, 119–24. Robert Solomon was a participant at the Washington meeting and helped draft its final communique.

[55] *Time* (March 29, 1968): 80.

[56] Arthur Okun OHM, Tape 1, p. 23, LBJL. On Guido Carli's role, see Frederick Deming OHM, Tape 2, p. 29, LBJL.

[57] "Communique," March 17, 1968, National Security File, NSCH, Box 53, LBJL; Theodore C. Sorensen, *Kennedy* (New York, 1965), 407.

[58] U.S., President, *Public Papers*, Johnson, 1968–69, 1: 33; Joseph Barr OHM, Tape 2, p. 10, LBJL.

commitment to a reform already in the works—the creation of a new form of international reserves, the Special Drawing Rights (SDR), designed to serve as a form of paper gold to meet the liquidity needs of an expanding world economy. Indeed, it was, as the Washington Communique explicitly stated, the prospect of the SDR that allowed the creation of the two-tier system. With the SDR on the horizon, the central bankers of the gold pool states could agree that the existing stock of monetary gold was sufficient and that they would no longer need to buy gold from the market.[59] The international reserves needed for future economic growth could come from the new paper gold, which would be used alongside real gold and the dollar for settling international accounts.

It is clear that the concept of the SDR was already well advanced by the time of the March crisis. The congressional Joint Economic Committee had in 1962 urged the creation of new methods for routinely increasing international liquidity, and discussions on the matter continued among both the Group of Ten and the International Monetary Fund in the mid-1960s. The IMF approved an outline proposal for the creation of the Special Drawing Rights at its meeting in Rio de Janeiro in September 1967, but working out the final details proved to be a difficult and contentious task.[60] Early in 1968, *Time* reported, "There is one big hang-up: these 'S.D.R.s' will probably not be activated until the U.S. and Britain markedly reduce their balance of payments deficits." *Business Week* agreed that "the plan can't be ratified before next year at the earliest."[61] More devoted to the primacy of gold than other nations, France in particular seemed to be dragging its feet.

Once again, the March crisis had an effect, more accelerative than causal in the case of SDRs but significant nonetheless. A Group of Ten meeting in Stockholm at the end of March finally settled the SDR issue. In the judgment of Treasury Secretary Fowler, the gold crisis of mid-March had pointed up the danger of continuing to depend on increased supplies of gold at $35 an ounce as the monetary system's source of additional liquidity: "The gold crisis was draining away from, and reducing, the quantity of gold held in the reserves of Central Banks. So there was a source of diminishing liquidity. This underscored and, indeed, highlighted the need for the Special Drawing Rights facility."[62]

U.S. policymakers believed that the Washington Gold Accord of mid-March and the innovations that underpinned it—the two-tier system, the full commitment of the U.S. gold stock, the development of the SDR—were necessary expedients that provided much-needed breathing room; but, as Arthur Okun, LBJ's new chairman of the CEA, pointed out, the accord was "futile unless we get a tax increase." In the end, Wilbur Mills triumphed. Johnson ended the long struggle by signing the Revenue and Expenditure Control Act of 1968 into law on June 28, 1968—two and a half years after CEA chairman Gardner Ackley had first warned of economic overheating.[63] The administration gained a retroactive 10 percent surcharge on

[59] "Communique," March 17, 1968, National Security File, NSCH, Box 53, LBJL.

[60] Odell, *U.S. International Monetary Policy*, 129; Solomon, *International Monetary System*, 128–50; and Frederick Deming OHM, Tape 2, pp. 34–45, LBJL.

[61] "Dollar Is Not as Bad as Gold," 17; "Gold Fever Rises to Record Heat," *Business Week* (March 16, 1968): 31.

[62] Henry Fowler OHM, Tape 3, p. 31, LBJL.

[63] Arthur Okun to Johnson, memo, March 23, 1967, National Security File, NSCH, Box 53, LBJL.

individual and corporate income taxes but at the price of agreeing to $6 billion in immediate spending cuts for fiscal year 1969, a reduction of $10 billion in new obligational and loan authority for fiscal year 1969, and a future $8 billion recision in unobligated balances of obligational and loan authority carried over from previous years.

The March gold crisis contributed significantly to the final outcome of the tax-hike struggle. The tax compromise was a difficult one for Johnson and the liberals in his administration to accept, for it cut to the heart of the Great Society—the reductions would come from domestic programs as well as non-Vietnam defense expenditures. Wilbur Mills believed that the dramatic impact of the March gold crisis helped LBJ accept the hard bargain that Mills and his allies had forced upon him: "President Johnson ... was scared almost out of his body when he woke up to the fact that people in Europe were having trouble exchanging dollars for foreign currency." For his part, Johnson agreed that the crisis provided an important impetus, but he emphasized its impact on *his* opposition: "The international crisis had done what we could not do: arouse the American public and many congressional leaders to the need for decisive action." Mills did indeed subsequently report that the "severe run on the dollar in the international market during the early months of 1968" and the "drastic outflow of gold" were "important to ... [the Ways and Means Committee] in reaching a decision to agree to the surtax proposal." In retrospect, the March crisis moved both sides toward a resolution of the fiscal impasse. Treasury Undersecretary Deming correctly observed that "the prime mover in getting action was the fact that the international monetary system seemed to be going to hell in a handbasket."[64]

In this fashion, the worst economic crisis since the Great Depression was resolved. Changes—significant but not truly radical—were made to buttress the Bretton Woods regime, and hard choices were decided on in the name of fiscal responsibility. In the short run, the innovations seemed to work. Johnson touted the development of the SDR as a "historic step" that "will prepare us for the era of expanding world trade and economic opportunity that unfolds before us." At the end of July, Okun reported to the president that "there is less of a crisis atmosphere now than at any time in the past year"; in September, he noted that the "economy is advancing strongly" and that "the unhealthy boomy pace of the first half has already moderated." Ironically, the balance of payments improved dramatically over the course of 1968. The New Year's program and the tax hike helped to some extent, as did the unrest in Europe when France suffered its May riots and the Soviets invaded Czechoslovakia. As a result, Joseph Barr (who replaced Fowler as treasury secretary in December 1968) recalled, "all the money ran out of Europe and came to the United States so we ended up really in amazing statistical fashion."

On the outcome of the tax struggle, see Kettl, "Economic Education of Lyndon Johnson," 70–71; and Charles Zwick OHM, Tape 2, pp. 5–9, LBJL.

[64] Wilbur Mills OHM, Tape 1, p. 35, LBJL; Johnson, *Vantage Point*, 451; Wilbur Mills, speech at England, Arkansas, August 27, 1968, Box 420, Mills Papers; Frederick Deming OHM, Tape 1, p. 34, LBJL.

By the end of the year, the United States enjoyed a small surplus in its balance of payments, calculated on both the liquidity and the official transactions basis.[65]

Looking back, however, it is clear that the resolution of the 1968 economic crisis bought breathing room but settled little. An analysis of how the basic sources of the crisis played out in its aftermath makes the point. The balance of payments quickly turned downward again, as even the trade account (basically, exports and imports of goods and raw materials), long a source of U.S. strength, sank into deficit in the face of stagnating productivity at home and increased global competition.[66] The Vietnam War continued to generate inflationary pressures that would plague the economy, and policymakers, into the 1970s and beyond. Johnson's tax surcharge proved to be too little too late and appears to have had only a small effect on consumer and business spending.[67] Moreover, it was offset, much to the chagrin of Wilbur Mills, by the easing of credit by monetary authorities in the latter half of 1968.[68] Finally, despite the revamping during 1968, the Bretton Woods international monetary regime was doomed by the continued economic and political resurgence of Europe and Japan; and, after another global monetary crisis in 1971, President Richard M. Nixon closed the gold window, thereby ending the era of dollar-gold convertibility. By 1973, a new regime based on floating exchange rates had taken shape.[69]

Thus the 1968 crisis illuminated trends that could be accommodated and moderated but not arrested or reversed. It both revealed and contributed to the passing of postwar U.S. economic hegemony; and it marked the beginning of an awkward transition from the postwar boom to a new era of economic stagnation cum inflation—stagflation—that emerged unmistakably by the mid-1970s. (Indeed, the suggestion of such a transition puts the Nixon presidency in a new light and offers a new context and criterion for evaluating its record, in addition to those provided by Watergate and the Cold War.)[70]

THE 1968 ECONOMIC CRISIS had a similarly significant impact in the wider world of political economy, where economics connects with the political culture and the social fabric. By early 1968, LBJ's attempt to fight a war in Southeast Asia while

[65] U.S., President, *Public Papers*, Johnson, 1968–69, 1: 545–46; Okun to Johnson, memo, July 29, 1968, White House Central Files, EX FI 9, Box 53, LBJL; Arthur Okun, Notes for Cabinet Meeting, September 5, 1968, Cabinet Papers, Box 14, LBJL; Joseph Barr OHM, Tape 1, p. 28, LBJL.

[66] Gordon, *Economic Instability and Growth*, 179–85. Conventional wisdom dates the decline in productivity growth in the 1970s, but most scholars find the postwar decline beginning in the mid to late 1960s. See William J. Baumol and Kenneth McLennan, "U.S. Productivity Performance and Its Implications," in *Productivity Growth and U.S. Competitiveness*, William J. Baumol and Kenneth McLennan, eds. (New York, 1985), 7; and Edward N. Wolff, "The Magnitude and Causes of the Recent Productivity Slowdown in the United States: A Survey of Recent Studies," in Baumol and McLennan, *Productivity Growth and U.S. Competitiveness*, 32.

[67] Robert Eisner, "Fiscal and Monetary Policy Reconsidered," *American Economic Review*, 59 (December 1969): 897–905; and Eisner, "What Went Wrong?" *Journal of Political Economy*, 79 (May–June 1971): 629–41.

[68] Wilbur Mills OHM, Tape 1, p. 12, LBJL.

[69] Solomon, *International Monetary System*, 176–234.

[70] See Thomas L. Friedman, "A Nixon Legacy Devalued by a Cold War Standard," *New York Times*, May 1, 1994.

building the Great Society at home had stretched the U.S. political economy to the breaking point. The economic crisis that culminated in March coincided with the shock of the Tet Offensive in Vietnam, which began on the last two days of January but continued to dominate the war action through February and March. The combined weight of these economic and military reversals finally wrecked Johnson's guns-and-butter policy. As a result, the administration was forced to cap both the long escalation of the Vietnam War and the expansion of the Great Society.

The Tet Offensive, Secretary of Defense Clark Clifford later recalled, "really . . . threw gasoline on the fire."[71] Communist forces struck at district headquarters, provincial capitals, and cities and towns across the length of South Vietnam. Although the military tide turned quickly when the Americans and South Vietnamese counterattacked and inflicted devastating losses on the Communists, especially on the irregulars of the Vietcong, the impact of the enemy's initial success proved impossible to erase. The Tet Offensive crystallized doubts and reservations that had been gathering for months and years among both policymakers and the general public. The war was far from over; any light at the end of the tunnel—in General William Westmoreland's unfortunate phrase—was much dimmer than optimistic official assessments had suggested; clear-cut military victory now seemed either impossible or unacceptably costly.

As if to punctuate the bad tidings, Westmoreland, the U.S. commander in Vietnam, and General Earle Wheeler, the chairman of the Joint Chiefs of Staff, in February requested the commitment of an additional 205,000 troops to Vietnam.[72] The request for more troops touched off a controversy within the administration that became a public debate when word of the proposal was leaked to the press, resulting ultimately in a fundamental reassessment of U.S. policy in Vietnam. Coming at precisely the moment when the economic crisis of 1968 came to a head in the March run on gold, the reexamination of war policy involved economic considerations fully as much as political calculation and military strategy.

The economic implications of the troop request were troubling. To provide the requested reinforcements for Vietnam would require the rebuilding of the military's seriously depleted strategic reserve as well, and so the Westmoreland-Wheeler request would necessitate the call-up of over a quarter-million reservists, increased draft calls, and the extension of terms of service for many already in uniform—altogether, the addition of 511,000 to the active duty armed forces by June 30, 1969. This was the war mobilization long sought by the military and thus far assiduously avoided by Johnson. The cost would be $2.5 billion in fiscal year 1968 and $10 billion in fiscal year 1969, raising the annual price of the war by roughly 40 percent. The adverse impact on the balance of payments was projected

[71] Clark Clifford OHM, Tape 4, p. 33, LBJL.

[72] Earle Wheeler to Johnson, memo, February 27, 1969, Tom Johnson's Notes of Meetings, Box 2, LBJL. The origins of the February 1968 troop request have been the stuff of controversy. See "The Origins of the Post-Tet 1968 Plans for Additional American Forces in RVN," November 9, 1970, Declassified and Sanitized Documents from Unprocessed Files, Box 3, LBJL; William C. Westmoreland, *A Soldier Reports* (Garden City, N.Y., 1976), 350–59; Mark Perry, *Four Stars* (Boston, 1989), 173–89; and Clark Clifford with Richard Holbrooke, *Counsel to the President: A Memoir* (New York, 1991), 472–83.

to be $500 million.[73] Moreover, all such costs were *additions* to a basic defense budget whose projections for fiscal year 1970 had already been labeled "a shock" by Budget Director Charles Zwick. "Now this on top of the already enormous burden we were carrying," Clark Clifford subsequently recalled, "the dollar had gone through a period of vulnerability in the early part of '68, and in the spring this would put a lot more pressure on it, put a lot more pressure upon our balance of payments problem, which was already acute, so that all these matters began to come in that day by day caused me growing concern."[74]

Other top policymakers shared the defense secretary's anxiety about the economic cost of the war. Before leaving office at the end of February 1968, Clifford's predecessor, Robert McNamara, had noted the importance of doing "whatever we can to prevent the financial requirements [of any proposal for post-Tet Vietnam reinforcements] from ruining us in foreign exchange in our domestic economic situation [*sic*]."[75] Secretary of State Rusk cautioned, "We have ... got to think of what this troop increase would mean in terms of increased taxes, the balance of payments picture, inflation, gold, and the general economic picture."[76] Treasury Secretary Fowler observed that events in Vietnam and developments in "the international financial picture" were "interacting" and warned that the troop increase would hurt both the economy and the dollar and likely necessitate further cuts in Great Society programs, especially those dealing with poverty and urban problems.[77] Even LBJ's resolutely hawkish national security adviser, Walt Rostow, admitted that, without a tax increase, the proposed Vietnam build-up "may be very tough on the dollar."[78] U.S. policymakers clearly recognized a connection between the future prosecution of the war in Southeast Asia and the economic crisis that had emerged in the early months of 1968.

As word of the troop request leaked out to the press, observers outside government made the connection as well. "The gold crisis ... and a continuing threat to the dollar," wrote Hobart Rowen in the *Washington Post*, "are bringing President Johnson face to face with basic questions on Vietnam war policy. It is now clear that there are real limits to our financial resources." Writing in *The New Republic* that the sending of more troops to Vietnam would risk "a collapse ... of the international monetary system," Edwin Dale announced: "Someone had better tell the President, in so many words, that if he puts into Vietnam the number of

[73] "Notes of the President's Meeting with Senior Foreign Policy Advisers," March 4, 1968, Tom Johnson's Notes of Meetings, Box 2, LBJL.

[74] Charles Zwick to Johnson, March 2, 1968, Clark Clifford Papers, Box 1, LBJL; Clark Clifford OHM, Tape 3, p. 15, LBJL.

[75] "Notes of the President's Meeting with Senior Foreign Policy Advisers," February 9, 1968, Tom Johnson's Notes of Meetings, Box 2, LBJL.

[76] "Notes of the President's Meeting with Senior Foreign Policy Advisers," March 4, 1968, Tom Johnson's Notes of Meetings, Box 2, LBJL.

[77] Fowler to Johnson, memo, March 1, 1968, National Security File, NSCH, Box 53, LBJL; "Difficulties and Negative Factors in the Course of Action," n.d., Tab. G, Box 1, Clifford Papers, LBJL. See also Henry Fowler, "Economic and Financial Problems and Measures," memo, March 3, 1968, Box 1, Clifford Papers, LBJL.

[78] Rostow to Johnson, March 11, 1968, National Security File, Memos to the President (Rostow), Box 30, LBJL.

troops that now seem required to restore and improve the situation there, he may throw away the fruits of a generation of brilliant economic progress."[79]

Johnson received just that message on a number of occasions in March when he sent his immediate advisers to take the pulse of Congress on the troop request and related Vietnam issues. When Clifford and Wheeler canvassed key congressional leaders, they found little support for either a major troop commitment or a large reserve call-up. Both hawks and doves feared the economic consequences of an escalation. Clifford subsequently reported that Stuart Symington, a Democratic senator from Missouri and Cold War stalwart, "thinks we should get out. He thinks the dollar will depreciate." Johnson's successor as Senate majority leader, the dovish Mike Mansfield, explained in a memo forwarded to the president that expanding the U.S. role in Vietnam would mean "more inflation, more balance of payments complication, and possibly financial panic and collapse."[80]

Still casting about for advice in late March, Johnson convened a group of elder statesmen known as the "Wise Men." The members of the group constituted a virtual "who's who" of the foreign policy establishment. They had advised him before on the war (with "hawkish" results), and he turned to them again to gauge just how much opinion had changed in the wake of recent events. One key member was McGeorge Bundy, former national security adviser to both Kennedy and Johnson. Bundy, too, recognized the connection between the economic and the political. "I now understand," he wrote to Johnson, "that the really tough problem you have is the interlock between the bad turn in the war, the critical need for a tax increase, and the crisis of public confidence at home." The most imposing, and imperious, of the Wise Men, Dean Acheson, conveyed a similar opinion personally to Johnson in mid-March and spoke forcefully when the Wise Men met with the president on March 26. The United States, Acheson asserted, could not prevail in Vietnam in a reasonable time with the means available. That fact, he reasoned, "together with our broader interests in SEA [Southeast Asia], Europe, and in connection with the dollar crisis, requires a decision now to disengage within a limited time." For Acheson, as for others, the matter of resources and limits had become critical. "The gold crisis," the former secretary of state wrote a friend, "has dampened expansionist ideas. The town is in an atmosphere of crisis." Clark Clifford subsequently observed, "Speaking almost *ex officio* as the leader of the foreign policy establishment, and with his customary authority, Acheson had an unquestionable impact on the President."[81]

In the end, the decision on the troop request was Lyndon Johnson's to make.

[79] Hobart Rowen, "Gold, Dollar Threats Affecting War Policy," *Washington Post*, March 24, 1968; Edwin L. Dale, Jr., "The Gold Rush," *The New Republic*, March 23, 1968.

[80] Clifford, *Counsel to the President*, 498; "Notes of the President's Meeting with His Foreign Advisers at The Tuesday Luncheon," March 19, 1968, Tom Johnson's Notes of Meetings, Box 2, LBJL; Mike Mansfield, "Reports of Requests for an Additional 200,000 Men in Vietnam," memo, March 13, 1968, Meeting Notes File, Box 2, LBJL.

[81] Bundy quoted in Larry Berman, *Lyndon Johnson's War: The Road to Stalemate in Vietnam* (New York, 1989), 193; Dean Acheson, "Confidential Memorandum: DA's Views Regarding Vietnam as of March 26, 1968 (As Expressed at the State Department and White House on March 26, 1968)," Series IV, Box 67, Dean Acheson Papers, Yale University Library, New Haven, Connecticut; Dean Acheson to John Cowles, March 14, 1968, Series IV, Box 88, Acheson Papers; Clifford, *Counsel to the President*, 518.

And, for LBJ, the economic context of Vietnam decision-making proved inescapable and mattered greatly: "We were struggling with one of the most serious financial crises of recent years," he later wrote. "These monetary and budgetary problems were constantly before us as we considered whether we should or could do more in Vietnam. It was clear that calling up a large number of troops, sending additional men overseas, and increasing military expenditures would complicate our problems and put greater pressure on the dollar."[82] Mindful of such economic concerns, an improving military situation in Vietnam, and the declining political support at home for both the war and his presidency, Johnson decided in a tentative and halting fashion over the course of March to scale back dramatically any deployment of additional forces to Vietnam or mobilization of reserves.[83]

By the time Johnson met with Rusk and Generals Wheeler and Creighton Abrams (who was soon to replace Westmoreland as U.S. commander in Vietnam) on March 26, the basic decisions for a reorientation of U.S. war policy had been made, and the tone of the meeting was elegiac. Their common endeavor was about to take a new turn, and Johnson seemed to need to explain to his generals why he had not met the military's request for a dramatic escalation of the war. He also sought to assure them that the new course had been forced on him by dastardly enemies and large, impersonal forces, rather than by his past mistakes or theirs. "It is the civilians [in the Pentagon]," he told Wheeler, Abrams, and Rusk, "that are cutting our guts out." Press leakers and Georgetown liberals, the *New York Times* and the *Washington Post*, Edward and Robert Kennedy, an uncooperative Congress—all suffered the president's opprobrium. But, in a revealing lament, Johnson laid bare the larger forces dictating so fundamental a shift in his Vietnam policy.[84]

The political economy of the war, Johnson told his generals, had turned against them. "Our fiscal situation is abominable," he reported. The fate of the tax bill remained uncertain, and the administration faced a possible deficit of over $30 billion. Such a large shortfall would force interest rates up and endanger both the British pound and the dollar. "Unless we get a tax bill . . . [the situation] will be unthinkable." But LBJ's predicament did not end there. The price of congressional approval for his tax increase would likely be the sort of concomitant spending cuts demanded by Mills. Johnson expected to be forced to make half the cuts in non-Vietnam defense expenditures. "That will cause hell with Russell [Senator Richard Russell, chairman of the Senate Armed Services Committee]. If we don't do that we will have hell. What happens when you cut poverty, housing and education?" Every way Johnson turned, his choices looked grim.[85]

The request for Vietnam reinforcements and a large-scale mobilization only exacerbated the administration's plight. "That would cost $15 billion. That would hurt the dollar and the gold [*sic*]," Johnson explained. "How can we get the job

[82] Johnson, *Vantage Point*, 406.

[83] A first-rate scholarly account of the Tet decisions is David M. Barrett, *Uncertain Warriors: Lyndon Johnson and His Vietnam Advisers* (Lawrence, Kan., 1993), chap. 4. Detailed firsthand accounts include Johnson, *Vantage Point*, chap. 17; and Clifford, *Counsel to the President*, chaps. 27–28.

[84] "Notes of the President's Meeting with General Earle Wheeler, JCS, and General Creighton Abrams," March 26, 1968, Tom Johnson's Notes of Meetings, Box 2, LBJL.

[85] "Notes of the President's Meeting with General Earle Wheeler, JCS, and General Creighton Abrams," March 26, 1968, Tom Johnson's Notes of Meetings, Box 2, LBJL.

done?" he asked plaintively. "We need more money in an election year, more taxes in an election year, more troops in an election year and more cuts in an election year." There was, he added pointedly, "no support for the war."[86]

Johnson concluded the meeting with his military leaders by asserting, "I would give Westmoreland 206,000 men if he said he needed them [to stave off a disastrous defeat] and if we could get them."[87] But Westmoreland could not honestly couch his request in such terms. And the president realized that to fulfill such a request would be to risk further disasters both economic and political. In the end, the lessening of the immediate military pressure in Vietnam as the Communist gains of the Tet Offensive were rolled back, the difficulty in envisioning a likely scenario for American military victory by doing "more of the same," the erosion of popular support for the war, and the realization that the costs of further escalation were unacceptable at a time when the economy's performance and institutional underpinnings were already overstrained all came together to seal LBJ's decision to try a new tack in Vietnam.

On March 31, 1968, Johnson announced that the new troop commitment to Vietnam would be limited to 13,500 additional support troops to bolster the 11,000 combat troops already airlifted to Vietnam immediately after the Tet attack.[88] Johnson also reported that new emphasis would be placed on expanding South Vietnam's role in its own defense. To help secure a political resolution of the war, he named a new peace ambassador, Averell Harriman, and ordered a bombing halt over most of North Vietnam. Although American forces would remain in combat in Vietnam for nearly five more years, the long, gradual escalation of U.S. involvement was at last capped. Henceforth, emphasis would shift from prosecution of the war to extrication from it. The decision to halt the escalation of the war was as much economic as it was political or military.[89]

[86] "Notes of the President's Meeting with General Earle Wheeler, JCS, and General Creighton Abrams," March 26, 1968, Tom Johnson's Notes of Meetings, Box 2, LBJL.

[87] "Notes of the President's Meeting with General Earle Wheeler, JCS, and General Creighton Abrams," March 26, 1968, Tom Johnson's Notes of Meetings, Box 2, LBJL.

[88] A limited reserve call-up of 20,000 men took place shortly thereafter, in May 1968. Stanley Resor OHM, p. 19, LBJL. Resor was secretary of the army from 1968 to 1971.

[89] This interpretation appears fleetingly in David Halberstam, *The Best and the Brightest* (New York, 1972), 604, but scholars have since pursued at least four other emphases in explaining the March 1968 decision to deescalate. Don Oberdorfer, *Tet!* (Garden City, N.Y., 1971), views the policy shift as the inevitable, or at least predictable, result of the shock generated by the Tet Offensive. Several studies emphasize the palace revolt of a handful of administration doves led by Clark Clifford. See Townsend Hoopes, *The Limits of Intervention: An Inside Account of How the Johnson Policy of Escalation in Vietnam Was Reversed* (New York, 1969); and Herbert Y. Schandler, *The Unmaking of a President: Lyndon Johnson and Vietnam* (Princeton, N.J., 1977). The significance of the defection of the so-called Establishment is stressed in Walter Isaacson and Evan Thomas, *The Wise Men: Six Friends and the World They Made; Acheson, Bohlen, Harriman, Kennan, Lovett, McCloy* (New York, 1986). For the impact of the antiwar movement, see Melvin Small, *Johnson, Nixon, and the Doves* (New Brunswick, N.J., 1988), 129–32; Tom Wells, *The War Within: America's Battle over Vietnam* (Berkeley, Calif., 1994), 4, 261; and Tom Hayden, *Reunion: A Memoir* (New York, 1988), 501.

For the dimension of political economy presently under discussion, see Lloyd Gardner, "Lyndon Johnson and Vietnam: The Final Months," in *The Johnson Years*, Volume 3: *LBJ at Home and Abroad*, Robert A. Divine, ed. (Lawrence, Kan., 1994), 198–238. Halberstam notes correctly that the war never cost more than 3.5 percent of the gross national product, and he concludes that it was not the war but rather "the essentially dishonest way in which it was handled" that "destroyed the economy" (*Best and the Brightest*, 610).

IN 1968, THE ECONOMIC CRISIS also directly influenced developments at home. As he moved to cap the escalation of the war in Southeast Asia, Johnson came under increasing pressure to throttle back his domestic reforms as well. On the Saturday morning in mid-March when central bankers from the gold pool nations gathered at the Federal Reserve Building in Washington to salvage the international monetary regime, the president spoke to a meeting of business leaders across town at the Sheraton Park Hotel: "We must tighten our belts. We must adopt an austere program . . . Hard choices are going to have to be made in the next few days. Some desirable programs of lesser priority and urgency are going to have to be deferred."[90] The continuing failure to resolve the nation's fiscal impasse and the threatened collapse of the international monetary order forced on the administration exactly the sort of "discipline of stringency" that LBJ's guns-and-butter policy had sought to avoid.

Admittedly, economic woes were not the only impediment to the expansion of the Great Society in early 1968. Administrative difficulties, hardening racial attitudes on all sides, and the apparent intractability of problems such as poverty contributed to the slowing of the administration's reform surge. The War on Poverty had proven to be politically divisive even among old-line Democrats, and Johnson's own reform ardor sometimes showed signs of flagging. He was convinced that the poverty warriors of the Office of Economic Opportunity were personally disloyal.[91] Moreover, in the spring of 1968, the president occasionally voiced bitter disappointment at the disaffection (and, by implication, the ingratitude) of blacks and the young, two groups he felt had benefited most from his reform efforts in civil rights, poverty, and education.[92]

Personal pique notwithstanding, however, Johnson remained committed, in both word and deed, to his Great Society vision. In late 1967, he told reporters that he wanted to leave as his legacy "a social consciousness in concrete." He had not enjoyed complete success in moving his programs through Congress, he admitted, but, "It's only half-time now; there is still another session of the 90th Congress to go."[93] As 1968 began, Johnson continued to press, in the words of a key aide, "almost frenetically" for further reform. During the first two months of the year, he sent to the Hill the largest manpower program and most ambitious housing bill in U.S. history. He asked for a $290 million increase in appropriations for the Office of Economic Opportunity's poverty program and in April signed into law the fair housing legislation he had been seeking since 1966.[94] The pace of reform, though no longer dizzying, remained substantial.

The face and substance of reform were changing, however, as financial exigency

[90] U.S., President, *Public Papers*, Johnson, 1968–69, 1: 404.

[91] Daniel P. Moynihan, *Maximum Feasible Misunderstanding: Community Action in the War on Poverty* (New York, 1969); Wilbur Cohen OHM, Tape 3, p. 10, and Tape 4, pp. 5, 9, LBJL.

[92] See, for example, "Notes on Meeting of the President with Senator Robert Kennedy, April 3, 1968"; and "Memorandum of Conversation: The President, Senator Robert F. Kennedy, Theodore Sorensen, Charles Murphy, and W. W. Rostow, 10:00 a.m., April 3, 1968," both in Diary Backup, Box 94, LBJL.

[93] "Notes of the President's Meeting with Lyle Denniston, Bob Walters, and Jack Horner of the Washington Evening Star," November 15, 1967, Tom Johnson's Notes of Meetings, Box 1, LBJL.

[94] Califano, *Triumph and Tragedy*, 258; U.S., President, *Public Papers*, Johnson, 1968–69, 1: 46–53, 248–63, 509–10.

chipped away at the administration's reformist resolve even before economic events reached crisis proportions in March 1968. In formally requesting his tax surcharge from Congress in August 1967, Johnson had tried to sweeten the deal by promising to make spending cuts. Britain's devaluation of the pound in November increased the pressure on the administration to trim expenditures. At a special meeting called to assess the devaluation, Johnson told his Cabinet, "This weekend has made it even more obvious that we must try to slash and stick with reductions in the Budget if we are to save the Great Society and try to get a Tax Bill . . . if we are not to suffer seriously." Speaking of "a new era of economic challenge," he exhorted his department heads to "sharpen your pencils and be prepared." Joseph Califano, LBJ's chief domestic aide, urged the president to emphasize to the Cabinet that "this program of cuts is designed to *preserve* the Great Society programs" from those who would use the failure to reach a compromise on the tax bill as an excuse to roll back earlier Great Society triumphs entirely.[95] In short, the administration remained committed to reform, but, under the pressure of a variety of forces, not the least of them economic, the definition of that commitment shifted increasingly from expanding reform to preserving it.

The reorientation from expansion to preservation was halting and uncertain. Sometimes, Johnson talked as though the two goals were interchangeable, but when on occasion he paid lip service to both in the same breath, the tension between them became evident. "There is a philosophy in the Congress," Johnson told his Cabinet in December 1967, "that we have done enough . . . that we should slow down and tighten up what we have done rather than undertake any new legislation . . . I don't agree." But he added immediately, "Whatever else we do, we have got to have a price tag on everything we come up with . . . We have got to know what every new proposal costs and who will pay for it . . . All of you have got to ask that question. We are all good at saying what we need but we don't know who will pay for it."[96]

The shift from expanding the Great Society to fighting to preserve it touched off a season of political contention for the administration and its liberal constituency. The issuance in February 1968 of the National Advisory Commission on Civil Disorders report on the urban riots of the previous summer constituted an opening round. The commission, headed by Illinois governor Otto Kerner, called for a massive expansion of governmental programs to deal with the ravages of white racism; its report made over 150 recommendations, which Johnson estimated privately would add between $75 and $100 billion to the federal budget over several years.[97] The commission's implicit indictment of previous efforts stung Johnson, and he instructed Califano to pass the word that the report was "destroying the President's interest in things like this."[98] Johnson's pique was familiar to those who

[95] U.S., President, *Public Papers*, Johnson, 1967, 2: 733–40; Cabinet Meeting Minutes, November 20, 1967, Cabinet Papers, Box 11, LBJL; Joseph Califano to Johnson, November 20, 1967, Cabinet Papers, Box 11, LBJL.

[96] Cabinet Meeting Minutes, December 6, 1967, Cabinet Papers, Box 12, LBJL. See also Sargent Shriver to Johnson, December 22, 1967, Aides Files, Califano, Box 8, LBJL. On Johnson's backing and filling at this point, see Califano, *Triumph and Tragedy*, 255–56.

[97] *Report of the National Advisory Commission on Civil Disorders* (New York, 1968); *New York Times* (March 2, 1968): 15; Cabinet Meeting Minutes, March 13, 1968, Cabinet Papers, Box 13, LBJL.

[98] LBJ quoted in Califano, *Triumph and Tragedy*, 261.

worked with him, a reaction to which he often succumbed and which he also often overcame. More daunting were the fiscal realities the president now confronted. "I am more practical," he told a delegation of black editors and publishers, "than some of those who wrote the report and some of the staff who sent it to me. First thing we have got to do is find the money. They didn't touch upon that problem. It's like saying we need sirloin steaks three nights a week, but only have the money to pay for two steaks." "I will never understand," he wrote later, "how the commission expected me to get this same Congress to turn 180 degrees overnight and appropriate an additional $30 billion for the same programs that it was demanding I cut by $6 billion."[99]

Organized labor pressed Johnson in a similar fashion. The American Federation of Labor cautioned against any "moratorium on domestic progress" and called instead for "a resurgence of a national determination to create an ever-better society in America." The AFL-CIO program for 1968 included legislation to make the federal government the employer of last resort and denounced the very idea of cuts in social spending. Nor was the AFL-CIO leadership sympathetic to the administration's fears regarding the international economy. Califano reported to Johnson that AFL-CIO president George Meany and his staff "believe the worst [consequence of] separating the dollar from gold would be to shake up international trade for a year or two without any serious repercussions here at home."[100] In the end, the union agreed that the need for a tax increase was overwhelming, and it therefore grudgingly and silently acquiesced in the $6 billion spending cut demanded by Mills and others as the quid pro quo for congressional action.[101]

Liberals carried the fight to the administration's inner councils. Califano kept up a steady drumbeat urging Johnson to "fight both the Congress and [Treasury Secretary] Fowler on anything like a $6 billion expenditure cut." Johnson's legislative liaison, Barefoot Sanders, shaken by the assassination of Martin Luther King, Jr., and the rioting that followed in early April, warned the president, "If, in the face of *more numerous and more vocal calls* for additional government action, the government appears to do less, by cutting appropriations in order to solve the financial crisis, we run the risk of leaving these people who want more done without any hope for accomplishing their programs within either the Democratic or Republican parties." Following Sanders's lead, Califano promptly took the offensive by suggesting that any budget cuts come from such "low priority areas" as the supersonic transport airplane program, the Apollo program, and federal highway expenditures. He implored Johnson to ask for an even greater tax hike and to direct an additional $3 to $5 billion to "relatively quick impact [social] programs." "The argument against [such a course]," he admitted, "is the balance of payments, the tax bill and Wilbur Mills." But perhaps the conventional wisdom of the Treasury Department regarding the relationship between the balance of payments, fiscal

[99] "Notes on Meeting with Negro Editors and Publishers," March 15, 1968, Diary Backup, Box 93, LBJL; Johnson, *Vantage Point*, 173.

[100] George Meany to Johnson, December 29, 1967, Aides Files, Califano, Box 8, LBJL; Califano to Johnson, March 28, 1968, Aides Files, Califano, Box 16, LBJL. See also Victor Riesel, "Inside Labor: Inside the White House; Labor Chiefs Warn LBJ; Budget Slash Plays into Hands of Kennedy and McCarthy," syndicated column dated May 16, 1968, in Aides Files, Califano, Box 17, LBJL.

[101] Califano to Johnson, May 29, 1968, Aides Files, Califano, Box 17, LBJL.

policy, and domestic priorities was based on false assumptions that had over time hardened into a "mythology" opposed to social welfare. Califano suggested that LBJ undertake "a thorough reassessment in the balance of payments and domestic priorities area—a reassessment of the same magnitude you have gone through with respect to Vietnam."[102] But Johnson's angry marginal comments on Califano's memo were unambiguous: "No!" "I don't agree." "Tell him to forget it—" "Ha! Ha!" "Forget it."[103]

In the end, Califano and his fellow Great Society all-outers failed to persuade LBJ on the issue of domestic priorities. Frightened by the March gold crisis, Johnson decided that the tax surcharge was "the most urgent issue facing the country" next to Vietnam. "I knew," he later wrote, "that any call for increased spending would give my opponents the excuse they sought to call me a reckless spender and kill the tax bill. If that happened, it could bring on an uncontrollable world monetary crisis of 1931 proportions and consequences." Moreover, the president realized that any such crisis would incite conservatives to destroy the Great Society rather than merely contain it. As Okun advised, "If a moderate expenditure cutback can achieve the tax bill, it would offer the best possible protection for our social programs."[104]

Johnson thus found himself fighting a two-front war. As he struggled against a recalcitrant Congress to minimize the expenditure reductions demanded for the passage of the tax hike, he also fought to gain the support of liberals for whatever expenditure-reduction deal he would finally strike. In both campaigns, Johnson used what Califano characterized as "Okun's Chamber of Horrors" approach.[105] Importuning Mills to agree to a compromise spending limitation, Johnson told the Ways and Means chairman that "whether he realized it or not, the country's economy was about to go down the drain and we had to write a tax bill that we could both live with."[106]

Johnson carried the same message to his friends. In mid-May, he exposed the liberals in his Cabinet to a dire analysis by the chairman of the CEA. "If the political realities are a tax bill with a $6 billion cut or no tax bill," Okun told them, "if that is the choice . . . I am ready to say by a definite margin that our economy is much better off with this overdose of fiscal restraint than none at all." He drew heavily on the recent crisis experience to drive home his point: "The international consequences of a tax bill failure would be very great indeed. It could be a calamity. We could have a sharp rise in speculation in the American dollar and another gold run." The bitter choice then, Okun warned, might be between suspending the convertibility of the dollar or increasing the price of gold. "We could get a real explosion in the world financial community . . . It may undermine all our gains and jeopardize the complete world political situation." Okun's conclusion was self-evident, but Johnson drew him out even further. "Therefore?" asked the president. Okun

[102] Califano to Johnson, April 3, 1968, Aides Files, Califano, Box 17, LBJL; Barefoot Sanders to Johnson, April 5, 1968, Diary Backup, Box 95, LBJL; Califano to Johnson, April 10, 1968, Aides Files, Califano, Box 16, LBJL.

[103] LBJ quoted in Califano, *Triumph and Tragedy*, 282–83.

[104] Johnson, *Vantage Point*, 451; Okun to Johnson, April 27, 1968, Diary Backup, Box 97, LBJL.

[105] Califano to Johnson, May 20, 1968, Aides Files, Califano, Box 54, LBJL.

[106] Johnson, *Vantage Point*, 453.

answered, "Take a tax bill with the $6 billion cutback. It's hard advice to give but I think it's the best advice. It is the only advice I can give."[107] Swallowing hard, Johnson and the liberals took it.

The Revenue and Expenditure Control Act of 1968 forced on the administration's domestic agenda a discipline of stringency not unlike that already visited upon the administration's war policy. Wilbur Mills took satisfaction in what he perceived to be "the anguished cries of Federal administrators who are feeling the sharp bite of these legislative incisors."[108] Yet the outcome was more complicated than Mills's crowing allowed. The administration worked hard to shield its most critical social programs from budget cuts; Congress could agree to trim only slightly less than $4 billion from fiscal 1969 expenditures, and the president refused to make further reductions on his own.[109] Indeed, aggregate social welfare spending continued to rise, in 1969 and throughout the Nixon years. But the 1968 episode did constitute a sea change, because it shifted the emphasis from an expansion of the Great Society to its preservation. In fiscal year 1969, federal social welfare expenditures (in constant dollars) grew at a rate less than half that of 1965.[110] As historians Irwin and Debi Unger have written, "In June 1968 the Great Society, already badly wounded at the hands of its friends and enemies alike, lost its forward movement and its inner spirit."[111] What was left was not the powerful reform surge of mid-decade but only its inertia.

In its aftershocks, the economic crisis of 1968 left a deep imprint on both U.S. foreign affairs and domestic policy, on the history of a momentous year and a remarkable era. Growth liberalism—the interpenetration of liberal politics and growth economics—was a defining feature of the 1960s and the apotheosis of the postwar optimism that undergirded the notion of an American Century. In 1968, growth liberalism came a cropper and the American Century came to an end. The forces at work were many, the pattern of causation complex. But matters of political economy were central. The experience and consequences of the economic crisis of 1968 remind us that the history of the 1960s was not written entirely in the streets.

[107] Minutes of Special Cabinet Meeting, May 14, 1968, Cabinet Papers, Box 13, LBJL.
[108] Wilbur Mills, Remarks to Little Rock Rotary Club, August 29, 1968, Box 420, Mills Papers.
[109] Califano, *Triumph and Tragedy*, 288.
[110] Sar A. Levitan and Robert Taggart, *The Promise of Greatness: The Social Programs of the Last Decade and Their Major Achievements* (Cambridge, Mass., 1976), 21.
[111] Unger and Unger, *America in the 1960s*, 45.

Robert M. Collins is a professor of history at the University of Missouri, Columbia, where he teaches recent U.S. history. He has also taught at North Carolina State University and the University of Manchester. Collins earned his PhD at Johns Hopkins University under the supervision of Louis Galambos. He has written a number of articles on American historiography, including "The Originality Trap: Richard Hofstadter on Populism," in the *Journal of American History* (1989). In the area of political economy, he is the author of *The Business Response to Keynes, 1929–1964* (1981) and "Growth Liberalism in the Sixties," in *The Sixties: From Memory to History*, edited by David Farber (1994). The article in this issue is part of a larger project he is presently completing, a study of the political economy of growth in post–World War II America.

PRESIDENTIAL ADDRESS

"Peoples Quite Apart": Americans, South Vietnamese, and the War in Vietnam*

GEORGE C. HERRING

The interaction between Americans and South Vietnamese is one of the least developed areas in the burgeoning literature of the Vietnam War. In much of the writing on the war, the South Vietnamese are conspicuous by their absence, and virtually nothing has been done on their dealings with the United States. Yet analysis of the relations between these two allies—"peoples quite apart," former Ambassador to the United States Bui Diem once perceptively labeled them—can tell us much about why the war took the course it did.[1] It can also tell us Americans a great deal about the way we relate to other peoples and about the impact of our intervention on other nations.

The dilemmas and frustrations that would confront the United States and South Vietnam in their dealings with each other were painfully apparent in the hopelessly tangled and ultimately tragic relationship between the John F. Kennedy administration and Ngo Dinh Diem, president of the Republic of Vietnam from 1955 to 1963. In one sense, at least, Diem met the American criterion for leadership of South Vietnam: he was intensely nationalistic, certainly the most nationalistic of any South Vietnamese leader. Far more than his successors, he was wary of American influence and extremely sensitive to the dangers of a large-scale American presence in South Vietnam. He perceived that too great an American influence in his government would taint him in the eyes of his countrymen. He staunchly refused to accept conditions in return for U.S. assistance. He firmly resisted

---

*SHAFR presidential address delivered at San Francisco, 29 December 1989. The author would like to thank Robert Hodges for help with the research, Andy McIntire for critical comments, and especially Dottie Leathers for her varied and invaluable assistance in the preparation of this article and throughout his year as SHAFR president.

[1] Quoted in Stephen T. Hosmer et al., *The Fall of South Vietnam: Statements by Vietnamese Military and Civilian Leaders* (Santa Monica, 1978), 33.

the introduction of American troops. South Vietnam would "not be a protectorate," he adamantly insisted.[2]

The problem, of course, was that Diem also had a well-developed penchant for self-destruction. His flaws of leadership were manifest from the outset—a "messiah without a message," one U.S. diplomat labeled him in 1954.[3] Stubborn, narrow-minded, and unable to relate to his own people, he was fatally nepotistic in his reliance on his family, especially his brother Ngo Dinh Nhu, his theoretician and political strongman whom some Americans suspected of madness. He was also so convinced of the rightness of his cause, complained one frustrated American, that he "might easily carry the whole edifice to perdition because it was right to do so."[4] By 1961, U.S. officials were certain that if he did not change his ways the war would be lost.

The Kennedy administration could devise no solution for this conundrum. In late 1961, the United States attached conditions to its offer of additional economic and military assistance, but when Diem balked it quickly retreated. U.S. officials saw no real alternative—"Diem is Diem and the best we've got," Kennedy ruefully lamented.[5] To push him too far ran the risk of losing him—and the war. Yet Americans feared that giving in to him might deprive them of the means to win the war. The United States also lost support among non-Communist South Vietnamese opposition groups who could not understand why it would permit itself to be manipulated by Diem against its own interests.[6] Americans perceived, moreover, that they lost face with Diem, and as representatives of the world's greatest power they keenly resented being the puppet of their puppet.

As the war dragged on and the gap between the United States and South Vietnam widened, tensions increased on both sides. Even without the Ngos, there were problems deriving from history and culture. The two nations differed fundamentally in their approaches. By nature impatient, the Americans "were anxious to get on with the job." "Proud and stubborn, the Vietnamese didn't relish taking advice, especially from Occidentals." Each side was persuaded that the other was not doing enough to prove its commitment and loyalty. "We always felt that you Americans wanted to test us too much," Madame Nhu told journalist Robert Shaplen. "We have our whole lives and experience behind us in Vietnam. Why do you keep asking us to prove ourselves?" Beyond the surface distrust, Shaplen added, "was the whole tragic overlay of history, of colonialism and 'neo-colonialism,' of white men versus yellow men, and of the sort of deep miscomprehension

---

[2]Frederick Nolting to State Department, 18 November 1961, John F. Kennedy Papers, National Security File, box 195, John F. Kennedy Library, Boston, Massachusetts.

[3]Robert McClintock to State Department, 4 July 1954, *Foreign Relations of the United States, 1952–1954* (Washington, 1979), 13: 1783–84

[4]Howard Sochick, "Report From Viet-Nam," n.d., Kennedy Papers, Official File, box 128.

[5]Quoted in Benjamin Bradlee, *Conversations with Kennedy* (New York, 1975), 59.

[6]Bui Diem with David Chanoff, *In the Jaws of History* (Boston, 1987), 96–98.

that could only be resolved—perhaps—in time of peace, but surely not in time of war."[7]

The Buddhist crisis of 1963 brought the conflict with Diem to a head and added a new and inscrutable piece of the puzzle. Skilled propagandists, the Buddhists quickly learned how to use the American media to advantage, and their fiery protests forced Vietnam into the consciousness of the American public for the first time, adding new and compelling pressures for decisive action. Anti-Diemist Vietnamese protested that oppression of the Buddhists was made possible by U.S. aid and insisted that the United States must displace Diem. Furious at being led "around by the nose" by Diem and Nhu, American officials had to show the Vietnamese, in Roger Hilsman's words, that "we are not and cannot be their complete puppets."[8]

But a solution now appeared even more difficult. Americans could never discover exactly what the Buddhists were about or what they wanted. Embassy officers "despaired of cutting through their obscure, fog shrouded rhetoric," Chester Cooper later observed, and even when the State Department sent to them a Foreign Service officer who was a Buddhist he could do little better.[9] In any event, efforts to persuade Diem to rid himself of Nhu and accommodate the Buddhists were unavailing.

Kennedy and his advisers eventually solved the problem by authorizing the ill-fated coup that brought the deaths of Diem and Nhu. As some U.S. officials had predicted, however, the "solution" produced greater problems. The demise of Diem left a vacuum that the United States itself would have to fill. Americans were probably relieved to take over the war rather than continue to work through a feckless and intractable ally. But the pervasive Americanization of the war that took place in 1965 produced a whole new set of problems and a more complex and ultimately equally fateful relationship with the South Vietnamese.

The overthrow of Diem opened the way to a series of revolving-door governments that changed with startling rapidity. Indeed, for much of the period from November 1963 to May 1965, it was impossible to tell the players without a scorecard. The ascendancy of the so-called Young Turks, Nguyen Van Thieu and Nguyen Cao Ky, offered cold comfort to perplexed U.S. policymakers. The flamboyant Ky resembled a character from a comic opera. "A Hollywood central casting bureau would have grabbed him for a role as a sax player in a second-rate Manila night club," Cooper later observed. Secretary of Defense Robert McNamara "seemed momentarily dazed and bemused" at his first sight of Ky, Cooper recalled, and another American standing nearby was overheard to mutter: "At least no one could confuse him

---

[7]Robert Shaplen, *The Lost Revolution: The U.S. in Vietnam, 1946–1966* (New York, 1966), 162, 151–52.

[8]Roger Hilsman memorandum on meeting with Peter Lisagor, Hugh Sidey, and Marguerite Higgins, 2 September 1963, Kennedy Papers, National Security File, box 198–99.

[9]Chester A. Cooper, *The Lost Crusade: America in Vietnam* (New York, 1970), 209–10.

with Uncle Ho!"[10] The Ky-Thieu directorate "seemed to all of us the bottom of the barrel," William Bundy later remarked, "absolutely the bottom of the barrel."[11]

Throughout the period 1963–1965, U.S. officials became increasingly and painfully aware of the chronic, deeply rooted deficiencies of their ally. A National Security Council (NSC) study in late 1964 highlighted the "atypical features" of South Vietnam that dogged U.S. efforts at nation-building: a "bad colonial heritage," inadequate preparation for self-government, a nationalist movement that had been taken over by Communists, and a rival government that had inherited "much the better military force and far more than its share of talent."[12] In cables to Washington detailing the problems in South Vietnam, Ambassador to Saigon Maxwell Taylor repeatedly complained of the "chronic factionalism, civilian-military suspicions and distrust, absence of national spirit and motivation, lack of cohesion in the social structure, [and] lack of experience in the conduct of government."[13]

By the spring and early summer of 1965, South Vietnam verged on collapse. The armed forces were "close to anarchy," General William Depuy warned General William Westmoreland, and unless the "generals stopped fighting over the spoils there will soon be no spoils over which to fight."[14] "I don't think we ought to take this government seriously," former Ambassador Henry Cabot Lodge told a top-level meeting on 21 July 1965. "There is no one who can do anything." A more charitable President Lyndon B. Johnson evaluated the South Vietnamese leaders in the political context he knew best. "They're like Republicans," he said, "who try to stay in power, but don't stay there long."[15]

The weakness of South Vietnam was the overriding issue facing U.S. leaders in the summer of 1965. For months, the Johnson administration had hesitated to escalate the war for fear that North Vietnam would deal a crippling blow to the beleaguered Saigon regime. Indeed, the foremost opponent of escalation, Undersecretary of State George Ball, even used the incompetence of the Government of Vietnam as a justification for U.S. withdrawal. Dismissing the South Vietnamese leaders as "clowns," Ball warned that the United States could not build anything on such a "totally

---

[10]Ibid., 281.

[11]William Bundy oral history interview, Lyndon Baines Johnson Library, Austin, Texas.

[12]Senate Subcommittee on Public Buildings and Grounds, *The Pentagon Papers (The Senator Gravel Edition)*, 4 vols. (Boston, 1971), 3:625.

[13]Taylor to Dean Rusk, 5 January 1965, Lyndon Baines Johnson Papers, National Security File, National Security Council Histories, Deployment of Forces, Vol. 1, Tabs 1–10, box 40, Johnson Library.

[14]General William Depuy to General William Westmoreland, 13 April 1965, William Depuy Papers, folder D(65), U.S. Army Military History Institute, Carlisle Barracks, Pennsylvania.

[15]Notes on meeting, 21 July 1965, Johnson Papers, Meeting Notes File, box 1.

fragile political base." Reminding his colleagues that President Dwight D. Eisenhower had conditioned the original promise of U.S. aid on South Vietnamese performance, he urged that the United States pull out because the South Vietnamese had not lived up to their part of the deal.[16]

In the top-level discussions of June and July 1965, Ball was a minority of one. Other officials shared his view of South Vietnamese deficiencies. But they were more concerned with the risks of national humiliation from withdrawal, and, like Secretary of State Dean Rusk, they were certain that U.S. skill and resources could somehow make up for South Vietnam's weakness.[17] In a curious reversal of arguments the main obstacle to intervention in 1964 became the main reason for intervention in 1965: The perceived ineptitude of the South Vietnamese government and armed forces.

Significantly, if not surprisingly, in escalating the war the United States virtually ignored the object of its concern, its South Vietnamese ally. The Saigon government was scarcely consulted on the decisions to bomb North Vietnam and enemy base areas in South Vietnam, bring U.S. Marines to Vietnam to guard air bases, and dispatch major increments of U.S. combat troops. The most that was done was to request its concurrence and brief its leaders on decisions already made. Looking back on the fateful days of 1965, Bui Diem has rightly noted the absence of communication between the United States and its ally, the "unself-conscious arrogance" of the United States, and the impotence of the South Vietnamese, who acquiesced in a large-scale U.S. presence against their better judgment and despite the fact that they had just emerged from years of foreign domination. "The Americans came in like bulldozers," Diem observed, "and the South Vietnamese followed their lead without a word of dissent, for the most part without a thought of dissent."[18]

The United States took over the war in a big way in the summer of 1965. To throw money, men, and resources at a problem is an entirely American way of doing things, of course, and in this instance the perceived incompetence of the South Vietnamese provided an added incentive. Thus, between 1965 and 1967, the United States inundated South Vietnam with men, money, and material. It imposed its views and ways on its hapless ally, undermining a fragile political culture with the largesse of the affluent society. It reduced the Saigon government to a "submissive order taker" that lost respect and credibility in the eyes of its own people.[19] Unwittingly, it induced a form of dependency in a client whose independence it had professedly gone to war to defend. Yet despite its overwhelming presence, the United States still had difficulty getting the South Vietnamese to do its bidding. And as the American presence grew, tensions between the allies also increased, threatening an already tenuous relationship.

---

[16]David D. Leo, "Rethinking Containment: George Ball's Vietnam Dissent," unpublished ms. in possession of author, 162, 182.

[17]Ibid., 182.

[18]Diem, *Jaws of History*, 127, 153.

[19]Quoted in Hosmer, *Fall of South Vietnam*, 28.

America's approach to its ally was manifest in decisions made early in the war on the command structure and the assignment of missions. Westmoreland had originally thought in terms of a combined command such as the one used in Korea. Experience seemed to commend it, and it appeared a way to buck up a faltering ally. The South Vietnamese resisted such an arrangement, however, perceiving it as a form of neocolonialism. Westmoreland deferred to Saigon's sensitivities, probably eagerly, seeing all too clearly the difficulties in shaping up the South Vietnamese armed forces and the complications stemming from direct involvement with them.[20]

The decision on command structure significantly influenced the assignment of missions. The lack of a unified command made combined operations of any sort impractical and even put a premium on separating the forces of the two allies into clearly delineated zones with different missions and objectives. Because of the demonstrated weakness of the South Vietnamese armed forces, moreover, U.S. officials concluded early on that the war could best be won by using American air and ground forces in a campaign of attrition against North Vietnam. U.S. ground forces were thus given the most important military mission—search-and-destroy operations against North Vietnamese Army (NVA) and National Liberation Front (NLF) main forces. Such a mission also accorded with what Russell Weigley has called the "American way of war," the traditional, offensive modus operandi of the U.S. Army that emphasized destruction of the enemy's main forces. In Westmoreland's view, it had the additional advantage of keeping U.S. troops away from the population centers where friction might develop with the South Vietnamese.

The assignment of missions also reflected cultural prejudices. The Vietnamese could not handle "complex, detailed U.S. conceived programs," the Joint Chiefs of Staff (JCS) insisted, and should therefore be giver simpler tasks. In addition, pacification was not an "action word" and was "too slow" for the Americans, who preferred an offensive strategy and quick results.[21] Certain in any event that the Army of the Republic of Vietnam (ARVN) could not win the war, U.S. officers preferred to have it out of the way and relegated it to the secondary missions of pacification and population security. Old soldier Maxwell Taylor shrewdly warned that by becoming the "primary doer," the United States would absorb the highest casualties, thus threatening domestic support for the war, and would demoralize the South Vietnamese. But Westmoreland and the JCS overrode his objections. South Vietnamese officers had reservations about U.S. strategy, but in general said nothing.[22] We "depended so heavily on the Americans for almost everything that it was difficult to get our opinions taken into account," General Cao Van Vien later observed.[23]

---

[20]Jeffrey J. Clarke, *Advice and Support: The Final Years, 1965–1973* (Washington, 1988), 87–93.

[21]Ibid., 120.

[22]Ibid., 121–22.

[23]Diem, *Jaws of History*, 155.

The separated commands impeded the effective conduct of military operations in a variety of ways. North Vietnamese and NLF forces were able to exploit the "seams" between administrative areas where the authority of one commander began and another ended. A verbal agreement between the two commands to coordinate operations failed to ensure that coordination actually took place. U.S. and South Vietnamese forces frequently surprised each other with military initiatives. The lack of coordination hindered the ability of each to respond to enemy attacks and occasionally resulted in the accidental shelling of friendly forces.[24] The emphasis given the U.S. combat mission meant that, in terms of equipment and training, South Vietnamese forces were neglected and the modernization program languished. South Vietnamese officers would also later claim that relegation of their units to security duties eroded their combat effectiveness and left them ill prepared to fight the big-unit war that would be forced upon them.[25]

Americanization of the war also produced among the South Vietnamese what was called the "takeover effect." U.S. officials vigorously debated in early 1965 whether the infusion of American forces would bolster flagging ARVN morale or encourage the South Vietnamese to step aside, and the answer was not long in coming. As early as 8 March 1965, the day the Marines landed at Danang, a South Vietnamese general expressed concern that his forces were showing a "tendency to 'let the Americans do it.'"[26] Many officers and men found the pacification mission demeaning and assumed it without enthusiasm, and they were quite content to sit back and let the United States run the war. "Why should we fight," Ky heard one soldier remark. "The Americans are doing the fighting for us."[27] Some Vietnamese even concluded after 1965 that they were fighting for the United States in a war that was America's, not theirs. Many of the better ARVN officers sat out the war in Saigon, frequenting the nightclubs and amassing personal fortunes from the corruption that pervaded every nook and cranny of South Vietnamese life.[28] The takeover effect was dramatically apparent in South Vietnamese performance. A study by John Paul Vann in late 1967 indicated that South Vietnamese small-unit operations had dropped off sharply in number and effectiveness after the Americans entered the war. ARVN forces were not providing security for pacification, and only in a small percentage of operations were they making contact with the enemy.[29]

The U.S. command imposed its own ways on its ally. Training programs were based on American models, and although the South Vietnamese army was assigned pacification duties, it was still organized and

---

[24]James J. Wirtz, "Explaining an Instance of Intrawar Intelligence Failure: The American Military Response to the 1968 Tet Offensive" (Ph.D. diss., Columbia University, 1989), 185–91.

[25]General Cao Van Vien and Lt. General Dong Van Khuyen, *Reflections on the Vietnam War* (Washington, 1980), 80–81, 57.

[26]Depuy memorandum for the record, 9 March 1965, Depuy Papers, folder D(65).

[27]Nguyen Cao Ky, *How We Lost the Vietnam War* (New York, 1984), 151.

[28]Clarke, *Final Years*, 230–31

[29]Ibid., 253.

trained to fight conventional warfare in the American mold. The ARVN in time became a carbon copy of the U.S. Army, with a huge, unwieldy logistics "tail" and one combat soldier for every five support troops. The South Vietnamese were encouraged to call upon U.S. forces for fire and air support and for backup when they encountered difficulties. They emulated their mentors in the lavish and often careless use of resources, particularly in the overreliance on firepower and air support. Bringing to their alliance with the world's greatest power an inferiority complex and a "blind confidence" in the United States, the South Vietnamese watched their ally and concluded that its way of fighting was the correct way.[30] More dangerous, perhaps, the high standard of living of American forces rubbed off on those Vietnamese who worked closely with them.

U.S. dominance of South Vietnam was almost complete. The United States controlled the fighting, financed the country, and selected or influenced the selection of leaders down to the village level. Even at the level of district chief, every South Vietnamese official had a full-time American adviser, and thus the entire governmental apparatus was paralleled by an American structure. The United States paid, clothed, and equipped the South Vietnamese army. American officers drew up military plans and submitted them to the South Vietnamese Joint General Staff, which translated them into Vietnamese and passed them on to its units for implementation. The American presence was so powerful and pervasive that many Vietnamese viewed their own government as a puppet, devoid of national prestige, and frequently referred to the U.S. ambassador as "the Governor General." In fact, as Jonathan Schell observed, the Government of Vietnam was less a puppet government than a "balloon government," which owed its very existence to a foreign master. "When a balloon government is puffed up by its master," Schell noted, "it may look fairly impressive. But when the air is let out it doesn't so much collapse as reveal that it hardly existed in the first place."[31]

The American treatment of South Vietnam's leaders in itself speaks volumes about the nature of the relationship. When Secretary of Defense McNamara met with South Vietnamese officials on the eve of the administration's troop decision in July 1965, he made no apparent effort to size up Prime Minister Ky. "I wondered," Bui Diem later wrote, "if Ky simply did not matter to him." At Honolulu in February 1966, when Ky committed South Vietnam to attack ignorance and disease, President Johnson responded with unabashed enthusiasm, "Boy, you speak just like an American," perhaps the highest praise the president could lavish on him, Ky later acknowledged. At Guam in March 1967, however, when an angered Johnson chastised the Vietnamese leader for his public protests about U.S. restrictions on military operations above the demilitarized zone, David Lilienthal observed the smaller Ky, seated on a sofa between Johnson and

[30]Diem, *Jaws of History*, 210.

[31]Hosmer, *Fall of South Vietnam*, 29–30; Ky, *How We Lost the Vietnam War*, 123–24, 137–38; Jonathan Schell, *Observing the Nixon Years: "Notes and Comments" from the New Yorker on the Vietnam War and the Watergate Crisis, 1969–1975* (New York, 1989), 4, 91.

Secretary of State Rusk, "his eyes cast downward like a boy being scolded." Ky's successor, Nguyen Van Thieu, was infuriated and felt that he had lost face with his own people when President Richard M. Nixon insisted that they meet at isolated Guam rather than in Washington or even Honolulu.[32]

The sudden infusion of one half million American troops, hundreds of civilian advisers, and billions of dollars had a profoundly disruptive effect on a weak and divided nation. The buildup was so rapid and vast that it threatened to overwhelm South Vietnam. Saigon's ports were congested with ships and goods, and vessels awaiting unloading were backed up far out to sea. The city itself became a "thorough-going boom town," Robert Shaplen remarked, its streets clogged with traffic, its restaurants "bursting with boisterous soldiers," its bars as "crowded as New York subway cars in the rush hour."[33]

Signs of the American presence appeared everywhere. Vietnamese children wore Batman tee shirts. Long strips of seedy bars and brothels sprang up overnight around base areas—the one at Bien Hoa came to be called Tijuana East. In a remote village near Danang, Marine Lieutenant Philip Caputo encountered houses made of discarded beer cans: "red and white Budweiser, gold Miller, cream and brown Schlitz, blue and gold Hamm's from the land of sky-blue waters."[34] Returning to Vietnam in 1965 after a two-year absence, John Vann expressed outrage at the "ugly transformation" of the country.[35]

American spending had a devastating effect on the vulnerable South Vietnamese economy. Prices increased by as much as 170 percent during the first two years of the buildup. The United States eventually controlled the rate of inflation by paying its own soldiers in scrip and by flooding the country with consumer goods, but the corrective measures themselves had harmful side effects. Instead of using American aid to promote economic development, South Vietnamese importers bought watches, transistor radios, and Hondas to sell to people employed by the United States. The vast influx of American goods destroyed South Vietnam's few native industries and made the economy even more dependent on continued outside aid. By 1967, much of the urban population was employed providing services to the Americans, and the American presence absorbed much of the country's skilled labor.[36]

In the bonanza atmosphere, crime and corruption flourished. Corruption was not new to South Vietnam or unusual in a nation at war, but by 1966 it operated on an incredible scale. Government officials rented land to the United States at inflated prices, required bribes for drivers' licenses, passports, visas, and work permits, extorted kickbacks for contracts to build

---

[32]Diem, *Jaws of History*, 152; Ky, *How We Lost the Vietnam War*, 81; David Lilienthal, *The Journals of David Lilienthal*, 7 vols. (New York, 1964–1983), 6:417.

[33]Robert Shaplen, *The Road from War: Vietnam, 1965–1970* (New York, 1970), 24.

[34]Philip Caputo, *A Rumor of War* (New York, 1977), 107.

[35]Neil Sheehan, *A Bright and Shining Lie: John Paul Vann and America in Vietnam* (New York, 1988), 617.

[36]Vien and Khuyen, *Reflections*, 50–57.

and service facilities, and took part in the illicit importation of opium. The black market in scrip, dollars, and stolen American goods became a major enterprise. On Saigon's infamous PX Alley, an open-air market covering two city blocks and comprising more than one hundred stalls, purchasers could buy everything from hand grenades to scotch whiskey—even tanks—at markups as high as 300 percent. The pervasive corruption undermined the U.S. aid program and demoralized the society.[37]

American officials could find no way to contain the problem, much less resolve it. Ky candidly admitted that "most of the generals are corrupt. Most of the senior officials in the provinces are corrupt." But, he added calmly, "corruption exists everywhere, and people can live with some of it. You live with it in Chicago and New York."[38] The embassy pressed the government to remove officials known to be corrupt, but with little result. "You fight like hell to get someone removed and most times you fail and you just make it worse," a frustrated American explained. "And then on occasions [when] you win, why hell, they give you someone just as bad."[39]

Indeed, paradoxically, despite its vast power and overwhelming presence, the United States could not get the South Vietnamese to do what it wanted. Americans in fact found to their chagrin that as their commitment increased, their leverage diminished. Concern with corruption and inefficiency was always balanced by the fear that tough action might alienate the government or bring about its collapse, and the Saigon government effectively neutralized the limited U.S. leverage by going through the motions of reform or appearing to do things the American way, all the while resisting real change.[40]

U.S. officials could never decide how to deal with the problem. In fact, they faced an insoluble dilemma. If they took charge, they diluted the purity of the South Vietnamese cause. If they did not, things did not get done. John Vann urged that the United States simply take over and run the government until the war had been won. Ambassador Henry Cabot Lodge and General Westmoreland were not inclined to go that far, however, preferring to deal with the situation as it was, and, in Westmoreland's case, concentrate on military operations. The inability or unwillingness of U.S. officials to exploit the limited leverage available to them was, in Lawrence Grinter's words, "the fundamental operational failure of our experience with South Vietnam."[41]To the South Vietnamese, at the same time, the United States presented "an inconstant, often self-contradictory force," always "tip-toeing

---

[37]See, for example, *New York Times*, 16 November 1966; and Abraham Ribicoff to Robert McLellan, 15 January 1969, and memorandum, 15 January 1970, Abraham Ribicoff Papers, box 432, Manuscript Division, Library of Congress, Washington, DC.

[38]Harry McPherson to Lyndon Baines Johnson, 13 June 1967, Johnson Papers, Aides File: Harry McPherson, box 29.

[39]David Halberstam, "Return to Vietnam," *Harpers* 235 (December 1967): 52.

[40]Lawrence E. Grinter, "Bargaining between Saigon and Washington: Dilemmas of Linkage Politics during War," *Orbis* 18 (Fall 1974): 837–67.

[41]Ibid., 865; Clarke, *Final Years*, 193.

along a delicate tightrope between intervention and non-intervention. The U.S. government never seemed to quite figure out whether or not it was proper to intervene and as a result it brought itself and its Vietnamese ally the worst of both positions."[42]

As the American presence grew and the relationship with South Vietnam became more complex, tensions between Americans and South Vietnamese increased. In the early years, many U.S. advisers had developed a sentimental attachment to the Vietnamese, living with them, sharing their food, and imbibing their culture. In the aftermath of the U.S. buildup, some Americans continued to work effectively with the Vietnamese, establishing themselves as *co-van*, or trusted friend.[43] This was especially true at the lower levels and in combat situations and among those advisers who served in remote villages. Lieutenant David Donovan, a senior district adviser in the Mekong Delta, even accepted membership in a secret society of Hoa Hao warriors, one of the initiation rites of which was to eat coagulated duck blood.[44]

For the most part, however, as the American presence became pervasive, mutual suspicion and resentment increased. The two peoples approached each other with colossal ignorance. "My time in Vietnam is the memory of ignorance," one GI later conceded. "I didn't know the language. I knew nothing about the village community. I knew nothing about the aims of the people—whether they were for the war or against the war."[45] For the Americans, the elemental task of distinguishing friend from foe became a sometimes impossible challenge. "What we need is some . . . kind of litmus paper that turns red when it's near a communist," one U.S. officer half seriously, half jokingly, told journalist Malcolm Browne.[46] The Vietnamese found American culture incomprehensible, and knew little more about American history than some clichés about the Marshall Plan and anticommunism.[47] "We went to war side by side, puzzled by each other," Nguyen Cao Ky later wrote, "a country of yesterday and a country of tomorrow, each trying to keep in step with the other."[48]

The ethnocentricity of both peoples emphasized profound cultural differences. The Americans were forward looking, optimistic, and impatient, the Vietnamese closely tied to their past, resigned and cautious, and infinitely

---

[42]Diem, *Jaws of History*, 111.

[43]John Grider Miller, *Bridge at Dong Ha* (Annapolis, 1989), 13–14; Sheehan, *Vann*, 65. See also Hosmer, *Fall of South Vietnam*, 35.

[44]David Donovan, *Once a Warrior King: Memories of an Officer in Vietnam* (New York, 1985), 241–42. The South Vietnamese thought cooperation between the two peoples was closest at the lowest levels, especially among combat soldiers, and worst at the middle levels. See Hosmer, *Fall of South Vietnam*, 35.

[45]Quoted in Clark Dougan and Stephen Weiss, *The American Experience in Vietnam* (New York, 1988), 62.

[46]Malcolm W. Browne, *The New Face of War* (Indianapolis, 1968), 46.

[47]Hosmer, *Fall of South Vietnam*, 33.

[48]Ky, *How We Lost the Vietnam War*, 12.

patient.[49] The Americans had a blind faith in technology; the Vietnamese clung to age-old superstitions. A story told by Ky graphically illustrates the differences. On one occasion when a U.S. adviser proposed using tear gas to clear out an enemy stronghold, his Vietnamese counterpart protested that it was the windy season and if the wind blew the tear gas away the attack would fail. The American insisted that that was no problem. There was plenty more gas and the attack could be resumed when the wind died down. "But if the wind blows the gas away," the Vietnamese responded, "everyone in the area will believe that God is on the side of the Communists."[50]

Although fighting in a common cause, the two peoples grew increasingly suspicious and resentful of each other. The more the Americans assumed the burden of the fighting, the more they demeaned the martial abilities of their ally. "I wish the southern members of the clan would display the fighting qualities of their northern brethren," a senior U.S. officer observed with obvious scorn.[51] Although shunted aside as a direct result of a U.S. policy decision, the ARVN became an object of ridicule, its attack mode best depicted, according to a standard American joke, by the statue of a seated soldier in the National Military Cemetery. "They have too few Nathan Hales," an adviser complained. "They want to make babies during and after the conflict. They do not equate their dying for their country as a necessity for the future."[52]

Among many GIs, the South Vietnamese people also became an object of scorn. Some Americans perhaps expected to be greeted like their fathers who had liberated France in World War II, but instead found themselves treated like an invading army. The seeming indifference of many Vietnamese, while Americans were dying in the field, provoked resentment and hatred. Americans viewed with contempt the poverty in which many Vietnamese lived. The "filth . . . was beyond any one's wildest dreams," one soldier wrote home; the people "live like pigs," remarked another.[53] Americans expressed contempt for the consumer culture they had created and for the apparent determination of the South Vietnamese to exact the last possible dollar from it. "The war has brought out all the venality imaginable in these people," observed GI Thomas Pellaton.[54] "Everywhere I looked," John Ketwig added, "I found a society of murderers, thieves, and carnival hucksters."[55]

---

[49]Ibid., 126–27, 135.

[50]Ibid., 127.

[51]General A. S. Collins to Edward F. Smith, 15 November 1966, A. S. Collins Papers, U.S. Army Military History Institute.

[52]Curtis Herrick diary, 17 November 1964, Curtis Herrick Papers, U.S. Army Military History Institute.

[53]Bernard Edelman, ed., *Dear America: Letters Home from Vietnam* (New York, 1985), 54.

[54]Ibid., 150.

[55]John Ketwig, . . . *And a Hard Rain Fell: A GI's True Story of the War in Vietnam* (New York, 1985), 29.

Among the most serious problems was a basic lack of trust. Because of chronic security leaks, the United States kept Vietnamese off its major bases, and Vietcong infiltration of the ARVN's top ranks compelled U.S. officers to keep from their Vietnamese counterparts the details of major military operations. The unerring ability of the villagers to avoid mines and booby traps that killed and maimed Americans led to charges of collusion with the enemy. The people were "treacherous," one GI wrote. "They say 'GI number one' when we're in the village, but at night the dirty little rats are VC." "Everybody in this fucking country is VC," John Ketwig recalls a buddy saying. "During the day they'll smile and take your money. At night they'll creep in and slit your throat."[56]

The Vietnamese attitude toward the foreigners was at best ambivalent. Although many Vietnamese undoubtedly appreciated American generosity, they were also bewildered by the opulence and waste. Sometimes, they found amusement in the curious ways of their allies. The Americans were going to cement over the entire country, went a standard joke, and in that way win the war because there would be no people left. Those Vietnamese who fought against the intrusion of American culture only became more aware of its pervasiveness. Nguyen Duc Thang, a friend of Edward Lansdale, launched a one-man crusade against the use of American slang by Saigon's street kids. When he accosted one youth and asked him to speak "polite Vietnamese" instead, the child looked at him in amazement and responded: "My! How did you American learn to speak such good Vietnamese?"[57]

More often, the American presence provoked anger and resentment. Vietnamese naturally resented the way the Americans looked down on them and imposed American methods on a presumably inferior people. They were angered by American impatience. "They want everything done yesterday, not tomorrow," General Lu Mong Van later complained.[58] They envied the high life of the Americans, their air-conditioned bars and clubs, the PXs where Vietnamese were not permitted to shop. They complained that American soldiers "acted despicably" toward them, tearing up roads and endangering the lives of civilians by deliberately reckless handling of vehicles and firearms. An ARVN major protested that Americans trusted only those Vietnamese who accepted without question their way of doing things and doled out their aid in the "same way as that given to beggars."[59] Most of all, the South Vietnamese resented their growing dependence on the United States and its increasing visibility in every facet of their lives. They wondered how South Vietnam could maintain its identity if the Americans dominated everything from the economy to the manner of waging war.[60]

---

[56]Edelman, *Dear America*, 109–10; Ketwig, *Hard Rain Fell*, 29.

[57]Cecil B. Currey, *Edward Lansdale: The Unquiet American* (Boston, 1989), 302, 312.

[58]Quoted in Al Santoli, *To Bear Any Burden: The Vietnam War and Its Aftermath in the Words of Americans and Southeast Asians* (New York, 1985), 117, 119.

[59]Weekly Psyops Field Operation Report, 2 December 1967, John Paul Vann Papers, U.S. Army Military History Institute.

[60]Diem, *Jaws of History*, 208.

The result was a strange mix of feelings. Many Vietnamese recognized their need for U.S. help, and some were probably grateful for it. Others were quite content to let the United States assume responsibility for their survival. At the same time, many Vietnamese came to consider the U.S. "occupation" a "demoralizing scourge," even theorizing that "if we could only get rid of the Americans, then we could worry about the Viet Cong."[61] Thoughtful Vietnamese perceived that the Americans were not "colonialists," Shaplen commented. But, he added, "there has evolved here a colonial ambience that can sometimes be worse than colonialism itself."[62]

As with so many other areas of the war, the Tet Offensive of 1968 was a turning point in U.S.-South Vietnamese relations. Despite their profound differences, the two nations to this point had at least agreed on the fundamental goal of preserving an independent, non-Communist South Vietnam. After Tet, survival remained the name of the game for the Saigon regime. Some American officials, however, increasingly began to look for a way out, even at the expense of the original, long-standing goal of U.S. policy. At a minimum, in the aftermath of Tet, the Johnson administration sought to shift the burden of attaining that goal back to the Vietnamese, thus lowering U.S. casualties and decreasing political pressures at home. The widening gap in goals and especially in methods heightened the already considerable tensions between the two allies.

Shrewd strategist that he was, the North Vietnamese general, Vo Nguyen Giap, clearly perceived the divisions between the United States and South Vietnam, and his masterstroke, the Tet Offensive, was designed to exploit them. Keenly aware of the "contradictions" between the "U.S. imperialists" and the "country-selling Vietnamese traitors," Giap sought to increase the discord between them, causing them to "destroy each other." The Tet Offensive was aimed at the weak link, South Vietnam, with the hope of igniting a mass uprising among the people and forcing the collapse of the ARVN, thus limiting the ability of the United States to continue the war. At the same time, Hanoi held out the lure of negotiations to the United States, hoping to intensify pressures for a change of American policy and exacerbate the differences between Washington and Saigon.[63]

Giap's strategy worked, although not in the way he intended. The mass uprising did not occur, and the South Vietnamese government and armed forces did not fall apart. The former responded more effectively to the crisis and the latter fought better than anyone dared expect. Using enormous firepower, American and South Vietnamese forces beat back the NVA/NLF assaults in every area, inflicting huge casualties. Still, the Tet Offensive added significantly to the pressures on each ally, widening the divisions between them and heightening the mutual suspicions and resentment.

---

[61]Browne, *New Face of War*, 338.

[62]Shaplen, *Road from War*, 154.

[63]Patrick J. McGarvey, ed., *Visions of Victory: Selected Vietnamese Communist Military Writings, 1964–1968* (Stanford, 1969), 76; *Vietnam Documents and Research Notes, Document No. 18* (Saigon, 1968).

The sheer physical destruction of the fighting of Tet caused added Vietnamese antagonism toward the United States. Indeed, old Vietnam hand Edward Lansdale thought the war was lost at this point. The ability of Americans to discriminate between friend and foe, never well developed, was lost totally amid the fury of the combat during Tet. The extensive and indiscriminate use of firepower killed friend as well as enemy, "making hundreds of people hate Americans and be afraid of them."[64]

Tet also delegitimized South Vietnam in the eyes of many Americans, especially some top officials. The ease with which the enemy penetrated the very centers of U.S.-South Vietnamese power raised profound questions about the viability and staying power of the Saigon government. The brutal street execution of a Vietcong captive by the Saigon police chief—an event brought home to Americans through the candid cameras of photographer Eddie Adams and NBC television—disconnected the United States from its ally in an important way. White House staffer Harry McPherson recalled that the event signified to him "that we were involved up to our necks in a war among very alien peoples with whom we shared few values."[65]

The most important result of Tet was a retreat from the Americanization of the war. In late 1967, several of Johnson's key advisers and a group of establishment figures meeting under the auspices of the Carnegie Foundation had urged scrapping Westmoreland's costly search-and-destroy strategy, employing U.S. troops for population security, and turning back to the Vietnamese a greater share of the fighting.[66] Pressures to "Vietnamize" the war increased in the aftermath of Tet. Growing public impatience made clear that from a long-range standpoint the only possible way to achieve U.S. goals was for South Vietnam to take on greater responsibility for its own survival. The ARVN's relatively good performance during Tet, along with a huge dose of wishful thinking, enabled some U.S. policymakers to conclude that Vietnamization might work. Thus, while putting a lid on further escalation of the war and offering to negotiate with North Vietnam, the Johnson administration decided that additional U.S. assistance would be conditioned on South Vietnam's putting its own house in order and assuming a greater burden of the fighting. The decision marked a step back toward the policies that prevailed before 1965 and a move toward the policy of Vietnamization later institutionalized by Richard Nixon.

For a time at least, the exigencies of Tet compelled closer cooperation between the United States and South Vietnam. The prospect of defeat galvanized the South Vietnamese into action as nothing had before and made them more receptive to U.S. advice. "It concentrated their minds

[64]Currey, *Lansdale*, 319.

[65]Quoted in David Culbert, "Television's Vietnam and Historical Revisionism in the United States," *Historical Journal of Film, Radio and Television* 8:3 (1988): 257.

[66]See, for example, Jim Jones notes on meeting, 2 November 1967, Johnson Papers, Meeting Notes File, box 2; McGeorge Bundy to Johnson, 10 November 1967, Johnson Papers, Diary Backup, box 81; and "Carnegie Endowment Proposals," 5 December 1967, Matthew B. Ridgway Papers, box 34A, U.S. Army Military History Institute.

wonderfully," one U.S. official remarked.[67] Thieu got rid of some of his most incompetent corps commanders and implemented a mobilization plan long urged by American advisers. The United States retrieved the ARVN from the demeaning population security mission and reassigned it to a conventional combat mission to be shared with U.S. forces. Major efforts were made to improve the coordination of operations by the two armies.[68]

Even in a crisis atmosphere, however, there were sharp limits to allied cooperation. Shortly before leaving office, McNamara urged that a unified command system be implemented, but Westmoreland and his successor, General Creighton Abrams, rejected the proposal as too "cumbersome" and fraught with language and security problems.[69] In developing plans for the possible future withdrawal of U.S. forces and the modernization of South Vietnamese forces, American officials rarely consulted with their South Vietnamese counterparts, going no further than to bring senior officers into the discussions.

Those Americans most eager to press ahead with Vietnamization quickly became disillusioned with South Vietnam's progress. Secretary of Defense Clark Clifford returned from Vietnam in the summer of 1968 "oppressed" by the "pervasive Americanization" of the war. The United States was still doing most of the fighting and paying the cost, he warned Johnson. "Worst of all," he concluded, "the South Vietnamese leaders seemed content to have it that way."[70]

Vietnamese-American tensions increased significantly after Tet. The South Vietnamese protested that they had been railroaded into negotiations before they were ready and expressed bitter fears that they would be left at the mercy of the NLF and North Vietnam. American peace initiatives, they said, were meant to serve the interests of the United States without regard for the needs of South Vietnam, the nation whose survival was at stake.[71] For their part, American servicemen manifested the accumulated frustrations of fighting a war they could not win in an increasingly hostile environment, and the savagery of the battles of Tet inflamed anti-Vietnamese feelings. A gallows' humor solution that went the round of fire bases and bars typified the attitude of some GIs. "What you do is, you load all the Friendlies onto ships and take them out to the South China Sea. Then you bomb the country flat. Then you sink the ships."[72] The murder of more than two hundred civilians, including women and children, in the village of My Lai by

[67]Grinter, "Bargaining between Saigon and Washington," 865.

[68]Clarke, *Final Years*, 303, 308.

[69]Ibid., 304–5.

[70]Clark Clifford memorandum for Johnson, 16 July 1968, Clark Clifford Papers, box 5, Johnson Library; Clark Clifford, "A Viet Nam Reappraisal," *Foreign Affairs* 47 (July 1969): 614–15.

[71]Bui Diem would later observe of his own experience in Paris: "The Future of South Vietnam was now on the table at which the Americans sat on one side and the North Vietnamese on the other, while I hovered somewhere on the sidelines. The whole arrangement shouted, 'This is an American War.'" Diem, *Jaws of History*, 230.

[72]Michael Herr, *Dispatches* (New York, 1978), 59.

an American company under the command of Lieutenant William Calley in March 1968 starkly revealed the hostility that some Americans had come to feel for all Vietnamese.

At the end of 1968, the United States and South Vietnam openly feuded for the first time. In a desperate effort to end the war and elect Democratic presidential candidate Hubert Humphrey, chief negotiator W. Averell Harriman laboriously constructed a complex arrangement to deescalate the war and move the peace talks off dead center. The South Vietnamese naturally feared a sellout, and Thieu was encouraged by Republican candidate Richard Nixon to hold out until after the election. Proclaiming that his government was not a "car that can be hitched to a locomotive and taken anywhere the locomotive wants to go," Thieu insisted that the American-arranged understanding was a "clear admission of defeat." Hanoi must negotiate directly with the Government of Vietnam.[73]

South Vietnamese intransigence doomed any hopes of a peace settlement. The Johnson administration announced a bombing halt on 31 October without South Vietnamese concurrence and subsequently forced Thieu to send negotiators to Paris. Once the South Vietnamese joined the negotiations, however, they raised further obstructions, rejecting an ingenious solution devised by Harriman to bring them together with representatives of the NLF. By the time this procedural issue was resolved, the Johnson administration was in its final days and any possibility of an agreement had ended. It seems doubtful that Saigon's obstructionism prevented an end to the war—too many issues remained unsettled. Still, the open disagreements between the two allies vastly complicated an already difficult situation and further strained an already tenuous relationship.

The institutionalization of Vietnamization by the Nixon administration brought the differences into sharp relief. The South Vietnamese conceded that domestic political pressures required a change in U.S. policy, but they resented not being consulted. Thieu was especially outraged, feeling that Nixon owed him better treatment for his cooperation in 1968. The Vietnamese were alarmed with the time frame for U.S. withdrawals. From their perspective, Vietnamization had come too late and was imposed too abruptly. ARVN officers complained that they had to cover more territory with fewer troops, and they worried what would happen when the Americans "who are still pressing the buttons and calling the shots in combined operations leave Vietnam."[74] A mild-mannered individual, once staunchly pro-American, protested to Shaplen: "You created an economic Frankenstein monster here by making this a big war, and now you are telling us that we have to learn almost overnight to be austere and take care of ourselves."[75] Vietnamese found the very term "Vietnamization" demeaning, protesting that they had been fighting for years before the Americans became involved and

---

[73]Shaplen, *Road from War*, 243.
[74]Ibid., 318.
[75]Ibid., 316–17.

even after 1965 had "sacrificed and suffered the most."[76] Some cynically referred to it as the "U.S. Dollar and Vietnamese Blood Sharing Plan." Most saw it as a fig leaf for U.S. abandonment.[77]

For the United States, Vietnamization did nothing to ease the frustrations of dealing with a difficult ally. Abrams attempted to integrate operations between the two armies, but Americans were reluctant to work with Vietnamese units, regarding them as "more likely to cause problems . . . than be helpful."[78] Despite an apparent increase in leverage from its future departure, the United States was no better able than before to get things done. Americans perceived that the presence of incompetent officials in top positions hampered the conduct of government operations, damaged U.S. credibility, and made a sham of Vietnamization. Still, they would not or could not do anything about it. South Vietnamese resistance to change had become a way of life, and the Americans fussed and fumed but got little accomplished.[79]

Among the GIs, resentment grew into outright hostility. The morale of the U.S. Army deteriorated drastically under the surreal conditions of Vietnamization, and some Americans vented their anger on the Vietnamese. Soldiers fired weapons at civilians, hurled rocks and cans at villagers, and drove their vehicles in life-threatening ways.[80] GIs increasingly referred to the United States and other places outside Vietnam as "the world," as though Vietnam "were on another planet." "Many armies have dealt harshly with enemy populations," Jonathan Schell wrote in 1971, "but ours is certainly the first to deal so harshly with its allies." Although critical of the Americans, Schell refused to blame them or their officers. They had been sent to protect the South Vietnamese, he explained, only to find that their help was not wanted. Unable to tell friend from foe, they came to regard the entire population as the enemy and began to make war "against the people whom they were supposed to be saving but who didn't want to be saved."[81]

More and more resigned to an unfavorable outcome, each side increasingly blamed the other. The South Vietnamese protested that the United States had made them dependent and then deserted them. Reluctant to concede that the sacrifice of so much blood and treasure had been in vain, Americans attributed their failure to Saigon's ineptitude and its refusal to heed U.S. advice and contented themselves that they had given the South Vietnamese enough to defend themselves. "We've done what we can," Abrams would say, shrugging his shoulders in resignation.[82]

---

[76]Nguyen Duy Hinh, *Vietnamization and the Cease-Fire* (Washington, 1980), 19; Vien and Khuyen, *Reflections*, 91.

[77]Nguyen Tien Hung and Jerrold L. Schecter, *The Palace File* (New York, 1986), 224; Hosmer, *Fall of South Vietnam*, viii, 9–10.

[78]Clarke, *Final Years*, 392.

[79]Ibid., 489.

[80]Collins debriefing, 7 January 1971, Collins Papers.

[81]Schell, *Observing the Nixon Years*, 18–19, 61, 86.

[82]Clarke, *Final Years*, 469, 487.

The most bitter conflict between the two nations developed over the 1973 Paris agreements. By the fall of 1972, with an election approaching, the Nixon administration felt compelled to extricate the United States from its longest and one of its most divisive wars. Concern for the preservation of an independent, non-Communist South Vietnam took a back seat to getting out, and chief U.S. negotiator Henry Kissinger privately let it be known that he sought only a cynical "decent interval" between the U.S. departure and the anticipated fall of South Vietnam. The United States did not consult with the Thieu government in negotiating with North Vietnam and, indeed, did not even keep it well informed of what was happening. More important, the Nixon administration made concessions it had previously resisted, permitting North Vietnamese troops to remain in the south and in other ways compromising the already precarious position of the Thieu government. Kissinger sought to ram the October 1972 agreement down the throats of his allies, and when Thieu balked Nixon used heavy-handed pressure to compel him to sign, even reminding the embattled leader in one letter of the fate of Diem in 1963.[83]

To the South Vietnamese, of course, the Paris agreements represented the worst form of betrayal. The United States had callously used South Vietnam for its own purposes, then cynically cut a deal with its mortal enemy. "When the Americans wanted to enter, we had no choice, and now [when] they are ready to leave, we have no choice," Thieu lamented.[84] The South Vietnamese resented not being consulted on the negotiations. They first learned the terms from captured NLF documents, and they were infuriated by the way Kissinger tried to impose the agreement on them. Thieu refused to sign without getting major changes in the text, and even then insisted on lavish additional aid and solemn, secret pledges from Nixon to come to his aid if the North Vietnamese violated the agreements. He signed, Ambassador Bui Diem later noted, only after a "rather painful exchange of messages" and a warning from Nixon "couched in the toughest language that diplomatic practice has ever seen."[85]

Implementation of the agreements widened the gap still further. Whether Nixon intended to keep his secret pledges to Thieu will probably never be known. In any event, his own actions made living up to them impossible. Consumed by the Watergate scandal, he was helpless to do anything more than protest North Vietnamese violations of the Paris agreements. In the meantime, a war-weary and increasingly budget-conscious Congress ruthlessly slashed aid to South Vietnam. And in the spring of 1975, Nixon's successor Gerald R. Ford stood by helplessly while the Thieu government collapsed.

---

[83]These events are chronicled from very different perspectives in Hung and Schecter, *Palace File*, 62–145; and Henry Kissinger, *White House Years* (Boston, 1979), 1301–1470. The Nixon letter that refers to Diem is quoted in Hung and Schecter, *Palace File*, 73–74.

[84]Hung and Schecter, *Palace File*, 145.

[85]Hosmer, *Fall of South Vietnam*, 5–15.

The U.S. withdrawal had a devastating impact on the South Vietnamese armed forces. Because the United States had done so much during the peak years of its involvement, its departure left a gaping vacuum. The oppressive sense of dependency persisted, and many officers still insisted that the Americans must be consulted before any action was taken. South Vietnam's entire way of warfare had been premised on unlimited U.S. support, and the cutback in assistance demoralized officers and troops and severely hampered their ability to fight. Constructed on American models with a command system long dominated by the Americans, the ARVN had no strategy and doctrine, and some officers felt no need for them because, it was assumed, the United States would return in a crisis. The removal of American advisers had a critical impact on planning, follow-up, and evaluation, and it was impossible to train Vietnamese replacements in such areas as intelligence on short notice. The U.S. pullout removed the firepower and air support upon which the ARVN had come to rely. The South Vietnamese had also become dependent on U.S. equipment—they had "forgotten how to walk"—and the U.S. withdrawal and subsequent aid cuts denied them the equipment they were used to and the technical expertise needed to maintain it. The South Vietnamese protested, understandably, that they had been taught to wage war in a lavish, expensive manner and then not provided with the means to fight the only way they knew how.[86]

The South Vietnamese felt abandoned. They protested that the United States had made decisions that affected their very existence on the basis of its own geopolitical needs with "only the slightest nod to those whose protection it had gravely undertaken." They could not comprehend U.S. tolerance of North Vietnamese violations of the treaty.[87]

Paradoxically, South Vietnam's feelings of abandonment went hand in hand with an unshakable conviction that, as in 1968 and 1972, the United States would rescue it from disaster. In the Confucian tradition, the higher a man's status, the greater his duty to honor his promises and Thieu treated Nixon's secret letters like a sacred bond, hiding them in his bedroom.[88] Similarly, in the eyes of the South Vietnamese, as a responsible great power the United States must accept the consequences of its actions and therefore help South Vietnam out of a situation the presence of American troops had helped to create. "The Americans could not simply call it quits after putting the whole house of Vietnam in shambles."[89] In a more practical vein, the South Vietnamese surmised that the United States, having spent so much in South Vietnam, would not stand idly by and squander its investment. And as a superpower, it could not afford the loss of face that would result if South Vietnam fell. Thus, in their hour of peril, the South Vietnamese looked

[86]For extensive commentary on these points see Hosmer, *Fall of South Vietnam*, 28–30, 38–39, 46; Hung and Schecter, *Palace File*, 208–9, 221, 297, 323; Hinh, *Vietnamization*, 71, 73, 78–79; Vien and Khuyen, *Reflections*, 134.

[87]Diem, *Jaws of History*, 298–99.

[88]Hung and Schecter, *Palace File*, 153–54.

[89]Bui Diem quoted in Hosmer, *Fall of South Vietnam*, 33.

toward Washington. Tragically, even as North Vietnamese tanks closed in on Saigon, they remained certain that the B-52s would again come back and save them.[90]

At the end, scapegoating became the order of the day. As early as the summer of 1971, a substantial majority of Americans approved the removal of U.S. troops from South Vietnam even if the result was a Communist takeover.[91] Americans willingly, perhaps eagerly, endorsed cuts in aid to South Vietnam. A self-styled "fed-up taxpayer" saw no reason to continue supporting a corrupt and wasteful government and insisted that it was time for South Vietnam to stand on its own feet.[92] Congressmen argued that U.S. aid was an instrument of repression and a major source for the rampant corruption in South Vietnam. They blamed Thieu for prolonging the war and rationalized that aid cuts might end a long and bloody conflict by compelling him to negotiate. Ignoring the onrushing North Vietnamese army, some starry-eyed congressmen even rationalized that by forcing Thieu's withdrawal, aid cuts would promote the long-standing U.S. goal of political freedom in South Vietnam. Americans concluded that South Vietnam's peril was largely of its own making. The United States had met its obligations, Representative David Evans (D-IN) concluded, and it was "time to close out the open-ended checking account."[93] Angry and frustrated at what was widely perceived as their first defeat in war, Americans conveniently shifted the blame to South Vietnam.

The South Vietnamese in turn blamed the United States. Thieu denounced America's desertion as an "inhumane act by an inhumane ally." "It is easy to be an enemy of the United States," he lamented, "but so difficult to be a friend."[94] Generals and politicians blamed the United States for making South Vietnam dependent and then abandoning it. A storeowner summed up a widespread attitude toward the Americans. "When they wanted to come, they came. And when they want to leave, they leave. It's as if a neighbor came over and made a shambles of your house, then all of a sudden he decides the whole thing is wrong, so he calls it quits. How can they just do that?"[95] "You don't get deeply involved in our country, say it was a mistake, and run away," protested another South Vietnamese.[96]

The debacle of April 1975 cannot be understood apart from the troubled history of the U.S.-South Vietnamese alliance. From the outset, neither nation really understood the other, and the interaction between them hindered

---

[90]Ibid., 10–15, 118.

[91]Louis Harris, *The Anguish of Change* (New York, 1973), 72–73.

[92]Mrs. J. S. Mozzanini to James J. Kilpatrick, 6 February 1975, James J. Kilpatrick Papers, box 5, University of Virginia Library, Charlottesville, Virginia.

[93]*Congressional Record*, 94th Cong., 1st sess., 1975, 121, pt. 3:3121. See also the extensive commentary on this issue in ibid., 93d Cong., 2d sess., 1974, 120, pt. 22:29177–80, 29553, 29556–58, and 94th Cong., 1st sess., 1975, pt. 3:2646–47, 2658–59, 2701, 2919–20, 3121, 3514, 3818, 3869–70, pt. 4:4101, 4422, 4562–66.

[94]Hung and Schecter, *Palace File*, 333.

[95]Diem, *Jaws of History*, 342.

[96]Hung and Schecter, *Palace File*, 327.

the achievement of goals that, at least for much of the war, they shared. At all levels, Americans scarcely concealed their contempt for their weaker ally. Many South Vietnamese viewed the United States as a "gigantic but somewhat blind and often oppressive 'super-ally' who did not clearly understand the nature of the war, the nature of the South Vietnamese society, the nature of the enemy, or the needs of South Vietnam if it was ever to become socially viable and militarily able to face the enemy at the same time."[97] Still, they could only give way before their more powerful defender, and in doing so they buried their resentments, swallowed their national pride, and surrendered responsibility for their destiny to outsiders. Thus, Stephen Hosmer has concluded, "US-Vietnamese interaction was caught in many webs of misunderstanding from the beginning and never improved, eventually dissolving altogether."[98]

Most likely, there was no solution to the problems the United States took on in Vietnam. The chronic weakness that afflicted South Vietnam was the product of powerful historical forces that may have been beyond alteration. South Vietnam's weakness required a degree of U.S. intervention that undermined the national identity that was an indispensable ingredient for survival. The South Vietnamese regarded the American presence as oppressive and stultifying, but its removal left a void they could not fill.

Given the obvious weakness of South Vietnam, the United States might better have adhered to the time-honored rule of European diplomacy to refrain from intervention unless the people to be supported showed the capacity to stand on their own feet. The experience of Vietnam raises an even more fundamental moral issue: however noble the goals of an outside nation may be, the act of intervention may bring more grief than benefit to the people who are to be saved. And the uncertainty whether the commitment to intervene can be sustained over the long haul makes it a fragile reed upon which to lean and therefore of dubious morality in the first place.

Despite Vietnam, such interventions may well occur again, and it might be useful to draw some additional conclusions from the difficult and ultimately tragic interaction between these "peoples quite apart." First, the intervening nation does not promote independence by imposing on the weaker nation a form of dependence. Perhaps, for the short run, it is easier to take over and do the job for the peoples being supported, but it is destructive over the long run. Second, situations like Vietnam must be viewed in their political as well as military dimensions, and the impact of the two on each other must be understood. By the nature and magnitude of its intervention, by the destructiveness of its way of war, the United States, in the unfortunate words of the defender of Ben Tre, destroyed the society and political structure it was trying to save. Third, if a fundamental rule of warfare is to know your enemy, an equally important rule might be to know your ally. Ignorance at

[97]Hosmer, *Fall of South Vietnam*, v.

[98]Ibid., 41.

all levels of the peoples the United States was trying to help did grave, perhaps irreparable, damage to the cause.

Finally, Americans *must* be more sensitive to the way their intervention affects others. "My advice to small nations considering U.S. aid is that they should be wary of the U.S.," Bui Diem observed in 1983. "We small nations can end up losing higher stakes than the U.S. because for the Americans you can turn the page and say, 'Well, it is an unhappy chapter for U.S. history.' But that is not the same now for the South Vietnamese."[99] Referring to the casual, almost whimsical, way the United States during the 1980s extended and then withdrew its aid, a leader of the Nicaraguan contras, the lineal descendants of the South Vietnamese, raised the question in even more compelling terms: "But have you been aware that you're playing with the life and blood of a people and a country?"[100] It is a question we should ask ourselves over and over when we ponder and debate issues of intervention.

---

[99]Statement at the Wilson Center, January 1983, quoted in George C. Herring, "Some Legacies and Lessons of Vietnam," *Virginia Quarterly Review* 60 (Spring 1984): 211.

[100]Quoted in James LeMoyne, "Can the Contras Go On?" *New York Times Magazine*, 4 October 1987, 68.

THE 'VIETNAM SYNDROME' AND AMERICAN FOREIGN POLICY

By GEORGE C. HERRING

During the past few months, a new phrase has entered the American political vocabulary. It is called the "Vietnam syndrome." It was apparently coined by Richard Nixon. As employed by the Reagan administration, it presumably means that America's failure in Vietnam and the backlash from it have been primarily responsible for the malaise that has allegedly reduced the United States to a state of impotence in a menacing world. Doctor Reagan and his associates seem determined to cure the disease. Some of the administration's defenders have even justified intervention in El Salvador as essential to that end; and although the White House and State Department may not go that far, their public statements leave no doubt of their determination to exorcise the Vietnam syndrome.

The notion of a Vietnam syndrome presupposes a view of the war which, although rarely articulated in full, nevertheless clearly influences the administration's foreign policy. Reagan himself has stated—contrary to a long-prevailing view—that Vietnam was "in truth a noble war," an altruistic attempt on the part of the United States to help a "small country newly free from colonial rule" defend itself against a "totalitarian neighbor bent on conquest." He and Secretary of State Alexander M. Haig, Jr. have also insisted that it was a necessary war, necessary to check the expansionist designs of the Soviet Union and its client states and to uphold the global position of the United States. They have left no doubt that they regard it as a war that we should have won. America failed, Reagan recently stated, not because it was defeated but because the military was "denied permission to win." Haig has argued that the war could have been won at any of several junctures if American leaders had been willing to "apply the full range of American power to bring about a successful outcome." The defeat was thus self-inflicted, and the consequences have been enormous. "America is no longer the America it was," Haig has stated, and "that is largely attributable to the mistakes of Vietnam."

These views are not, of course, new, nor is it suprising that they have gained credence in recent years. The aggressiveness of the Soviets and the Hanoi regime have made it easier for us to justify our own actions morally and in terms of national security. An explanation of failure which places blame on ourselves rather than elsewhere is probably easier for us to live with. Scholars had begun to revise conventional dovish views of the war well before Reagan took office, and films such as the *Deerhunter*, whatever their artistic merit, promoted a form of redemption. What *is* significant is that this now seems to be the official view and is also a partial basis for major policy decisions. Equally important, it is getting little challenge from Congress and the media, the centers of respectable dissent in the late 1960's and early 1970's. From all appearances, to apply an Oriental usage, 1981 is the year of the hawk.

It seems particularly urgent, therefore, that we examine this view critically in terms of the following very difficult questions: was Vietnam a just and necessary war as is now being proclaimed? Was it a winnable war, our failure primarily the result of our own mistakes? Has the so-called Vietnam syndrome been responsible for our recent inability to control world events and meet foreign challenges?

Let me begin with a caveat. The questions I have just raised cannot now be answered definitively. We are still very close to Vietnam, and it is difficult to appraise the war with the sort of detachment and perspective we would like. The evidence is far from complete. We have no more than roughly 15 percent of the documentation on the American side, and Hanoi has given no indication that it plans to initiate a freedom of information act. More important, some of the major questions concerning the war can never be answered with finality. We cannot know, for example, what would have happened if we had not intervened in Vietnam or if we had fought the war differently. We can do no more than speculate, an inexact science at best.

With these qualifications in mind, we can turn to the essential questions that have been raised about the war and its consequences. For many of those who experienced the Vietnam era, Reagan's "noble war" statement seemed so far off the wall that it could not be taken seriously. But it touched a responsive chord, and this is not surprising. The charges of American atrocities and war guilt that echoed across the land just a few years ago ran across the grain of our traditional sense of our own righteousness. Every war has its elements of nobility, moreover, and it is perhaps proper and even necessary for us to recognize the acts of heroism, sacrifice, and compassion that were as much a part of Vietnam as the atrocities. Certainly it was wrong for us to lay on the veterans the guilt which all of us share in one way or another, and Reagan's statement may have been addressing this point, at least obliquely.

His argument was based on the specific premise that we intervened in defense of a "free government" against "outside agression," however, and this interpretation badly distorts the origins and nature of the war. In fact, we tried to contain an indigenous revolution that, although Communist led, expressed the deepest and most powerful currents of Vietnamese nationalism. The

Vietnam conflict cannot be understood by looking at the situation in 1965, when the major U.S. commitments were made. It is necessary to go back to 1945 or even earlier. The revolution that erupted in Vietnam at the end of World War II sought to eliminate French colonialism and to unify a country that had been divided for several centuries. During the ensuing war against France, the revolution generated widespread popular support, and its leader, Ho Chi Minh, came to symbolize for many Vietnamese the spirit of national independence just as George Washington did for the revolutionary generation of Americans. Ho's Vietminh defeated the French in 1954, despite the massive aid given France by the United States. It would probably have unified Vietnam after 1954, had the United States not stepped in and helped to make permanent a division at the 17th parallel the Geneva Conference had intended to be temporary. The Vietcong revolution, which erupted spontaneously in the south in the late 1950's, and subsequent North Vietnamese support of it, were extensions of the revolution of 1945, a fact which explains their unusual staying power in the face of tremendous adversity. This is not to endow the revolution with a higher morality, as the rhetoric of the antiwar movement frequently did. Its leaders were ruthless in pursuit of their goals and were capable of great brutality toward their own people and others. The point rather is that throughout much of the 30-year war, Ho's revolution represented the most powerful political force in Vietnam, and we can talk of outside aggression only in the most narrow, ahistorical sense.

Moreover, the governments we supported—by and large our own creations—were free primarily in the sense that they were non-Communist. It should be recalled in this connection that our first crucial commitment in Vietnam came in 1950 in support of French colonialism. When the French departed after Geneva, we inherited what was left of the puppet government they had created in 1949. We grafted onto it the trappings of Western-style democracy and gave it a measure of international respectability. But in fact, the governments of Ngo Dinh Diem and his successors were narrowly based oligarchies, held up mainly by American power, at times quite repressive, and generally unresponsive to the needs and concerns of the predominantly rural population of southern Vietnam. It can be argued, of course, that they were better than their counterpart in the north and provided an alternative to the many Vietnamese who did not want Communism. This may well be true, but it blurs the issue, and we should be wary in the aftermath of the war of endowing the governments we supported with qualities they did not have.

A third point that must be stressed is this: whatever our intent, the way we conducted the war had a devastating impact on the land and people we professed to be serving. In trying to ennoble our cause, we must not forget the consequences of our actions. We prolonged for as much as 20 years a war that might have ended much earlier, with losses of human lives that ran into the millions. The heavy bombing and artillery fire of the high-technology war we fought permanently scarred the landscape of southern Vietnam, obliterating an area roughly the size of Massachusetts and leaving an estimated 21 million craters. Along with Vietcong terrorism, our military operations made refugees of nearly one-third of the population of South Vietnam. We destroyed the economic and social fabric of the nation for which we had assumed responsibility. Despite the moral pretensions on both sides, it seems evident, as Henry Kissinger once observed, that in Vietnam, no one had a "monopoly of anguish and no one . . . had a monopoly of moral insight."

Finally, I would argue that the major American decisions in Vietnam were made primarily on the basis of self-interest, not altruism. This is a sticky wicket, to be sure. It is difficult to separate the two, and American policy makers certainly felt they were acting on the basis of principle as well as self-interest. To put it another way, however, had it been merely a matter of saving a free people from outside aggression, they would not have acted as they did. At every step along the way, they were convinced that the national interests of the United States required them to escalate the commitment.

What were these interests and why were they felt to be so compelling? From 1950 at least into the late 1960's, we viewed Vietnam primarily in terms of the Cold War and the doctrine of containment, the overarching principle of our Cold War foreign policies. The basic assumption of that policy was that we faced a monolithic, tightly unified world Communist movement, orchestrated by Moscow, and committed to world revolution. We viewed the world as split into two hostile blocs, irreconcilably divided by ideology and existing in a precarious equilibrium. Particularly after the fall of China to communism in 1949, we saw the Cold War as a zero sum game in which any gain for communism was automatically a loss for what we called the "free world." To contain the global Communist menace, we constructed a world-wide network of alliances, intervened freely in the affairs of other nations, and went to war in Korea.

From the beginning to near the end, we viewed the conflict in Vietnam primarily from this perspective. Because the revolution was led by Moscow-trained Communists, we assumed it was but an instrument of the Kremlin's drive for world domination. In the early stages, we felt it necessary to block Communist conquest of Vietnam lest it set off a domino effect which could cause the loss of all of Southeast Asia, with presumably incalculable strategic, political, and economic consequences for the United States. Later, we escalated the commitment because of a felt need to uphold our credibility. We had to prove that we would stand by our commitments to dissuade the Communists from further aggressions that could drastically undermine our global position or perhaps plunge us into a global war.

II

This leads directly to question number two: were these assumptions valid? Was the war necessary, as many now allege, to stop the advance of communism and uphold our world position? It is impossible to answer these questions with absolute certainty because we can never know precisely what would have happened if we had not intervened. It seems probable that there would have been war of some kind and that Vietnam would have been unified by force. What then? Would the dominoes have fallen in Southeast Asia? Would there have been a new wave of aggression elsewhere? Obviously, we can never know. I would argue, however, that we badly misperceived the nature of the struggle in Vietnam and that we may have exaggerated the possible consequences of a Communist victory.

The containment policy was misguided both generally and in its specific application to Vietnam. The simplistic, black and white assumptions from which it derived never bore much resemblance to reality. Soviet goals were (and remain) as much the product of traditional Russian nationalism as ideology, and they fell considerably short of world domination. The so-called Communist bloc was never a monolith—it was torn by divisions from the start, and the fragmentation has become more pronounced. In the Third World, nationalism and resistance to any form of outside influence have been the driving force. And there has never been a zero sum game. What appeared to be a major victory for the Soviet Union in China in 1949, for example, has turned out to be a castastrophic loss. In most parts of the world, neither the Soviet Union nor the United States has prevailed, and pluralism and fragmentation have been the norm.

In applying the containment policy to Vietnam, we drastically misjudged the internal dynamics of the conflict. We attributed the war to an expansionist communism bent on world domination. In fact, as I have suggested, it began as a revolution against French colonialism. Ho Chi Minh and his cohorts were Communists, to be sure, rigid and doctrinaire in their views and committed to structure their society along Marxist-Leninist lines. But they were never mere instruments of Moscow. The Soviet Union did not instigate the revolution and in fact exerted very little influence on it until after the United States initiated the bombing in 1965. The Chinese Communists exerted some influence in the early stages, but traditional Vietnamese suspicions of China, the product of a long history of Chinese imperialism, restricted the closeness of these ties. "I would rather sniff French dung for a few years than eat Chinese for a lifetime," Ho Chi Minh once said, expressing Vietnam's deep-seated fear of its larger northern neighbor. Throughout the 30-year war, the Soviet Union and China supported Vietnam when it was expedient to do so, but they also abandoned it at several critical junctures. North Vietnam played the two off against each other for essentially Vietnamese ends—to rid the country of foreign influence and unify it under one government.

Our rigid application of the containment doctrine in Vietnam had fateful consequences. By placing ourselves against the strongest force in an otherwise politically fragmented country, first in the war against France, later on our own, we may have ensured our ultimate failure. By ascribing the war to international rather than local forces, we underestimated the enemy's commitment, a vital point to which I will return later. Our intervention probably gave the war an international significance it did not have at the outset. Indeed, we may have driven the Vietnamese closer into the arms of their Communist allies than they would have preferred to go.

I also believe that we exaggerated the possible consequences of nonintervention. We will never know whether the domino theory would have operated if Vietnam had fallen earlier, but there is reason to doubt that it would have. Nationalism has proven the most potent and enduring force in recent history, and the nations of Southeast Asia, with their long tradition of opposition to China and Vietnam, would have resisted mightily. By making the war a test case of our credibility, we may have made its consequences greater than they would otherwise have been. By rigidly adhering to a narrow, one-dimensional world view, without adequately taking into account the nature and importance of local forces, we may have placed ourselves in an untenable position.

III

Question number three: was Vietnam a winnable war, our failure there primarily the result of our mistakes, our lack of will, the disunity within our society? Because it has such profound implications for future policy decisions, this is the most important of our questions and deserves the most extended commentary. Those who argue that our defeat was self-inflicted focus on the misuse of our admittedly vast military power. Instead of using air power to strike a knockout blow against the enemy, they contend, Lyndon Johnson foolishly hedged it about with restrictions, applied it gradually, and held back from the sort of massive, decisive bombing attacks that could have assured victory. Similarly, they argue, had Johnson permitted U.S. ground forces to invade North Vietnamese sanctuaries in Laos, Cambodia, and across the 17th parallel, General Westmoreland's strategy of attrition could have worked and the war could have been won.

These criticisms are not without merit. Johnson's gradual expansion of the bombing did give North Vietnam time to disperse its resources and develop a highly effective air defense system, and the bombing may have encouraged the will to resist rather than crippled it as Johnson had intended. A strategy of attrition could not work as long as the enemy enjoyed sanctuary. If losses reached unacceptable proportions, the enemy could simply retreat to safety, regroup and renew the battle at times and places of his own choosing. He retained the strategic initiative.

To jump from here to the conclusion that the unrestricted use of American power could have produced victory at acceptable costs raises some troubling questions, however. Could an unrestricted bombing campaign have forced North Vietnam to accept a settlement on our terms? Obviously, there is no way we can ever know, but there is reason to doubt that it would have. The surveys conducted after World War II raised some serious doubts about the effect of bombing on the morale of the civilian population of Germany and Japan, and the capacity of air power to cripple a pre-industrial society such as North Vietnam may have been even more limited. There is evidence to suggest that the North Vietnamese were prepared to resist no matter what the level of the bombing, even if they had to go underground. The United States could probably have destroyed the cities and industries of North Vietnam, but what then? Invasion of the sanctuaries and ground operations in North Vietnam might have made the strategy of attrition more workable, but they would also have enlarged the war at a time when the United States was already stretched thin. Each of these approaches would have greatly increased the costs of the war without resolving the central problem—the political viability of South Vietnam.

We must also consider the reasons why Johnson refused to expand the war. He feared that if the United States pushed North Vietnam to the brink of defeat, the Soviet Union and/or China would intervene, broadening the war to dangerous proportions, perhaps to a nuclear confrontation. Johnson may, of course, have overestimated the risks of outside intervention, but the pressures would certainly have been large and he would have been irresponsible to ignore the dangers. And even if the United States had been able militarily to subdue North Vietnam without provoking outside intervention, it would still have faced the onerous, expensive, and dangerous prospect of occupying a hostile nation along China's southern border.

Those who argue that the war was winnable also emphasize the importance of American public opinion in sealing our defeat. They shift blame from those who waged the war to those who opposed it, contending that an irresponsible media and a treacherous antiwar movement turned the nation against the war, forcing Johnson and later Nixon to curtail U.S. involvement just when victory was in grasp. As much mythology has deveoped around this issue as any other raised by the war, and we probably know as little about it as any. Studies of public opinion do indicate that despite an increasingly skeptical media and noisy protest in the streets, the war enjoyed broad, if unenthusiastic support until that point early in 1968 when it became apparent that the costs might exceed any possible gains—and, even then, Nixon was able to prolong it for four more years. Until the early 1970's, moreover, the antiwar movement was probably counterproductive in terms of its own goals, the majority of Americans finding the protestors more obnoxious than the war. Indeed, it seems likely that the antiwar protest in a perverse way may have strengthened support for the government. After 1969, public opinion and Congress did impose some constraints on the government, and the media probably contributed to this. But to pin the defeat on the media or the antiwar movement strikes me as a gross oversimplification.

The problem with all these explanations is that they are too enthnocentric. They reflect the persistence of what a British scholar has called the illusion of American omnipotence, the traditional American belief that the difficult we do tomorrow, the impossible may take awhile. When failure occurs, it must be *our* fault, and we find scapegoats in our own midst: the poor judgment of our leaders, the media, or the antiwar movement. The flaw in this approach is that it ignores the other side of the equation, in this case, the Vietnamese dimension. I would contend that the sources of our frustration and ultimate failure rest primarily, although certainly not exclusively, in the local circumstances of the war: the nature of the conflict itself, the weakness of our ally, the relative strength of our adversary.

The Vietnam War posed extremely difficult challenges for Americans. It was fought in a climate and on a terrain that were singularly inhospitable. Thick jungles, foreboding swamps and paddies, rugged mountains. Heat that could "kill a man, bake his brains, or wring the sweat from him until he died of exhaustion," Philip Caputo tells us in *Rumor of War*. "It was as if the sun and the land itself were in league with the Vietcong," Caputo adds, "wearing us down, driving us mad, killing us." Needless to say, those who had endured the land for centuries had a distinct advantage over outsiders, particularly when the latter came from a highly industrialized and urbanized environment.

It was a people's war, where the people rather than territory were the primary objective. But Americans as individuals and as a nation could never really bridge the vast cultural gap that separated them from all Vietnamese. Not knowing the language or the culture, they did not know what the people felt or even how to tell friend from foe. "Maybe the dinks got things mixed up," one of novelist Tim O'Brien's bewildered G.I.s comments in *Going After Cacciato* after a seemingly friendly farmer bowed and smiled and pointed the Americans into a minefield. "Maybe the gooks cry when they're happy and smile when they're sad." Recalling the emotionless response of a group of peasants when their homes were destroyed by an American company, Caputo notes that they did nothing "and I hated them for it. Their apparent indifference made me feel indifferent." The cultural gap produced cynicism and even hatred toward the people Americans were trying to help. It led to questioning of our goals and produced a great deal of moral confusion among those fighting the war and those at home.

Most important, perhaps, was the formless, yet lethal, nature of guerrilla warfare in Vietnam. It was a war without distinct battlelines or fixed objectives, where traditional concepts of victory and defeat were blurred. It was, Caputo writes, "a formless war against a formless enemy who evaporated into the morning jungle mists only to materialize in some unexpected place." This type of war was particularly difficult for Americans schooled in the conventional warfare of World War II and Korea to fight. And there was always the gnawing question, first raised by John Kennedy himself—how can we tell if we're winning? The only answer that could be devised was the notorious body count, as grim and corrupting as it was unreliable as an index of success. In time, the strategy of attrition and the body count came to represent for sensitive G.I.s and for those at home killing for the sake of killing. And the light at the end of the tunnel never glimmered. "Aimless, that's what it is," one of O'Brien's G.I.s laments, "a bunch of kids trying to pin the tail on the Asian donkey. But no . . . tail. No . . . donkey."

Far more important in explaining our failure is the uneven balance of forces we aligned ourselves with in Vietnam. With the passage of time, it becomes more and more apparent that in South Vietnam we attempted a truly formidable undertaking on the basis of a very weak foundation. The "country" to which we committed ourselves in 1954 lacked most of the essential ingredients for nationhood. Had we looked all over the world, in fact, we could hardly have found a less promising place for an experiment in nation-building. Southern Vietnam lacked a viable economy. The French had destroyed the traditional political order, and their departure left a gaping vacuum, no firmly established political institutions, no native elite capable of exercising effective political leadership. Southern Vietnam was rent by a multitude of conflicting ethnic and religious forces. It was, in the words of one scholar, a "political jungle of war lords, bandits, partisan troops, and secret societies." When viewed from this perspective, there were probably built-in limits to what the United States or any outside nation could have accomplished there.

For nearly 20 years, we struggled to establish a viable nation in the face of internal insurgency and external invasion, but the rapid collapse of South Vietnam after our withdrawal in 1973 suggests how little was really accomplished. We could never find leaders capable of mobilizing the disparate population of southern Vietnam. We launched a vast array of ambitious and expensive programs to promote sound and effective government, win the support of the people, and wage war against the Vietcong. When our client state was on the verge of collapse in 1965, we filled the vacuum by putting in our own military forces. But the more we did, the more we induced a state of dependency among those we were trying to help. Tragically, right up to the fall of Saigon in 1975, the South Vietnamese elite expected us to return and save them from defeat. This is not to denigrate the leaders or people who sided with us or to make them the scapegoats for our failure. The point rather is that given the history of southern Vietnam and the conditions that prevailed there in 1954, the creation of a viable nation by an outside power may have been an impossible task.

IV

The second point central to understanding our failure is that we drastically underestimated the strength and determination of our adversary. I do not wish to imply here that the North Vietnamese and Vietcong were supermen. They made blunders. They paid an enormous price for their success. They have shown a far greater capacity for making war than for building a nation. In terms of the balance of forces in Vietnam, however, they had distinct advantages. They were tightly mobilized and regimented and fanatically committed to their goals. They were fighting on familiar soil, and they employed methods already perfected in the ten years' war against France. The Vietcong were close to the rural population of South Vietnam, adapted its ideology and tactics to traditional Vietnamese political culture, and used the American presence to exploit popular distrust of outsiders. North Vietnam skillfully employed the strategy of protracted war, perceiving that the Americans, like the French, could become impatient, and if they bled long enough they might tire of the war. "You will kill ten of our men, but we will kill one of yours," Ho once remarked, "and in the end it is you who will tire." The comment was made to a French general in 1946, but it could as easily have been said of the Second Indochina War.

Our fatal error, therefore, was to underestimate our adversary. We rather casually assumed that the Vietnamese, rational beings like ourselves, would know better than to stand up against the most powerful nation in the world. It would be like a filibuster in Congress, Lyndon Johnson speculated, enormous resistance at first, then a steady whittling away, then Ho Chi Minh hurrying to get it over with. Years later, Henry Kissinger confessed great surprise with the discovery that his North Vietnamese counterparts were "fanatics." Since our own goals were limited and from our standpoint more than reasonable, we found it hard to understand the total, unyielding commitment of the enemy, his willingness to risk everything to achieve his objective.

The circumstances of the war in Vietnam thus posed a dilemma that we never resolved. To have achieved our goal of an independent non-Communist South Vietnam required means that were either morally repugnant to us, posed unacceptable risks, or were unlikely to work. Success would have required the physical annihilation of North Vietnam, but given our limited goals, this would have been distasteful and excessively costly, and it held out a serious threat of Soviet or Chinese intervention. The only other way was to establish a viable South Vietnam, but given the weak foundation we worked from and the cultural gap, not to mention the strength of the internal revolution, this was probably beyond our capability. To put it charitably, we may very well have placed ourselves in a classic, no-win situation.

For reasons closely related to the problems we have discussed, I think it would also be wrong for us to attribute our recent woes exclusively to Vietnam. The war has affected us profoundly, to be sure, but our failure there was not so much the cause of our present plight as a symptom of our general decline from world preeminence, the result of broad historical forces beyond our control. Our great power in the years immediately after World War II was to a considerable degree an aberration, the result as much of the devastation wrought by the war in the rest of the world as of our own intrinsic strength. Inevitably, that power has declined, as the Soviet Union has matched us in military and nuclear hardware, as the industrialized nations have regained a competitive position, and as the new nations recently emerged from colonialism have gained in assertiveness. In a variety of different ways, Vietnam demonstrated the new limits to our power, and as much as we long nostalgically for the "good old days," we cannot reverse the forces of history.

As I stated at the outset, the current official view of Vietnam is being articulated at least in part to exorcise the presumed Vietnam syndrome as a first step toward a new global policy. The Reagan administration seems to favor a return to the days of global containment, relying on a massive military buildup and intervention in the world's trouble spots to check Soviet expansion and regain the position we have lost.

I believe that such an approach defies the experience of Vietnam and is both dangerous and ultimately futile. Soviet military power and aggressiveness pose a very real threat to us and may in many instances require a stern response. To assume that the Soviets are responsible for most of the crises that beset today's world, however, is to ignore as we did in Vietnam the local circumstances from which revolutions and regional conflicts derive and which may determine their outcome. To assume that these conflicts can best be dealt with through a form of containment can make bad situations worse. Reagan is probably right in saying that El Salvador will not become another Vietnam, but this may be a clever way of justifying actions that cannot otherwise be justified. The containment approach, in El Salvador, as elsewhere, can lead to unwise and possibly counterproductive commitments to governments which are anti-Communist but also unpopular and instable. To attempt to bolster such governments through military aid can prolong conflicts which might be ended earlier, inflict great harm on people we are presuming to help, and polarize still fluid situations, driving the insurgents into the arms of the Soviets or Cubans. In Central America, it will likely revive a latent, powerful anti-Americanism, the product of years of gunboat diplomacy.

To adapt to the new and more complex situation we face today requires at a minimum a greater tolerance for revolution, even though it may be leftist, greater patience and restraint, and a more subtle and sophisticated approach than was applied in Vietnam and is being applied in El Salvador. The first question we need to ask in judging crises in the Third World is to what extent they derive from local conditions and to what from Soviet initiative. Assuming that Soviet involvement is not decisive, as may be likely in most cases, we should work quietly and indirectly for a political settlement without making an irrevocable commitment to either, side. Should Soviet involvement be the critical factor, we still need to ask whether Soviet success is likely, and if so whether over the long haul it will significantly alter the global balance of power. It may be that what appears a short-term success can turn out over the long term to be a source of weakness rather than strength. Assuming that a Soviet victory would endanger our security, we must still ask whether the local balance of forces is such that success on our part can be achieved with limited external assistance. If that is not enough, the dispatch of American forces is not likely to do the job either and could make things much worse. Rapid escalation, the "win" approach Reagan seems to think should have been tried in Vietnam may not be the solution either, since it may enlarge the conflict without providing any means to resolve it and might result in a protracted war which could lose support after the usual rally-round-the-flag phenomenon has run its course.

I therefore believe it is urgent for us to ask these

questions and think in these terms. The world is more complex, confusing, and explosive than at any time in recent memory and will remain so for the forseeable future. Our power to manage events will probably continue to decline, and a military buildup of the most mammoth proportions will not change this. To those who insist that we must rid ourselves of the Vietnam syndrome and get about our business, I would respond that understanding of and perspective on the Vietnam experience is an essential basis for shaping a constructive and realistic foreign policy.

PRESIDENTIAL ADDRESS

Historical Memory and Illusive Victories: Vietnam and Central America*

THOMAS G. PATERSON

We are, the truism tells us, captives of our pasts, destined, for good or ill, whether we want to or not, to use history to find clarity in the blurred events swirling around us.[1] Because history is our memory, it is also the most familiar and steady guide in our quest to understand and explain. Comparisons, parallels, and analogies are always springing to mind. For some, history is a cookbook that provides a host of recipes. For others, as Henry A. Kissinger put it, history "teaches by analogy and forces us to decide what, if anything, is analogous."[2] Americans frequently remark that "history teaches," and they have been quick to draw lessons from the past, sometimes fixing them as "syndromes."

At the same time, Americans are notoriously lacking in an informed historical consciousness, and they shun close historical analysis. They may know whose statue adorns the town park, but they have only the faintest notion of the hero's place in their community's development. They may cherish the bicentennial medallions squirreled away in their treasure boxes, but they seldom ask why people rebel. Ignorance, we know too well, abounds. Americans' understanding of the past is selective and discriminatory. Commemoration often becomes celebration. Negatives, failures, and embarrassments become mere aberrations in the march of progress. And the lessons they draw from such a reading of history are necessarily flawed and misleading. As historians we have both the obligation and opportunity to see that

---

*SHAFR presidential address delivered at Washington, DC, 29 December 1987.

[1] For studies of how Americans use history see Göran Rystad, *Prisoners of the Past?: The Munich Syndrome and Makers of American Foreign Policy in the Cold War Era* (Lund, Sweden, 1982); Robert Jervis, *Perception and Misperception in International Politics* (Princeton, NJ, 1976); Richard E. Neustadt and Ernest R. May, *Thinking in Time: The Uses of History for Decision-Makers* (New York, 1986); and Ernest R. May, *"Lessons" of the Past: The Use and Misuse of History in American Foreign Policy* (New York, 1973).

[2] Henry A. Kissinger, *For the Record* (Boston, 1981), 124.

Americans and their leaders get the story right, form intelligent, reasonable conclusions, and draw credible analogies based upon the fullest documentary record available.

In this essay, I have attempted to explore a case of linkage between past and present. Several questions have guided me. First, what perspectives do Americans now hold regarding the Vietnam War? What lessons have they drawn from that wrenching experience? Second, how viable is the lesson most conspicuously touted by President Ronald Reagan and his conservative allies that the Vietnam War could have been won? Was it a winnable war? Third, how sensible is the Reagan view that the U.S. role in Central America in the 1980s is not analogous to Vietnam and that triumph in the hemisphere is quite possible? And, fourth, how sound is the contrasting belief, articulated by critics of U.S. intervention in Central America, that the nation is again trudging into a Vietnam-type quagmire fraught with peril? In short, does the analogy make sense? My fundamental assumption is that advocates on both sides of the debate over Central American policy in the 1980s hold views that have been greatly shaped by their perspectives on the Vietnam War.

Soviet leaders, masters of an "evil empire," asserted President Reagan, stood prepared "to commit any crime, to lie, to cheat" in order to achieve a Communist world.[3] In a display of raw anticommunism reminiscent of early Cold War days, Reagan claimed that an expansionist Soviet Union "underlies all the unrest that is going on. If they weren't engaged in this game of dominoes, there wouldn't be any hot spots in the world."[4] The president and his advisers quoted the Truman Doctrine, resuscitated the domino theory, and embraced the enduring themes of bipolarism, global containment, and Cold War confrontation, altogether happy to discard the "Vietnam syndrome" and the limits it seemed to place on the exertion of American power. Soon the Reagan Doctrine committed the United States to the active support of anti-Communist movements near and far.

The Reagan administration's attention fastened on Central America. Blaming turmoil in the region on the "Moscow-Havana axis," Reagan officials set out to defeat leftist insurgents in El Salvador, topple the Sandinista government in Nicaragua, and draw Guatemala and Honduras into closer military alignment with the United States.[5] As the president predicted victory over "communism" in Central America, critics predicted another Vietnam. "El Salvador is Spanish for Vietnam," read one bumper sticker. The veteran diplomat George Ball, an in-house dissenter on Vietnam in the 1960s, dissented again; Reagan's policy toward El Salvador, he insisted, was a case of

[3]Strobe Talbott, *The Russians and Reagan* (New York, 1984), 32; *Public Papers of the Presidents of the United States, Ronald Reagan, 1981* (Washington, DC, 1982), 57.

[4]Hedrick Smith, "Reagan: What Kind of World Leader?" *New York Times Magazine*, 16 November 1980.

[5]Harold Molineu, *U.S. Policy toward Latin America* (Boulder, CO, 1986), 176.

"plagiarization."[6] Representative Clarence D. Long (D-MD) said that "the similarity of Vietnam is so close it is almost uncanny. There is the unwillingness of people to fight, incompetent, corrupt leadership, and calling everyone a Communist."[7] Senator Christopher Dodd (D-CT) decried the "ignorance" of Reagan officials, who seemed "to know as little about Central America in 1983 as we knew about Indochina in 1963."[8] Economic underdevelopment, poor medical care, illiteracy, poverty, and a rigid class structure, not Communist plotting, underlay Central American unrest, argued Dodd. Reagan not only generated debate by plunging the United States into civil wars and regional disputes, he also sparked controversy by triggering memories of Vietnam when he declared it a "noble cause."[9] This time, in Central America, Reaganites bragged, the United States would stay the course and win. Policymakers and critics alike, then, summoned the Vietnam legacy to their debate over Central America. As a major survey has discovered, American leaders' attitudes toward the Vietnam War are the best predictors of their foreign policy views in the 1980s.[10]

"Still in Saigon, still in Saigon, still in Saigon, in my mind," went the words of a 1981 song.[11] But which Vietnam has stayed in American minds? That is, which lessons have Americans learned from the war that might guide them into or out of Central America? Although no consensus has formed, at least four general perspectives have become identifiable. First, the noninterventionist, "no more Vietnams" school of thought. This school holds that the United States should never again intervene in a Third World country undergoing national rebellion or civil war, because it cannot solve problems indigenous to other peoples. Americans may have the money, but they do not have the knowledge, sensitivity, patience, or muscle to rearrange other governments, especially those distant from U.S. power. Let others learn from their own mistakes; let Americans learn their own limits. Wisdom, then, lies in ending America's penchant for being the world's teacher, social worker, banker, and policeman.[12]

George C. Herring, "Vietnam, El Salvador, and the Uses of History," in *The Central American Crisis*, ed. Kenneth M. Coleman and George C. Herring (Wilmington, DE, 1985), 99.

David Fromkin and James Chace, "What *Are* the Lessons of Vietnam?" *Foreign Affairs* 63 (Spring 1985): 734.

New York Times, 28 April 1983.

Ibid., 19 August 1980. Reagan's view seemed at odds with American opinion. In a respected poll taken in 1982, 72 percent of the respondents considered the Vietnam War fundamentally wrong and immoral. See Chicago Council on Foreign Relations, *American Public Opinion and U.S. Foreign Policy 1983* (Chicago, 1983), 29.

Ole R. Holsti and James N. Rosenau, "Consensus Lost, Consensus Regained?: Foreign Policy Beliefs of American Leaders, 1976–1980," *International Studies Quarterly* 30 (December 1986): 393.

John C. Pratt, ed., *Vietnam Voices* (New York, 1984), 668.

Ole R. Holsti and James N. Rosenau call this position "semi-isolationism" in their *American Leadership in World Affairs: Vietnam and the Breakdown of Consensus* (Boston, 1984).

A second perspective resembles the first but is more radical—the "inevitability" point of view.[13] According to this reasoning, the United States is destined to repeat Vietnam-type experiences for several reasons. Americans must import scarce commodities and export American products; economic lifelines must be secured. Americans will likely insist on remaining "Number One," whatever that means, and this psychological factor compels an activist, interventionist foreign policy. Americans will continue, as well, to exaggerate the Communist threat and thus interpret local crises derived from internal sources as Cold War contests demanding impositions of the containment doctrine. So long as a national security bureaucracy perpetuates a warmaking machine and the imperial presidency overwhelms the checks-and-balances system and misleads the American people through deliberate "disinformation," Vietnams will darken America's future.

The third perspective we might call the "diplomatic intervention" school: the United States must be interventionist because it is a great power with global interests that must be protected against all threats, and because Americans have an obligation to help others establish democratic, prosperous states. But the means should be diplomatic rather than military. Washington should negotiate with leftist and nationalist regimes to reduce potential threats and use foreign aid to foster conditions compatible with American interests and principles. In this way, by nurturing nationalism, the United States could build a non-Communist world and, at the same time, guarantee American prosperity and security. In other words, Americans must reject the extremes of "Fortress America" (isolationism) and "Atlas America" (global policeman) in favor of "Participant America."[14] President Jimmy Carter's initial openness to the leftist government in Nicaragua and his negotiation of the Panama Canal treaties seemed to reflect this thinking. Americans, Carter once said, had to put their "inordinate fear of Communism" behind them.[15]

The fourth perspective, often labeled the "win" or "revisionist" school, largely emerged from military officers who served in Vietnam and from conservatives and others who came to believe that the Vietnam War could have been won.[16] Some of them promoted a "stab-in-the-back" thesis: biased journalists, antiwar critics, and meddlesome members of Congress broke America's staying power and thus assisted the enemy. America supposedly

---

[13]A provocative example is Richard J. Barnet, *Roots of War: The Men and Institutions behind U.S. Foreign Policy* (New York, 1972).

[14]Marina V. N. Whitman, "Leadership without Hegemony," *Foreign Policy*, no. 20 (Fall 1975): 138.

[15]John Lewis Gaddis, *Strategies of Containment: A Critical Appraisal of Postwar American National Security Policy* (New York, 1982), 345.

[16]For examples see Guenter Lewy, *America in Vietnam* (New York, 1978); Norman Podhoretz, *Why We Were in Vietnam* (New York, 1982); David H. Petraeus, "Lessons of History and Lessons of Vietnam," *Parameters* 16 (Autumn 1986): 43–53; Richard Nixon, *No More Vietnams* (New York, 1985); W. Scott Thompson and Donaldson D. Frizzell, eds., *The Lessons of Vietnam* (New York, 1977); and George F. Will, "Vietnam: Another Version," *Hartford Courant*, 11 May 1981.

lost its will. "I don't think we were driven out of Vietnam," claimed Ambassador Jeane J. Kirkpatrick. "I think we left."[17] According to such thinking, political leaders hampered the military through gradualist methods and should have pursued all-out war. "It takes the full strength of a tiger to kill a rabbit," lectured former General William C. Westmoreland when he made a case against incrementalism.[18] "Remember," advised a former battalion commander, "we're watchdogs you unchain to eat up the burglar. Don't ask us to be mayors or sociologists worrying about hearts and minds. Let us eat up the burglar our own way and then put us back on the chain."[19] Too often, but especially after the 1968 Tet Offensive, these "win" advocates have argued, the United States failed to follow up on military advantages to hurl defeat at the enemy. The military, Ronald Reagan concluded, was "denied permission to win."[20] In short, military answers are appropriate and they can work. Others in this school of thought have declared that the war *should* have been won because it was a moral war; that is, it was quite moral for the United States to resist the tyranny of North Vietnam, whose aggression against Kampuchea and repression of Vietnamese after 1975 have revealed the Communists' brutalities.[21]

Because Reagan's foreign policy appeared to be fueled at least in part by the notion that Vietnam was fought in the wrong way and could have been won, and hence that Central America was not a potential Vietnam, the question of victory in Vietnam became compelling. Could the war have been won with another 500,000 soldiers, billions of dollars more, unrestrained B-52 bombing raids, better counterinsurgency methods, additional equipment, and perhaps even nuclear weapons? Would all of this have delivered victory, or would the United States actually have lost more, destroying even more of what it was trying to save? Asked still another way: How could the Communist Vietnamese (the Vietcong in the South and Vietnamese of the North), outnumbered seven to one in military forces, lacking advanced weapons and bombers, using almost primitive means of communication and transportation, and receiving comparatively little foreign aid from the Soviet Union and China—how could this diminutive enemy have turned back the world's military giant?

When adherents to the "win" point of view have spoken of victory, they usually have meant either keeping a non-Communist government in power in South Vietnam or uniting under U.S. guidance the two Vietnams

[17] Flora Lewis, "Vietnam and Salvador—A Battle for Hearts and Minds," *New York Times*, 21 February 1982.

[18] William C. Westmoreland, "Vietnam in Perspective," *Military Review* 59 (January 1979): 42.

[19] "Vietnam: Yesterday's War, Today's Lessons," *Washington Post National Weekly Edition*, 29 April 1985.

[20] George C. Herring, "The 'Vietnam Syndrome' and American Foreign Policy," *Virginia Quarterly Review* 57 (Fall 1981): 595.

[21] For an "official" statement of this point see George Shultz, "The Meaning of Vietnam," U.S. Department of State *Bulletin* 85 (June 1985): 13–16.

that had been divided by the Geneva Accords of 1954. Could either have been achieved? Many analysts have thought not. and have argued that "win" enthusiasts have failed to contend with some troubling questions and inescapable facts.[22]

To many analysts, victory would have come only through an American invasion of North Vietnam in order to cripple Hanoi's warmaking capability. As Secretary of Defense Robert McNamara came to realize, the massive bombings of the Ho Chi Minh Trail, Laos, Kampuchea, and North Vietnamese cities had not forced the adversary to capitulate and had not halted the flow of arms and men to the South. The air terror inflicted tremendous losses on the enemy, of course, but did not break it. American planes dropped 6.7 billion tons of bombs on Indochina in 1965–73, or three times the total tonnage dumped on all enemy nations during the Second World War. Strategic bombing, we have been told, seldom works against a nonindustrialized country. When Richard Nixon entered the White House in early 1969, he surmised that there were only two ways he could deliver a "knockout blow."[23] One was to bomb the North's irrigation dikes, probably killing 100,000 civilians. The other was to use tactical nuclear weapons. He ruled out both options, in part because he recoiled from the domestic and international uproar that surely would have met such steps, and in part because either action would have wrecked the détente he hoped to cultivate with the People's Republic of China (PRC).

Even if the United States had destroyed cities, dikes, factories, and farms in North Vietnam, then what? An invasion and occupation of the territory north of the 17th parallel probably would still have been necessary. American troops would have had to slash their way across the Demilitarized

---

[22]For critiques see Terry Nardin and Jerome Slater, "Vietnam Revised," *World Politics* 33 (April 1981): 436–48; Herring, " 'Vietnam Syndrome' "; David E. Kaiser, "Vietnam: Was the System the Solution?" *International Security* 4 (Spring 1980): 199–218; Earl C. Ravenal, *Never Again: Learning from America's Foreign Policy Failures* (Philadelphia, 1978); Walter LaFeber, "The Last War, the Next War, and the New Revisionists," *democracy* 1 (January 1981): 93–103; Fromkin and Chace, "What *Are* the Lessons"; Frank A. Burdick, "Vietnam Revisioned: The Military Campaign against Civilian Control," *democracy* 2 (January 1982): 36–56; Marilyn B. Young, "Revisionists Revisited: The Case of Vietnam," Society for Historians of American Foreign Relations *Newsletter* 10 (June 1979): 1–10; Gary R. Hess, "The Military Perspective on Strategy in Vietnam: Harry G. Summers's *On Strategy* and Bruce Palmer's *The 25-Year War*," *Diplomatic History* 10 (Winter 1986): 91–106; Paul M. Kattenburg, "Reflections on Vietnam: Of Revisionism and Lessons Yet to be Learned," *Parameters* 14 (Autumn 1984): 42–56; and Barbara Tuchman, *The March of Folly: From Troy to Vietnam* (New York, 1984). I have profited from the following reviews of Vietnam literature: Christopher C. Lovett, " 'We Held the Day in the Palm of Our Hand': A Review of Recent Sources on the War in Vietnam," *Military Affairs* 51 (April 1987): 350–62; Fox Butterfield, "The New Vietnam Scholarship," *New York Times Magazine*, 13 February 1983; George C. Herring, "Vietnam Remembered," *Journal of American History* 73 (June 1986): 152–64; Herring, "America and Vietnam: The Debate Continues," *American Historical Review* 92 (April 1987): 350–62; Stephen Pelz, "Alibi Alley: Vietnam as History," *Reviews in American History* 8 (March 1980): 139–43; and Sandra Taylor, "Taking Aim on Saigon: Rambo, Writers, and the Vietnam War," Organization of American Historians *Newsletter* 14 (February 1986): 4–6.

[23]Richard Nixon, *RN: The Memoirs of Richard Nixon* (New York, 1978), 347.

Zone into the Democratic Republic of Vietnam, where a reserve army of perhaps half a million soldiers waited, and where "the whole population is dug in, with individual foxholes and an efficient civil defense."[24] American casualties would have been staggering. Assuming the improbable, a successful invasion, the United States would have been forced to conduct an expensive and bloody occupation of indeterminate duration against a hostile people defending their homeland, probably through guerrilla warfare. And, having paid the price in lives and treasure once, would Americans have been ready to reintervene if resistance to outside authority, in the North or the South, flared significantly again? Given all of these prospects, it seems quite unlikely that an invasion would have delivered victory.

American leaders appreciated the difficulty of invading and controlling the North, but they might have opted for that drastic course had they not feared provoking a Soviet or Chinese intervention. If U.S. forces crossed the 17th parallel, Beijing had warned, the PRC would come to North Vietnam's defense. The Soviet Union, Hanoi's primary supplier, might have been dissuaded from saving its ally, but no president could gamble that both the Soviets and Chinese would stand aside. American fears were anything but casual, based as they were on prior experience in Korea, intelligence data, and strategic calculations. At the very least, an invasion would have derailed the simultaneous movement toward détente with the two Communist giants. At worst, it would have elevated a regional war to a great power conflagration. It is difficult to see, of course, how turning Vietnam into a world war would have led to an American victory.

Advocates of the "win" thesis also overlook the negative international political consequences the United States would have incurred had it prosecuted the war more vigorously. America's European allies already thought Washington had lost its senses by investing resources in a region peripheral to the West's vital interests. Members of the North Atlantic Treaty Organization became resentful and restless, further weakening the alliance. Only four of the United States' forty worldwide allies sent troops to help in Vietnam (South Korea, Thailand, Australia, and New Zealand). The Third World that the United States was trying hard to woo soured even further toward Washington, as votes against the United States in the United Nations, restrictions on American corporations, and terrorist acts against American citizens and property starkly testified. When radical Islamic students stormed the American embassy in Tehran, Iran, in 1979, one of the attackers snarled to a blindfolded captive: "We're paying you back for Vietnam."[25]

To have won the war, moreover, the United States would have had to reform significantly the Saigon government, which claimed little popular following and existed at Washington's sufference. The clique of Southern leaders routinely jailed critics, fixed elections, refused land reform, and, as nationalists, ignored or rejected American advice. A series of conspiracies,

---

[24]Roger Hilsman, "Must We Invade the North?" *Foreign Affairs* 46 (April 1968): 430.
[25]Doyle McManus, *Free at Last!* (New York, 1981), 16.

coups, attempted coups, and American covert actions destabilized Vietnamese politics, while America's client, Ngo Dinh Diem, polarized politics by smashing the Buddhists, leaving the extreme choices of the National Liberation Front or the Saigon regime.

The American-assisted plot in 1963 to oust Diem in order to improve the chances for reform only produced more instability. By 1965, George Ball concluded, South Vietnam had only an army, not a government. "I don't think we ought to take this government seriously," Ambassador Henry Cabot Lodge told a White House meeting that same year. "There is simply no one who can do anything."[26] South Vietnamese leaders, moreover, came to resent American criticism and bristled against their dependency upon American aid. The United States struggled with a dilemma: if it pressed Saigon to reform and manipulated the government to enhance its political standing, it risked making Southern officials appear to be puppets. Doing so would undermine the very objective of building a strong, independent government that could command popular support. In the end, American officials abandoned reform, and the weak South Vietnamese regime continued to hinder victory.

Many Vietnamese refused to fight and die for this corrupt, American-backed government and its self-serving leaders. Nor would they sacrifice for the Americans, who seemed increasingly willing to take on the responsibilities of fighting and bleeding. Marine officer Robert Muller remembered: "I served as an adviser to three separate ARVN [Army of the Republic of Vietnam] battalions, every one of which every time we were in combat, split. Not most of the time, every time!" Muller realized that "the writing was on the wall."[27] One-third of the men in combat units deserted each year, and this high rate, not warfare or disease, accounted for the biggest loss of manpower for America's ally. ARVN forces were afflicted with the same problems that troubled their government: poor morale, corruption, self-serving politics, and nepotism.[28]

In short, South Vietnam lacked the stable political foundation that was necessary for victory. The United States had no reliable, internal instrument for the implementation of containment and no chances of building one in the midst of a major war. As Ball has reflected, "we failed not from military ineptitude but because there was no adequate indigenous political base on which our power could be emplaced."[29]

This incontestable evidence of the instability and ineffectiveness of the Southern government should make us doubt the postwar prescriptive analysis

---

[26]George McT. Kahin, *Intervention: How America Became Involved in Vietnam* (New York: 1986), 372.

[27]"After Vietnam: This War Was Different," *Washington Post*, 25 May 1980.

[28]Ronald H. Spector, *Advice and Support: The Early Years of the U.S. Army in Vietnam, 1941–1960* (New York, 1985); Spector, "U.S. Army Strategy in the Vietnam War," *International Security* 11 (Spring 1987): 133.

[29]Ravenal, *Never Again*, 25. On the importance of the weakness of the South Vietnamese government see Stanley Hoffmann et al., "Vietnam Reappraised," *International Security* 6 (Summer 1981): 3, 4; Herring, " 'Vietnam Syndrome,' " 607–8; and Gabriel Kolko, *Anatomy of a War: Vietnam, the United States, and the Modern Historical Experience* (New York, 1985).

of Colonel Harry G. Summers, Jr., and others that a deployment of American forces just below the Demilitarized Zone along routes into the South and a blockade of Northern ports would have stopped the movement of soldiers from the North and cut lines of supply. Under such conditions the Vietcong supposedly would have withered away. In military terms, sealing off a 900-mile frontier against a determined and versatile enemy demonstrably adept at infiltration would have been extremely difficult at best, requiring great numbers of troops. Even if such a blocking operation had worked, the fact of tortured politics and popular discontent with the Saigon coterie would have remained to ensure disarray and insurgency in the South and handicap the war effort. A different military strategy would not have altered political realities.[30]

Another problem dogs the "win" perspective. From the postwar works of military officers and others, it seems evident that victory never could have come without a reformation of the American military establishment.[31] The generals pursued a kill-and-destroy strategy and war of attrition that failed. Their "can-do," "no-harm-in-trying" attitude prevented them from warning the president about the serious obstacles to victory. The Joint Chiefs of Staff labored under a "group-think" or consensual approach; in order to speak with one voice to the president, they buried objections. Nor could military authorities articulate an alternative strategy for the president, because they themselves were confused about the war's objectives. They kept calling for more men and more bombs. The enemy was never beaten down to the point of surrender: hurt, to be sure, but not conquered. Their war of attrition also presumed incredible patience on the part of the American people, who eventually sensed what postwar analysts have since emphasized: American strategy was not working, and more of the same would not deliver success.

The military brass, too, sent soldiers into a war of insurgency after having trained them for combat in Europe or for an encounter similar to the Korean War. The United States largely fought a conventional war, stressing massive fire-power and technology rather than light infantry. Although the U.S. Army trained and used some special units and seemed to embrace counterinsurgency methods, its conversion to this type of warfare was "largely cosmetic."[32] The enemy lost when it tangled with Americans in a conventional battle, but it seldom fought that way, preferring quick attacks and skirmishes in the jungles and mountains. The rotation system for officers—one year in

---

[30] Harry G. Summers, Jr., *On Strategy: A Critical Analysis of the Vietnam War* (Novato, CA, 1982); Bruce Palmer, *The 25-Year War: America's Military Role in Vietnam* (Lexington, KY, 1984). On this point see Gary Hess's critique in "The Military Perspective," 104–5.

[31] Andrew F. Krepinevich, *The Army and Vietnam* (Baltimore, 1986); Palmer, *The 25-Year War*; Spector, "U.S. Army Strategy"; Drew Middleton, "Vietnam and the Military Mind," *New York Times Magazine*, 10 January 1982; Douglas Kinnard, *The War Managers* (Hanover, NH, 1977); Summers, *On Strategy*.

[32] Spector, "U.S. Army Strategy," 131. Summers disagrees in "The Army after Vietnam," in *Against All Enemies: Interpretations of American Military History from Colonial Times to the Present*, ed. Kenneth J. Hagan and William R. Roberts (Westport, CT, 1986), 361–73.

Vietnam to "punch your ticket"—only compounded the problem: it broke continuity and squandered whatever experience had been gained. Burdened with these and other factors, the United States enjoyed tactical victory but endured strategic defeat.

The American military also engaged in deceit that made it difficult for officials in Washington to assess accurately the course of the war. Examples are legion, but a few will suffice. For twenty months, military authorities suppressed reports of the massacre of Vietnamese women, children, and elderly men at My Lai in March 1968. They played games with data, too. In jest, but illustrating the point, one former policymaker created a fictional encounter in which a military officer informed a 1967 White House meeting on the effectiveness of the air war: American planes "knocked out 78 percent of North Vietnam's petroleum reserve; since we had knocked out 86 percent three days ago and 92 percent last week, we were doing exceptionally well."[33] In addition, military men faked body counts. Major William Lowry recalled that the "duplicity became so automatic that lower headquarters began to believe the things they were forwarding to higher headquarters. It was on paper; therefore, no matter what might have actually occurred, the paper graphs and charts became the ultimate reality."[34] Colonel John B. Keeley, who commanded an infantry battalion in the Mekong Delta in 1967–68, provided an example: "One day my battalion spent the whole day beating the bush and flushed and killed four VC [Vietcong]. Another battalion was doing the same thing and killed two VC. We sent the number four and the number two to brigade for its body count report. There, the numbers were put side by side to make 42, not the six we actually killed."[35]

A variety of discontents not unlike those bedeviling American society back home also troubled the American military in Vietnam. Racial tensions and drugs were rife. By spring 1971, reported American officials, 10 percent of American GIs were taking heroin, while a higher percentage was smoking marijuana. In the period 1969–72 roughly one thousand cases of fragging were registered—assaults on officers with the intent to kill, harm, or intimidate. In the years 1965–72 some 550,000 American soldiers deserted and another 570,000 American men evaded the draft. Could this military, with all its problems, from the high-level strategist in the Pentagon to the "grunt" in the field, have won the war? Reforming the behemoth military during a war that was going badly was probably impossible, yet without reform America's chances of winning remained remote.

The American people and their doubts also must figure into any discussion of why victory eluded the United States. How could their ardent support have been aroused and maintained over a long period? Summers and others have argued that a declaration of war would have mattered. It would

---

[33]James C. Thomson, Jr., "Minutes of a White House Meeting, Summer, 1967," in *Who We Are*, ed. Robert Manning and Michael Janeway (Boston, 1975), 43–44.

[34]James Fallows, *National Defense* (New York, 1981), 26.

[35]*Washington Post*, 6 July 1981.

have focused national attention on the distant war, stimulated patriotic passions, permitted the placement of restraints on television journalists, ensured adequate mobilization, and forced dissenters to rally around the flag.[36] This argument is questionable on several scores. Americans, as the Korean War demonstrated, become impatient with limited war. As one historian has remarked, "protracted and inconclusive ground warfare will not for a long period of time command public support."[37] Congress might not have declared war in 1965, when escalation began in earnest. At that time South Vietnam had hardly entered American consciousness as vital to the national interest. The Gulf of Tonkin incident of the year before lacked the stunning force of Pearl Harbor and could not have generated a prowar consensus. A declaration of war would not have changed the dismal status of the South Vietnamese government and military, American strategy, the continued loss of international friends, or the obstacles to invasion and occupation of the North.

Just as unlikely would have been a prolonged public tolerance for governmental controls over the flow of information. Television would probably still have brought into American homes enough pictures of death and destruction to convince many American citizens that their nation's conduct of the war was morally disgraceful. Although the credibility gap already had opened wide by 1967, Americans supported their government's decisions for a long time—not until 1970 did a majority favor withdrawal.[38] By then many believed that their leaders had deceived them. Would a declaration of war have prevented deception? Would not Americans, with or without a declaration of war, eventually have grown weary of the returning coffins, disruptions of family life, and higher taxes? And for how long could decision makers persuade Americans that they should oppose communism in Vietnam while Washington sought détente with the two primary Communist nations, the Soviet Union and China, the latter supposedly the real enemy in Vietnam?

Data also reveal a pale popular endorsement of the war and suggest that a declaration of war and greater mobilization might have exacerbated rather than diminished protest. In addition to illegal draft evasions, lawful educational and employment deferments exempted some nine million men from the draft.[39] A prolonged, declared war might very well have pushed up the desertion, evasion, and avoidance statistics, created a draft crisis, and

---

[36]In addition to Summers, *On Strategy*, 23–24, 37, and Palmer, *The 25-Year War*, 190, see General Maxwell Taylor in *New York Times*, 21 April 1987. Hess provides a critique in "The Military Perspective," 98–99.

[37]Ernest R. May quoted in Hoffmann, "Vietnam Reappraised," 4.

[38]John E. Mueller, "Trends in Popular Support for the Wars in Korea and Vietnam," *American Political Science Review* 65 (June 1971): 358–75; Mueller, *War, Presidents and Public Opinion* (New York, 1973); William M. Lunch and Peter W. Sperlich, "American Public Opinion and the War in Vietnam," *Western Political Quarterly* 32 (March 1979): 21–44.

[39]About 27 million men were eligible for the draft (ages 19–26). 6.6 million of that number were disqualified. Paul M. Kattenburg, *The Vietnam Trauma in American Foreign Policy, 1945–75* (New Brunswick, NJ, 1980), 273, 284n.40.

sparked more street demonstrations. In short, to have won the war, Washington would have had to undertake the daunting task of mobilizing the American people.

The obstacles to invasion and occupation of the North, the absence of allied support, the many problems besetting the American army and ARVN, the debilities of the South Vietnamese government, and the American people's shrinking endorsement of the never-ending war—all help to explain why the U.S. venture into Indochina ended in defeat. But even if the United States had overcome this litany of problems, victory would have remained elusive, because American leaders proved woefully ignorant about Indochina. They knew little and seemed not to want to know about the Vietnamese people and their ancient culture, particularly their traditional and largely successful resistance to foreign influence. American policymakers failed as well to study the long experience or heed the cautionary advice of the French, belittling their predecessors as the quitters of World War II, brutal and failed colonialists, and technologically deficient warriors. By failing to appreciate the difficulties imposed by terrain and climate on modern warfare, and by discounting the character and history of the people on whose land they were fighting, American leaders invited the disappointment they ultimately suffered.

Three points merit special consideration here. First, the environment itself was hostile. American forces had to operate in a jungle terrain of thick grasses and bamboo, leeches, and weather that alternated between hot sun and drenching rain. Boots and human skin rotted, and diseases flourished. "It is as if the sun and the land itself were in league with the Vietcong," recalled Marine officer Philip Caputo, "wearing us down, driving us mad, killing us."[40] The Vietnam veteran Oliver Stone's provocative movie *Platoon* (1987) revealed the inhospitable country that partially negated American technological superiority. Well-hidden booby traps blasted away parts of the body, and snipers made every step of a grunt or "bonnierat" precarious.[41] The enemy was everywhere but nowhere, often burrowed into elaborate underground tunnels or melded into the population, where every Vietnamese might be a Vietcong. No place in Vietnam seemed secure. Many veterans later suffered "post-traumatic stress disorder," an illness of nightmares and extreme nervousness.

The United States lost the war as well because its conduct alienated the Vietnamese people, some one-third of whom became refugees. Bomb craters scarred the land: the chemical defoliant Agent Orange denuded it. GIs tagged Vietnamese "gooks," and did not always distinguish between peasant farmers and the enemy. Some even sliced off Vietnamese ears as trophies. The Americans used napalm freely, blasted to bits with artillery and air strikes hamlets from which American troops had received small-arms fire, and torched villages considered friendly to the Communists. "Free-fire zones," within which any person was considered the enemy, trapped the innocent. Most American

---

[40] Philip A. Caputo, *A Rumor of War* (New York, 1977), 100.

[41] See, for example, John M. DelVecchio, *The 13th Valley: A Novel* (New York, 1982).

soldiers were not committing atrocities, but the record is replete with enough examples to support the conclusion of one American official that "it was as if we were trying to build a house with a bulldozer and wrecking crane."[42] Before leaving office, Secretary McNamara complained about the bombing: "It's not just that it isn't preventing the supplies from getting down the trail. It's destroyed the countryside in the South. It's making lasting enemies."[43] As for the village of Ben Tre, "it became necessary to destroy the town to save it," remarked an American officer.[44]

The strategic hamlet program, begun in 1962, also uprooted people from ancestral lands and relocated them in guarded quarters surrounded by barbed wire. Although American leaders may have deliberately created a refugee population in order to separate the people from the National Liberation Front, in reality the policy meant the growth of a discontented populace and reduced agricultural production.[45] As well, the huge influx of Americans disrupted the Vietnamese economy and helped support a debasing underworld of prostitution, drugs, and the black market. Vietnam's fragile society, already profoundly divided between Catholics and Buddhists, became further fragmented. The United States in the end was destroying the very place it was trying to defend. It is no wonder that Washington could not build a strong, popular government in the South.

The United States lost, finally, because it faced a people deeply committed to their cause, who seemed to have no "breaking point."[46] When an American veteran returned to Vietnam as a journalist in the early 1980s, he interviewed soldiers about their endurance of great sacrifices during the war. They invariably quoted Ho Chi Minh: "Nothing is more important than independence and freedom."[47] Although probably harboring some doubts about whether these noble aspirations had been satisfied, given the ruthlessness and warrior-state mentality of their Communist leaders in recent years, these soldiers believed in the 1960s that they were defending their divided nation against outsiders, as their ancestors had done for centuries against the Chinese, French, and Japanese. "Not only do the Viet Cong units have the recuperative

[42]George C. Herring, *America's Longest War*, 2d ed. (New York, 1986), 155.

[43]Leslie H. Gelb and Richard K. Betts, *The Irony of Vietnam: The System Worked* (Washington, DC, 1979), 169–70.

[44]George McT. Kahin and John W. Lewis, *The United States in Vietnam*, rev. ed. (New York, 1969), 373. The fate of the six thousand residents of Ben Suc, where the Vietcong had dug a huge tunnel network, illustrates the destruction of South Vietnamese village life. The residents were rounded up and sent to a refugee camp, where enemy suspects were apparently tortured and murdered. According to the official Army history: "As the villagers and their belongings moved out, bulldozers, tankdozers, and demolition teams moved in. . . . When the village had been flattened by the engineers. . . . a large cavity was scooped out near the center of the area, filled with ten thousand pounds of explosives . . . and then set off. . . . The village of Ben Suc no longer existed." Bernard W. Rogers, *Cedar Falls-Junction City* (Washington, DC, 1974), 41.

[45]Nardin and Slater, "Vietnam Revised," 449.

[46]John E. Mueller, "The Search for the 'Breaking Point' in Vietnam," *International Studies Quarterly* 24 (December 1980): 497–519.

[47]William Broyles, Jr., *Brothers in Arms* (New York, 1986), 267.

power of the phoenix," General Maxwell Taylor reported in late 1964, "but they have an amazing ability to maintain morale."[48] General Bruce Palmer remembered that "their will to persist was inextinguishable."[49] Vietnamese nationalism and a commitment to revolution combined to thwart American victory. General Taylor summarized the general problem when he said that "we didn't know our ally. Secondly, we knew even less about the enemy. And, the last, most inexcusable of our mistakes, was not knowing our own people."[50]

These "mistakes," Americans have been assured in the 1980s, were being avoided in El Salvador, where American military advisers and economic and military aid were at work to defeat a leftist insurgency against a conservative, American-backed government. "There is no comparison with Vietnam. There isn't going to be anything like that in this," asserted President Reagan.[51] But critics warned against another Vietnam. "The White House did not appreciate how rapidly El Salvador would take off in the minds of the press as a Vietnam," remarked a presidential assistant.[52]

Has the Vietnam analogy made sense, or, as some analysts have argued, was Vietnam so unique that reasonable comparisons cannot be made? Whatever our answers, Vietnam has emerged as a reference point in the debate over policy toward Central America.[53] President Reagan seemed to think that the victory denied in Vietnam could be achieved in El Salvador. As one senator put it, El Salvador seemed a place where the United States could "win one for a change."[54] According to Robert White, a former ambassador to El Salvador, the administration "thought it was like rolling a drunk."[55] Why would Reagan and his advisers have thought so? Because the differences between Vietnam and El Salvador seemed favorable to a U.S. venture into Central America.

The strategic, economic, and historical contexts were quite different. Unlike Vietnam, which had China, El Salvador had no large Communist state at its border to provide supplies and sanctuary. Salvador's neighbors, Guatemala and Honduras, were actually staunch and well-armed American allies.

48Kahin, *Intervention*, 249. See also 399–400.

49Palmer, *The 25-Year War*, 176.

50Michael Maclear, *The Ten Thousand Day War* (New York, 1981), 354.

51News conference statement, 27 July 1983, quoted in Waltraud Queiser Morales, "El Salvador and Vietnam: Analogy for American Foreign Policy?" (Paper, National Endowment for the Humanities Summer Seminar for College Teachers, University of Connecticut, 1983), 1.

52Sidney Blumenthal, "Marketing the President," *New York Times Magazine*, 13 September 1981.

53For examples of discussions of Central America in the context of Vietnam see "El Salvador and Vietnam," *Wall Street Journal*, 5 March 1981; Lewis, "Vietnam and El Salvador"; Strobe Talbott, "El Salvador: It Is Not Viet Nam," *Time* 119 (22 February 1982): 33–34; "The Talk of the Town," *The New Yorker* 59 (2 May 1983): 29; Richard Nixon, "Don't Let Salvador Become Another Vietnam," *Wall Street Journal*, 2 May 1983; John D. Waghelstein, "Choices in Central America," *New York Times*, 7 August 1984; Herring, "Vietnam, El Salvador"; and works cited earlier. See also the Icaras film, *El Salvador: Another Vietnam* (1981).

54*New York Times*, 26 April 1981.

55Marvin E. Gettleman et al., eds., *El Salvador* (New York, 1981), 355.

El Salvador, moreover, was a small country about the size of Massachusetts, with only five million people. The U.S. Navy enjoyed easy access to the nation: this proximity made logistics far simpler than was the case of Vietnam, some 12,000 miles away. The Salvadoran rebels were hardly a replica of the disciplined, tenacious Vietminh or Vietcong who became battle-hardened from years of war against the French before Americans ever became combatants. The insurgents were internally divided, seemed unable to gain wide popular support, and failed to control much territory. The nationalism that drove the Vietnamese was aroused and invigorated by anticolonialism. It was not a force the Salvadoran revolutionaries could draw upon, for El Salvador already existed as a nation and no immediate colonial master lurked in the recent past, even if some Salvadorans considered the United States an imperialist intruder.

American economic and strategic interests in Central America, unlike Vietnam, were longstanding and large. The Caribbean and Pacific sea lanes were vital to U.S. trade. North American investment in and trade with the region had always been substantial. Since the early twentieth century the United States had intervened regularly in Central America and had established strong ties with military establishments in the area. A good number of American officers spoke Spanish, whereas few had learned Vietnamese. The president of El Salvador, José Napoleón Duarte, had attended the University of Notre Dame in South Bend, Indiana. All in all, American leaders knew Central America; they had a clear view of U.S. interests; they considered it a place where Americans would no doubt fight with a staying power lacking in Vietnam. They also had a justification for intervention in the Monroe Doctrine, which had evolved by the early 1980s into a statement of U.S. hegemony in the hemisphere. Reagan officials revitalized the dormant doctrine—the conservative publicist William Buckley called it a "re-baptism"—although they sounded more like Theodore Roosevelt than James Monroe.[56] For the Vietnam War, American leaders could not muster a declaration of such longevity, self-interest, and emotional appeal. For all of these reasons, then, presidential advisers could tell Reagan, the chances for victory in El Salvador—without the introduction of American combat troops—seemed good and certainly much better than the chances had been in Vietnam.

The Reagan administration, however, did find one difference between Vietnam and El Salvador restraining. American citizens repeatedly indicated to pollsters and members of Congress that they opposed sending American soldiers to Central America. In 1964, President Lyndon B. Johnson was able to get the Tonkin Gulf Resolution without much congressional debate, and in 1965 he was able to send American troops to Vietnam without much public

---

[56] Walter LaFeber, "The Evolution of the Monroe Doctrine from Monroe to Reagan," in *Redefining the Past: Essays in Diplomatic History in Honor of William Appleman Williams*, ed. Lloyd C. Gardner (Corvallis, OR, 1986), 139. See also LaFeber, *Inevitable Revolutions: The United States in Central America* (New York, 1983); and Gaddis Smith, "The Legacy of the Monroe Doctrine," *New York Times Magazine*, 9 September 1984.

discussion. In the 1980s, however, Americans were much more alert to Central American events and the prospects of an expanded American military presence. Congress cautioned the president and even, at times, prohibited U.S. aid to the contras, the anti-Sandinista forces using Honduras as a base to attack Nicaragua. Some military leaders expressed reluctance to become involved in another counterinsurgency, if only because they feared that the American people again would tire of the effort. "Remember one lesson from the Vietnam era," General William A. Knowlton lectured the 1985 Army War College class. "Those who ordered the meal were not there when the waiter brought the check."[57] Some conservatives have agreed that the United States could not intervene militarily in Central America without a public mandate. "You first commit the nation before you commit the troops," the Texas billionaire H. Ross Perot told Colonel Oliver North of the National Security Council, who was running a clandestine aid program for the contras.[58]

Critics of U.S. intervention in Central America believed that the similarities to Vietnam were more striking than the differences. The way American officials thought about global politics constituted the first similarity. They saw events in Central America as part of an East-West contest. As in the case of Vietnam, Washington's leaders elevated a local conflict into an international crisis. They invoked the containment doctrine to turn back "a textbook case of indirect armed aggression by Communist powers."[59] If fear of "another China" drove decision makers in Vietnam, so fear of "another Cuba" generated policy toward Central America. Reaganites refurbished the domino theory, charging that Nicaragua, Cuba, and the Soviet Union were plotting to tip dominoes in the United States' own backyard. Remember, President Reagan said, "we are the last domino."[60] Such threat exaggerations were typical during the Vietnam War, as were the denunciations of critics as unpatriotic apologists for Communist misdeeds.[61] The "can-do" feeling also reemerged—the time of "self-doubt is over"—to blind leaders to the obstacles in the way of victory in another civil war.[62] However chastened by Vietnam, American policymakers once again seemed to believe that they had answers for other people's problems.

Strategic arguments in the 1980s also resembled those of the 1960s. If Secretary of State Dean Rusk worried that China would use Vietnam as a platform for expansion into Asia, threatening such American allies as Japan and the Philippines, Secretary of State George Shultz declared that the Soviet

---

[57]Petraeus, "Lessons of History," 45.

[58]David Remnick, "The Billionaire Boy Scout," *Washington Post National Weekly Edition*, 27 April 1987.

[59]Department of State *Bulletin* 81 (March 1981): 7.

[60]William M. LeoGrande, "A Splendid Little War: Drawing the Line in El Salvador," *International Security* 6 (Summer 1981): 45.

[61]For an example see Shultz, "The Meaning of Vietnam," 15.

[62]Reagan quoted in *New York Times*, 28 May 1981.

Union was trying to use Nicaragua as a "stepping stone."[63] Yet another similarity with Vietnam was that few U.S. allies stood with the Reagan administration. The major nations in the region, Mexico and Venezuela, have opposed Washington's emphasis on military solutions. Joining with the other members of the Contadora group, Colombia and Panama, they have urged negotiations to resolve the Salvadoran and Nicaraguan crises, which threatened to engulf all of Central America in war. But U.S. officials have rebuffed the Contadora group's repeated overtures and plans and have flatly rejected revolutionary Salvadorans' calls for negotiations.

Still another similarity between Vietnam and Central America, claim opponents of intervention, lay in the unreliability and unsavory character of America's local allies. The contra leadership included a number of former Somoza family henchmen and National Guardsmen who had been overthrown in 1979 in large part because Nicaraguans had grown intolerant of the Somocistas' corruption and violence. Washington officials frequently have had to press the contras to reform so that they could present a better public image. In their war against the Sandinista government the contras have committed atrocities, practiced fraud with American money, and squabbled vigorously among themselves. By the late 1980s they had not demonstrated any ability to command popular support in Nicaragua. In El Salvador, although Duarte won with the help of American financing, politics remained corrupt and unpredictable, and the military and wealthy retained power. The government appeared incapable of stopping the ravaging death squads that silenced critics of all kinds. Yet another similarity flowed from these ties to local leaders: a credibility gap. If Americans came to doubt that officials were telling them the truth in the Vietnam years, they also came to question Washington's exaggerated rhetoric about Central America. Reagan's depiction of the contras as "freedom fighters" and his assurances that "democracy" was developing and "human rights" were improving in El Salvador seemed ludicrous. The official *White Paper* of 1981 on El Salvador was so riddled with errors and unsubstantiated generalizations about Communist intrigue that the administration soon shelved it. Finally, there is the issue of international law. If the United States had violated the Geneva Accords in Vietnam, the World Court in 1986 ruled that the United States had violated international law by aiding the contras and should pay reparations to Nicaragua. Washington dismissed the court ruling and questioned its jurisdiction, even though a few years earlier American officials had appealed to that same court to punish Iran for taking Americans hostage.

As of this writing, the outcome of U.S. intervention in Central America remains uncertain. Certainly the scenario will not follow each step of the Vietnam experience. The analogy does not work in all respects, and Reagan has vowed never to send American troops to Central America. But if the critics are right, as they seem to be, the United States will stumble in Central

[63]Department of State *Bulletin* 87 (March 1987): 16.

America for some of the same reasons it fell in Vietnam. The regions contrast sharply, but American assumptions have not changed and the drive for victory is relentless. Local conditions, once again, promise to determine the outcome. Once again the exaggerated image of a ubiquitous Communist threat takes the United States into a civil war for which there are seldom outside answers. The past directs and continues to mislead. "Here we go again," groaned Republican Senator Mark Hatfield of Oregon, "old men creating a monster for young men to destroy."[64]

[64] *New York Times*, 13 August 1986.

The Last War, the Next War, and the New Revisionists

WALTER LAFEBER

As if to prove Lord Acton's dictum that "the strong man with the dagger is followed by the weak man with the sponge," a remarkable rewriting of the Vietnam war's history is under way. It is especially remarkable because the new revisionists are either ignorant of American policy in the conflict or have chosen to forget past policies in order to mold present opinion. More generally, they are rewriting the record of failed military interventionism in the 1950 to 1975 era in order to build support for interventionism in the 1980s. More specifically, the new revisionists are attempting to shift historical guilt from those who instigated and ran the war to those who opposed it.

Immediately after South Vietnam fell in 1975, Secretary of State Henry Kissinger urged Americans to forget the quarter-century-long war. That advice was no doubt related to his other concern at the time: committing U.S. military power to Angola and the Horn of Africa. Congress had fortunately learned from experience and stopped Kissinger from involving the country in an African Vietnam. The next year, however, influential authors began to discover that Vietnam's history was more usable than Kissinger had imagined. General William Westmoreland, who commanded U.S. forces during the worst months of fighting in the 1960s, set the line when he argued in his memoirs and public speeches that the conflict was not lost on the battlefield, but at home where overly sensitive politicians followed a "no-win policy" to accommodate "a misguided minority opposition . . . masterfully manipulated by Hanoi and Moscow." The enemy, Westmoreland claimed, finally won "the war politically in Washington."

Part of Westmoreland's thesis was developed with more scholarship and cooler prose by Leslie H. Gelb and Richard K. Betts in *The Irony of Vietnam: the System Worked.* It was not the "system"—that is, the Cold War national security establishment—that failed, the authors argued. Failure was to be blamed on the American people, who never understood the war and finally tired of it, and on the Presidents who supinely followed the people. Thus the "system" worked doubly well: the professional bureaucrats gave the correct advice, as they were paid to do, and the Presidents followed the public's wishes, as democratic theory provides that they should.

Westmoreland's argument that the antiwar groups wrongly labeled Vietnam an illegal and immoral conflict was developed by Guenter Lewy's *America in Vietnam*. Lewy, however, was so honest that his own evidence destroyed the thesis. Although he wrote that U.S. soldiers followed civilized modes of war even though this sometimes meant virtual suicide, Lewy also gave striking examples of how the troops ruthlessly destroyed villages and civilians. "It is well to remember," he wrote, "that revulsion at the fate of thousands of hapless civilians killed and maimed" because of American reliance upon high-technology weapons "may undercut the willingness of a democratic nation to fight communist insurgents." That becomes a fair judgment when "thousands" is changed to "hundreds of thousands." Lewy nevertheless held grimly to his thesis about the war's morality and legality, even as he reached his closing pages: "the simplistic slogan 'No more Vietnams' not only may encourage international disorder, but could mean abandoning basic American values." It apparently made little difference to Lewy that those basic American values had been ravaged at My Lai, or at Cam Ne, where a Marine commander burned down a village and then observed in his after-action report that "It is extremely difficult for a ground commander to reconcile his tactical mission and a people-to-people program." Lewy's conclusions, not his evidence, set a tone that was widely echoed, particularly after the foreign policy crises of late 1979.

The Soviet invasion of Afghanistan was seized upon with almost audible sighs of relief in some quarters. *Commentary*, which had publicly introduced Lewy's argument in 1978, published a series of essays in early 1980 that developed some of his conclusions, especially the view that if the Vietnam experience inhibited future U.S. interventions, it "could mean abandoning basic American values." In an essay that thoughtfully explored the meaning of his own antiwar protests in the 1960s, Peter Berger nevertheless drew the conclusion that the American defeat in Vietnam "greatly altered" the world balance of power, and that "American power has dramatically declined, politically as well as militarily." Charles Horner condemned President Jimmy Carter's early belief that Vietnam taught us the limits of U.S. power. "That view," Horner claimed, "is the single greatest restraint on our capacity to deal with the world, and that capacity will not much increase unless the view behind it is changed, thoroughly and profoundly."[1] Horner did his best to reinterpret the meaning of Vietnam,

1 Charles Horner, "America Five Years After Defeat," *Commentary*, April 1980. Horner was special assistant to Senator Daniel P. Moynihan.

but it was *Commentary's* editor, Norman Podhoretz, who best demonstrated how history could be rewritten to obtain desired conclusions.

"Now that Vietnam is coming to be seen by more and more people as an imprudent effort to save Indochina from the horrors of Communist rule rather than an immoral intervention or a crime," Podhoretz wrote in the March 1980 issue, "the policy out of which it grew is also coming to be seen in a new light." He believed that the "policy—of defending democracy [*sic*] wherever it existed, or of holding the line against the advance of Communist totalitarianism by political means where possible and by military means when necessary," was based on the Wilsonian idea that "in the long run," U.S. interests depended on "'the survival and the success of liberty' in the world as a whole." This revisionist view of Vietnam, Podhoretz argued, is helping to create a "new nationalism"—the kind of outlook that "Woodrow Wilson appealed to in seeking to 'make the world safe for democracy' and that John F. Kennedy echoed."[2]

Podhoretz's grasp of historical facts is not reassuring; the essay has three major errors in its first three pages.[3] George A. Carver, Jr.'s essay subtitled "The Teachings of Vietnam," in the July 1980 issue of *Harper's*, only adds to that problem. An old C.I.A. hand who was deeply involved in Vietnam policy planning, Carver is identified in *Harper's* only as "a senior fellow" at Georgetown University's Center for Strategic and International Studies. That identification is nevertheless of note, for the Center serves as an important source of personnel and ideas for what passes as Ronald Reagan's foreign policy program. In the article, Carver set out to "dispel Vietnam's shadows" so the United States could

2 Norman Podhoretz, "The Present Danger," *Commentary*, March 1980.

3 (1) "The . . . Cold War began in 1947 when the United States, after several years of acquiescence in the expansion of the Soviet empire, decided to resist any further advance. . . . Up until this point the Russians had enjoyed a free hand." They actually did not enjoy a "free hand" in parts of Central Europe (for example, Germany), or even Eastern Europe. In 1946 the United States exerted strong pressure to get the Russians out of Iran, then helped the Iranians renege on the deal that the Soviets had accepted in return for agreeing to leave. The United States also sent warships to the Eastern Mediterranean in 1946 to reinforce its policy that Russia should not have new rights of control over the Dardanelles. The United States certainly was not passive in 1945–1946. (2) "The Korean War [broke] out as a result of American encouragement" to the Communists "in the form of an announcement by Secretary of State Dean Acheson seeming to suggest that the defense of South Korea was not a vital American interest." Podhoretz is referring to Acheson's speech of January 12, 1950. That speech clearly announced that the United States would help defend such areas as South Korea "under the Charter of the United Nations"—which is what the United States did in the Korean War. (3) "In refusing to do more in Korea than repel the North Korean invasion . . . Truman served notice on the world that [the United States] had no intention of going beyond containment to rollback or liberation." In truth, of course, Truman did change containment to attempted liberation when he ordered U.S.-U.N. forces across the thirty-eighth parallel and into North Korea in late summer, 1950. That order proved to be a disaster; it produced the overwhelming majority of the war's casualties, led to war with Chinese armies, and produced a new McCarthyite response in the United States.

again exercise great power and influence. When he mentioned earlier policy, Carver simply postulated that South Vietnam fell to North Vietnamese conventional forces, not to "any popular southern rebellion," and that "the press and media, and their internal competitive imperatives" misrepresented the real progress the U.S. forces were making in the war. Beyond that, the analysis consists of empty generalizations (Americans are encumbered in their foreign policy by "theological intensity" and "childlike innocence"), and it climaxes with the insight that "the world is cruel."

Read closely, Carver's warning about the dangers of "theological intensity" contradicts Podhoretz's call for a new Wilsonianism. But in the wake of the Iranian and Afghanistan crises, few read these calls to the ramparts of freedom very closely. The essays were more valuable for their feelings than for their historical accuracy. The new revisionists wanted to create a mood, not recall an actual past, and their success became dramatically apparent when that highly sensitive barometer of popular feelings, commercial television, quickly put together a new sitcom on the war, "The Six O'Clock Follies." One reviewer labeled it a "gutlessly cynical comedy," signaling that "suddenly we are supposed to be able to laugh at Vietnam."[4] As the *Washington Post*'s critic observed, however, since the conflict has "been deemed a safe zone . . . all three networks have Vietnam sitcoms in the works" for 1980–1981. Television was placing its seal of approval on a revisionism that promised to be commercially as well as ideologically satisfying.[5]

Given this new mood, it was natural that those who wielded, or planned to wield, power were also prepared to help wring the sponge. In 1978 Zbigniew Brzezinski had lamented privately to Senate staff members that the floundering administration needed a *Mayagüez* incident so Carter, as Ford had in 1975, could get tough with Communists (preferably, apparently, from a small country), and rally Americans behind a battle flag. By the end of 1979, Carter had not one but two such opportunities with the Iranian hostage issue and the Soviet invasion of Afghanistan, and as usual Americans indeed closed ranks behind the President. In mid-December, Brzezinski observed that the country was finally getting over its post-Vietnam opposition to military spending and overseas intervention.

Three months later, Ronald Reagan, in his only major foreign policy speech prior to the Republic Convention, urged a return to Wilsonianism—what one reporter characterized as a belief that Americans have "an inescapable duty to act as the tutor and protector of the free world in confronting . . . alien ideologies."[6] To carry out this mission, Reagan proclaimed, "we must rid

4 *Washington Post*, April 24, 1980, p. D15.

5 Future plans for Vietnam sitcoms are also noted in *Washington Post*, April 24, 1980.

6 John M. Goshko, "World Speculates on Nature of a Reagan Foreign Policy," *Washington Post*, July 12, 1980, p. A8.

ourselves of the 'Vietnam syndrome.'"[7] He of course meant the old "syndrome," not the new syndrome of the revisionists that the war was to be admired for its intent if not its outcome. A frustrated job seeker at the Republican Convention best captured the effects of the new revisionism. A reporter teased Henry Kissinger about his prediction in the early 1970s that if the war did not end well for Americans there would be a fierce right-wing reaction. "It turned out just about the way I predicted it would," Kissinger replied.[8] The former Secretary of State, however, contributed to the mood that threatened to confine him to academia. In recent writings and speeches, Kissinger has argued that if the Watergate scandal had not driven Nixon from office, South Vietnam would not have been allowed to fall. His claim cannot, of course, be completely disproved, but it is totally unsupported by either the post-1973 military and political situation in Vietnam, or the antiwar course of American policies, including Nixon's, that appeared long before the Watergate scandal paralyzed the administration.

The arguments of the new revisionists—or the new nationalists, as some prefer to be called (in perhaps unconscious reference to the New Nationalism of Theodore Roosevelt and Herbert Croly that pledged an imperial "Big Stick" foreign policy)—dominated the foreign policy debates and, indeed, the Carter-Brzezinski foreign policies in early 1980. Because those arguments rest heavily on interpretations of the Vietnam conflict, their use of the war's history deserves analysis. This can be done on two levels: the new revisionists' explicit claims, and the events they choose to ignore.

The most notable explicit theme is captured by Westmoreland's assertion that the war was lost because of pressure from a "misguided minority opposition" at home, or by Peter Berger's more careful statement that "the anti-war movement was a primary causal factor in the American withdrawal from Indochina." Since at least the mid-1960s, detailed public opinion polls have existed that show that Americans supported a tough policy in Vietnam. In this, as in nearly all foreign policies, the public followed the President. As Herbert Y. Schandler concluded after his careful study of public opinion between 1964 and 1969, "If the administration is using increasing force, the public will respond like hawks; if it is seeking peace, the public responds like doves."[9] When Lyndon Johnson tried to convince doubters by whipping out the latest opinion polls showing support for the war, he did not have to make up the figures. George Ball has testified that the antiwar protests only "dug us in more deeply" and in-

7 Quoted in ibid.

8 Robert Kaiser, "Kissinger Keeps His Distance from Reagan on Foreign Policy," *Washington Post*, July 16, 1980, p. A12.

9 Herbert Y. Schandler, *The Unmaking of a President: Lyndon Johnson and Vietnam* (Princeton: Princeton University Press, 1977), p. 179, fn.

tensified the administration's determination to win. Ball, who served as Under Secretary of State under Johnson, rightly calculated that "only late in the day did widespread discontent . . . appreciably slow the escalation of the war."[10] Even those who dissented in the 1960s were more hawk than dove. Richard Scammon and Ben Wattenberg's analysis of the 1968 election concluded that a plurality of the Democrats who voted for Eugene McCarthy in the primaries supported George Wallace in November, and that finding is corroborated by polls revealing that a majority of those who opposed the conduct of the war also opposed protests against the war. Westmoreland's "misguided minority opposition" was of significantly less importance than a much larger group that wanted him to have whatever he needed to end the war. It simply is not true, as Barry Goldwater claimed at the 1980 Republican Convention, that the "will" to win the war was missing in the 1960s.

By 1970–1971, antiwar opposition had increased, but it did not stop Nixon from expanding the conflict into Cambodia and Laos. One statistic stands out: before Nixon sent in the troops, 56 percent of college-educated Americans wanted to "stay out" of Cambodia, and after he committed the forces, 50 percent of the same group supported the Cambodian invasion. When Nixon carpet-bombed North Vietnam two years later and for the first time mined the North's ports, 59 percent of those polled supported the President, and only 24 percent opposed him, even though it was clear that the mining could lead to a confrontation with the Russians and Chinese, whose ships used the harbors.

The effectiveness of the antiwar movement has been greatly overrated by the new revisionists, and the movement has consequently served as the scapegoat for them as well as for the national security managers whose policies failed in Vietnam. Given the new revisionist arguments, it needs to be emphasized that the United States lost in Vietnam because it was defeated militarily, and that that defeat occurred because Americans could not win the war without destroying what they were fighting to save—or, alternatively, without fighting for decades while surrendering those values at home and in the Western alliance for which the cold war was supposedly being waged. The antiwar protesters only pointed up these contradictions; they did not create them.

The new revisionists argue that the nation has largely recovered from the disaster. Carl Gershman writes that "as the polls reveal, the American people have now overwhelmingly rejected the ideas of the new [Carter-Vance-Young] establishment."[11] The strategy of the post-Vietnam "establishment" is to con-

10 Quoted in *New York Times Magazine*, April 1, 1973, p. 43.

11 Carl Gershman, "The Rise and Fall of the New Foreign Policy Establishment," *Commentary*, July 1980. Gershman is executive director of Social Democrats, U.S.A.

tain communism only in selected areas, and by using nonmilitary means if possible. The polls actually reveal considerable support for this strategy. In January 1980, after the invasion of Afghanistan, a CBS/*New York Times* survey showed that about two-fifths of those polled wanted to respond with nonmilitary tactics, two-fifths wanted to "hold off for now," and less than one-fifth favored a military response.[12] Lou Harris discovered that within six weeks after the seizure of the hostages in Iran, support for military retaliation dropped off sharply.[13] Quite clearly, if the new nationalists hope to whip up public sentiment for using military force wherever they perceive "democracy" to be threatened, they have much work yet to do. Most Americans have not overwhelmingly rejected nonmilitary responses, even after being shaken by the diplomatic earthquakes of 1979–1980. And they appear too sophisticated to agree with Podhoretz's Wilsonian assumption that "American interests in the long run [depend] on the survival and the success of liberty in the world as a whole." A majority of Americans seem to agree with that part of the post-Vietnam "establishment" represented by Vance and Young that it is wiser to trust nationalisms in the Third World than to undertake a Wilsonian crusade to rescue those nationalisms for an American-defined "liberty."

There is a reason for this confusion among new revisionist writers. They focus almost entirely on the Soviet Union instead of on the instability in Third World areas that the Soviets have at times turned to their own advantage. Such an approach allows the new revisionists to stress military power rather than the political or economic strategies that are most appropriate for dealing with Third World problems. The new nationalists, like the old, pride themselves on being realists in regard to power, but their concept of power is one-dimensional. Once this military dimension becomes unusable, nothing is left. A direct military strategy is appropriate for dealing with the Soviets in certain cases—for example, if the Red Army invaded Western Europe or Middle East oil fields. That strategy, however, has existed since the days of Harry Truman; the Vietnam war, regardless of how it is reinterpreted, has nothing new to teach us about that kind of massive response. A quarter-century ago, when the United States took its first military steps into Vietnam, Reinhold Niebuhr warned that the policy placed "undue reliance on purely military power" and therefore missed the fundamental political point: a U.S. military response was incapable of end-

12 "The Hardening Mood Toward Foreign Policy," *Public Opinion*, February/March 1980, p. 13.

13 Ibid.

ing "the injustices of [Asia's] decaying feudalism and the inequalities of its recent colonialism."[14] Niebuhr's advice was of course ignored. The supposed realists of the day proceeded to commit military power in Vietnam—*to contain China*. For, in the mid-1960s, China was the villain for the national security managers, as the Soviets are now for the new revisionists.

The reason for the failure of U.S. military power was not that it was severely limited. Lyndon Johnson bragged that he put 100,000 men into Vietnam in just one hundred and twenty days. Those troops were supported by the most powerful naval and air force ever used in Asia. Laos became the most heavily bombed country in history, North Vietnam's ports and cities were bombed and mined almost yard by yard, and Nixon dropped a ton of bombs on Indochina for every minute of his first term in the White House. Neither the will nor the power was missing. As Michael Herr wrote in *Dispatches*, "There was such a dense concentration of American energy there, American and essentially adolescent, if that energy could have been channeled into anything more than noise, waste and pain, it would have lighted up Indochina for a thousand years." Vietnam provides a classic lesson in the misuse of military power, but that lesson is being overlooked by the new revisionists.

And if they have misunderstood the conflict's central political and military features, so have the new revisionists lost sight of the historical context. They stress that Vietnam caused the decline of American power. It is quite probable, however, that when historians look back with proper prospective on the last half of the twentieth century, they will conclude that U.S. foreign policy problems in the 1970s and 1980s resulted not from the Vietnam experience, but more generally from political misperception and from an overestimation of American power. The *hubris* produced by the American triumph in the Cuban missile crisis contributed to such misestimation, but the problems also resulted from the failure to understand that U.S. power began a relative decline in the late 1950s and early 1960s. It was during those earlier years that the American economy and international trade began a decline that only accelerated—not started—in the 1970s; that such important allies as Japan and West Germany directly attacked American markets and helped to undermine the dollars; that the Western alliance displayed its first signs of slipping out of Washington's control; and that the Third World rapidly multiplied its numbers and decided—as the creation of OPEC in 1960 demonstrated—that it no longer had to join either one of the superpower camps. Future historians will consequently see the Vietnam war as one result, not a cause, of the relative decline of American power that began in the late 1950s. They will also probably conclude that space ventures, and the achievement of independence by nearly one hundred nations in the Third

14 Reinhold Niebuhr's 1955 essay "The Anatomy of American Nationalism" is reprinted in his *The World Crisis and American Responsibility* (New York: Associated Press, 1958), pp. 61–63.

World, were of greater historical significance than the Vietnam conflict or the U.S.-USSR rivalry that obsesses the new revisionists.

Even with their narrow focus on the lessons of Vietnam, it is striking how much the new revisionists omit from their accounts of the war. They say relatively little about the South Vietnamese. The war is viewed as an eyeball-to-eyeball confrontation between Americans and Communists, and the turn comes when the Americans, undone by what Carver calls their "childlike innocence," blink. This approach resembles watching two football teams but not noticing the ball that is being kicked and passed around. The new revisionists have downplayed the inability of the South Vietnamese to establish a stable and effective government amid a massive U.S. buildup, the Vietnamese hatred for the growing American domination, and the massive desertions from the South's army in 1966-1967, even when the U.S. forces arrived to help. As early as 1966, non-Communist student leaders accurately called the country's presidential elections "a farce directed by foreigners."[15] By 1971, a Saigon newspaper ran a daily contest in which readers submitted stories of rape or homicide committed by Americans. As Woodrow Wilson learned in 1919, some people just do not want to be saved—at least by outsiders with whom they have little in common.

The new revisionists also overlook the role the allies played in Vietnam. There is a good reason for this omission: of the forty nations tied to the United States by treaties, only four—Australia, New Zealand, South Korea, and Thailand—committed any combat troops. The major European and Latin American allies refused to send such forces. We later discovered that the South Koreans, whom Americans had saved at tremendous cost in 1950, agreed to help only after Washington bribed them with one billion dollars of aid. The key Asian ally, Japan, carefully distanced itself from the U.S. effort. This was especially bitter for American officials, for Truman and Eisenhower had made the original commitment to Vietnam in part to keep the area's raw materials and markets open for the Japanese. Relations between Tokyo and Washington deteriorated rapidly. When Lyndon Johnson asked whether he could visit Japan in 1966, the answer came back, "inconceivable."[16] An article in the authoritative *Japan Quarterly* stated that if the United States became involved in another war with China, divisions in Japanese public opinion "would split the nation in two" and lead to "disturbances approaching a civil war in scale."[17]

As Jimmy Carter admitted in early 1980, the United States needs strong support from allies if it hopes to contain the Soviets in the Middle East. It would

15 Quoted in *New York Times*, October 10, 1967, p. 6.

16 Quoted in George R. Packard III, "Living With the Real Japan," *Foreign Affairs*, October 1967, pp. 200–01.

17 Quoted in *New York Times*, January 22, 1966, p. 1.

be well, therefore, to note carefully the allied view of U.S. policy in Vietnam and elsewhere before embarking on a Wilsonian crusade to make "democracy" safe everywhere. Having chosen to ignore the lesson that Vietnam teaches about the allies, the new revisionists resemble traditional isolationists, who, as scholars have agreed, were characterized by a desire for maximum freedom of action, minimum commitment to other nations ("no entangling alliances"), and a primary reliance on mlitary force rather than on the compromises of political negotiations.

Finally, these recent accounts neglect the war's domestic costs. The new revisionists stress the decline of the American "will" to win, but they say little about how the economic disasters and a corrupted presidency produced by the war influenced that "will." As early as January 1966, Lyndon Johnson admitted that "Because of Vietnam we cannot do all that we should, or all that we would like to do"[18] in building a more just society at home. As the phrase went at the time, Americans—those "people of plenty"—suddenly discovered they could not have both guns and butter. The butter, or, more generally, the Great Society program, was sacrificed. A Pentagon analysis drawn up under the direction of Secretary of Defense Clark Clifford after the 1968 Tet offensive faced the problem squarely. It concluded that militarily the war could not be won, "even with the 200,000 additional troops" requested by Westmoreland. A drastic escalation, moreover, would result not only in "increased defiance of the draft," but in "growing unrest in the cities because of the belief that we are ignoring domestic problems." A "domestic crisis of unprecedented proportions" threatened.[19] If the new revisionists and Reagan Republicans plan to manipulate the war's history to obtain higher defense budgets and unilateral commitments overseas, they should discuss this crucial characteristic of the war's course: it was determined less by campus protesters than by the growing realization that the costs worsened the conditions of the poorest and most discriminated against in American society until an "unprecedented" crisis loomed. Clifford turned against the war after businessmen he respected suddenly became scared and dovish. Clifford learned, but there is little evidence that the new revisionists understand the choices that were embedded in what they dismiss as the "Vietnam syndrome."

As persons who attack centralized power in the federal government, the new revisionists and the Reagan Republicans should at least discuss the effect of Vietnam on the imperial presidency. They could note, for example, that nothing centralizes power more rapidly than waging the cold war militarily, unless it is waging hot war in Korea and Vietnam. In 1967, Under Secretary of

18 Quoted in Walter LaFeber, *America, Russia, and the Cold War, 1945–1975* (New York: John Wiley, 1976), p. 262.

19 Neil Sheehan et al., *The Pentagon Papers* (New York: Times Books, 1971), p. 614.

State Nicholas Katzenbach told the Senate that the power given by the Constitution to Congress to declare war was "an outmoded phraseology." In 1969–1972, Nixon used "national security" as the rationale for ordering a series of acts that resulted in nearly forty criminal indictments. Vietnam raised the central question in American foreign policy: How can the nation's interests be defended without destroying the economic and political principles that make it worth defending? In their extensive study of Vietnam, the new revisionists have chosen to ignore that question.

They have instead concentrated on an objective that is as simple as it is potentially catastrophic: the removal of the restraints of history, so that the next war can be waged from the start with fewer limitations. They are offering a particular interpretation of the last war, so the next war can be fought differently. This purpose helps explain why these writers stress the narrow military aspects of the war and ignore the larger problems of historical context, the Western allies, economic costs, and political corruption. Westmoreland again set the tone with his remark that "If we go to war . . . we need heed the old Oriental saying, 'It takes the full strength of a tiger to kill a rabbit' and use appropriate force to bring the war to a timely end."[20] In his reassessment of the tragedy, Ambassador Robert Komer condemned the "institutional factors—bureaucratic restraints" that made success impossible.[21] Lewy argued that the struggle was considered a mistake at the time because of "the conviction that the war was not being won and apparently showed little prospect of coming to a successful conclusion." If only the restraints had been lifted, the new revisionists imply, the war—which they consider morally and politically justified—could have been fought to a successful conclusion. This inference is drawn with little attention to either the inherent contradictions in Vietnam military strategy (for example, that villages had to be destroyed to be saved) or the nonmilitary aspects of the conflict. It comes perilously close to an end-justifies-the-means argument.

By trying to make the last war more acceptable, the new revisionists are asking us to make the next war legitimate, even before we know where it will be or what it will be fought for. A Chinese official once told Henry Kissinger that "One should not lose the whole world just to gain South Vietnam."[22] Nor, it might be added, should men with sponges try to legitimize their global cold-war policies by whitewashing the history of the war in South Vietnam.

20 The remarks were reprinted in *Congressional Record* (Senate), March 5, 1979.

21 Komer's views are given in Willard Scott Thompson and Donald D. Frizzell, eds., *The Lessons of Vietnam* (New York: Crane-Russak, Co., 1977), especially pp. 266–68.

22 Quoted in Theodore Draper, "Kissinger's Apologia," *Dissent*, Spring 1980, p. 248.

The Post-Vietnam Formula under Siege: The Imperial Presidency and Central America

KENNETH E. SHARPE

The Iran-contra affair made public an abuse of executive authority that began in 1981. The deeper issues raised by the trading of arms for hostages and the diversion of profits to the contras, however, harken back to the Vietnam period. The impact of the Vietnam war on our constitutional democracy, which culminated in the Watergate scandal and Richard Nixon's resignation, served as a warning of the dangers of an imperial presidency. This article evaluates the lessons learned, the reforms instituted in the aftermath of Vietnam, and indicates what it is necessary to do now.

Different people drew different lessons from the Vietnam-Watergate scandals. Some blamed the abuse of executive power on the character flaws of the President and his closest advisers, and saw the solution as their removal from office. Others saw the problem as weak laws and sought legislation to strengthen Congress's power to check executive abuses and to legislate foreign and domestic policy. Reforms that I loosely call the post-Vietnam-Watergate formula were enacted to ensure that presidential abuse of power would be less likely to again endanger constitutional democracy in the United States. Others, like Senator J. William Fulbright, supported legislative action but argued that this was not enough. The problem, they argued, was political, not legal. Congress lacked the will to enforce its constitutional authority in foreign policy. An exercise of that will required a challenge to the direction of foreign policy, and the president, drawing on his often self-

KENNETH E. SHARPE is a professor of political science at Swarthmore College and co-editor (with Morris Blachman and William LeoGrande) of *Confronting Revolution: Security through Diplomacy in Central America.*

proclaimed authority as commander in chief, was often able to take foreign policy steps that created a *fait accompli* and made the exercise of that will even harder. As long as a condition of permanent cold-war crisis prevailed, it would be difficult to defend the authority of Congress against usurpation by the president and the national security bureaucracy he managed.

The Reagan administration's conduct of Central American policy provided the first sustained test of the post-Vietnam-Watergate formula. It demonstrated the continued willingness of the executive branch to abuse its authority in foreign policy and suggested the limits of legislative reform when not backed by a strong congressional will.

The Imperial Presidency and the Post-Vietnam-Watergate Formula

> In no part of the constitution is more wisdom to be found, than in the clause which confides the question of war or peace to the legislature, and not to the executive department. . . . [T]he trust and the temptation would be too great for any one man. . . . War is in fact the true nurse of executive aggrandizement. In war, a physical force is to be created; and it is the executive will, which is to direct it. In war, the public treasures are to be unlocked; and it is the executive hand which is to dispense them. In war, the honours and emoluments of office are to be multiplied; and it is the executive patronage under which they are to be enjoyed. . . . The strongest passions and most dangerous weaknesses of the human breast; ambition, avarice, vanity, the honourable or venial love of fame, are all in conspiracy against the desire and duty of peace. [James Madison][1]

The Constitution leaves fundamental issues to be settled by practice, precedent, and judicial review. There has been continual dispute over the balance of power in foreign policy making. One of the major conflicts has been over efforts to reconcile the war-declaring power of Congress and the war-making power of the president. The decision to declare war was given to Congress for the reasons Madison outlines above. Yet the Founding Fathers understood that this restriction would not impede the executive from repelling attacks against the country in the absence of a formal declaration of war. Over the decades presidents drew on their constitutional authority as commander in chief to claim increasingly unchecked authority in the case of such "defensive" wars. But what did it mean to repel an attack? Was it just to defend American borders from actual invasion? Did it include preventive wars to stop a possible attack? And who was to determine how likely that possibility was? Was an attack on U.S. citizens or property outside the United States the kind of attack a president could by himself decide to repel? What was the distinction between a "defensive" war and a "preventive war"? Were such wars justified only in areas immediately bordering the United States? Or any place in the hemisphere? Or the world?

The system of checks and balances in the foreign policy arena was in Edwin

[1] Cited in Christopher H. Pyle and Richard M. Pious, *The President, Congress and the Constitution* (New York: The Free Press, 1984), 287.

S. Corwin's words "an invitation to struggle for the privilege of directing American foreign policy."[2] Over more than two centuries of struggle a pattern has emerged: the executive has enlarged its foreign policy powers at the expense of Congress; and Congress has reacted to reassert its constitutional prerogatives when the dangers to its institutional authority have become clear. The long-term effect of such conflicts, however, has been the gradual enlargement of executive power.

The shift in the balance toward the executive began to take on alarming proportions in the cold-war decades that followed World War II. The executive developed a large independent peacetime national security apparatus whose centerpiece was the National Security Council (NSC) created in 1947. Also critical was the establishment of the Defense Department (which integrated all the services) and the giving of legislative authority to a Joint Chiefs of Staff system and to the Central Intelligence Agency (CIA).

As the security apparatus grew and cold-war tensions mounted, the executive branch became increasingly unaccountable to Congress, the press, and the public in the making of foreign policy. Congress generally acquiesced. The rough consensus over foreign policy goals and the seeming imperatives of national security muted fundamental criticism of the shift of power to the executive. The executive branch increasingly bypassed the treaty-making authority of Congress through the use of secret executive agreements. The CIA developed into an apparatus that not only gathered intelligence but secretly carried out foreign policy, often using covert operations to overthrow foreign governments and assassinate foreign leaders. The president, the Pentagon, the CIA, the NSC, and even the State Department felt less obliged to give Congress and the public information about foreign policy issues.

President Lyndon B. Johnson's commitment of half a million U.S. troops to Vietnam under the Tonkin Gulf Resolution demonstrated how far Congress had abdicated its constitutional prerogative. In 1969 President Richard M. Nixon took the executive interpretation of war powers even further than Johnson by authorizing the bombing of Cambodia. The next year, in the face of clear congressional sentiment to terminate the war in Indochina, he authorized a U.S. invasion of Cambodia, claiming authority as commander in chief and invoking the need to protect U.S. troops. A few years later the Watergate revelations showed that the problem of executive secrecy and abuse of power went even further, putting, Henry Steele Commager wrote, other fundamental principles at risk.

> By countenancing burglary, wiretapping, *agents provocateurs*, the use of the Federal Bureau of Investigation, the Central Intelligence Agency and even the Internal Revenue Service to punish "enemies," Mr. Nixon sought to substitute his own fiat for law.
>
> By attempting to impose, for the first time in our history, prior censorship of the press, by threatening hostile television stations with deprivation of their licenses . . . Mr. Nixon presented the most dangerous threat to the Bill of Rights in the whole of our history.

[2] Edward S. Corwin, *The President: Office and Powers* (New York: New York University Press, 1940), 200.

> By corrupting presidential elections through the solicitation of illegal contributions, by a systematic campaign of mendacity, trickery and character assassination against opponents . . . Mr. Nixon gravely endangered the integrity of our republican system of government.[3]

The reaction was growing support for impeachment and an attempt to strengthen constitutional democracy. A set of three related commitments—a post-Vietnam formula—were embodied in new laws, procedures, and institutional arrangements. One commitment was to get access to information about executive activities, a necessary condition for checks and balances to work. A second was to restore congressional legislative authority in foreign policy and strengthen congressional checks on potential abuses of authority at home and abroad. A third commitment was to limit the possibilities for political repression and violations of civil liberties and civil rights, about which I have written elsewhere.[4] This article will focus on the first two commitments.

Access to information. The conflict between secrecy and disclosure has had a long history. The recurrent pattern was demonstrated in 1798 when Benjamin Franklin Bache of the Philadelphia *Aurora* published a secret dispatch from the French to the secretary of state in order to show that the French wanted peace and the John Adams administration wanted war. He was arrested for seditious libel, and Congress was spurred to pass the Sedition Act. The issue then and for later generations was not the government's right to secrecy; *The Federalist* No. 64 argued that executive secrecy was vital in diplomatic negotiation and in "the business of intelligence." Rather it was whether or not the suppressed information was really vital or was suppressed in order to prevent an informed citizenry from making its own decisions and to protect the government from public opposition. When Congress passed the Espionage Act in 1917, it sought to prevent its misuse by overzealous presidents when it rejected a provision that would have made it a crime to publish information that "might" be used by the enemy. Instead it demanded proof that the person disclosing information had "reason to believe" it could be used "to the injury of the United States or to the advantage of any foreign nation."[5] Congress's power to gain access to information through investigation was strengthened by a 1927 Supreme Court decision stating that a legislative body "cannot legislate wisely or effectively in the absence of information respecting the conditions which the legislative is intended to affect or change. . . ."[6] But the problem of the balance between secrecy and disclosure deepened during and after World War II with the development and expansion of a classification system for information, a specialized national security bureaucracy with a vested interest in secrecy, and the widespread fear of Communist agents and subversion.

[3] Henry Steele Commager, *The Defeat of America* (New York: Simon and Schuster, 1974), 155–156.

[4] Morris Blachman and Kenneth Sharpe, "De-Democratizing Foreign Policy: Dismantling the Post-Vietnam Formula," *Third World Quarterly* 8 (October 1986).

[5] Cited in Arthur Schlesinger, *The Imperial Presidency* (Boston: Houghton Mifflin, 1973), 338.

[6] McGrain V. Daugherty, 273 U.S. 135, 175 (1927).

Only a few members of Congress were willing to take up the battle of disclosure versus secrecy during this time. But Congress was shaken out of its lethargy by Vietnam and Watergate.

One legislative response was to require certain critical information. The 1973 War Powers Resolution demanded that the president inform Congress in writing within forty-eight hours of introducing troops (in the absence of a declaration of war) into areas of hostilities or where imminent involvement in hostilities was likely. The reasons for introducing the troops, the legal authority justifying the introduction, and the scope and duration of the commitment had to be specified.

The 1974 Hughes-Ryan Amendment (amended again in 1980) required that the president report in "a timely fashion" all CIA covert operations other than intelligence gathering to appropriate committees. And legislation in 1976 and 1977 created Select Intelligence Committees in the Senate and House respectively. This allowed some oversight and control by the Congress, and there were mechanisms under certain circumstances for public disclosure of the classified information given to the committees.

The ability of the president to make secret executive agreements was limited by the Case-Zablocki Act of 1972, which required all executive agreements to be reported to Congress. In 1974 Congress also required that arms sales be so reported. If the president declared a national emergency, Congress required him to inform it of the specific laws under which he proposed to act, to file with Congress all executive agency rules and regulations, and to account for expenditures. Congress also strengthened the Freedom of Information Act in 1974 to provide for judicial review of decisions by executive agencies to keep all parts of a document classified.

Perhaps more important than the specific statutes was the general commitment Congress made to watch presidential actions more carefully and to use its existing powers as leverage to demand that foreign policy decisions be shared. The greater size and foreign policy expertise of staff members were also important. Such staff provided independent sources of information and allowed concerned members of Congress to use existing mechanisms better to provide oversight of foreign policy.

Restoring Shared Control. The new commitment to get access to information was aimed at allowing Congress increased participation in the making of foreign policy and a greater ability to check executive excesses. Constitutionally, much of the necessary power was already in the hands of Congress: the authority to declare war, to advise and consent on treaties and appointments, and the ultimate "check" through its power of the purse. But Congress was concerned about the various mechanisms or precedents that had developed to allow the president to circumvent congressional control. Of particular concern was an old problem in the struggle over foreign policy—the ability of the president to create situations that *forced congressional acquiescence* and created an antecedent, a *fait accompli*, which limited Congress's will and ability to use its existing powers. Alexander Hamilton had recognized that "the executive in the exercise of its constitutional powers, may establish an antecedent state of things, which ought to weigh in the legislative decision," a situation which Madison feared could create a dangerous shift in the congressional balance.[7]

In 1846 President James Polk sent U.S. troops into an area contested by Mexico and Texas. When they were predictably attacked by Mexican soldiers, he forced Congress's hand. In 1907 Theodore Roosevelt sent the fleet around the world in the face of strong congressional opposition, but Congress had to give the funds for fuel and supplies to bring it back. During and after World War II, congressional acquiescence allowed a dangerous growth of the president's prerogative as commander in chief. Corwin wrote after the war:

> there is Presidential initiative *and* Presidential initiative—that type which, recognizing that Congress has powers—great powers—in the premises, seeks to win its collaboration; and that type which, invoking the "Commander-in-Chief" clause proceeds to stake out Congress's course by a series of *faits accomplis*.[8]

In the cold-war years this kind of initiative, in which the president presented Congress with a *fait accompli*, grew more and more common. Presidents involved the United States in full-scale war by first committing troops to foreign lands (Truman in Korea, Kennedy and Johnson in Vietnam) and then arguing that the troops could not be abandoned or that commitments made had to be honored to protect American credibility. Presidents increasingly made secret executive agreements that bound the United States to certain foreign policies without congressional debate and authorization. Presidents ordered covert operations that involved the United States in policies that Congress could disown only at the risk of seeming to undermine national security. By the late 1960s the president had an unprecedented ability to create an antecedent state of things; and the argument that Congress had to stand by presidential commitments had a much more important place in U.S. foreign policy than in the past.

Congress attempted to hold the president accountable by insisting on full consultation and shared decision making *before* the policy die was cast. Some of this was handled legislatively. For example the War Powers Act aimed to "insure that the collective judgement of both the Congress and the President will apply" to the decision to send U.S. troops into hostilities by insisting that the president consult with Congress "in every possible instance" *before* the troops are introduced.[9] The Senate Foreign Relations Committee described the resolution as "an invitation to the executive to reconsider its excesses, and to the legislature to reconsider its omissions, in the making of foreign policy."[10]

Congress also established procedures by which the new access to information

[7] Cited in Schlesinger, *The Imperial Presidency*, 19.

[8] Edward S. Corwin, *Total War and the Constitution* (New York: Knopf, 1947), 33.

[9] The War Powers Resolution, Public Law 93-148, 93rd Congress, 1st sess., J.J. Res. 542, 7 November 1973; reprinted in Pat M. Holt, *The War Powers Resolution, The Role of Congress in U.S. Armed Intervention* (Washington, D.C.: The American Enterprise Institute, 1978), 43-48.

[10] Cited in Holt, *The War Powers Resolution*, 4.

could be used to insist on participation or to stop the president. For example, the Senate and House Intelligence Oversight Committees could try to dissuade the CIA from continuing covert operations by using their control of authorizations for intelligence activities, or by revealing such operations, or by taking the issue to the House or Senate to pass legislation specifically forbidding or cutting appropriations for the activity. The Clark Amendment in 1976 (abolished in 1985), for example, prohibited assistance for military or paramilitary operations in Angola. Similarly, Congress could block or force the modification of executive agreements by denying funds to implement them.

Perhaps the strongest measure was the provision of the War Powers Resolution that required the unauthorized use of troops to stop automatically. The resolution recognized that a president might have to act without congressional authorization in emergencies, but did not want such extraordinary circumstances to become an ordinary route for circumventing Congress. The War Powers Resolution required the president to terminate any unauthorized use of troops within sixty days unless Congress took affirmative action to approve it. The sixty days starts upon submission of the required report to Congress—a wrinkle that puts the starting of the clock in the hands of the president.

The new formula that emerged after Vietnam and Watergate represented concern both about the *process* of foreign-policy decision making and about the *content* of foreign policy. There was an awareness in Congress, and later in the Carter administration, that Third World turmoil was often caused by local conditions of poverty and repression, and that a "North-South" perspective was more realistic than an "East-West" perspective. Critics of the Vietnam policy were wary of sending U.S. troops to fight in Third World countries where the goals were not clearly defined and the conflict was unpopular at home. Many were opposed to supporting corrupt, repressive regimes and sought instead to condition foreign military and economic aid on a regime's human rights performance.

These new commitments to both process and content allowed Congress to take a more aggressive role in shaping Central American policy than it had in shaping early Vietnam policy. In the Carter administration this was most visible in the compromises and policy changes the administration was forced to accept in order to get congressional approval of the Panama Canal treaties and of economic assistance to the new Sandinista regime in Nicaragua. But a much more serious and sustained test came when the Reagan administration took office. Its willingness to aid repressive regimes facing domestic turmoil troubled many in Congress, and its emphasis on a military strategy in Central America raised the spectre of the involvement of U.S. troops in "another Vietnam." Moderates in Congress were particularly worried that the commitments being made to El Salvador (and later to Honduras and to the Nicaraguan exile army) would eventually draw in U.S. troops. They did not count on the War Powers Resolution alone; they understood that presidential initiatives could make it difficult to oppose the President if he sent troops. They wanted to participate from the very beginning in shaping policy.

Central America: A Test Case for the Post-Vietnam Formula

The post-Vietnam formula, like the Constitution itself, was open to interpretation. Would Congress share in shaping the overall direction of foreign policy, in the "takeoffs" as well as the "crash landings"?[11] Would Congress be able to prevent the executive from creating a crisis—an antecedent state of things—over which it could not easily exert its constitutional authority? Could Congress expect the executive to be forthright and candid in providing information about what it was doing and why? Would the executive respect congressional statutes and stay within the bounds of the law?

El Salvador

From 1981 until 1984, Congress attempted to participate in shaping El Salvador policy by making military aid conditional on certain requirements. The president had to certify that the Salvadoran government was "making a concerted . . . effort to comply with internationally recognized human rights," was "achieving substantial control over all elements of its armed forces, so as to bring an end . . . to indiscriminate torture and murder," was "making continued progress in . . . land reform," and was "committed to the holding of free elections."[12]

The conditionality requirement was weak: once the president certified, aid was automatically released. But the requirement made clear the broad opposition in Congress to aid for a repressive, reactionary regime; and it underlined the widespread belief that real reform was the only way to stop revolution. Presidential certification every six months also forced a certain public accountability, and the congressional hearings around each certification provided for careful scrutiny of administration facts and stimulated through media coverage public debate and education.

The administration, however, provided false and misleading information in order to certify that the conditions required for aid existed, despite overwhelming evidence to the contrary. Further, it refused to put serious pressure on the Salvadoran military to end its human rights abuses. To pick but one example, it repeatedly denied the well substantiated charges (confirmed by its own internal documents) that thousands of civilian noncombatants were being killed by government forces and "death squads" organized or aided by top military officials.[13] When Congress

[11] Senator Arthur Vandenberg had advised President Truman: "Let us in on the takeoffs if you want us in on the crash landings." Cited in James Sundquist, *The Decline and Resurgence of Congress* (Washington, D.C.: Brookings Institution, 1981), 300.

[12] U.S. House of Representatives, 97th Cong., 1st sess., International Security and Development Cooperation Act of 1981, Section 728(b).

[13] See Jim Leach et. al., *U.S. Policy in Central America: Against the Law?* (Washington, D.C.: Arms Control and Foreign Policy Caucus, 11 September 1984), 9–13; The Central America Crisis Monitoring Team, *In Contempt of Congress, The Reagan Record of Deceit and Illegality on Central America* (Washington, D.C.: Institute for Policy Studies, 1985), 32–37.

renewed the certification requirement in November 1983, Reagan pocket vetoed the bill while Congress was not in session and, therefore, had no opportunity to override it. The congressional response to such efforts to undercut or eliminate certification was weak. A majority would not support strengthening such legislation, and there was only limited willingness to use the power of the purse to cut aid even when the certification conditions were being violated.

The Reagan administration sought to avoid further scrutiny and opposition by refusing to comply with the requirement of the War Powers Resolution that the president report to Congress within forty-eight hours of when U.S. troops are introduced "into hostilities or into a situation where imminent involvement in hostilities is clearly indicated by the circumstances." While such reporting had also been avoided by Ford and Carter, neither had presented such systematically false information about the actual situation of U.S. troops. The Reagan administration maintained "we are not putting our people in a situation where there is any imminent danger of hostilities."[14] But in fact, U.S. military personnel were stationed in brigade headquarters throughout zones of conflict, traveled to the site of combat, came under fire on at least eight separate occasions by early 1985, flew reconnaissance missions over Salvadoran battlefields, and participated in naval interdiction activities in the Gulf of Fonseca.[15] Congressional critics pointed to the evidence, but they were unable to generate widespread concern.

Congress's ultimate leverage in the foreign policy process is in the power of the purse. From 1981 until mid-1984 a majority in Congress often did seek to limit military appropriations to El Salvador. The President, however, used a number of mechanisms to increase vastly military assistance outside the regular or supplemental appropriations process. In March 1981, for example, he used his defense drawdown authority to tap special funds earmarked for military emergencies and increased congressionally authorized military aid to El Salvador by $20 million. Congress had only appropriated $5.5 million. He then used his authority to reprogram budgetary allocations to send another $5 million in military aid and $44.9 million in economic support funds. For fiscal year (FY) 1982, Congress only appropriated $27 million and turned down an administration supplemental request for another $35 million. But in February 1982, the White House, claiming that the guerrilla destruction of aircraft at the Ilopango air base created an emergency situation, used its special defense drawdown authority to dispatch $55 million to El Salvador—over twice the amount Congress had authorized.

In each case the President was obeying the letter but not the spirit of the law. The special funds he drew on for military aid were put aside by Congress for use in emergency situations at presidential discretion. Although there was no emer-

[14] Langhorne Motley, before the House Subcommittee on Western Hemisphere Affairs, 2 May 1984; cited in Central America Crisis Monitoring Team, *In Contempt of Congress*, 39.

[15] Jim Leach, George Miller, Mark O. Hatfield, *U.S. Aid to El Salvador: An Evaluation of the Past, A Proposal for the Future* (Washington, D.C.: Arms Control and Foreign Policy Caucus, February 1985), 6, 24.

gency in these cases, the President defined them as such in order to circumvent a congressional debate on supplemental appropriations that he was likely to lose. Similarly, reprogramming – which requires only that the appropriations committees be informed of executive budget reallocations and not object within fifteen days – was designed to give the bureaucracy flexibility in reallocating funds among budget categories, not to provide a way to circumvent congressional debate on controversial aid authorizations. Yet the large volume of often legitimate reprogram requests makes it nearly impossible for the committees to quickly evaluate how funds are being allocated.[16] House leaders eventually grew critical of such circumventions. In 1983, the Appropriations Committee cut the reprogramming request for $60 million down to $30 million. House leaders warned the President not to continue to use his special drawdown authority to fund unauthorized military aid to El Salvador.

The administration tried another tack. In early 1984 it came to Congress with a request for an emergency supplemental appropriation for $93 million; Congress approved $61.75. Secretary of State George Shultz claimed that the Salvadorans were "running out of supplies right now" and other officials stated that "without these funds, the El Salvadoran Armed Forces will either go back to the barracks or collapse."[17] It turned out there was no emergency; $32 million of military aid already in the pipeline could have been diverted if necessary, and much of the emergency supplemental aid was used to expand the army by building new units.[18]

The 1984 and 1985 elections in El Salvador radically changed the character of congressional-executive relations. The election of José Napoleón Duarte, a recognized reformer, reinforced the administration's definition of the government as centrist and reformist. Many moderates grew reluctant to oppose aid, despite evidence that the military, not Duarte, was still the real power in El Salvador and that military corruption and repression were continuing. Congress approved the administration's aid requests. This aid, and particularly the aggressive air mobile tactics it provided, enabled the Salvadoran military severely to limit the guerrillas' offensive capabilities. This, in turn, reassured Congress that the aid was not making U.S. military intervention more likely. The admistration continued to provide misleading and false information about the economic and political situation in El Salvador, the growing isolation of Duarte from his own supporters, and above all the repression by the military. There was some decline in politically-targeted death squad killings, but the White House denied the documented killing and forced

[16] Initially the committees treated all such requests as routine and trusted the executive to use this budgetary discretion reasonably. The first full analysis of the reprogramming abuses was not done until the Senate Democratic Policy Committee Special Report, "Foreign Aid to Central America FY 1981-1987," 18 February 1987.

[17] Leach et.al., *U.S. Aid to El Salvador*, 4.

[18] Ibid., 4–5.

displacement of civilians by air and ground operations. Congress made few attempts to scrutinize administration claims publicly.[19]

Honduras

Administration attempts to avoid congressional scrutiny and debate by circumventing the normal appropriations process and tightly guarding information were even more serious in the case of aid to Honduras. During U.S. maneuvers in Honduras, for example, the Defense Department used funds out of a budget category called Operations and Maintenance (which is supposed to function as petty cash, not major military financing) to train and equip Honduran forces and to build permanent basing facilities. In 1984 the House Committee on Appropriations protested:

> the Comptroller General found that funds appropriated for operation and maintenance of our armed forces were used for military construction projects, security assistance activities, and civic action and humanitarian assistance. The Committee believes such diversion of funding from properly appropriated purposes is unwarranted and directs that the Department of Defense take such steps as necessary to prevent recurrence of such improprieties in the future.[20]

Furthermore, the maneuvers, which began in August 1981, turned out to be nearly continuous and thus had the effect of permanently stationing 700 to 1000 U.S. military personnel in Honduras and thousands more on ships off the coast—all without congressional consultation or authorization. As the character of these activities became public, some in Congress raised their voices.[21]

Although the issue was generally fought on narrow legal grounds, the larger concern involved the circumvention of Congress on foreign policy decisions of major importance. The administration was in effect using the maneuvers to put military pressure on the Sandinistas and to turn Honduras into a forward basing area for possible use against Nicaragua and perhaps El Salvador. In doing so, it was not only militarizing Honduras, but putting U.S. military personnel geographically close to such areas of high conflict as the Nicaraguan border. Had the administration presented this larger plan to Congress for funding in 1982, it would have been brought under great scrutiny given the concern over war powers. The presence of fifty-five advisers in El Salvador was frequently scrutinized and became an informal limit. When Congress tried to bring such activities under its

[19] See, for example, Kenneth E. Sharpe, "El Salvador Revisited," *World Policy Journal* 3 (Summer 1986): 473–494.

[20] H.R. Rep. No. 1086, 98th Cong., 2d sess. 40–41 (1984).

[21] Representative Ronald Dellums (D. Calif.) and Senator James Sasser (D. Tenn.), for example. See Philip L. Shepherd, "Honduras" in Morris J. Blachman, William M. LeoGrande and Kenneth Sharpe, *Confronting Revolution: Security Through Diplomacy in Central America* (New York: Pantheon Books, 1986), 133.

scrutiny in 1984 by requiring prior notification as to "the complete U.S. construction plan for the region," the administration supplied as little information as possible.[22] A January 1986 follow-up report by the General Accounting Office showed some compliance with congressional requirements but documented a series of new accounting procedures and mechanisms that allowed further circumvention.[23]

Nicaragua

U.S. policy making toward Nicaragua illustrates graphically how emerging patterns of congressional-executive relations are undermining the intent of the post-Vietnam formula. If one began the examination of congressional participation in Nicaragua policy in 1985 or 1986, it would seem that the administration had at least respected the important procedural commitments of the post-Vietnam formula. The White House came to Congress and asked for money to aid Nicaraguan exiles fighting to overthrow the Sandinista regime. After long public debate, in 1985 Congress approved $27 million in nonlethal military support and logistical supplies, and in 1986, $100 million (70 percent military). But the story began much earlier. Indeed, if the President had come to Congress in 1981 and asked for funds to *create* an exile army to pressure or overthrow the Sandinistas, it would have been very difficult to have secured congressional authorization. What happened in the Nicaraguan case was the creation of an antecedent state of things that made it difficult (although not impossible) for Congress to say no by 1985. The mechanisms by which the administration got the funding that created this situation demonstrate even more clearly than the Honduras and El Salvador cases how secrecy, distortion, and circumvention were used by the executive to avoid accountability, consultation, and debate.

On 23 November 1981 President Reagan signed National Security Decision Directive 17 and a secret finding that was submitted to the House and Senate Intelligence Committees informing them that $19.95 million in CIA funds would be used to support 500 contras who would infiltrate Nicaragua to interdict purported arms flows to Salvadoran rebels. By so informing these congressional committees, the administration was carefully responding to the letter of the law. These committees did not protest, because the interdiction rationale made sense to members concerned to contain a leftist revolution supported by the Nicaraguans.

While some in the administration may have initially supported the program simply to interdict arms, major actors such as the exiles the CIA was funding, CIA operatives in the field, and hardliners in the administration had a very different purpose—to overthrow the Sandinista regime. This view became even more prevalent as the operation grew in 1982 and 1983. The so-called hard and soft liners,

[22] Leach, et. al., *U.S. Policy in Central America*, 31–32.

[23] Comptroller General of the United States, Report B-213137, "DOD Use of Operations and Maintenance Appropriations in Honduras," submitted to Representative Bill Alexander, 30 January 1986.

mostly in the State Department, did not approve of attempts to overthrow the Nicaraguan government, but saw building up the contras as a way of creating a credible threat with which to pressure the Sandinistas to bargain over security issues and ultimately over the internal character of their regime. But the broad purposes of Nicaragua policy were not presented to the congressional committees for scrutiny and debate. It was only in the following years, as congressional opposition built, that the administration quietly introduced the pressure logic. The President's public position until the 1985 congressional debates was that "we are not doing anything to overthrow the government of Nicaragua."[24]

An effort to misinform or deceive Congress was always an important element of administration policy. But secret wars are never secret from the people being warred on and are not long secret from Congress and the American public. As early as 4 December 1981, articles began to appear in the American press about the covert U.S. action. They were soon followed by information from Florida about training camps for the contras and then by reports from the field about contra activities. As the press revealed the scope and character of contra activities, the House Intelligence Committee sought to limit American aid to its original purpose. In December 1982, Representative Edward Boland (D. Mass.), chairman of the committee, introduced language (the Boland Amendment) into the Continuing Resolution for fiscal year 1983 prohibiting the use of funds "for the purpose of overthrowing the government of Nicaragua."[25]

The administration's response was to *expand* contra operations to include sabotage raids on such targets as oil supplies and port facilities. While acknowledging that the aim of the contras might be to overthrow the Nicaraguan government, the administration insisted that it was within the law because *its* purpose in giving the aid was arms interdiction, not overthrow.[26] The Democratic leadership in the House grew angry, and in 1983 the House Intelligence Committee voted to cut off all funds.

The Republican-controlled Senate Intelligence Committee refused to go along with a total cutoff, and a cap of $24 million was put on contra aid for fiscal year 1984. But the administration circumvented congressional spending limits: certain expenses like the mining of Nicaragua's harbors were charged to other accounts; an airfield for the contras was built in Aguacate, Honduras, as a part of a Defense Department exercise and then made available to the contras as a logistics and transportation center; and the Defense Department donated aircraft to transport sup-

[24] Doyle McManus and Robert Toth, "The Contras: How U.S. Got Entangled," *Los Angeles Times*, 4 March 1985.

[25] The language he introduced was the same as the language his Intelligence Committee had already introduced in its confidential statements to the administration shortly before the congressional debates. Boland publicly introduced his amendment to block other legislation that would have cut funds off completely. It was meant to warn the administration that its expansion of the program would not be tolerated; the committee was not yet ready to support the cutoff of all funds.

[26] Leach, et. al., *U.S. Policy in Central America*, 4.

plies to contra bases and transferred ships, planes, and guns to the CIA at little or no charge.[27]

Some members of the House and Senate Intelligence Committees were particularly disturbed in 1984 when they discovered that the administration had violated the reporting requirements of the 1980 Intelligence Oversight Act by failing to inform the committees of the decision to mine Nicaraguan harbors. In September 1984, Congress learned of a CIA manual entitled "Psychological Operations in Guerrilla Warfare." Its explicit instructions for "neutralizing" Sandinista officials and "creating martyrs" for the contra cause underlined reports from the press and human rights organization about contra terror. In October 1984, the House Intelligence Committee forced the Senate committee, in conference, to accept the Boland Amendment, now carefully worded to avoid administration circumvention:

> During the fiscal year 1985, no funds available to the Central Intelligence Agency, the Department of Defense, or any other agency or entity of the United States involved in intelligence activities may be obligated or expended for the purpose or which would have the effect of supporting, directly or indirectly, military or paramilitary operations in Nicaragua by any nation, group, organization, movement or individual.[28]

It was agreed that aid could only be restored by a majority vote in both houses after February 1985.

Again the administration circumvented the law. The National Security Council helped organize and advise a *private* aid network to fund the contras. According to some administration officials, the plan was approved both by National Security Adviser Robert C. McFarlane and the President. Marine Lt. Col. Oliver North, a member of the National Security Council staff, was put in charge. North helped reorganize and coordinate operations of the two main rebel groups, gave tactical advice, helped the contras raise millions in private and secret public funds, and arranged for supplies and contributions to reach the contras.

While there was consternation among contra aid critics and Congress threatened to hold hearings, nothing was done to sanction North and little could be done to undo his work. The White House, in the words of Representative Michael Barnes (D. Md.), stonewalled, refusing, for example, to release requested documents on its management of the private network and circumvention of the Boland Amendment. It was not until the Iran-contra affair broke in late 1986 that Congress and the press began to uncover the full details of the National Security

[27] See, for example, ibid., 5-6. In September 1984, for example, the Defense Department was discovered transferring three Cessna OA2 noncombat aircraft to a top secret Joint Chiefs of Staff operation code named "Elephant Herd." The planes were officially declared "excess" and dropped from the air force's inventory roster. Having officially disappeared, they were then flown to the New York State National Guard, and next to a CIA contractor who fitted the aircraft with rocket pods for combat. They were then delivered, via intermediaries, to the contras. Blaine Harden and Joe Pichirallo, "CIA Said to Supply Planes to Nicaraguan Rebels," *Washington Post*, 15 September 1984.

[28] Jonathan Fuerbringer, "U.S. Aide's Ties to Contras Challenged," *New York Times*, 5 September 1985.

Council's involvement in circumventing Congress. It became clear that millions of dollars in profits made on secret arms sales to Iran were diverted to supply the contras; that the NSC had been involved in secretly raising millions for the contras from foreign governments (Saudi Arabia, Brunei); and that National Security Adviser Admiral John Poindexter and a top official at the State Department (Elliot Abrams, assistant secretary of state for Latin America) and the CIA (including Director William Casey) were also involved. It was further revealed that the contra operation was the centerpiece of an even larger covert effort labelled "Project Democracy" authorized by President Reagan in the January 1983 National Security Decision Directive No.77; and that North and private individuals had set up "the enterprise," an extra-government agency (described by North as an "off-the-shelf, self-sustaining, stand-alone entity") to finance and carry out intelligence operations all over the world outside normal government control.[29]

Between 1984 and 1986, as the NSC was circumventing the congressional ban, the CIA was also secretly giving the Nicaraguan rebels aid. More than $1.5 million went for "political" operations to finance "security," a radio station, and to seek political and financial support in Europe and Venezuela. The CIA also helped carry out the elaborate contra supply operation run by the NSC (dramatically revealed after a plane was shot down in October 1986 and American mercenary Eugene Hasenfus was captured by the Nicaraguans and put on trial) and actively tried to reorganize and strengthen contra activities in Costa Rica.

Although full details did not emerge until late 1986 and early 1987, by early 1985 there was enough information for Congress to demand that future funding of the "covert" war be openly debated and legislated through normal channels. This debate was different from the one on El Salvador, because Congress viewed rollback much more critically than containment. U.S. involvement in overthrowing a foreign government raised both moral issues and fears of dragging U.S. troops into a quagmire.

When forced to fight openly for aid, the administration's strategy was to insist that there was no alternative to the contras—and that even the negotiations insisted upon by moderates needed the force of the contras to back them up. There were two elements to this strategy. One was a somewhat successful administration effort to impose its definition of reality on the situation. The internal character of the regime in Nicaragua was presented as so abhorrent and the security threat as so great that any opponent of Reagan administration efforts could be delegitimized as soft on both security and communism. The administration did not hesitate to lie and distort reality in order to create the image it wanted.[30] As

[29] John Tower, Edmund Muskie, and Brent Scowcroft, *The Tower Commission Report* (New York: Bantam Books and Time Books, 1987), appendix C, 450–479; Joel Brinkley, "Iran Sales Linked to Wide Program of Covert Policies," *New York Times*, 15 February 1987; Fox Butterfield, "North Says Casey Proposed Using Arms Profit for Fund Kept Secret from President," *New York Times*, 11 July 1987; Elizabeth Drew, "Letter from Washington," *New Yorker*, 31 August 1987, 71–89.

[30] See, for example, Americas Watch, *Human Rights in Nicaragua, Reagan, Rhetoric and Reality* (New York: Americas Watch, July 1985); Joel Brinkley, "Nicaraguan Army: 'War Machine' or De-

ideology and distorted information replaced fact, rational debate about the means and ends of U.S. policy toward Nicaragua became increasingly difficult. The more the Democrats accepted the purpose of policy as getting the Sandinista regime out of power (as opposed to negotiating security issues, for example), the more difficult it became to offer an alternative other than the contras.

The second element of administration strategy was systematically to scuttle all efforts at negotiated settlements—the efforts of the Contadora countries (Mexico, Venezuela, Colombia, and Panama) for example—that recognized the legitimacy of the Nicaraguan government.[31] By destroying all other alternatives, the contras were made to seem the only alternative.

Important to both elements of this whole strategy, however, was the fact that the contras already existed: this *fait accompli*, brought about covertly, was what gave the administration its leverage in the important votes in 1985 and 1986.

When contra aid came before Congress in April 1985, the House narrowly defeated the administration request. But on 12 June, seventy-three Democrats abandoned the House leadership and joined 175 Republicans in supporting a compromise package that banned lethal military aid and restricted CIA involvement in disbursing the aid. A number of the Democrats were conservative southerners who felt that voting against the aid would make them vulnerable to charges that they were "soft on communism." Alluding to this issue, majority leader Jim Wright (D. Tex.), who himself opposed the aid, said that "to some degree" the country was going through an era reminiscent of McCarthyism. "Nobody wants to be portrayed as friendly toward Communism."[32]

Many moderate Democrats and Republicans reversed their votes because they felt ill at ease at turning down the President's request in April without providing an alternative. "A good many of our guys," said Wright "don't believe in waging war to overthrow the Government of Nicaragua, but they feel some responsibility to those doing the fighting."[33] This was how the administration had defined the issue, and it was reinforced shortly after the April vote when Nicaraguan President Daniel Ortega flew to Moscow to ask for more aid. Representative Steward B. McKinney (R. Conn.), who reversed his vote, explained, "There are those of us here who have to recognize the fact that the contra movement against an oppressive dictatorial society does exist. We cannot walk away from it."[34] Others believed that the contras could provide leverage for a negotiated political settlement, which the President claimed he sought. Representative Bill Richardson (D. N.M.),

---

fender of a Besieged Nation?" *New York Times*, 30 March 1985; and Central America Crisis Monitoring Team, *In Contempt of Congress*, 11–29; and Blachman and Sharpe, "De-democratising Foreign Policy."

[31] See William M. LeoGrande, "Rollback or Containment?" *International Security* 2 (Fall 1986): 89-120.

[32] Steven V. Roberts, "House Reverses Earlier Ban on Aid to Nicaragua Rebels; Passes $27 Million Package," *New York Times*, 13 June 1985.

[33] Steven V. Roberts, "House Gets Compromise on Rebel Aid," *New York Times*, 9 May 1985.

[34] Steven V. Roberts, "A Consensus on Rebel Aid," *New York Times*, 14 June 1985.

who switched his vote, said, "I think the President of the United States for the first time is saying that he is for negotiations and meaning it."[35]

By the time the crucial vote for $100 million in contra aid came up in the House in March 1986 (it was defeated 222–210) and in June (it passed 221–209) the hook of commitment had already been sunk. While the majority of Democrats (about 183) opposed any aid, the thirty or so crucial swing votes accepted administration arguments that the contras could not be abandoned and that they were a useful tool for pressing negotiations.

In both June 1985 and June 1986, the arguments that swayed middle-of-the-roaders would not have made sense if a huge contra army had not already been created and if other alternatives had not been undermined or defined out of existence. Administration policies had created the very "antecedent state of things" that the post-Vietnam formula had sought to avoid by insisting that important foreign policy decisions be shared from the beginning by Congress and the president. This situation had been created by the kind of circumvention, secrecy, and deception the post-Vietnam formula had sought to check.

The efforts to win continued funding in late 1987 were still undecided as this article goes to press. The Iran-contra scandal seriously weakened the administration's credibility and angered Congress at the way in which lying, distortion and law breaking had been used to circumvent congressional authority. The peace plan proposed by President Oscar Arias of Costa Rica was signed by the five central American countries in August of 1987 (despite administration opposition) thus creating, at least temporarily, an alternative. The administration's arguments were the same as they had always been—and a crucial element was still the already existing state of things, but one to which Congress had now committed itself. "The Congress of the United States has made a moral commitment to these men," President Reagan argued in a speech to the Organization of American States. "It cannot just walk away."[36]

The Post-Vietnam-Watergate Formula Reconsidered

It took the shock of the Iran-contra scandal—the administration's trading of arms for hostages and the diversion of the profits to fund the contras—to finally move Congress into action against years of executive abuse of authority. Why did the post-Vietnam legislation itself fail to reestablish congressional balance and check such abuses? The implicit answer given by the congressional committees investigating the scandal was that the problem must have been either bad people or bad laws. Is "this unseemly chapter in our history" the result of "well-intentioned, patriotic zealots" asked Senator Daniel K. Inouye (D. Hawaii, chairman of the Senate committee), or are we here today because of the inadequacy of our laws and our Constitution?"[37]

[35] Ibid.

[36] "Reagan on Contras: 'Strive and Struggle,'" *New York Times*, 8 October 1987.

[37] "Closing Remarks by Leaders of Panels: A Litany of Mistakes," *New York Times*, 4 August 1987.

There is no question that individual character contributed to the violations and abuses. And better laws (tightening the War Powers Act, tougher regulations for CIA oversight, legally limiting the NSC staff to an advisory role) could help tame such individual abuses. But the problem is not simply one of laws. Arthur Schlesinger noted in 1973 that the president, like Gulliver, could break loose of even a thousand small legal strings. "The effective means of controlling the Presidency lay less in law than in politics. For the American President rules by influence; and the withdrawal of consent, by Congress, by the press, by public opinion, could bring any President down.[38]

This conclusion is apt today. When Congress, the press, and the public were willing to exercise political power, the post-Vietnam formula often worked. It helped Congress get access to information needed to participate in the making of foreign policy, and it ultimately helped cut off the private funding network in the aftermath of the Iran-contra revelations. But more often than not, Congress was unwilling to exercise its potential power. It did not demand to participate in ways that would have limited the president's ability to create an antecedent state of things or to break and circumvent the law.

Mistrust of executive information led members of Congress to use existing institutional mechanisms of oversight (requests for GAO reports on contra corruption, committee hearings on misuses of military maneuver and construction funds, etc.) and to create new mechanisms to generate and crosscheck information (the certification procedures on El Salvador). A number of reporters did investigative reports that in turn were used by members of Congress. Further, the requirement that the intelligence committees be informed of covert operations proved very important. Although information on the covert war was publicly available through the press almost immediately after it began, these committees provided an institutional locus for information gathering and accountability. Their recognition that the scope was expanding beyond arms interdiction, and later that serious actions had *not* been reported as the law demanded, led first to committee restrictions on aid, then to support of restrictive legislation on the floor of the House, and finally to a cutoff of funds.

But it is important to note that the public outcry and initial opposition in Congress to the covert war were stimulated by press coverage. The intelligence committees did not initially take leadership: they could have objected to the covert aid, warned the President that they would bring their objections to the floor for debate, and then, if the President still insisted, actively led a floor fight. Instead, these committees allowed themselves to be used by the President to create an antecedent state of things that then limited later debate on the contra war and on other major war-making operations carried out in Afghanistan, Cambodia, and Angola.

What of the post-Vietnam commitment to *restore constitutional checks and balances* in foreign policy? Congress only sometimes insisted on full consultation

[38] Schlesinger, *The Imperial Presidency*, 409–410.

and participation and rarely reacted forcefully to presidential efforts to break or evade the law. Congressional efforts to make the formula work were important in forcing a reluctant President to allow congressional participation in the making of policy toward El Salvador from 1981 to 1984. Congress ruled out the sending of U.S. troops to quell a leftist revolution. And until the Duarte election, Congress used the power of the purse to restrict funding. Congress, however, was unwilling to confront forcefully the actions of the executive that broke the letter of the law, violated its spirit, or circumvented the constitutional prerogatives of Congress. Congress did not blow the whistle on the certification charades or reprogramming circumventions in El Salvador. What happened in Honduras was worse, exactly what the post-Vietnam formula was designed to prevent: the creation of conditions, an antecedent state of things, which committed the United States to a foreign policy without the participation of Congress. But even when Congress discovered that the circumventions and legal violations were creating a *fait accompli*, it did little more than slap the hand of the executive, warn that such actions must not be done again, and put some restrictions on the use of funds. It did not authorize dismantling the bases, nor did it seriously interfere with the use of maneuvers to build infrastructure in Honduras or permanently station U.S. troops there.

The greatest violation of the spirit of the War Powers Act was in the Nicaraguan case. Not only did the contra effort pose an immediate danger of creating an antecedent state of things that could draw in U.S. troops, it also established a dangerous precedent for the conduct of foreign policy. Using covert action as a central instrument of American foreign policy, where the only congressional checks were intelligence committees whose oversight function was never meant to cover generalized war, meant that crucial foreign policies were initiated and conducted in a highly secret, unaccountable way. Misrepresenting the size and mission of the contras (arms interdiction) and failing to meet reporting requirements (the mining, the terror manual) made things worse. When Congress cut off funds, the White House circumvented Congress's power of the purse by helping to organize a private funding network and managing it for over two years.

An important foreign policy commitment was established with minimum scrutiny and public debate. Congress by and large acquiesced and failed to act, even when information was brought to it that private funding was circumventing its decisions and that high members of the National Security Council were helping to coordinate this effort. The few members who protested were unable to get enough support to investigate publicly, let alone stop such executive actions. The President, acting as commander in chief, took incremental actions that slowly created an antecedent state of things. Congress lacked the political will to block the small steps, even though legally it could have done much more. Gradually, commitment by accretion made it more difficult for Congress to share control of policy making.

Conclusion

The failure of the post-Vietnam formula to check executive abuse of authority was not simply due to the character of the legislation. Senator Fulbright's 1972 observation is just as true today: "It is not a lack of power which has prevented the Congress from ending the war in Indochina, but a lack of will."[39] We need to explain why Congress has not been more vociferous and forceful in using the institutional mechanisms and authority it has to prevent executive disregard for the commitments of the post-Vietnam formula. There are a number of explanations given in the general literature on Congress and foreign policy: the fragmentation of the foreign policy process within Congress, the president's ability to shape and present information, and the difficulty of rallying congressional opposition to small encroachments of its authority.

There is some truth in all of these explanations, but there is also a more fundamental problem. On the one hand, Congress faces a hard-to-control national security apparatus dedicated to maintaining U.S. hegemony and largely unchallenged by the post-Vietnam reforms. The powerful intelligence and security agencies created after World War II embodied norms of secrecy, speed, unity, and efficiency that were antithetical to constitutional democracy. On the other hand, there is no "anti-imperial" political coalition strong enough to force Congress to check the executive and to enforce legislation against the security bureaucracy.

A coalition to reform substantively the security apparatus must challenge the foreign policy that justifies the existence of the apparatus itself. Arthur Schlesinger has argued:

> The Imperial Presidency was essentially the creation of foreign policy. A combination of doctrines and emotions—belief in permanent and universal crisis, fear of communism, faith in the duty and the right of the United States to intervene swiftly in every part of the world—had brought about the unprecedented centralization of decisions over war and peace in the Presidency.[40]

While the post-Vietnam commitment did include a reluctance to commit troops and some tolerance for leftist regimes, moderates and conservatives still shared the same underlying strategic vision—revolutionary regimes of the left were antithetical to U.S. global interests. The U.S. still had the right and responsibility to maintain its hegemony and to minimize the chances of leftist outbreaks and takeovers. The difference between moderates and conservatives was over means, not ends. Moderates saw local repression and poverty as the causes of revolution and argued for human rights and economic development—a position similar to the old Alliance for Progress. Conservatives saw Soviet-backed intervention and subversion as the causes of revolution. They argued for primarily military responses to Third World revolutions. And no one argued for substantial change in the national security apparatus that planned and administered so much of foreign policy.[41]

[39] Senator J. William Fulbright, *The Crippled Giant, American Foreign Policy and its Domestic Consequences*, (New York: Vintage Books, 1972), 194.

[40] Schlesinger, *The Imperial Presidency*, 208.

[41] For a detailed discussion see Blachman, et al., *Confronting Revolution*, chaps. 12 and 13.

When the Reagan administration came into office it inherited the existing security bureaucracy and brought back the conservative version of the strategic vision. It emphasized not simply the containment but rollback of leftist governments ("The Reagan Doctrine"). In this context, the New Right and the Reagan administration could draw on a continued fear of communism and fears of declining U.S. power and hegemony once again to define debate in terms of cold-war assumptions. Such assumptions made it difficult for many of the middle-of-the-road swing voters in Congress to resist the President's persistent demands for a proxy army strategy against Nicaragua. Especially after he created an antecedent state of things, they found themselves trapped between their opposition to communism and their opposition to U.S. troop commitments, between "no more Cubas" and "no more Vietnams." Accepting the end of undermining the Sandinistas and seeing no alternative means except the contras, they were open to persuasion.

If cold-war assumptions make it difficult to challenge the executive on specific issues, they make it extremely hard even to put the restructuring of the national security bureaucracy on the political agenda, let alone to challenge its organization and vision against a well-organized and entrenched right. As long as moderates and conservatives both share the assumption that the United States has the right and responsibility to keep (or get) leftist revolutionary regimes out of power, they are trapped into supporting a chronic cold war and the means necessary to carry it out – a largely unaccountable and uncontrollable imperial president and the security apparatus he manages. As long as cold-war assumptions guide policy, Schlesinger argued, there will be a demand "for concentration of authority, secrecy, speed and discretion in the Presidency."[42] And "in a country chronically at war, as America has been for the last three decades" wrote Senator J. William Fulbright in 1972, "even the most energetic and ingenious means of reasserting Congressional prerogative will of themselves prove insufficient to the maintenance of constitutional government.[43]*

[42] Schlesinger, *The Imperial Presidency*, 298.

[43] Fulbright, *The Crippled Giant*, 241.

* This paper benefited from the research assistance of Eva Bertram and the critical comments of Charles Beitz, Douglas Bennett, Morris Blachman, Jeff Frieden, Sherle Schwenninger, and Richard Valelly. This article is adapted from a piece that will appear in Nora Hamilton, ed., *Crisis in Central America: Regional Dynamics and U.S. Policy* (Boulder, Colo.: Westview Press, forthcoming).

RHETORIC, FAILURE, AND THE PRESIDENCY: THE CASE OF VIETNAM

KENNETH S. ZAGACKI

Scholars have largely dismissed the postwar Vietnam rhetoric of American presidents. Rhetorical analysis of this discourse, however, reveals recurrent failure topoi used by Nixon, Ford, and Carter to console and compensate the nation after Vietnam. This study explores the limitations of these topoi in postwar situations. It argues that even as they purge the nation of wartime failure and reassert foundational myths and ideology, these topoi restrict historical judgments about the wartime experience and perhaps even perpetuate climates that make future confrontations likely. This essay concludes by locating the constraints upon presidential discoursing about failure within the culture and within the institution of the Presidency itself.

In the years since the Vietnam War, American presidents have been inclined to solidify an official view of our struggle in Southeast Asia. Ronald Reagan unabashedly recalled Vietnam as a war in which America was not "defeated" but its soldiers were "denied permission to win." In his speeches about the Iraqi conflict, President Bush struck a vainglorious profile when referring to Vietnam. He assured the American people their soldiers would triumph against Iraq; these combatants would not be asked to fight as Vietnam veterans were, with "their hands tied behind their backs." His rhetoric was a shrewd attempt to purge the nation of its bitter Vietnam memories and reaffirm America's technological and moral prowess. As Bush proclaimed after American forces had crushed Iraqi armies: "The specter of Vietnam has been buried forever in the desert sands of the Arabian Peninsula."[1] Comments like these should give us pause. We cannot dismiss the Vietnam War as we strive to understand the complex relationship between war and the Presidency, and the ways in which our national leaders cope with failure events like Vietnam.

Rhetorical critics have offered strong indictments of presidential rhetoric about the Vietnam war. Critics assailed Lyndon Johnson and Richard Nixon for what was taken to be the underhanded attempts by these Presidents to justify America's presence in Vietnam.[2] In the recent book, *Cultural Legacies of Vietnam*, Adi Wimmer complained that "No Senator or Congressman, and certainly no President or general, has ever publicly expressed sorrow and sympathy with the victims of America's awesome power in Vietnam."[3] Most of the other contributors to this volume also largely dismiss presidential rhetoric in favor of exploring what they see as the more meaningful discourses located in popular culture.[4] They dismiss presidential rhetoric not because it is inconsequential but because it is fundamentally deceptive and incapable of enlightening public opinion.

In this essay, I wish to quarrel not with the conclusions of these commentators, but with their assessment of the significance of presidential rhetoric. I believe it extremely important that we understand not just what American presidents said about Vietnam, but also *how* and *why* they spoke as they did. We must understand inventional resources and possibilities available for presidential speech during moments of failure. As Kathleen Hall Jamieson and Roderick Hart remind us, the public still looks to its presidents at times of crisis for consolation and compensa-

Kenneth S. Zagacki (Ph.D., University of Texas, 1985) is assistant professor in the Department of Speech Communication, Lousiana State University, Baton Rogue, LA. *The author wishes to thank Richard Cherwitz, Andrew King, and Kenneth Mihalik for their helpful comments on this manuscript.*

COMMUNICATION STUDIES, Volume 43, Spring 1992

tion.[5] Moreover, the Presidency continues to be a source of profound power for shaping public perceptions about American history and the direction of foreign and domestic affairs. To overlook how and why presidents talk during crises or the constraints imposed by the nature of the office itself—even if their rhetoric appears at first hopelessly formulaic—is to resubmit ourselves unquestionably to the influence of presidential discourse. As Karyln Kohrs Campbell and Jamieson point out, we require a deeper understanding of the "symbolic institutional needs" of the Presidency, for these needs and the ways in which presidents act upon them "are at least as powerful as the force of events."[6]

The decline and defeat of America in Vietnam presented Americans, in general, and Presidents Richard Nixon and Gerald Ford, in particular, with their most devastating example of national failure. As such, Vietnam created a complex rhetorical situation requiring a response that would have tremendous consequences for the Presidency and for the ways in which we continued to conceive of ourselves as a nation. My specific contention in this essay is that the post-Vietnam discourse of Presidents Nixon and Ford collectively failed to properly console and compensate the American public about the country's defeat in Vietnam. I maintain that this failure occurred because both presidents steadfastly employed traditional topoi associated with a genre of discourse called the "rhetoric of failure." The use of these topoi, constrained as they were institutionally and ideologically, resulted in the mis-representation of the Vietnam War experience. This mis-representation essentially prevented American audiences from achieving what Paul Fussell calls "public maturity" over the war; that is, the public's complete understanding of the historical and moral meaning of the struggle.[7]

THE RHETORIC OF FAILURE

One of the most important exigencies facing postwar rhetors is the lingering perception that nations involved in conflict have failed either in war itself, or in allowing the conflict to begin and escalate in the first place. These moments constitute serious threats to national self-confidence and identity. Such perceived or sensed failure creates what David Payne calls "rhetorical situations that require the purposes of consolation and compensation, and . . . these purposes are executed by drawing lines of argument, assertion and response from a set of basic topoi that constantly recur in therapeutic rhetoric."[8] Payne points out that communication about failure is a type of persuasion that functions to explain the unsuccessful experience and alleviate dissonance resulting from it. This rhetoric works "to console and/or to open the way to compensation" (42). For Payne, consolation refers to discourse that highlights "social value over personal loss, conditions and causes of the past over present failing, and spiritual meanings or orientations over material losses" (45). In consolation, a person is disassociated from the loss, since the emphasis is placed on other individuals, past successes, and spiritual gains or replacements for the material loss. "Consolation," Payne says, "looks back at the loss and proposes adaptations to that past" (45). Compensatory rhetoric, on the other hand, "stresses self-directed involvements or motives, future consequences or opportunities, and material values and orientations" (45). Compensation highlights a person's actions, possibilities for change or repair in the future, and material gain. Compensatory rhetoric "looks forward to future ways of balancing or eliminating or overcoming the loss" (45).

Payne argues that the rhetoric of failure contains several distinct topoi which indicate the traditional ways of performing consolation and compensation. These topoi indicate how rhetors cope with failure both culturally and symbolically; they show how we are to define our failures so that cooperative resolutions through discourse are possible. Failure topoi clarify means of comprehending failures, provide ways of talking about our understandings, and illustrate the "analytic headings that are commonly available to people who must deal with failure" (53).

According to Payne, the primary topoi of the rhetoric of failure include: *self-society*, *past-future*, and *spiritual-material*. To this I would add the topos of *actuality-potentiality*. Thus, we might find consolation from appeals that place blame for failure on social causes, on past conditions, or illustrate the future (or potential) spiritual gain to be derived from material loss. Likewise, compensation can be achieved by recognizing the immense actual or potential material strength possessed by an agent, even in the aftermath of failure. Other topical combinations are of course possible. As Payne suggests, each term in these pairs stands in a dialectical relationship to the other. Together, these topoi demonstrate the fundamental logic of consolation and compensation. As Payne argues, "Each side of each topos . . . can be either positively or negatively valued, and the sides of each pair can be set rhetorically in direct opposition to one another" (55). The value of one side or another depends upon the specific content an audience or rhetor associates with it; equally important is how that content is understood in relation to persons, institutions, and values. Payne adds that the topoi of failure are powerful resources for rhetorical invention. These topoi inform both the "logical and stylistic formulas that can be used to persuade about any failure" (56).

FAILURE AND THE RHETORICAL END TO VIETNAM

Nixon and the Rhetoric of "Peace with Honor"

The Vietnam War had two endings: the first under Richard Nixon after the 1973 Paris Peace accords; the second under Gerald Ford following the fall of Saigon in 1975. Nixon described his desire for an "honorable" cessation to hostilities early in his administration. He declared in his first inaugural that "We all hope . . . there's a chance that current negotiations may bring an honorable end" to war in Vietnam.[9] Essentially, Nixon promised to extricate America from Southeast Asia by gradually withdrawing troops, handing the fighting over to the South Vietnamese, and working toward a settlement that would preserve the sovereignty of the South without dramatic and costly incursions into the North. He defined this process as "peace with honor." By January 1973, after years of difficult negotiations, a bloody stalemate on the battlefield, and bitter divisions at home, a peace agreement was finally hammered out. The impetus for the treaty is well described by historian Stanley Karnow, whose characterization of Secretary of State Henry Kissinger's anguish over concluding the conflict aptly describes the rhetorical exigencies eventually to face Nixon:

> The specter of an ignominious finale in Vietnam haunted Kissinger. A humiliating collapse would shatter America's global credibility . . . [and would] 'leave deep scars on our society, fueling impulses for recrimination.' Constantly on his mind was the tragedy of the Weimar Republic . . . the democracy that had eventually been ripped asunder by the tensions that divided Germany after its defeat in World War I.[10]

What Kissinger's ruminations failed to appreciate, of course, was the extent to which the country had already been divided over Vietnam, and a growing sentiment, particularly among Vietnam veterans, that America had engaged in what veteran John Kerry and many others were calling a disastrous and "immoral" war.[11]

Nixon's motivations are debatable. Did he really see the treaty as a lasting and "honorable" settlement, or did he believe, at that time, that the United States had 'failed' in Vietnam? Some commentators have suggested that Nixon viewed the Paris Accords as a ceasefire that would yield an American "victory" as long as the North Vietnamese adhered to it, and the United States remained willing to enforce the agreement. Whatever his intent, Nixon was presumably aware of the fact that once the United States left Vietnam, the nation would suffer a tremendous after shock. Thus, it seems clear that he not only hoped his settlement would shift the conclusion of the war in America's favor, but would also reiterate his "peace with honor" imperative. Indeed, for Nixon, "peace with honor" became a shibboleth for acknowledging the struggles of American armed forces in Vietnam, as well as mitigating the growing wounds and divisions at home.

Nixon's first substantial effort toward these 'postwar' rhetorical goals occurred in his January, 1973 speech before the nation announcing the Paris Accords.[12] In this address, Nixon clearly called upon the *spiritual-material* topos. He found consolation and compensation in the assertion that, despite a harsh war, the nation had nevertheless remained committed to its democratic ideals. It had achieved a just settlement, bringing material stability (i.e., democratic government, lessened hostilities, the development of a large South Vietnamese army) to South Vietnam. He explained: "Throughout the years of negotiations, we have insisted on peace with honor . . . In the settlement that has now been agreed to, all the conditions that I laid down then have been met" (18–19). In short, Nixon attempted to console the American public by asserting that despite intense sacrifice and growing divisiveness at home, the United States can still be seem as firm and uncompromising on its ideals of freedom and self-government.

His denial of imperial ambitions on the part of Americans offered further consolation. Such denials overcame the deflating charge that the nation had expended great effort solely to press its own selfish designs. Nixon argued that the United States had not imposed its will upon the South Vietnamese. On the contrary, he noted that the U.S. government had consulted closely with representatives of the Republic of Vietnam and that "this settlement . . . has the full support of President Thieu and [his] Government" (19). Again, we are urged to take heart in Nixon's comments because they reduce any sense of failure to achieve our goals in Vietnam or any lingering doubt as to the moral rectitude of the nation. Nixon achieves this reduction by his inspiring portrayal of the United States as non-exploitive and non-imperialistic defenders of South Vietnamese sovereignty.

Nixon added another reassuring gesture—possibly to assuage skeptical audiences who believed that further American military participation in Vietnam was imminent—by promising to "aid South Vietnam within the terms of the agreement, and [supporting] efforts by the people of South Vietnam to settle their problems peacefully among themselves" (19). He offered the consoling opinion that future American sacrifices in Vietnam would involve mostly economic aid. This aid, when combined with the already extraordinary personal and spiritual sacrifices of the American people, would bolster the ability of the Vietnamese to resolve "peacefully" their differences "among themselves." Taken together, these statements suggest that Nixon saw his treaty as initiating material changes on the battlefield and in no way compromising, but in fact advancing, American principles. Thus, his treaty appeared worthy of the wearisome struggle required to obtain it.

Nixon hinted at further consolation and compensation by actually discussing direct military aid. He declared "that ending the war is only the first step toward building the peace. All parties must now see to it that this is a peace that . . . heals [and an] agreement [that] must be scrupulously adhered to" (19). These comments invoke the *past-future* topos to remind listeners of the long, arduous path to honorable peace; they indicate that the losses of war can be compensated by the "healing" that occurs after. Still, Nixon's inclusion of the term "scrupulously" raised the ominous and hardly reassuring possibility that more immolation might be necessary.

Other Nixon comments revealed an even more menacing tone. In a March 15 news conference, he responded to questions about alleged North Vietnamese infiltrations by rekindling memories of previous bombing sorties: "We have informed the North Vietnamese of our concern about this infiltration and of what we believe it to be, a violation of the cease-fire and the peace-settlement . . . based on my actions over the past 4 years . . . the North Vietnamese should not lightly disregard such expressions of concern when they are made with regard to a violation. That is all I will say about it" (205–206).[13]

In all of these instances, Nixon resorted to a rather imperious logic in attempting to produce a measure of consolation and compensation. By drawing from the *actuality-potentiality* topos, he demonstrated how a carefully worded warning might itself promote healing and self-respect after war. In essence, he offered the caveat that, despite a hard-fought conflict, the nation still possessed the actual military might reminiscent of "the actions over the past 4 years." Doubtless, Nixon used this indirect expression to his ordering of bombing sorties over Hanoi to compensate hawkish audiences worried that the war had eroded American power and the nation's determination to exert it. At the same time, Nixon remained circumspect about the application of this force. Consequently, the United States was made to appear exceptionally altruistic (a conciliatory touch for the doves) because it chose to negotiate treaties and issue admonitions rather than unleash a potentially furious assault. As consolation, then, this warning amounted to a moral proclamation that "even when our ire has been provoked we ask questions first and shoot second, because we are a noble and peace-loving people."

Nixon also utilized various failure topoi to console and compensate veterans and their families. In the Paris settlement announcement, he asked audiences to recognize the extremely difficult plight of Vietnam combatants, to "be proud of the 2 1/2 million young Americans" who, despite being involved in "one of the most selfless enterprises in the history of nations," served with "honor and distinction" (20). These are the warriors "who sacrificed, who gave their lives so that the people of South Vietnam might live in freedom and so that the world might live in peace" (20). Nixon utilized both the *spiritual-material* and *self-society* topoi in these statements. For him, consolation and compensation are found in the fact that individuals at home and those "selfless" soldiers abroad engaged in supreme material and spiritual sacrifice. They sacrificed so that a collective group (i.e., a besieged, democratic community abroad, as well as the threatened nation at home) could be saved and its sacred, democratic values preserved.

This theme of immolation and its consoling/compensatory virtue is replayed in other addresses to veterans and their families. In a March 23 speech about Veterans' Affairs, Nixon showed how the past sacrifices of Vietnam veterans created future peace: "Thanks to the sacrifices of our returning veterans . . . the chances for lasting peace in the world are greater today than ever before" (223).[14] Equally important for Nixon is the fact that the actions of veterans in Vietnam reflected the material power of the United States and its overall commitment to defending democracy abroad. As such, his comments are consoling because they reaffirm this spiritual commitment. They are compensatory insofar as they re-establish America's strategic, global position and the material presence of the nation's military elsewhere. As Nixon proudly asserted, because of our sacrifices and our show of resolve in Vietnam, "America's . . . strength is respected, all around the world" (223).

Payne notes that the arguments derived from failure topoi enable rhetors "to position [themselves] and situated audience in relation to the failure" (53). Nixon's comments concerning the homefront and the Vietnam war work precisely this way, distinguishing his supporters from his detractors. "Now that we have achieved an honorable agreement," he declared in his Paris treaty announcement, "let us be proud that America did not settle for a peace that would have betrayed our allies, that would have abandoned our prisoners of war, or that would have ended the war for us but would have continued the war for the 50 million people of Indochina" (20). These remarks drew their influence from the *past-future* and *spiritual-material* topoi. Consolation is derived from the realization that the past material sacrifices and the reigning spirit of Americans at home protected democratic principles overseas. Compensation is found in the recognition that these sacrifices allow for future material stability in Vietnam.

These comments and others from Nixon's treaty address also reveal a curious use of the *self-society* topos to distinguish friend from foe: "When others called on us to settle on any terms, you had the courage to stand for the right kind of peace so that those who died and those who suffered would not have died and suffered in vain, and so that . . . the next generation would know peace" (20). Thus, Nixon stationed himself and his supporters—the ubiquitous "you"—as individuals who carefully weighed the moral implications of the war and therefore contributed significantly to the "honorable agreement." However, Nixon's critics, the "others," were made to appear like an irresponsible and politically naive group that lacked spiritual resolve. This group sought only expedient solutions or peace "on any terms," that would have "betrayed our allies," denied our moral principles, and wasted the sacrifices of courageous individuals.

Overall, Nixon's rhetoric reveals an important paradox faced by postwar failure discourse. This rhetoric seeks scapegoats for failure, even as it attempts to console our loss. It tries to unify audiences torn by failure, while it creates divisiveness in its search for collective or individual guilt. Nixon's rhetorical maneuvering is paradoxical because as he reached out to reassure the public, he reached out only to those who supported his war policies. Nixon himself seemed unconcerned with this paradox. Perhaps his rhetoric was figured in such a way that, should his treaty have held and the peace maintained, he and his supporters could have taken credit for an American victory while, at the same time, allowing them to blame critics for the schisms and miscalculations that had constrained the war effort. If the treaty failed, Nixon could again castigate his critics for undermining America's resolve but also for the nation's inability to enforce the Paris settlement. In either case, guilt was shifted away from Nixon and his supporters and onto his detractors. In the process, consolation was achieved but division remained in the form of the culpable "others."

Ford and the Future of America After Vietnam

Not long after the Paris Peace Accords, Nixon found himself deeply embroiled in the Watergate conspiracy. Almost simultaneously, in the midst of numerous treaty violations by both the North and South Vietnamese governments, Congress passed resolutions preventing further military aid to Vietnam. Having thus found the United States in exactly the strategic position they desired, the North Vietnamese began to plan a decisive offensive in 1974 which, by April of 1975, resulted in the total capitulation of Saigon and the American-backed South Vietnamese government. When Gerald Ford took office in 1974 after Nixon's Watergate inspired resignation, he therefore could not have inherited a more untenable set of circumstances—the final and most dismal end of American involvement in Vietnam and the aftermath of Watergate.

Ford also inherited a number of failure topoi from Nixon. But his rhetorical goals were somewhat different. No longer working within the contraints of Nixon's Paris treaty, Ford's primary purpose was to relieve guilt and justify American involvment in a war that had finally come to a poignant conclusion. This ending had brought into sharp focus the nature of America's disastrous defeat. Thus, Ford found it more necessary than ever to define this failure in view of the nation's past history and its future material and spiritual progress.

Like Nixon, Ford attempted to console the American public by acknowledging that the United States' failure in Vietnam reduced neither America's moral resolve to support its allies abroad nor its material ability to make war. In a news conference on April 3, 1975, he made it abundantly clear that America is still "a reliable ally."[15] In fact, sounding as bellicose as his predecessor, Ford warned any adversaries that "they should not, under any circumstances, feel that the tragedy of Vietnam is an indication that the American people have lost their will or their desire to stand up for freedom anyplace [sic] in the world" (413). Like Nixon, then, Ford attempted to reassure the nation that the strenuous war in Vietnam has not drained America's significant resources. In fact, he emphasized his belief that the United States would remain a superior global power well into the future.

Ford's attempt at consolation utilized the *past-future* topos. He reaffirmed the worth of past presidential actions in the Vietnam war: "I believe that the program of the previous four or five Presidents . . . was a sound policy" (420). Ford also used his discourse to position himself and his audience in temporal relation to failure. "Unfortunately," he explained, certain "events that were beyond our control as a country have made it appear that [our] policy was wrong" (420). Of course, he still believed that from his enlightened historical vantage point, "that policy was right if the United States had carried it out" (420).

Like Nixon, Ford faced the important paradox inherent to many failure situations: He desired to unify (and work toward political consensus) yet required a tangible villain for the loss of Vietnam. The paradoxical nature of his dilemma is reflected in the way Ford equivocated on the question of responsibility. At one point during his news conference, he declared that Congress was to blame for the failure but then attributed this failure to "events beyond our control." Still later during his conference, he claimed not to affix "blame on anyone" (421). Moments later he asked his audience to be mindful of the fact "that in fiscal year 1974, there was substantial reduction made by the Congress in the amount of military equipment requested" and "appropriated for South Vietnam" (421). "Those are the facts," he concluded, "I think it is up to the American people to pass judgment on who was at fault or where the blame may rest" (421).

In the process of coping with paradox, then, Ford applied the *self-society*, *past-future*, and *spiritual-material* topoi. He consoled and compensated the public by asserting that their spiritual values and motives, as well as those "of the previous four or five presidents," were laudable. He added to their consolation by supplying a scapegoat for what he took to be the public's (and his) frustration. Americans, in his view, should feel comforted knowing that from the start of the war through the present and undoubtedly into the future, they and their presidents possessed the noble desire and material ability to aid South Vietnam. Congress, however, representing what Ford constructed as an irresponsible institution in the *self-society* topos, should rightfully have taken responsibility for the failure in Vietnam. Congress refused to exercise the moral will and material strength of a people united by common goals and tradition. Thus, Ford urged us to find solace in the fact that we and our presidents remained committed to winning even if our public representatives did not.

Later in his news conference, Ford again evoked the *past-future* topos. He claimed that both the people and the Congress should "in the weeks and months ahead . . . do what we can to work together to meet the problems of the future" (421). This assertion represented a concerted effort toward future healing and even transcendence. Moreover, it helped Ford leave the issue of past human or institutional culpability aside in the name of solving the more meaningful and pressing "problems of the future."

In later speeches, particularly in his April 23, 1975 address at Tulane University, Ford heralded the nation that redemption might be located in the future. Here, he invited his audience not to dwell too deeply upon the failure of Vietnam.[16] Ford juxtaposed the present with the past in order to illumine the future. He compared Vietnam with the War of 1812, where the United States also "suffered a humiliation and a measure of defeat" (569). Nevertheless, consolation was gained from the epic Battle of New Orleans, which "restored America's pride . . . Today, America can regain the sense of pride that existed before Vietnam. But it cannot be achieved by refighting a war that is finished as far as America is concerned" (569). For Ford, the key to restoration lay in the future: "the time has come to look forward to an agenda for the future, to unify, to bind up the Nation's wounds, and to restore its health and its optimistic self-confidence" (569). He consoled the nation by mentioning that although "we . . . are saddened by the events in Indochina . . . these events, tragic as they are, portend neither the end of the world nor of American leadership in the world" (570). In other words, Ford urged us to take comfort in knowing that our policies would eventually achieve their democratic aims and continue to reflect America's substantial world "leadership" for years to come.

Ford also drew upon the *potentiality-actuality* and *past-future* topoi. He advised his audience to "stop refighting the battles and the recriminations of the past" (569). Despite America's loss in Vietnam, the future for Ford held great promise.

Therefore, he encouraged the public to "look now at what is right with America, at our possibilities and our potentialities for change and growth and achievement and sharing" (569).

In these remarks, Ford illustrated one of Payne's observations: "When failure interrupts a sequence, one must find either an interpretation that reestablishes continuity between past and future, or discover some program of change that involves a productive pattern of making past and future discontinuous" (86). In a sense, Ford did both. On the one hand, he made the immediate past history of Vietnam discontinuous with the rest of American history, and especially with the robust economic and other future programs he outlined in his postwar speeches. He declared simply that America is "finished" with Vietnam and should "stop refighting the battles and recriminations of the past." These comments, along with earlier statements about Congressional lack of resolve and "forces beyond our control," tended to turn Vietnam into nothing more than a temporary anomaly. They made the war resemble what Ford called in an April 10 speech before a Joint Session of Congress, mere "setbacks and disappointments in foreign policy," and not an enervating defeat (460).[17]

On the other hand, his rhetoric proposed a model of historical continuity where Vietnam played a pivotal role. This is because the war in Vietnam, like the history of the War of 1812, represented for Ford what one would commonly expect from the cycle of America's short-term failures and long-term successes. In his discourse, Ford suggested that Vietnam is akin to the few "measured" defeats and humiliations of America's second war with Great Britain. But just as the Battle of New Orleans "restored America's pride," so too would the loss of Vietnam jettison the nation into a hopeful future. Thus, Ford offered consolation through his insistence that distant history revealed telling lessons, and compensation through his proposing a future of spiritual and material optimism. Ford's discourse argued for a movement toward greater progress; for a continual realization of the nation's potential. This progress, Ford maintained, was not so much interrupted as it was facilitated by events in Vietnam. Ford suggested that Americans after Vietnam, like Americans after the War of 1812, could heal and restore the nation, but only if they saw Vietnam in its proper historical perspective.

Finally, during an August 19 speech to the Veterans of Foreign Wars, Ford concentrated on the question of amnesty for draft evaders.[18] He combined consolation and compensation by distinguishing his just program from other "unconditional, blanket amnesty programs" (24). He acknowledged "a Power, higher than the people, who commands not only righteousness but love, not only justice but mercy" (24). He then illustrated how his own amnesty policy conformed to the conciliatory, yet just, nature of the divine "Power": Like President's Truman and Lincoln before him, "I found on my desk . . . the urgent problem of how to bind up the Nation's wounds. And I intend to do that" (24). The positioning of this justification relative to Ford's recognition of a higher "Power" was important. Ford appeared firm and compensatory by renouncing "unconditional, blanket amnesty," but consoled by acknowledging how his actions were still consistent with the greater, Divine force. By prescribing his own brand of amnesty—one premised on binding "up the nations wounds," on "righteousness," "love," "justice," and "mercy"—Ford appeared to invoke all the spiritual values necessary for forgiveness without compromising other principles of moral righteousness in war. Nor did he compromise the physical and spiritual suffering felt by those who believed in the sanctity of the war effort itself. In short, by appealing to Divine power, the President elevated the issue of amnesty to a transcendent level, where the world of the warrior and the protestor could ostensibly co-exist.

THE RHETORICAL LEGACY OF VIETNAM AND THE PRESIDENCY

Presidential postwar rhetoric following Vietnam revealed a general unwillingness to come to grips with the historical realities of Vietnam. This rhetoric and the topoi it employed, neither acknowledged America's diminished power after the war, nor confronted the horrors of war in general.

In essence, the post-Vietnam presidential rhetoric of Nixon and Ford was extremely protective of the prevailing ideology that contributed to, and indeed, justified participation in the war from the outset. Historian Loren Baritz has identified two foundational myths used by American presidents to support the country's involvement in Vietnam. The myth of "the city on the hill" distinguished the United States by its moral and spiritual superiority. The myth of American technological invulnerability pictured America's technological or material prowess as capable of solving any problem and as a resource greatly admired, feared, and desired by other less developed cultures.[19] Combined as they were in American foreign policy rhetoric after World War Two, Baritz argues that these two myths conferred upon the United States a sense of omnipotence. They also contributed to the belief, later echoed by President Kennedy, that Americans should bear any burden and pay any price in order to spread and protect democracy. These foundational myths were severely shaken by anti-war rhetoric during and immediately after Vietnam, yet there appears to be no departure from them in the presidential speeches examined here. On the contrary, the topoi which structured these speeches consistently reaffirmed the spiritual and material superiority of America, and made explicit the potential of the nation to carry out its international duties well into the future by wielding the nation's formidable moral and technological strengths. We can again recall Nixon's bold proclamation that because of America's noble commitment in Southeast Asia, its "strength is respected, all around the world."

Drawing upon these founding myths and reconstituting them in light of the rupture caused by war, post-Vietnam presidential rhetoric also reconstructed the past. This rhetoric forced Vietnam to recede into the reconceived past, as both a noble venture and a mere anomaly. When referring to the war, this rhetoric also highlighted the heroic aspects of the conflict while playing down the nature of disastrous failure. It thereby served an important though potentially damaging psychological function, especially for American audiences who had been conditioned since World War Two not to confront defeat. This discourse rendered the unthinkable in the best possible terms. As Vietnam-veteran Robert Muller astutely observed, Americans were too quick to forget or selectively interpret the meaning of the war: "Nobody likes to live with the pain of a really bad incident. We as a society are cleaning up our Vietnam experience to make it more palatable."[20] Presidential rhetoric following Vietnam made failure in war "more palatable."

Moreover, by structuring historical representation, post-Vietnam presidential rhetoric defined the war in a way that delimited other interpretations. Such ideological engineering functioned as a verbal memorial by drawing heavily upon conventional topical means to "clean up" the war experience. As Peter Ehrenhaus explains, reliance on conventional topoi may "block alternative interpretations of the past, of our community and our place in it. Our relationship to the community is explained and reconfirmed; we need not question or doubt our obligation to others or to the group."[21] Presidential rhetoric following Vietnam exploited the past by "blocking" other possible interpretations. It thereby inhibited inquiries into the legitimacy and long-term consequences of constructing our national and international duties as we do.

Finally, postwar presidential rhetoric following Vietnam also conveys the notion that we must learn to see all conflicts from an overall strategic perspective. In this sense, such rhetoric is marked by the unmistakably cold tint of the technocratic reasoning so characteristic of foreign policy elites. In this mode of reasoning, foreign affairs are divorced from moral, emotional, and other social/personal concerns. In fact, through the present writing, Nixon maintains that the loss of Vietnam must be seen from a "geopolitical" point of view. He argues in *In the Arena* that

> As a nation we must learn that in geopolitics the game never ends. There is no point at which all sides cash in their chips. No victory is ever permanent and no defeat irredeemable. A triumph or a loss marks only a shift into a new phase of the contest. To compete with [our enemies] we need to develop the resilience to bounce back after the reversals that great powers inevitably suffer from time to time.[22]

Nixon invites us to comprehend the loss of Vietnam from its proper "geopolitical" context—as part of a much larger strategic game. His use of the "game" metaphor to talk about war and its aftermath is not without its discomforting implications. Such a metaphor conveys a pragmatic view of foreign affairs. Yet in the framework of arguments about the war, it diminishes the meaning of the suffering of those Americans who played but lost "the game" in Vietnam. This metaphor invites us to equate the value of human suffering merely with the fact of our willingness to sacrifice for the game. The game metaphor also creates the impression that because foreign policy (and wars) are just games, we can afford to incur any losses in order to play. According to Nixon's logic, then, losses are less important than our willingness to engage the game. Finally, this metaphorical perspective on the loss of Vietnam is disturbing because it focuses attention in foreign policy on parallel terms such as "winning" and "competition," rather than on alternative metaphors and perhaps alternative failure topoi such as "compromise" and "cooperation." Surely, these alternative vehicles are equally vital to the way in which we engage in talk about our global, geopolitical aspirations.

CONCLUSION

The terrible costs of Vietnam should have produced a basic redefinition of our national identity and policy. True, the nation suffered tremendous humiliation and division resulting from the war; and the so-called "Vietnam syndrome" has caused us to ruminate more carefully over our military interventions in Central American and the Middle East. Still, it has not prevented these interventions. Nor did it prevent a huge military buildup under the Reagan administration, which itself reflected a conservative backlash designed to make any future ignoble defeats in military contests unlikely by virtue of the sheer weight of overwhelming force. The Vietnam war also ignited debates about our international place, although these disputes were mostly confined to leftist and rightist intellectuals. As the war concluded, the broad center of public and political opinion held to business as usual and seemed to dismiss the war experience as an aberration rather than a fundamental shattering of American myths of supremacy. In fact, the humiliation of defeat appears mainly to have created an even greater appetite for decisive victory in war.

Moreover, as this study suggests, postwar presidential rhetoric following Vietnam showed little of the introspection so characteristic of Germany after World War One. Perhaps this lack of introspection is good; Germany had a traumatic crisis of identity after the First World War for which the whole world paid only twenty years later. On the other hand, it seems reasonable to expect more introspection from our presidents than the perfunctory analysis offered in the rhetoric witnessed here. Surely, presidents are obliged to honor those who have suffered in war, to appraise the postwar situation in light of pressing geopolitical exigencies. Many of the failure topoi examined in this essay allow them to do so. But we might also expect from them a more transcendent, healing rhetoric. Such a rhetoric might mitigate the anguish and terror of loss in war in ways that seek something beyond strategic geopolitical maneuvering, something beyond continued confrontation with enemies or those who desire change.

One lesson we learn about our presidents' efforts to explain Vietnam is that, from a rhetorical point of view, the Presidency is a remarkably limited office. This institution is so molded by underlying myths about American superiority that presidents cannot easily come to grips with failure. These myths constrain what presidents can say to create a mature and honest understanding of the complex moral and historical implications of American failures. Thus, the highly constrained, highly formulaic presidential rhetoric about failure may contribute to a false sense of invulnerability, which itself can have serious historical consequences. Perhaps, after failure in war, we merely exhibit what Alan Minc finds characteristic of so much contemporary nationalistic rhetoric during crisis: "reflexes" rather than ideas.[23]

What is most vexing about this postwar rhetoric is the distinct possibility that as it attempts to reinvigorate the nation from the strains inflicted by war, it enhances the very atmosphere that makes future confrontations more likely. As Richard Slotkin says, cultures justify violent confrontations by depicting war as a means of *regenerating* themselves; this makes the regular occurrence of violence a necessity. Perhaps we should amend Slotkin's thesis by noting the role presidents play in describing a nation's process of regeneration after war, and propose alternative means by which they might undertake this project.[24]

We can only speculate about what therapeutic discourse could replace or supplement the presidential speeches we have been exploring. Clearly, for presidents, rhetoric about failure occurs within a highly charged celebration of history and ideology. In this rhetorical climate, a president's turn to alternative failure rhetoric that depicts a nation aspiring to different ends, would define him and his discourse as unfit for reconciling the nation to its ultimate historical purpose. Of course, leaders come to mind who creatively employed failure topoi in public. They were able to transcend the usual prescriptions of failure rhetoric and confront the terrible, perhaps even unrepresentable, realities of war. Among these are Presidents Lincoln and Wilson, along with Winston Churchill. These were leaders who, as Henry Fairlie once wrote of Churchill—by staring honestly at, and speaking eloquently about "the harshness of reality . . . (were able to) wring hope from the very brutality of the truth."[25] Yet, we live in a society where the rhetorical lenses of utopianism are designed to secure the separation of past, present, and future; they foreclose the imagination of possible worlds. In this present milieu, alternative presidential discourse about failure would probably be viewed as defying not only historical consciousness, but also a teleological reading that delivers the nation to a historical destination.

NOTES

[1] Reagan's quote is found in Kathleen Hall Jamieson, *Eloquence in the Electronic Age: The Transformation of Political Speechmaking* (New York: Oxford University Press, 1988), p. 157. Bush's quotes come from his "Address to the Nation on Operation Desert Storm," *Morning Advocate* January 17, 1991, 11A; and his "Radio Address to the United States Armed Forces Stationed in the Persian Gulf Region," *Public Papers of the Presidents*, 91 (March 11, 1991), 245.

[2]See, for example, Cal M. Logue and John Patton, "From Ambiguity to Dogma: The Rhetorical Symbols of Lyndon B. Johnson on Vietnam," in Theodore Windt and Beth Ingold, eds., *Essays in Presidential Rhetoric* (New York: Kendall/Hunt Publishing Co., 1987), pp. 194–210; Robert P. Newman, "Under the Veneer: Nixon's Vietnam Speech of November 3, 1969," in *Essays in Presidential Rhetoric*, pp. 226–239; Karlyn Kohrs Campbell, *Critiques of Contemporary Rhetoric* (Belmont, CA.: Wadsworth Publishing Co., 1972), pp 39–58.

[3]Adi Wimmer, "The American Idea of National Identity: Patriotism and Poetic Sensibility Before and After Vietnam" in *Cultural Legacies of Vietnam: Uses of the Past in the Present* Richard Morris & Peter Ehrenhaus, eds (Norwood, N.J.: Ablex Publishing Co., 1990).

[4]*Ibid.*

[5]Jamieson; also Roderick P. Hart, *The Sound of Leadership: Presidential Communication in the Modern Age* (Chicago: University of Chicago Press, 1987).

[6]Karlyn Kohrs Campbell and Kathleen Hall Jamieson, *Deeds Done in Words: Presidential Rhetoric and Genres of Governance* (Chicago and London: University of Chicago Press, 1990), p. 8.

[7]Paul Fussell, *Wartime: Understanding and Behavior in the Second World War* (New York: Oxford University Press, 1989), see especially chapters 1 and 16–18.

[8]David Payne, *Coping With Failure: The Therapeutic Uses of Rhetoric* (Columbia: University of South Carolina Press, 1989), p. 44. All other references are cited by page number in the text unless otherwise noted.

[9]Richard M. Nixon's 1968 "Inaugural Address," in Aaron Singer, ed., *Campaign Speeches of American Presidential Candidates 1928–1972* (New York: Frederick Unger Publishing Co., 1976), p. 359.

[10]Stanley Karnow, *Vietnam: A History* (New York: Penguin Books, 1983), p. 635.

[11]John Kerry, "Vietnam Veterans Against the War," in Will A. Linkugel, R.R. Allen, and Richard L. Johannesen, eds., *Contemporary American Speeches* (Dubuque, Iowa: Kendall/Hunt Publishing Co., 1978), pp. 288–293.

[12]"Address to the Nation Announcing Conclusion of an Agreement on Ending the War and Restoring Peace in Vietnam," *Public Papers of the Presidents: Richard M. Nixon, 1973* (Washington, D.C.: Government Printing Office, 1975), pp. 18–20. Hereafter all references to specific passages from various presidential speeches are cited in the text by page number.

[13]"The President's News Conference," *Public Papers of the Presidents: Richard M. Nixon, 1973*, 202–212.

[14]"Statement About the Vietnam Veteran," *Public Papers of the Presidents: Richard M. Nixon, 1973*, 220–223.

[15]"News Conference," *Public Papers of the Presidents: Gerald R. Ford, 1975* (Washington, D.C.: Government Printing Office, 1975), pp. 411–430.

[16]"Address at a Tulane University Convocation," *Public Papers of the Presidents: Gerald R. Ford, 1975*, 568–573.

[17]"Address Before a Joint Session of the Congress Reporting on United States Foreign Policy," *Public Papers of the Presidents: Gerald R. Ford, 1975*, 459–469.

[18]"Remarks to the Veterans of Foreign Wars Convention," *Public Papers of the Presidents: Gerald R. Ford, 1975*, 22–28.

[19]See Loren Baritz, *Backfire: A Study of How American Culture Led Us into Vietnam and Made Us Fight the Way We Did* (New York: Morrow, 1985).

[20]Quoted in Norman Kempster, "Loss in Vietnam Steers United States Policy," *The Austin American Statesman* April 28, 1985, 1C.

[21]Peter Ehrenhaus, "Silence and Symbolic Expression," *Communication Monographs* 55 (1988): 48.

[22]Richard M. Nixon, *In the Arena: A Memoir of Victory, Defeat and Renewal* (New York: Simon & Schuster, 1990), p. 380

[23]See Alan Minc as cited in Douglas Johnson, "French Cuffs," *New York Review of Books*, June 13, 1991, 41. Presidential postwar rhetoric reflects fundamental problems with our cultural attitude toward failure in general, problems which presidential rhetoric might perpetuate even as it is used to conceal these difficulties. In his insightful review of Payne's *The Rhetoric of Failure*, Harold Barrett notes that the major motivator of this age is "shame," not "guilt." Rhetoric about shame is also rhetoric "about protecting the self from critical judgment by one's self and others. To the generality of this culture, ideas like guilt, flaw, and fault have

limited personal meaning" (211). For Barrett, in an age where we are quick to fix blame on others, where we rarely ponder the personal responsibilities of our own acts, we should recognize shame as "the predominant rhetorical inspiration," which "would lead to acknowledgment of the prevalence and character of rhetorical dysfunction in these times, for the very force that instigates compensation and consolation will work counterproductively at times" (212). Barrett's diagnosis of our cultural ills translates to the level of presidential discourse about war. For this rhetoric works "counterproductively" precisely because, by restricting critical judgment, it fails to confront the sources of our failure, such as guilt, flaw, fault, or hubris. It does not challenge us to look beyond our traditional failure topoi and the rhetorical exigencies, like shame, that call them into existence. See Harold Barrett, "Review of *Coping With Failure*," *Quarterly Journal of Speech* 76 (1990): 210–12.

[24]See Richard Slotkin, *Regeneration Through Violence: The Mythology of the American Frontier, 1600–1860* (Middletown Conn.: Wesleyan University Press, 1973). For a similar point about America after World War Two, see Ray E. McKerrow, "Truman and Korea: Rhetoric in the Pursuit of Victory," *Central States Speech Journal* 28 (1977): 1–12.

[25]Henry Fairlie, "A Volcanic Flash," *The New Republic* December 6, 1988, 36. Both Hart and Jamieson have also called for greater eloquence on the part of presidents.

The Stab-in-the-Back Legend and the Vietnam War

JEFFREY P. KIMBALL
Miami University

Originating during the Vietnam War in the debate over U.S. policy and strategy, the stab-in-the-back theme developed into a full-fledged explanation for American defeat after the war ended and as another, related debate unfolded over the causes of failure and the future of policy. The existence of the legend—which condemns the antiwar movement, civilian strategists, Democratic presidents, Congress, leftists, liberals, and the press for snatching defeat from the jaws of victory—has not gone unnoticed. Several observers have made passing reference to an approximate similarity between the response of some Americans to defeat in that war and the response of some Germans to defeat in World War I—the best-known manifestation of the legend.[1]

The purpose of unearthing the stab-in-the-back legend about the war is to recognize and identify a phenomenon of American culture and of the history of the modern era, whereby some losers of wars consciously or unconsciously search for scapegoats. This search often results in the formulation of a myth that is not simply another harmless academic interpretation and much less an "objective" interpretation, but is one that has significant social, political, strategic, and civil-military implications. Many Americans, doubting the existence of a Vietnam War stab-in-the-back legend, might resent comparisons with post-World War I Germany. But in spite of the inflammatory nature of the subject, it seems safe to hypothesize that such legends are common responses to

ARMED FORCES AND SOCIETY, Vol. 14 No. 3, Spring 1988 433-458 defeat in war, and it should not be surprising that one appeared in connection with American defeat in that long and bitter conflict. The test of its existence is whether certain explanations of American defeat in Vietnam conform to the pattern of historical consciousness that is associated with the stab-in-the-back perspective. Even though history does not repeat itself precisely and patterns and analogies are never exact, similarities exist, and their recognition is part of historical memory and understanding.

Reflecting an ancient mythos about the betrayal of the virtuous, heroic, and otherwise invincible warrior, cultural manifestations of the stab-in-the-back legend are at least as venerable as the Old Norse *Nibelungensage* and the Medieval German *Nibelungenlied*, in which Hagen spears the hero Siegfried in his back. The modern, archetypal *Dolchstoss Legende* was born after the German defeat of 1918. Field Marshal Paul von Hindenburg, Gen. Erich Ludendorff, the Germany army, the political Right, and eventually the Nazi party all concocted a stab-in-the-back explanation of how the Great War had been lost: not on the battlefield but on the home front. The army, the war effort, and the nation, they asserted, were betrayed by disloyal, fainthearted, rebellious civilians who undermined the will of the people and the soldiers to continue the fight, and by the Left-leaning government that agreed to an armistice. "Like Siegfried, stricken down by the treacherous spear of savage Hagen," von Hindenburg wrote, "our weary front collapsed."[2]

The archetypal pattern represented by the twentieth-century German example may be said to include the circumstances of defeat in war and national humiliation. The accusers—advocates of the original war aims—were from the ranks of nationalistic intellectuals, those most responsible for the war's prosecution, those to some degree responsible for defeat, and some in the military and from the Right, who stood to gain by scapegoating others. The accused included the post-Kaiser, civilian, left-of-center government; socialists, Communists, revolutionary workers, and intellectuals; Jews; and, indirectly, the German people. The accusers, in blaming others for national defeat, salvaged their own reputations, countered the political power of the opposition, regained power, and revived the pursuit of right-wing social, economic, expansionist, and military aims.[3]

There were of course differences between Germany and the United States—in particular, in their history and culture, and in their circumstances, and in each's involvement in World War I and the Vietnam War, respectively. American military commanders did not enjoy the power and status possessed by the German command, and they were not fully in control of strategy. U.S. armed forces were not fully deployed, beaten militarily, or forced to surrender. The government, economy, and institutions of the United States were not on the verge of collapse. American territory was neither occupied nor lost, and American society was not threatened by fundamental social revolution.

Although there were differences in circumstances, there were also similarities. In Vietnam, American national policy and military strategy met with defeat, or at least with failure; thus, America lost the war or at least was unable to emerge victorious. Battles were lost at the small-unit, tactical level. The army was humiliated and under criticism, its morale in shambles. Two presidencies fell victim to the war; one major political party underwent an upheaval in leadership, and another seemed doomed to an even smaller minority status than it then held. To some at the time, American society seemed to be undergoing a social, intellectual, and political "revolution." In addition, the U.S. economy was under increasing strain, and American foreign and military policy doctrines were in tatters. There followed a postwar period of economic crisis and perceived political confusion. Then, in the presidential election of 1980, a rightist "counterrevolution" achieved power through allusions to betrayal in Vietnam and calls for the revival of patriotic pride, stronger foreign and military policies, and more law and order at home.

Myths explaining defeat need not correspond precisely to match a pattern or for historians to draw valid analogies. It is not a requirement of the legend, for example, that blame for the defeat in Vietnam is put upon a religious minority. In any case, the stab-in-the-back theme is not unique to the twentieth-century German experience, even though it has become synonymous with it. In recent European history, variants of this theme can be seen in the French army's response to defeat in the Franco-Prussian War and to the Dreyfus affair,[4] as well as in the French army's response to cumulative defeat in World War II, the First Indochina War, and the Algerian War.[5] In recent Southeast Asian history, the Democratic Republic of (north) Vietnam accused the People's Republic of China of back stabbing through its invitation to President Richard Nixon to visit China in 1972;[6] former Republic of (south) Vietnam allies of the United States accused certain American leaders of betrayal and of losing the war by their reductions in aid to South Vietnam after 1973.[7]

It is not uncommon to find elements of the stab-in-the-back legend in pre–Vietnam War-era U.S. history, despite the fact that Americans lost or met with policy failure in few wars besides that one: for example, the War of 1812, the Korean War, and, for the South, the Civil War.

For their roles in the failure of America to win all of its battles and to conquer Canada during the War of 1812, New England Federalists were accused of near-treasonous activity; the Congress and president of naïveté, confusion, and parsimony; and the nonprofessional, citizen-soldier militia of ineptitude. The defeat of the Confederacy in the Civil War was explained by some as having been caused by President Jefferson Davis' incompetent interference in military strategy, the states' rights sentiment of Southern politicians, the mistakes of Gen. Robert E. Lee's subordinates, and the excessively democratic and antimilitary attitudes of the Southern white masses.

For their alleged military unpreparedness and exclusion of South Korea from a Pacific defense perimeter, President Harry Truman and Secretary of State Dean Acheson were castigated for contributing to North Korean aggression. In his failure to liberate North Korea, Truman was also reproached for his rejection of Gen. Douglas MacArthur's strategic advice. Even after the victorious War of the American Revolution, there was the argument that the Continental Army was made to suffer deprivations, lose battles, and almost lose the war because of the inefficiency of the Continental Congress, the lukewarm support of the state governments, and the cowardice, wastefulness, and incompetence of the militia. For the loss of early battles and the excessive length of the otherwise victorious Civil War, President Abraham Lincoln was criticized for his alleged bungling interference in military generalship.

Many of these explanations for failure and defeat have some basis in fact but are nevertheless either demonstrably untrue in substantial part or simplistic in their interpretations of complex and misunderstood events. Accordingly, they not only recall ancient myths of betrayal in war, but also amount to distortions of historical fact. And beyond the realms of historical fallacy, cultural mythology, and misplaced pride, they represent tensions in civil-military relations and specific class, group, and ideological outlooks and interests. The reappearance of the stab-in-the-back theme in connection with the Vietnam War is but a repetition of a familiar pattern of response to defeat. The details may differ from both culture to culture and epoch to epoch, but the essential characteristics remain the same.

Anecdotal and quantitative evidence—personal conversations, "man-on-the-street" comments, the apparent popularity of militant statements by public figures, and public-opinion polls—suggest that a sizable *minority* of Americans in the postwar era accepted some of the essential beliefs of a stab-in-the-back perspective vis-à-vis the Vietnam War.

In March 1985, on the eve of the 10th anniversary of the end of the war, for example, a *Newsweek* poll found that 38 percent of Americans believed "the United States should have made an even greater military effort to win a victory."[8] A *New York Times* poll during the same period discovered that "18- to 22-year-olds were. . .among the most likely to share President Reagan's endorsement of the Vietnam War as a 'noble cause,' and to believe it 'taught us that military leaders should be able to fight wars without civilian leaders tying their hands.' " The *Times* polling analyst, Adam Clymer, also reported that "when asked if United States troops should be used in a list of [international] crises, support [among Americans] was higher in 1985 [than in the 1970s] in every case."[9] Thus the "Vietnam syndrome"—the postwar aversion of Americans to military intervention in crises, conflicts, and revolutions[10]—appeared to have subsided. (By way of contrast, an article in *Armed Forces and Society* in 1975 about public-opinion trends had reported the strengthening of acceptance of the "Vietnam analogy"—another term for the derogatory Vietnam syndrome.)[11] But Clymer warned that responses to questions were "deeply contradictory," compounded by ignorance and forgetfulness about the war.

As Clymer and others have pointed out, several factors complicate the interpretation of public-opinion trends concerning both the war and foreign policy issues: for example, the tendency of citizens to rally round the flag in a crisis, the interrelationship between domestic and foreign events, the impact of economic perceptions and realities on support for military endeavors, and the divergencies of responses to questions about hypothetical and real events.[12] Despite the elusiveness of public opinion, a shift seemed to occur among the young—from the 1970s to the 1980s—toward more support for intervention abroad and more militaristic answers regarding the Vietnam debacle, while opinions in other groups more or less held steady.

Elite views of the causes of defeat in the war are less difficult to identify and verify than popular views. Gen. Douglas Kinnard's 1974 survey of 173 Vietnam War Army generals unearthed a variety of self-critical analyses, contradicting the notion of a monolithic "military mind." Still, there was a clear consensus in this group about the adverse impact of media coverage of the conflict on the public and on government officials.[13] In broader-based surveys of elite opinion in 1976 and 1980, Ole Holsti and James Rosenau found evidence for the constancy of dissension among elite groups. Military and foreign-service officers, business executives, labor leaders, lawyers, public officials, educators, media leaders, the clergy, and others who had disagreed about the war and foreign policy in the past continued to do so into the 1980s. Ideology, occupation, and their policy positions on the Vietnam issue were "the most potent predictor[s] of [their] foreign policy beliefs." Compared with other elite groups, conservative Republicans, conservatives in general, military officers, and business executives tended toward "cold war internationalism," which, as a set of beliefs about foreign policy and the Vietnam defeat and in contrast to "post–cold war internationalism" and "semi-isolationism,"[14] included stab-in-the-back themes.

Qualitative evidence for the existence of an American stab-in-the-back perspective can be found in the literature, oratory, and cinematography concerning the U.S. failure in Vietnam. A sampling of this material strongly suggests that such a perspective did emerge in the postwar period. Although the outlook of an elite minority, it is influential.

A nearly pure form of the theory is represented in the writings and statements of Richard Nixon, Ronald Reagan, William Westmoreland, U.S. Grant Sharp, the John Birch Society, writers for *National Review*, and Accuracy in Media—to name some of the most conspicuous examples. All have a tenacious commitment to the containment doctrine, though some more than others; and all blame the press, the antiwar movement, leftists, liberals, Democratic presidents, Congress, and civilian strategy intellectuals for the defeat in Vietnam. As they see it, the war can best be understood as a war of aggression instigated by world communism, with the "nation" of North Vietnam as the instrument of the aggression against the "nation" of South Vietnam. They agree that the war aim of effecting the independence of the Republic of Vietnam was correct, but some question whether it was the right war in the right place at the right time.[15] All agree that, once committed, the United States should have pursued it to a victorious conclusion, though Nixon has some reservations on this score.

Almost exclusively emphasizing military force over other factors, these stab-in-the-back advocates claim that the war could have been won if the correct strategy had been followed and if certain of the civilian strategists had stood by South Vietnamese allies and allowed the U.S. military to fight the kind of war they were most experienced with. This would have involved calling up reserves and using more force, especially bombing the North more heavily and sooner; mining Haiphong harbor; destroying bridges to China; removing target restrictions in general; attacking "sanctuaries"; and invading the North and stopping "infiltration" from that area. Presidents, and especially the Democratic ones, they argue, pursued incorrect strategies and were overly concerned with politics, the achievement of domestic programs, the threat of Chinese and Soviet intervention, and world opinion.

Furthermore, they maintain, if the will of the American people had not been undermined by antiwar activists, students, professors, movie stars, and the press (notably during the Tet offensive), and if Congress had not had its share of critics and also lost its nerve after 1973, there would not have been the confusion that characterized civilian leadership. Nor would the morale of the armed forces have been lowered. Home-front criticism and turmoil had a particularly adverse effect on the army's efficiency and, in addition, encouraged the enemy to persevere. Losing the war was a terrible blow to the United States, and the Vietnam syndrome now threatens its great-power credibility.

Staunchest Proponents: Reagan, Westmoreland

While sharing a general perspective, the specific arguments and claims of the stab-in-the-back pleaders differ in emphasis and on minor details. Reagan and Westmoreland, for example, are probably among the purest and staunchest proponents of the thesis. The president's criticism of so-called back-stabbers has a long pedigree, dating to the Vietnam War era, when he alternately and contradictorily referred to antiwar demonstrators as "Communists," "cowardly little Fascist bands," and instruments of an "international conspiracy"; he also criticized the Johnson administration for sending "its young men to fight and die in a war the government is afraid to let them win."

In the postwar period before his election Reagan repeated earlier themes, maintaining that more B-52 bombings could have prevented defeat, accusing Congress of acting irresponsibly and of having "blood on its hands" for failing to support a stronger military effort and for tying President Nixon's hands with the War Powers Act, and blaming the "liberal press" for undermining the will of the people to support "wars of the Vietnam type. . . in the defense of freedom and our own country."[16] During the 1980 election campaign Reagan frequently declared to audiences: "There will be no more Taiwans. There will be no more Vietnams. There will be no more betrayals of friends by the United States."[17] As president he has referred to the Vietnam War as an effort at stopping Communist aggression by the nation of North Vietnam against the nation of South Vietnam—both of which were allegedly created by the Geneva Accords[18]—and as a war from which American soldiers "came home without a victory, not because they'd been defeated but because they'd been denied permission to win."[19]

General Westmoreland, who believes that "our Achilles' heel is our resolve"[20] and that the enemy won "the war politically in Washington," blames a "no-win policy" on partisan politicians who accommodated "a misguided minority opposition. . . masterfully manipulated by Hanoi and Moscow."[21] The former commander of Military Assistance Command Vietnam is probably most critical of two groups: "vocal antiwar elements" for rebuking the military, encouraging the enemy, and weakening congressional resolve; and the media for the impact of its "no-holds-barred," misleading, and defeatist reporting upon "timid" Washington officials and the public. He also indicts the Johnson administration, civilian strategists, diplomats, intellectuals, reformers, and Congress for faulty strategies, weak wills, and expedient policies, all of which had the effect of prolonging and losing the war.[22] In the end, "our erstwhile honorable country betrayed and deserted the Republic of Vietnam. . . . It was a shabby performance by America, a blemish on our history and a possible blight on our future. Our credibility has been damaged."[23]

Admiral Sharp, who was Commander in Chief Pacific from 1964 to 1968, is as staunch as Westmoreland but perhaps less strident in his explanation of defeat. Sharp is especially critical of the air-war strategy of "gradual escalation," which he attributes to President Johnson, then Secretary of Defense Robert McNamara, and civilian "antiwar advocates" within the Defense Department in offices such as International Security Affairs.

To Sharp, air power is a "potent tool. . . in power diplomacy through military action," and it could have been one of the main military components of victory through coercion in Vietnam. That it was not was due to the on-again, off-again application of bombing, which encouraged and strengthened the enemy. He blames the theoretical tinkerings of arrogant civilian strategists who ignored the practical advice of experienced, uniformed planners; Johnson's pursuit of peace with the carrot minus the stick; the fear of Chinese and Soviet intervention and of world opinion; the absence of national unity; and the shocking weakness of the public's will to support U.S. policy objectives.

Sharp intimates that the last two causes—national disunity and feeble public support—were the failures of political leadership, "a skillfully waged subversive propaganda campaign, aided and abetted by the media's bombardment of sensationalism, rumors and half-truths," antiwar activities in the streets, Congress, the Department of Defense, and a general dearth of concern for the responsibility and honor of world leadership.[24] In the foreword to Sharp's *Strategy for Defeat*, journalist Hanson Baldwin calls the book a "good companion piece to [Westmoreland's] *A Soldier Reports*," for these volumes and others provide proof that "the blame for the lost war rests, *not* upon the men in uniform, but upon the civilian policy makers in Washington."[25]

Also staunchly faithful to the lost possibility of military victory, but focusing on the so-called betrayals of the press, is the right-wing, press-watchdog group Accuracy in Media. AIM succeeded in winning an unprecedented opportunity to respond to the alleged historical misrepresentations of the Public Broadcasting Service series *Vietnam: A Television History* (broadcast in 1983). In an acridly critical film, *Television's Vietnam: The Real Story* (aired in 1985), AIM closely followed the stab-in-the-back view of the war's history, emphasizing television press distortions about Ho Chi Minh, Ngo Dinh Diem, the Geneva Accords, the National Liberation Front, the Tet offensive, the performance of American soldiers, the role of Congress and the media, Cambodia, and other issues and events. Amid backdrop scenes of the Vietnam War Memorial in the nation's capital, film narrator Charlton Heston concluded:

> The men whose names are chiseled into this marble [monument] were not sent on a fool's errand. . . . The purpose was noble but we failed. Our people and our leaders became confused and suffered a loss of will. . . . We were wrong to think the outcome would be decided by military strength. In the end words, disinformation, [and] deception were the deciding factors.[26]

The Nixon Version

Richard Nixon's version of the war's failure is predictably one of the more convoluted, coming as it does from one who presided over its denouement. With other stab-in-the-back purveyors, he accepts the tenets of the containment doctrine. But unlike most, he is critical of Westmoreland's World War II–like conventional strategy, which, he says, substituted masses of men and equipment for subtler political and psychological approaches in dealing with what Nixon concedes was a guerrilla war that had something to do with nationalism and revolution. Like other conservatives, he maintains that democracy is unsuited to fighting a prolonged war; thus, democracy has much to do with American failure in Vietnam. Among the citizenry and institutions of democracy, liberals, the antiwar movement, the press, and Congress receive particular opprobrium for having constrained the White House and encouraged enemies, and generally for engaging in near-treasonous activities.[27] Faulting neither himself nor President Dwight Eisenhower for earlier leading the United States into the Vietnam quagmire in the 1950s, he reproaches John Kennedy for plunging "impulsively" into the fray in the early 1960s.

Nixon is also critical of Johnson's countenancing of Cambodian and Laotian sanctuaries and of his strategy of air-war "gradualism," as well as of Johnson's lack of success in defending the war publicly. Not surprisingly, Nixon, like other stab-in-the-back theorists, asserts that his escalations of B-52 and fighter-bomber raids over the North and South and the mining of Haiphong harbor in 1972 produced positive results, having the effect of strengthening the hand of the United States in dealing with China and the Soviet Union, stopping the North Vietnamese Easter offensive, and forcing the enemy finally to accept the accords of 1973. Although Nixon presided over American foreign policy and military strategy at the time of America's failure, he claims to have won not only "peace with honor," but also victory, accusing Congress of "losing" the war by its supposed failure to support President Nguyen Van Thieu after 1973. To Nixon, it is not so much a case of the military having been betrayed as it is a matter of Nixon, the war effort, and containment militarism having been betrayed.[28]

Other Theorists

Significantly, other theorists—for example, *National Review* writers—do not seem to hold Nixon accountable for America's failure, or at least they do not press the point. When they criticize the Nixon administration's handling of the war, they direct most of their ire against his subordinate, Henry Kissinger,[29] or they blame a disembodied "Watergate scandal" for undermining Nixon's position. But they ignore his responsibility for Watergate and the relationship of Watergate to his personality and the Vietnam War itself. Ironically, they also sometimes imply that Watergate was the fault of the press and Congress alike, or that both institutions distorted its character. Some stab-in-the-back apologists even praise Nixon's strong will, demonstrated, they say, by his bombing of Hanoi, which in turn proved that the greater use of air power earlier in the war would have produced victory.[30] But in general their position concerning Nixon and the end of U.S. involvement is unclear and perhaps contradictory. On the one hand, they seem to recognize that the treaty of 1973 was a formal admission of failure;[31] on the other, they claim that the Christmas bombing brought the other side to terms and that more bombing sooner could have won better terms.[32] In any event, Congress and the protesters were finally to blame.[33]

Militaristic Values

Strong criticism of Johnson and of the wartime Democratic Congress compared with relative magnanimity toward Nixon suggests there are specific ideological and political sources of the stab-in-the-back outlook; namely, it is a partisan perspective founded on arch-conservative and militaristic assumptions and values. Most if not all of the apologists denigrate liberal Democrats, pacifists, and the Left, while simultaneously removing the burden of involvement and defeat from their own shoulders. Important too is the emphasis placed by some on faulty civilian decisions, which suggests a challenge to civilian advisers as makers of strategy and military policy, especially during wartime.

Assumptions and values represented in stab-in-the-back arguments include

- A we-they mentality;
- Belief in the efficacy of military force and national will;
- Theories of war and social turmoil that ascribe blame to conspiratorial evildoers and place trust in strong leaders, though they be corrupt, unpopular, and authoritarian;
- Mistrust of democracy and love of order;
- Rejection of the public's right to know if such information undermines a militant foreign policy;
- The equation of criticism of containment militarism with disloyalty, but a vigorous exercise of press freedom to rebuke foreign policy moderation; and
- Callousness toward the taking of human life in pursuit of nationalistic ends.[34]

Liberal and Leftist Explanations of Defeat

In the context of the Vietnam War, the theme of "betrayal" becomes conservative and militaristic because of its identification with the notion of disloyalty to both the nation and the institution of the armed forces. In contrast, liberal explanations of the defeat cite widely held misunderstandings about Vietnamese society, the nature of the war, and mistaken optimism about the utility of military force. Leftist arguments point to systemic contradictions in American society, foreign policy, and capitalism. This is not to say that all conservatives are stab-in-the-back pleaders, but it is to suggest that all adherents of the theory are on the Right, if not the far Right, of the ideological spectrum, at least concerning foreign policy and military affairs. (It is not to suggest, however, that all conservatives and military personnel are militaristic.) Quantitatively and qualitatively, the evidence seems to agree on these points.

The theory also has its historic roots in past debates over the war. For example, the U.S. Saigon mission, Diemists, and S.L.A. Marshall criticized press coverage of the war in the early 1960s.[35] In 1964, presidential candidate Barry Goldwater called for military victory and condemned Johnson's record of "fumbling and futility."[36] In 1966, the Joint Chiefs of Staff advocated more bombing while McNamara counseled less.[37] And in 1965, Westmoreland recommended escalation, later attempting to defend his responses to the 1968 Tet offensive.[38] Governor Reagan (of California) called for a declaration of war in order to punish alleged treasonous draft-card burners,[39] while Sen. Walter Judd warned in 1968 that peace demonstrations in the United States encouraged Ho Chi Minh, declaring that it was "humanitarian" to bomb dikes.[40] Further, in 1971 Col. Robert Heinl, Jr., attributed high desertion rates and poor morale, discipline, and battle-worthiness to sedition, subversion, and legal harassment.[41] Nixon, campaigning from 1965 to 1968, criticized Johnson's squandering of military power, and later—as chief executive—continued to accuse the antiwar movement of undermining the war effort.[42]

Before becoming president, Nixon had contributed to Johnson's political and military dilemma, as well as to public expectations of victory. Ironically, once in power, both he and Kissinger were worried about a possible public backlash against their ending of the war unless it could be done, as one correspondent put it, without making "a mockery of the loss thus far of more than 31,000 American lives."[43] By August 1972 Nixon believed "the Left" could be made to shoulder the responsibility for failure in Vietnam: "We've got the Left where we want it now," he told Kissinger. "All they've got left to argue for is a bug-out, and that's their problem." But he was shocked to learn that elements of the Right wanted him to end the war quickly, thereby complicating his pursuit of an "honorable" defeat and his *own* political and military dilemma. "When the Right starts wanting to get out, for whatever reason, that's *our* problem," he lamented.[44] After the war, Nixon was in the forefront of efforts to create a backlash against Democrats, doves, and the Left for having stabbed the pursuit of victory in the back.

Other critiques and policy recommendations that share common themes and origins with the Vietnam War stab-in-the-back legend preceded debates of that period: historiographical interpretations and political references to 1930s' appeasement and pre–World War II military unpreparedness; accusations that liberal Democrats surrendered to Stalin at Yalta and lost China to Mao; McCarthyite anticommunism; and cold war policy documents like NSC-68 and the Gaither report.[45] These policy critiques and recommendations crossed party lines; but to the extent that they originated from Democrats, they generally came from conservatives and militant policymakers, some of whom have frequently served the party in power.

The stab-in-the-back theory is more than merely a historiographically revisionist argument in the postwar debate over the causes and lessons of Vietnam and more than simply a folk response to defeat. It appears also to be an excrescence of containment militarism, which has intellectual, social, economic, political, and institutional roots in past and present elite struggles for and over political power, national strategy, and military and foreign policy. Its proponents stem from sectors of the military, the right wing of the Republican—and to a lesser extent the Democratic—party, militant national security managers, and the right-wing press and intelligentsia. AIM is one of the better examples of the last mentioned in the 1980s. But there are earlier examples, dating at least to the 1960s. Stab-in-the-back arguments, for example, were common in the pages of the John Birch Society's *American Opinion* and William F. Buckley, Jr.'s *National Review* in 1964 and continued to appear throughout the war. Like the criticisms of Nixon and other conservatives at the time, they constituted right-wing pressure on the Johnson administration to win the war militarily.[46]

If indeed there does exist in American currents of cultural perception an explanation about defeat in Vietnam that conforms to a stab-in-the-back pattern of thought, at issue is whether this view is valid or whether it comprises the stuff of myth and legend. Explanations of the war, and especially about the causes of American involvement, are often said to be divided between hawks, doves, and "moderates." In turn, these perspectives correspond in the *ideological* arena to shades of conservative, Left, and liberal views about the conflict, and in the *historiographical* realm to Right-revisionist, Left-revisionist, and centrist—or allegedly neutral—interpretations. In the literature explaining American defeat in the war, opinion is divided among hawk, dove, counterinsurgency, and limits-of-power schools of thought,[47] a breakdown that mirrors divisions within and without the U.S. government during and especially after the Tet offensive.[48] The stab-in-the-back thesis clearly represents a very hawkish point of view.

That there is "controversy" about the causes of American failure in the Vietnam War does not mean, however, that all explanations are equal or accurate. Thus, there remains the problem of determining which are demonstrably true in whole or substantial part and which are not, or at least which explanations are more uncertain than others. On its face, the stab-in-the-back plea distorts, oversimplifies, redefines realities, and ignores vast amounts of contradictory evidence; in addition, it is logically flawed, highly polemical, self-serving, and—in the end—fallacious. Those who disagree with the theory assert the following.

Dissenters from the Theory

Strategy

In general, the claim of stab-in-the-back theorists that victory was possible amounts to speculation founded upon hypothetical strategic scenarios, with "victory" understood to mean a military one. In particular, it is by no means certain that invasions of North Vietnam, Laos, and Cambodia, or the cutting of supply routes to the South, or heavier bombing of the North much earlier than 1972 would have "won" the war for the United States—even if those steps had been feasible.[49]

The establishment of a military cordon across the South/North Vietnamese border would have required the sending of many more American troops, besides resulting in an expansion of the war. An invasion of North Vietnam would have meant more American troops, a widened war, and (as all the U.S. presidents feared) the possible intervention of the Soviet Union and China. Had it been logistically possible, the earlier and heavier bombing of North Vietnam might also have brought on Soviet or Chinese intervention. And even if not, destruction through heavier bombing would still have left the United States with the problem of "pacifying" the country.

As it happened, wartime bombing seems at best to have enabled the United States to stalemate the war and postpone the end. The bombings of 1972 did not produce victorious results, and their consequences could be interpreted to demonstrate that, despite the enormous expenditure of American armaments, the other side was shaken but undaunted, with its political influence in the South Vietnamese countryside enlarged. The heavy bombing of the North, while physically destructive, was politically counterproductive.[50] Hawk and dove critics alike, moreover, pointed out not only that bombing was cost-ineffective but also that a greater escalation of it or of troop strength was logistically infeasible and undesirable in relation to their perceptions of America's global commitments.[51]

It is rather ludicrous to argue in any event that the military strategy pursued was one of gradualism, a concept that makes sense only in terms of American superpower potential. The dropping of several times the tonnage of bombs used in World War II, the introduction of 530,000 American troops in three years, the employment of tens of thousands of other "free world" troops, the creation of a large South Vietnamese army, and the employment of massive firepower and chemical weapons did not add up to a strategy of mere *gradualism*. The term fails to capture the reality and immensity of the American way of "capital-intensive" war.[52] Many critics argue that greater destruction would have caused an even greater erosion of the moral and political standing of the United States in the eyes of the world and its own people, a not inconsequential price to pay for hypothetical victory.

From a different but related perspective, the war was lost because the U.S. officials who waged it had not even learned the lessons of failed strategic bombing campaigns in previous wars and failed interventions in past revolutions; they did not understand its political, social, nationalistic, cultural, and revolutionary nature. By placing an excessive reliance on military methods and power, they revealed the strategic bankruptcy of "Americanizing" the war. Even before Americanization, their counterinsurgency approach was half-hearted, poorly coordinated, misguided, and overly military.[53]

Civilian Interference

With respect to the charge of *excessive* civilian interference, General Kinnard maintains

> There was not *enough* civilian participation in terms of asking the big questions about what we were really doing in Vietnam. In part, this was a matter of personality. . . . In part, it was also the "big war" mentality—let the military run it—in what was a very political affair indeed. Most of all, it was a lack of communication between civilians and military.

Moreover, the "can do" military ethos inhibited practical assessments of what was possible and what was not.[54] It would be simplistic to argue that the U.S. military command alone was responsible for the American failure in Vietnam, but it is nevertheless true that there were serious deficiencies in leadership, management, manpower policy, morale, tactics, and strategy attributable to the military command.[55]

The Press

The press did influence public opinion, but it was often the servant of the state, especially in the war's early stages, when it generally supported cold war visions and Third World interventions. Although both the print and broadcast media did write about and televise scenes of the carnage, the media told of and broadcast far fewer of the horrors than actually occurred. Editors of national organizations, moreover, often censored stories from the battle zone.

Throughout the conflict, the government tried to manipulate and pressure the press to hew to the administration line. During the Johnson years, for example, the administration persuaded "front" groups of distinguished citizens to profess support for the war.[56] During the Nixon watch, then Vice President Spiro Agnew verbally flayed the media. For its part, the press was far from monolithic; many, if not most, local newspapers and television stations, for example, editorialized in favor of the war.[57] Eventually—at least by 1968—the press had to come to grips with and report some of the tragic realities of the war.[58]

Even if the press distorted the war coverage—and this is subjective—it is another thing to say that such reportage undermined the people's support of the war, and that the weakening of public support caused American leaders to pursue a no-win policy. Some analysts argue that dinnertime television-news coverage inured American viewers to the bloodshed, numbing them into acquiescence.[59] In any case, the people have a right to decide to fight wars or not and to know what is being done in their name.

Antiwar Protest

Both the nature and degree of influence of the antiwar movement on the prosecution of the war are difficult issues to assess. Analyses of its impact range from the view that the movement was counterproductive, having the effect of increasing popular support for the war,[60] to the stab-in-the-back notion that it encouraged and was even inspired by the enemy, undermining the will and ability of the American people and government to wage and win the war.

The claim that the movement was counterproductive is most probably overstated, fails to take the complexity of the issues into account, begs empirical proof, and contradicts common sense, anecdotal evidence, personal experience, and the testimony of the war wagers. At the other extreme, the charge of foreign manipulation is groundless. Despite vigorous and sustained efforts, the government itself was never able to demonstrate that the antiwar opposition was inspired or controlled by international Communists or anyone else.[61] On the issue of whether antiwar activity encouraged the enemy, one scholar, generally unsympathetic to the antiwar movement, suggests that while it probably encouraged the Vietnamese, "the crucial consideration . . . is not whether the war protest was encouraging to the Communists but whether that encouragement was important to their ability to continue their war effort."[62] He and others deny its importance and point instead to the psychological commitment of the Vietnamese to the nationalist struggle, their willingness to endure heavy losses, and the greater interest of the Democratic Republic of Vietnam and the National Liberation Front in South Vietnamese politics rather than American politics. Other causes of American failure include the difficult terrain, flawed strategy, and the limits of military force in revolutionary wars.[63]

Scholars sympathetic with the antiwar movement maintain that it and other "rebellions" of the era had a "direct veto power" over the ability of the government to escalate the war.[64] Although they thereby provide grist for the mill of the stab-in-the-back accusers, these scholars argue from the point of view that antiwar protest—and protest in general—reflected the problems of American society and the general unpopularity of a senseless and immoral war in Southeast Asia: the war was but a symptom of the contradictions of U.S. government policies, and protest the cure. To some, the protesters deserve credit for saving American and Vietnamese lives and for stopping the war and should not cower and recant in the face of right-wing criticism.[65] Other analysts, however, regret the influence of the "romantic" elements in the movement.[66] The antiwar opposition was a home-front, overwhelmingly nonviolent "guerrilla army"; it achieved no decisive victories but nevertheless ate away at the government's position, gradually wearing it down.

Yet other sympathetic scholars hedge their assessment. Charles DeBenedetti concludes:

> [The] antiwar opposition performed two vital functions. First, it produced awareness of an alternative America that stripped away through dissent and resistance the rational, moral, and political legitimacy of Washington's war in Indochina. Second, it provided. . .a respectable haven for those many Americans who shifted against the war in the late winter of 1968. . . .[67] The dissidents did not stop the war. But they made it stoppable.[68]

From this perspective, the antiwar movement was a slap-in-the-face of the government, not a stab-in-the-back of the armed forces or the nation.

Although the true impact of the antiwar movement on policy is far from certain,[69] it seems safe to say that the argument of the stab-in-the-back purveyors is seriously wanting. Its perspective on the role of the opposition is flawed from the outset, for it fails to appreciate the war itself as the driving force of domestic reactions. The history of the period reveals that the war gave rise to antiwar protest, which grew as the war widened. Even though the heterogenous antiwar "movement" originated with a few core peace groups, they were of diverse origins and followed different agendas. As the war escalated, their attention focused increasingly on it, and the opposition in general grew. The movement evolved with fits and starts to encompass many different elements, united in opposition to the war but at odds on solutions and tactics. The opposition included pre-Vietnam-era peace activists; religious, secular, liberal, and radical pacifists; civil rights activists; the old and new Left; church groups; disaffected cold war and antimilitarist liberals; students; intellectuals; the politically conscious counterculture; politicians; portions of labor and business; soldiers; and, eventually, the nonactivist majority of the American people. Viewed developmentally, it was fundamentally the nature of the struggle and the failure of the war itself that produced disaffection. Although it exerted a powerful influence on popular and elite opinion, the peace movement alone did not give rise to weariness with America's longest war but was itself a symptom of it.

Conclusions

Civilian policymakers and strategists, the legislature, the press, the antiwar opposition, and the American people clearly had more influence on the waging of the Vietnam War than their counterparts in World War I Germany had on the conduct of the Great War. Nevertheless, the stab-in-the-back theory is so flawed in argument and so narrow in perspective that the real mystery is why it enjoys any acceptance. Part of the reason stems from its mythological character: it embodies the ideals and institutions of a segment of the society.

The ambiguity of failure in both the War of 1812 and the Korean War made it possible for some influential U.S. officials to overcome anticivilian explanations of defeat with declarations of moral, political, or military victory, consequently preserving the American myth of omnipotence, or at least that part of the myth claiming America had never lost a war. The certain knowledge of defeat in the Vietnam War, however, like the certainty of the South's defeat in the Civil War, has helped bring into being a myth of the Lost Cause, of which the stab-in-the-back legend is an essential part.

Rising from the ruins of the South's decidedly unambiguous military defeat in the Civil War—and fostered by former Confederate political leaders, military men, veterans, evangelical preachers, and Southern writers—the Lost Cause assumed mythical proportions in the late nineteenth century. A phrase originating with Sir Walter Scott's accounts of the "lost cause" of Scotland's independence, its meaning has changed with time. It involves defiance, vindication, nostalgia, escapism, chivalric romance, redemption, and an attempt to retrieve something from calamity. It is also a justification of decisions made and defeat incurred; a timeless ideal of the Southern spirit; an expression of the frustrations of defeat, poverty, and social upheaval; a search for order; an expression of the historical burden of defeat; a memory of loss; an attempt to interpret the place of the South in the nation; an effort to preserve the Southern way of life in spite of military defeat; an evangelical revival; an assertion of moral superiority; and a literary "search for a system of beliefs in the aristocratic legend of the Old South."[70]

Key elements in the South's myth of the Lost Cause include stab-in-the-back themes, such as criticisms of Southern diplomats, civilian leaders, politicians, and others. General Lee, the central figure of the myth—the symbol of the superiority of Southern character, the invincible hero of the war—is portrayed as a tragic figure who, though superior to Ulysses S. Grant and other Northern generals, was defeated by the betrayals of the Confederate government and of subordinates like James Longstreet.[71] As Albion W. Tourgeé observed about post-Reconstruction American fiction concerning Southern Civil War history, "The downfall of empire is always the epoch of romance."[72]

By the 10th anniversary of the end of the war in Southeast Asia, a Vietnam War version of the Lost Cause had arisen, threatening to become, as did the post-Civil War Lost Cause, a civil religion.[73] At least one U.S. president ritualistically declared the war to have been a noble, honorable, idealistic, humanitarian, lost cause.[74] Veterans struggled with memory, frustration, loss, and the burden of defeat, while Rambo-like films symbolically refought the war and won (to popular acclaim), simultaneously exploiting veterans' anguish, prisoner-of-war mistreatment, and grief over those missing in action.[75]

Soldier-of-fortune magazines paid tribute to the memory of professional prowess and bravery, affirming the good cause, recommending the avoidance in future conflicts of mistakes made in Vietnam, and lamenting that soldiers had not been allowed to win[76]—at the same time publicizing mercenary camps and sending "freedom fighter" instructors to Third World hot spots.[77] Right-wing evangelists bemoaned the abandonment of the war, the alleged fulfillment of the domino theory, and the victory of "peaceniks"; they called for a redeeming revival of pre-1960s traditional values.

Former, allegedly weak presidents were ridiculed. Youngsters sported jungle-fatigue apparel, now chic.[78] War toys, war games, and the ROTC made a comeback. Militarism was equated with patriotism. A new, nationalistic fervor called for vindication. Defeat was transformed into anger, which itself was transmuted into a desire to strike out—to win one for our side. National security officials, foreign policy committees, and foundations took encouragement from public-opinion polls said to show that Americans shifted from "pacifism" to "patriotism" in the post-Vietnam War era,[79] and they drew on popular sentiment about the war's Lost Cause to call for a return to militant containment policies, the rehabilitation of America's declining place in the world, and the reestablishment of American hegemony.[80] At stake for these former and present policymakers was the issue of whether the Vietnam syndrome would hinder containment militarism and counterrevolutionary interventionism.

Despite its quasi-historical nature, the stab-in-the-back argument enjoys some currency because it represents the ideals and interests of a segment of society, which, in the wake of defeat in Vietnam, can use its not insignificant resources to tap the national sense of tragedy, guilt, and decline. Another example of how the history of the past is used to shape the perceptions of the present and policies of the future, it is an ersatz premise, a poor substitute for sound history. It mirrors the Vietnam War itself, which was, in a sense, an ersatz conflict, invented for protecting artificially conceived vital interests.

Notes

1. See Richard Dean Burns and Milton Leitenberg, eds., *The Wars in Vietnam, Cambodia and Laos, 1945–1982: A Bibliographic Guide* (Santa Barbara, Calif.: ABC-Clio Information Services, 1984), p. 141; Marvin E. Gettleman et al., eds., *Vietnam and America: A Documented History* (New York: Grove Press, 1985), p. xv; George C. Herring, "American Strategy in Vietnam: The Postwar Debate," *Military Affairs* 46, 2 (April 1982): n. 8; Guenter Lewy, *America in Vietnam* (New York: Oxford University Press, 1978), p. vi; Evan Thomas, "West Point Makes a Comeback," *Time*, 4 November 1985, p. 32.
2. Quoted in Telford Taylor, *Sword and Swastika* (New York: Simon and Schuster, 1952), pp. 32-33.
3. On the origins of the German stab-in-the-back legend, see Gordon Craig, *Politics of the Prussian Army, 1640–1945* (New York: Oxford University Press, 1956), and

John W. Wheeler-Bennett, *The Nemesis of Power: The German Army in Politics, 1918-1945* (London: Macmillan & Co., 1964).

4. Jean-Denis Bredin, *The Affair* (New York: George Braziller, 1986), pp. 532-533.

5. John Steward Ambler, *Soldiers Against the State: The French Army in Politics* (New York: Anchor Books, 1968; first pub. 1966), p. 308.

6. William J. Duiker, "Applying the Lessons of Vietnam: The View from Hanoi," *Indochina Issues*, no. 68, August 1986, p. 2.

7. See "The Vietnamese," in *Vietnam Reconsidered: Lessons from a War*, ed. Harrison E. Salisbury (New York: Harper & Row, 1984), pp. 214-240.

8. "A Newsweek Poll: The Voice of the Vietnam Generation," *Newsweek*, 15 April 1985, p. 37.

9. Adam Clymer, "What Americans Think Now," *New York Times* Magazine, 31 March 1985, p. 34. Cf. George Gallup, Jr., *The Gallup Poll: Public Opinion 1985* (Wilmington, Del.: Scholarly Resources, 1986), p. viii; *Newsweek*, 15 April 1985, p. 37.

10. On the Vietnam syndrome, see George C. Herring, "The 'Vietnam Syndrome' and American Foreign Policy," *Virginia Quarterly Review* 57, 4 (1981): pp. 594-612; and Michael T. Klare, *Beyond the "Vietnam Syndrome": U.S. Interventionism in the 1980s* (Washington, D.C.: Institute for Policy Studies, 1981).

11. James A. Nathan and James K. Oliver, "Public Opinion and U.S. Security Policy," *Armed Forces and Society* 2, 1 (Fall 1975): pp. 58-59.

12. John E. Mueller, *War, Presidents and Public Opinion* (New York: John Wiley & Sons, 1973); John M. Benson, "The Polls: U.S. Military Intervention," *Public Opinion Quarterly* 46, 4 (Winter 1982): pp. 592-598; and Nathan and Oliver, "Public Opinion," pp. 46-62.

13. Douglas Kinnard, "Vietnam Reconsidered: An Attitudinal Survey of U.S. Army General Officers," *Public Opinion Quarterly* 39, 4 (Winter 1975-1976): pp. 445-456; and Douglas Kinnard, *The War Managers* (Hanover, N.H.: University Press of New England, 1977).

14. Ole R. Holsti and James N. Rosenau, *American Leadership in World Affairs: Vietnam and the Breakdown of Consensus* (Boston: Allen and Unwin, 1984), pp. 16-17, 108-173, 206-209.

15. William C. Westmoreland, "Vietnam in Perspective," *Military Review* 59 (January 1979): p. 35, and "The Handling of the Vietnam Episode Was a Shameful National Blunder," (Louisville) *Courier-Journal*, 26 March 1978, pp. D-1, D-3; Richard M. Nixon, *The Real War* (New York: Warner Books, 1980), pp. 100-102.

16. Quoted in Ronnie Dugger, *On Reagan: The Man and His Presidency* (New York: McGraw-Hill, 1983), pp. 240, 244, 343-349, 512-514.

17. Quoted in Laurence I. Barrett, *Gambling with History: Ronald Reagan in the White House* (New York: Penguin Books, 1984), p. 207.

18. *Public Papers of the Presidents of the United States: Ronald Reagan, 1982*, Book I (Washington, D.C.: GPO, 1983), pp. 184-185.

19. Ibid., *1981*, p. 155.

20. Quoted in Robert Pisor, *The End of the Line: The Siege of Khe Sanh* (New York: Ballantine, 1983), p. 50.

21. Quoted in Walter LaFeber, "The Last War, the Next War, and the New Revisionists," *Democracy* 1, 1 (January 1981): p. 93.

22. William C. Westmoreland, *A Soldier Reports* (Garden City, N.Y.: Doubleday, 1976), pp. 357-358, 410; "If We'd Kept Pressure On, We'd Have Won It," *USA Today*, 18 April 1985, p. 11A; Westmoreland, "Vietnam in Perspective," pp. 34-42; Westmoreland, "Handling of the Vietnam Episode," pp. D-1, D-3.

23. Westmoreland, "Vietnam in Perspective," p. 34.

24. U.S. Grant Sharp, *Strategy for Defeat: Vietnam in Retrospect* (San Rafael, Calif.: Presidio Press, 1978), pp. xvii, 1-4, 133-134, 165-166, 205, 242, 268, 267-271; "How to Win the War in South Vietnam," *US News and World Report*, 28 March 1966, pp. 38-41; and "Airpower Could Have Won in Vietnam," *Air Force Magazine* 54 (September 1971): pp. 82-83.

25. Hanson W. Baldwin, "Foreword," in Sharp, *Strategy for Defeat*, pp. xii-xiii.

26. In a sequel, *Television's Vietnam: The Impact of Media* (1985), Accuracy in Media took even more direct aim at the television press for its supposed misrepresentations of the Tet campaign, the battle of Khe Sanh, and the My Lai massacre.

27. In *RN: The Memoirs of Richard Nixon* (New York: Grosset & Dunlap, 1978), p. 387, Nixon claims approvingly that Eisenhower told him that the leaking of classified information in war or peace was treasonable.

28. Richard M. Nixon, *No More Vietnams* (New York: Arbor House, 1985), passim; Nixon, *The Real War*, pp. 22, 86, chap. 5; *RN*, pp. 269, 274, 344-350, 387-388, 393, 752, 754, 757. Jerry W. Sanders used the phrase "containment militarism" in *Peddlers of Crisis: The Committee on the Present Danger and the Politics of Containment* (Boston: South End Press, 1983), p. 11, meaning not merely containment of communism but also the projection of American political and economic hegemony through military force.

29. See *National Review*, 11 May 1972, pp. 510-511; and *American Opinion*, July-August 1970, pp. 91-96. But *American Opinion* was often critical of Nixon; see ibid., pp. 1-18. It tended to be more conspiratorial in its interpretations and more critical of Nixon and U.S. strategy than *National Review*. See also Phyllis Schlafly and (rear admiral) Chester Ward, *Kissinger on the Couch* (New Rochelle, N.Y.: Arlington House, 1975), pp. 127-128, 153-156, 205-210, 272.

30. *National Review*, 16 February 1973, p. 188, and 2 March 1973, p. 278.

31. *National Review*, 16 March 1973, pp. 192, 298-299, 303; *National Review*, 30 March 1973, p. 383; *National Review*, 11 May 1973, pp. 510-511; *American Opinion*, July-August 1970, pp. 91-96, regarded Vietnamization as a rationale for an American pullout from Vietnam. Some writers for both *National Review* and *American Opinion* considered any negotiated settlement as a sellout: *National Review*, 7 September 1965, p. 65; *American Opinion*, June 1968, p. 64.

32. *National Review*, 19 January 1973, p. 82. On several occasions, *National Review* advocated the use of nuclear weapons in Vietnam; see, e.g., *National Review*, 9 March 1965, pp. 187-188, 196.

33. See *National Review*, 5 January 1973, p. 11, and 11 May 1973, pp. 510-511.

34. On the latter point, see *National Review*, 19 January 1973, pp. 74-75.

35. Peter Braestrup, *Big Story: How the American Press and Television Reported and Interpreted the Crisis of Tet 1968 in Vietnam and Washington*, vol. 1 (Boulder,

Colo.: Westview Press, 1977), pp. 4-5; S.L.A. Marshall, "Press Failure in Vietnam," *New Leader*, 10 October 1966, pp. 3-5.

36. Barry Goldwater, *Where I Stand* (New York: McGraw-Hill Book Co., 1964), pp. 28-29.

37. "Joint Chiefs' Memo Disputing McNamara View on Bombing," 14 October 1966, *The Pentagon Papers* as published by the *New York Times* (New York: Bantam Books, 1971), pp. 552-553.

38. Memo, Westmoreland to CINCPAC, 13 June 1965, *The Senator Gravel Edition, The Pentagon Papers: The Defense Department History of United States Decision-making on Vietnam*, vol. 4 (Boston: Beacon Press, 1971), pp. 606-609; *Report on the War in Vietnam (As of 30 June 1968)*, Section II: *Report on Operations in South Vietnam, January 1964–June 1968* by (general) W. C. Westmoreland, commander, U.S. Military Assistance Command, Vietnam (Washington, D.C.: GPO, 1968).

39. Dugger, *On Reagan*, p. 240.

40. Speech, 18 February 1968, Miami University, Oxford, Ohio.

41. Lower on his list of causes were racial tension and drugs; Robert D. Heinl, Jr., "The Collapse of the Armed Forces," *Armed Forces Journal*, June 1971, pp. 30-37.

42. Nixon, *RN*, pp. 269-274; Presentation to the Platform Committee at the Republican National Convention, 1 August 1968, in *Vietnam: Anthology and Guide to a Television History*, ed. Steven Cohen (New York: Alfred A. Knopf, 1983), pp. 309-311.

43. Quoted in Henry A. Kissinger, *White House Years* (Boston: Little, Brown, 1979), pp. 288-289.

44. Quoted in ibid., p. 969.

45. See Sanders, *Peddlers of Crisis*.

46. *National Review*, 10 March 1964, pp. 186, 210; *National Review*, 2 June 1964, pp. 435-436, 441-446; *National Review*, 16 June 1964, p. 475; *National Review*, 22 February 1985, pp. 136-137, 493; *National Review*, 1 June 1965, p. 456; *American Opinion*, April 1965, pp. 3-4; *American Opinion*, February 1968, p. 74; *American Opinion*, May 1968, pp. 1-14; *American Opinion*, June 1968, p. 64; *American Opinion*, April 1969, pp. 39, 41.

47. Herring, "American Strategy in Vietnam," pp. 57-63. See also Wallace J. Thies, *When Governments Collide: Coercion and Diplomacy in the Vietnam Conflict, 1964-1968* (Berkeley: University of California Press, 1980), pp. 215-222.

48. Sanders, *Peddlers of Crisis*, p. 133.

49. See James Clay Thompson, *Rolling Thunder: Understanding Policy and Program Failure* (Chapel Hill: University of North Carolina Press, 1980); "The Air War in North Vietnam, 1965–1968," chap. 1 of *Senator Gravel Edition, Pentagon Papers*, vol. 4, and see esp. "The JASON Summer Study Reports," ibid., pp. 115-124; Raphael Littauer and Norman Uphoff, eds., Air War Study Group, Cornell University, *The Air War in Indochina*, rev. ed. (Boston: Beacon Press, 1972), pp. 35-36ff.

50. Guenter Lewy, "Some Political-Military Lessons of the Vietnam War," *Parameters* 14, 1 (Spring 1984): p. 13; Dorothy C. Donnelly, "A Settlement of Sorts: Henry Kissinger's Negotiations and America's Extrication from Vietnam," *Peace and*

Change 9, 2/3 (Summer 1983): pp. 55-79; Truong Nhu Tang, *A Vietcong Memoir* (New York: Harcourt Brace Jovanovich, 1985), pp. 165-175, 205-209.

51. Sanders, *Peddlers of Crisis*, p. 141.

52. See Bernard Brodie, "Vietnam: Why We Failed," chap. 5, *War and Politics* (New York: Macmillan, 1973), pp. 187-190; Littauer and Uphoff, eds., *The Air War in Indochina*; Pisor, *End of the Line*, passim; Fred Branfman, "Beyond the Pentagon Papers: The Pathology of Power," *Senator Gravel Edition, Pentagon Papers*, vol. 5: *Critical Essays Edited by Noam Chomsky and Howard Zinn*, pp. 294-315.

53. David G. Marr, "The Rise and Fall of 'Counterinsurgency,' 1961-1964," *Senator Gravel Edition, Pentagon Papers*, vol. 5, pp. 202-210; John Shy and Thomas W. Collier, "Revolutionary War," chap. 27 of *Makers of Modern Strategy: From Machiavelli to the Nuclear Age*, ed. Peter Paret (Princeton, N.J.: Princeton University Press, 1986), pp. 854-856. For a critical assessment of American performance based on a study of Vietnamese politics and strategy, see William S. Turley, *The Second Indochina War: A Short Political and Military History, 1954-1975* (New York: New American Library, 1987), pp. 194-201.

54. Kinnard, *The War Managers*, pp. 163-164.

55. See *Study on Military Professionalism* (Carlisle Barracks, Pa.: U.S. Army War College, 30 June 1970); The BDM Corporation, *A Study of Strategic Lessons Learned in Vietnam: Omnibus Executive Summary* (1980); Richard P. Gabriel and Paul L. Savage, *Crisis in Command: Mismanagement in the Army* (New York: Hill & Wang, 1979); Robert J. Graham, "Vietnam: An Infantryman's View of Our Failure," *Military Affairs* 48, 3 (July 1984): pp. 133-139.

56. "Vietnam, Committee to Support the Administration Position," Confidential File ND 19/CO 312, Box 73, Lyndon B. Johnson Library; John P. Roche, 1966-68, Office Files of the President, Box 11, LBJ Library.

57. J. William Fulbright, *The Pentagon Propaganda Machine* (New York: Vintage Books, 1971), pp. 106-107.

58. Analyses of the role of the press are legion; it is useful to begin with "Reporting Vietnam: Eight War Correspondents Rebut S.L.A. Marshall's 'Press Failure in Vietnam,' " *New Leader*, 21 November 1966, pp. 3-16; Phillip Knightley, *The First Casualty: From the Crimea to Vietnam, the War Correspondent as Hero, Propagandist, and Myth Maker* (New York: Harcourt Brace Jovanovich, 1975), chaps. 16, 17; Lawrence W. Lichty, "Comments on the Influence of Television on Public Opinion," in *Vietnam as History: Ten Years After the Paris Peace Accords*, ed. Peter Braestrup (Washington, D.C.: University Press of America, 1984), pp. 158-160; Kathleen J. Turner, *Lyndon Johnson's Dual War: Vietnam and the Press* (Chicago: University of Chicago Press, 1985); James A. Wechsler, "The Press and the War," *Progressive*, June 1967, pp. 18-19; Susan Welch, "Vietnam: How the Press Went Along," *Nation*, 11 October 1971, pp. 327-330; Jules Witcover, "Where Washington Reporting Failed," *Columbia Journalism Review* 9 (Winter 1971): pp. 7-12.

59. Michael Arlen, *Living Room War* (New York: Penguin Books, 1982), p. xiv.

60. Mueller, "Reflections on the Vietnam Antiwar Movement and on the Curious Calm at the War's End," in *Vietnam as History*, ed. Braestrup, pp. 151-157.

61. Charles DeBenedetti, "A CIA Analysis of the Anti-Vietnam War Movement: October 1967," *Peace and Change* 9, 1 (Spring 1983): pp. 31-41.

62. Mueller, "Vietnam Antiwar Movement," in *Vietnam as History*, ed. Braestrup, p. 155.

63. Russell F. Weigley, "Reflections on 'Lessons' from Vietnam," in *Vietnam as History*, ed. Braestrup, pp. 115-124; Herring, "The 'Vietnam Syndrome,' " pp. 594-612.

64. Todd Gitlin, "Seizing History: What We Won and Lost at Home," *Mother Jones*, November 1983, pp. 32-38, 48.

65. See Gettleman et al., eds., *Vietnam and America*, pp. 291-297, 335-338.

66. Gitlin, "Seizing History," pp. 38, 48.

67. DeBenedetti, *The Peace Reform in American History* (Bloomington: Indiana University Press), p. 174.

68. DeBenedetti, "On the Significance of Peace Activism: America, 1961–1975," *Peace and Change* 9, 2/3 (Summer 1983): p. 14.

69. Melvin Small, "The Impact of the Antiwar Movement on Lyndon Johnson, 1965–68: A Preliminary Report," *Peace and Change* 10, 1 (Spring 1984): p. 1.

70. Thomas L. Connelly and Barbara L. Bellows, *God and General Longstreet: The Lost Cause and the Southern Mind* (Baton Rouge: Louisiana State University Press, 1982), p. 4.

71. Thomas L. Connelly, *The Marble Man: Robert E. Lee and His Image in American Society* (New York: Alfred A. Knopf, 1977).

72. Albion W. Tourgeé, "The South as a Field for Fiction," *Forum* 6 (1888–1889): p. 412.

73. In *Baptized in Blood: The Religion of the Lost Cause, 1865–1920* (Athens: University of Georgia Press, 1980), Charles Reagan Wilson argues that the Lost Cause became a civil religion—a set of semi-institutionalized public beliefs and values embodying historical mythology.

74. *Public Papers of the Presidents: Ronald Reagan, 1981*, pp. 155-156; ibid., *1982*, p. 1445; ibid., *1983*, p. 255; Herring, "American Strategy," p. 57; Barrett, *Gambling with History*, p. 41; "President Promises. . . ," *Journal-News* (Hamilton-Fairfield, Ohio), 20 July 1986, p. A-1.

75. *Rambo: First Blood Part II* (1985); *Missing in Action* (1984). Some 1980s motion pictures tapped Vietnam War stab-in-the-back and Lost Cause themes even though their immediate subject matter was not about Vietnam: e.g., *Red Dawn* (1985) and *Amerika* (1987).

76. See *Vietnam Combat*, Spring 1986, and *Back to Battle: Vietnam* (published by *Soldier of Fortune*), February 1986.

77. "Militarism in America," Center for Defense Information, *The Defense Monitor* 15, 3 (1986): p. 7.

78. "Costume Party!" *J.C. Penney's Christmas 1986 Catalogue*, pp. 403, 410-411, blends sexism, racism, and militarism.

79. Sanders, *Peddlers of Crisis*, p. 193, quoting Norman Podhoretz.

80. Christopher Hitchens, "Home is Where the Enemy Is: Oliver North's 'Lessons' of Vietnam," *In These Times*, 25-31 March 1987, pp. 12-13; and Oliver L. North testimony before the Select Committee on Secret Military Assistance to Iran and the Nicaraguan Opposition, 9 July 1987, in *Taking the Stand: The Testimony of Lieutenant Colonel Oliver L. North* (New York: Pocket Books, 1987), pp. 269-271.

JEFFREY P. KIMBALL teaches U.S. military, diplomatic, and peace history at Miami University. He has published articles in such journals as *Military Affairs*, *Peace and Change*, and *Old Northwest*; he has also contributed to the *Encyclopedia of Southern History* and *Great Events in American History*. He is associate editor of the journal *Diplomatic History*.

Once again— Did the press lose Vietnam?

A veteran correspondent takes on the new revisionists

by CHARLES MOHR

At about 3 A.M., January 31, 1968, reporters sleeping in hotels and apartments near Saigon's Lam Son square were awakened by the sound of multiple explosions and heavy small arms fire. Such sounds were not especially unusual, but the volume was. I dressed and left my hotel, but was waved back by a jeepload of nearly hysterical American military police shouting, "Get off the streets, we're under attack." After going up to the hotel roof for a few minutes and watching tracer fire over large areas of the city, I again left the hotel and trotted a couple of blocks to the Associated Press office, which was manned twenty-four hours a day. There I learned that fighting was reportedly taking place in many areas of the city, including near the gates of the Vietnamese Presidential Palace. (Reports of attacks on South Vietnamese provincial and district capitals also began to come in. In an apparent misunderstanding of their orders, the Viet Cong had attacked seven towns the night before.) Even more startling was word that the United States embassy was under attack; my friend Peter Arnett of the AP was checking it out. The Tet, or lunar new year, truce proclaimed by the South Vietnamese government had come to a noisy end.

At first light a small group of reporters and cameramen was huddled with military police at the corner of Hai Ba Trung and Thong Nhat streets near the entrance of the walled United States embassy. A Viet Cong sapper squad had gotten onto the embassy grounds, and some were still alive and holding out. One of the M.P. sergeants told us that the V.C. were also in the chancery building. We heard M.P. radio traffic making the same statement. As it turned out, the report was not true.

As U.S. Army helicopters landed one at a time on the embassy roof and discharged a platoon of riflemen from the 101st Airborne division, another friend, Mert Perry of *Newsweek*, said, "Do you realize we are watching American troops assault our own embassy?"

By about 9 A.M. the embassy compound had been retaken; a talk with the U.S. Mission Coordinator, George Jacobson, who had been trapped in a villa in the compound, had provided a vivid, partly eyewitness, story; and I was at a typewriter banging it out. I was also already slightly behind normal deadline.

In a mixture of journalistic conservatism and sloppiness I waited until the sixteenth paragraph of the story before writing that some of the attackers were "said" to have held lower floors of the chancery building for several hours.

Six hours had elapsed.

The test of Tet

I hope to make several points with the above narrative.

In early 1982, another journalist wrote: "It is charged the American press turned an enemy defeat into a political victory for North Vietnam by concentrating on one brief and unsuccessful Communist action, the attack on the United States embassy." He added that this "emphasis, it is argued, reinforced pressure at home for a negotiated settlement." A number of neoconservative essayists, New Right polemicists, and other Vietnam revisionists, to whom I shall return, have made similar arguments, as part of a larger framework of complaint about Vietnam War journalism.

As I hope to make clear in this article, I believe the performance of the news media during the Tet offensive — and, indeed, throughout the entire course of the Vietnam War — is open to legitimate criticism. It is also worthy of some praise. But let the criticism be legitimate. Some of the criticism of Vietnam war correspondents, it appears, has not been based on a careful re-examination of the journalistic product.

At 9 A.M. on January 31 the Vietnam press corps was in no position to declare a result, victory or otherwise, in the Tet offensive (we were not even calling it

Pinned down: *the author under shellfire near An Loc, Easter offensive, 1972*

Charles Mohr is a New York Times *reporter who, between 1962 and 1973, spent a total of four years covering the Vietnam war.*

that yet), a complex event that was to continue for many weeks of intense combat. We had not yet had breakfast on the first day of what was to be a prolonged adventure; we had not yet even had a formal news briefing by Military Assistance Command Vietnam on the situation in Saigon and in South Vietnam as a whole. But by then we knew that much of Saigon was overrun by Viet Cong, and that many towns had also been overrun, although most government and U.S. military compounds in the towns were holding out.

No professional, serious journalist could have ignored the embassy attack. Not many overplayed it; there was no significant overemphasis on it. My own story was a sidebar to the main war roundup which another *New York Times* reporter, because of the time difference between Saigon and New York, had written the night before, and which he was updating on deadline that morning.

By 9 A.M. of the first day of the offensive the reporters were essentially finished with the embassy story. The next day I corrected in *The New York Times* the deplorable error about the Viet Cong having been in the chancery (an error made by all news organizations, as far as I know, but unfortunately not corrected by all). And I subsequently wrote a couple of other stories about embassy security when facts on that subject that were embarrassing to the U.S. Mission came to light. But I and other reporters did not give the embassy attack prolonged, obsessive coverage while ignoring the subsequent course of battle. If some failed to report Viet Cong losses adequately in subsequent weeks, this was not a consequence of their having reported a six-hour attack by a nineteen-man sapper squad. The thesis that there was such a connection is only one of scores of myths about Vietnam journalism that, together, constitute a larger and pernicious myth.

More is at stake in this debate than wounded journalistic egos.

Almost twenty-two years have elapsed since the administration of John F. Kennedy involved the United States in what was called "combat support" in South Vietnam, a concept that brought thousands of military advisers and hundreds of helicopters to assist in the prosecution of a proxy war. Less than four years later

UPI

The shock of Tet: *When the Viet Cong invaded the U.S. embassy compound (above) in Saigon in January 1968, Americans were stunned. They would have been less stunned, critics charge, if the press had not overplayed the story.*

it had become a real war for United States combat troops.

The ultimate failure (I have chosen that word with care — United States troops were never defeated militarily and, until very late in the war, no sizable South Vietnamese unit ever broke, was overrun, or defected) of that enterprise became undeniable by April of 1975, when Saigon fell to North Vietnamese troops. So painful was the Vietnam experience that both the U.S. Army and civilians seemed to want to put Vietnam out of memory.

In the last few years, however, there has been a resurgence of interest in the war. A number of historical treatments and analytical discussions of the conflict have been published. Even a controversy about the design of the emotionally moving Vietnam memorial in Washington aroused controversy about the way the war was fought, the way it was supported or obstructed by Congress and the public — and the way it was reported by American journalists. The ambitious public television series *Vietnam: A Television History*, which is being broadcast this autumn, will almost certainly increase the interest of adults who had tended to expunge Vietnam from their memories and to interest people too young to have experienced or understood the war.

Unfortunately, much of the discussion of the war has involved a kind of revisionist "history" which, in fact, comes from people who are not historians and who are not using historical methods.

This does not apply to such careful work as *Vietnam: A History*, Stanley Karnow's recently published history of the war (he was also chief correspondent of *A Television History*.) Nor does it apply to Peter Braestrup's *Big Story*, a lengthy study of how journalism covered the Tet offensive. Braestrup, who himself was an able Vietnam correspondent and a witness to Tet, may have annoyed some of his colleagues with his thesis that Tet was such an "extreme" event and reportorial challenge that it simply overwhelmed the Vietnam press corps. But Braestrup first carefully reread the journalistic record: the product. He then reprinted most of it. If his thesis is thought debatable, or only disagreeable, by some, it at least rests on a foundation of evidence. Being reminded of what we said, and did not say, proves in some cases to be embarrassing. It is less troubling, however, than the surly critiques of the polemicists.

Notable among the critics, writing and speaking with varying degrees of bitterness and coherence, have been the editorial page of *The Wall Street Journal*, Robert S. Elegant (a former *Los Angeles Times* reporter), William F. Buckley, John P. Roche, Walt W. Rostow, William C. Westmoreland, Richard M. Nixon, and Henry A. Kissinger. This is not meant to be a full list, nor do I intend to focus my rebuttal specifically on those I have named. Certain of these critics have also constructed a pontoon bridge from the Vietnam quagmire to Central America by contending that reporters now covering Central America are falling into the same bad habits the critics attribute to the reporters who covered Vietnam.

Some of these critics have drawn conclusions that bear little relation to the actual conduct of mainstream journalists for major news organizations in the years 1961 to 1975. Some of their conclusions also reflect an astonishing misrepresentation, or at least misunderstanding, of the nature of the war. This can be especially disturbing when it comes from former civilian officials who helped to manage and prosecute the war. There is also confusion about the manner in which events actually unfolded, the problems of Vietnam war correspondence, and what the journalists *actually* said and wrote.

The making of a myth

Although I like to argue that wars are not lost in the newspapers (or in television broadcasts), the revisionist argument goes far toward making that claim. In some cases it is flatly made. The core of the complaint is complicated, and not always quite coherent. Although to answer the critics it is necessary to discuss the entire course of the war, it is also convenient to focus on Tet.

One element of the revisionist argument is that Tet was not only a "victory" for the U.S.-South Vietnamese coalition, but that this was clearly and unmistakably true, and that willful misrepresentation by reporters caused a collapse of United States domestic morale in the first days of the offensive.

Certainly, massive erosion both of domestic American public support for the war, and of public confidence in the country's policymakers, did eventually follow the Tet offensive.* Such erosion was already well advanced among the members of the antiwar movement. But, in its magnitude, the loss of support among the general public to some extent genuinely surprised me and a number of other "veteran" Vietnam war correspondents. The revisionists ascribe the erosion to hysterical reporting from Vietnam; my own belief is that it was the result of strong public shock following the highly optimistic public claims of progress by American officials in the fall of 1967. A few journalists lost their composure, but most Vietnam correspondents did not. I and most others, even in the earliest hours of the offensive, did not believe that the enemy was going to "win" a military victory, capture the Saigon post office, and bayonet us and the allied high command in our beds. No fair reading of the body of news stories produced in early 1968 will sustain that myth.

* In the latest edition of his book, Braestrup cites poll data which casts strong doubt on the assertion that early Tet reports from Vietnam caused a significant loss of support for the war among the general public.

I did not share the sentiments of Senator John Stennis, who said a few days after the Tet kickoff that it was "embarrassing" and "humiliating" to the United States. But I could sympathize with him. Like Arthur Krock of *The New York Times* in 1963 at the time of the battle of Ap Bac, Stennis had tended to support — and for all I know, believe — the official optimism, and now felt betrayed.

In *Big Story*, Braestrup wrote that the press "emphasized the political and psychological effects" of the enemy attacks. (So poisonous was domestic feeling at that time that the mere use of the word "enemy" to describe men who were killing American troops usually drew angry letters. And when, at the end of the three-week battle for the ancient imperial capital of Hue, I wrote of the "liberation" of Hue, one reader angrily denounced me for doing so.) Braestrup's argument, it seems to me, was far more true of stories written in the United States than of those filed by relatively objective reporters in Vietnam, who did not believe it was their job to assess political effects in the United States, but who did speculate about the V.C.'s desire for a psychological victory.

Like many other journalists in Vietnam, I assumed and wrote, early in the offensive, that it was logical to believe that North Vietnam and the Viet Cong were seeking a psychological victory, since it was difficult to believe that they seriously thought they could achieve an actual military victory by pitting a nationwide assault force estimated at about 35,000 men against a force of more than one million regular United States and South Vietnamese troops.* This was not a political or ideological notion, but the conclusion of a reporter who had begun to gain some military sophistication.

There followed an irony, or perhaps a paradox. Senior officials of the U.S. Mission Vietnam came to dislike it that a reporter for an influential paper was

* It subsequently also seemed absurd when MACV in the first few days claimed that more than 30,000 V.C. had been killed in action.

writing that the enemy had probably not sought a military victory, even though the reporter did so because he believed that the possibility of success had been so inherently remote. Subjectively, the argument that the V.C. had sought, but had been denied, a purely military victory became very attractive to the officials. And objectively, captured documents indicated that the communist leadership had really believed in the concept of a "general uprising" by the South Vietnamese civilian population that could bring about both the collapse of the Saigon government and the forced evacuation of American troops. Some American officials, whose intellectual honesty was respected by the reporters, then met at length with some of us to argue the thesis that the Vietnamese communists had indeed believed in the general uprising and had sought not "merely" the destruction of an already frayed domestic American support for the war, but a clear-cut military victory. The relationship between the journalists and these unquestionably honest members of the official mission was never as hostile or adversarial as some revisionists have painted it. Most of the reporters, including me, came to accept the general-uprising theory and to describe it in news stories.

Were official views muffled?

This suggests several other significant elements in the discussion of the role and performance of journalists over the long haul in Vietnam. As early as late 1961, when the great Homer Bigart arrived in Vietnam for *The New York Times*, a degree of tension developed between some officials and most of the then tiny press corps. These differences, however, were not over the "morality" of the war or the desirability of winning (a concept not easy to define, then or later). Essentially, the dispute involved optimism versus pessimism, growing out of conflicting views about the way the war was being prosecuted and about the viability of the South Vietnamese government in a revolutionary conflict.

This debate was not essentially, as some seem to believe, a quarrel between the press and U.S. officials in Vietnam. It was, rather, a quarrel between factions within the U.S. Mission. For the most part, field advisers closest to the action

UPI

Calling it quits: *On March 21, 1968, in the wake of the Tet offensive, President Johnson announced he would not run for reelection. Was growing disenchantment with the war in part a result of biased reporting from Vietnam?*

and to the Vietnamese took the pessimistic view. Some of the more senior officials in Saigon, who were reporting to Washington on the progress of the programs they were themselves administering, were publicly and persistently optimistic. The reporters quickly became aware of this dispute because brilliant younger field officials and officers, as exemplified by the late John Paul Vann, increasingly turned to the journalists. The reporters did not invent the somber information that sometimes appeared in their stories. Nor did they relentlessly emphasize it.

One of the persistent myths about Vietnam journalism is that the copy was deeply colored by ideology, that it was loaded with strong advocacy, and that it muffled the voice and views of officialdom. Again, this misrepresents the actual news product. Much of it was cautious and bland — probably, in retrospect, too bland. For practical reasons, journalists always reported the claims, appraisals, and statements of the senior officials who asserted that "progress" was being made. These stories almost always got prominent play. At many points in the war, progress *was* being made and many journalists could see and agree that this was taking place. Less often, and seldom in shrill tones, correspondents also reported the countervailing views of Americans who were eager to place greater pressure on the South Vietnamese for better management of their war. It is mostly the latter stories that the revisionists and embittered officials, now retired, seem to remember today.

There is also the persistent argument that, because of television, Vietnam "was the first war that came into people's living rooms" and that TV coverage caused a fatal revulsion for the war. Several aspects of this argument fascinate me. It is often advanced by pro-war people who suggest that "seeing" the war did not bother them, but that other Americans could not be expected to withstand such a shock to the emotions. It also seems to reflect how isolated and safe America has been for most of its history. Most wars literally, not merely photographically, go through people's living rooms. The awesome casualty lists of World War I, the London Blitz, the stark still photography of World War II have never seemed to me to be less psychologically important than Vietnam TV coverage.

Rereading the Tet coverage, I am struck by how much space and emphasis were given to claims of "victory" when they were made. But, as we shall see, officials spent much of that period not claiming victory, but warning of harder fighting ahead and ominous enemy threats.

A victory concealed?

The most serious charge made by the revisionists, and one of the most frequently repeated, is that the Vietnam press corps failed to report an allied victory at Tet and, indeed, concealed its existence. There were, unquestionably, flaws in the purely military coverage; and not all of them were sins of omission. But in its raw form the charge does not seem to hold up.

I believe that Tet represented a serious *tactical* defeat for the Viet Cong and their North Vietnamese superiors. But this did not ultimately constitute a strategic victory for South Vietnam. That should be obvious. It is also argued that Tet shattered, nearly destroyed, the indigenous guerrillas and forced North Vietnam to continue the war with its own regular army troops. This was to a large extent true; but it was also what almost all serious journalists reported (though anyone who was around at the time of the 1973 "truce" quickly learned that there were still many Viet Cong in the countryside five years later).

In early January of 1969, I wrote a story, which was printed on the front page of the *Times*, that began: "After days of overoptimism, false starts, half-completed programs and lost opportunities, the allied forces in Vietnam appear to be making major progress against the enemy." The story also said that officials with reputations for intellectual honesty and skepticism "believe they see a drastic decline in the fighting quality and political abilities of the Viet Cong guerrillas and modest improvements in South Vietnamese and American prosecution of the war. Taken together, these may have broken the stalemate of previous years." (The story also contained plenty of qualifications and warnings that great problems persisted.)

Did the story come too late, as I suspect some revisionists would argue? Perhaps. But, although I was proud of my willingness to follow my reporting to any conclusions to which that reporting led, the real point today is that the story turned out to be essentially wrong. It appeared in print just before Nixon and Kissinger took office. They adopted a policy of "Vietnamization" of the war. And although the pace of American withdrawal seemed too slow to many people in this country, it seemed fatally rapid to some journalists in Vietnam. Then, in 1973, Kissinger signed a peace treaty that left some 140,000 regular North Vietnamese troops on South Vietnamese soil. Together, these steps guaranteed ultimate collapse. The stalemate of previous years was broken, but in an entirely different way.

As for the argument that the reporters were much too slow to accept the concept of at least a purely military victory at Tet, re-examination of the record is again revealing. Claims of victory were faithfully reported, often on the front page; apparently, Congress and the public were no longer so willing to believe. In the meantime, officers and officials in Vietnam kept warning that "second wave" attacks were likely, that the enemy was still full of fight. I and some other reporters tended journalistically to declare the battle for Saigon over within a few days — and we kept being fooled. Space will permit only a small sample of hundreds of incidents. On February 21, 123 troops were killed in heavy fighting at the city line. On March 4, forty-eight Americans were killed in an ambush near the airport. On March 12, General Westmoreland predicted "very heavy fighting" in the northern provinces. On May 5, the "second wave" struck and the notorious police chief, General Loan, was seriously wounded on a downtown bridge. Casualties soared. (Shortly thereafter several journalists were killed in the Cholon section, an American armed helicopter accidentally killed the mayor of Saigon in an airstrike against Communist troops not far from downtown, and, during a spooky jeep reconnaissance of the city, Arnett and I discovered the bodies of several Korean reporters executed by V.C. at a gasoline service station.) In one two-week period in May, more than 1,100 American troops were killed in action, the worst losses in any such a period in the entire war.

The revisionists often suggest that the journalists failed to take into account the heavy enemy losses; in fact, the reporters in Vietnam did report that the Viet Cong were suffering staggering casualties. In any case, I doubt that the journalists can be accused of concealing a transparently clear allied victory — one which did not seem so clear until autumn, even to officials. Only in the postwar era have they tried to rehabilitate their reputations with such assertions.

Of trust and distrust

As both its practitioners and critics should recognize, journalism is an imperfect instrument. The Vietnam reporters were far from blameless. Some stateside editors and executives also failed, both early and late, to assign enough staffers, or any staffers, to the story. The Vietnam press corps was woefully short on language skills (the reporters now covering Central America seem to me better equipped, both linguistically and intellectually, for their assignment). Many were not sophisticated militarily, and too many posed as ordnance experts, ready to pronounce on the caliber of an incoming shell.

Before and after Tet, the story did often tend to overwhelm the essentially conventional journalistic methods we employed. Much went unreported, although this may have been unavoidable in a sprawling nation of forty-four provinces and scores of allied divisions and brigades.

Granted that much went unreported, that factual errors were not rare, that sometimes we were too argumentative and skeptical (although much of the time we were far too gullible), that we spent too much time covering American troops and too little with the South Vietnamese. Still, in a broad sense, the coverage seems sound in retrospect. Not only ultimately, but also at each major milestone of the war, the weight of serious reporting corresponds quite closely to the historical record. Revisionists seem to fault correspondents for distrusting the version of events propounded by the most optimistic senior officials in Vietnam. But what if the correspondents had believed that version and had been guided by it in carrying out their assignment? In that case, the reporters' reputations, which are not unblemished, would be irredeemably tarnished. ■

Journal of Broadcasting
Volume 28:4, Fall 1984

An Analysis of Television Coverage of the Vietnam War

Oscar Patterson III

Between 1965 and 1975 no other single event so dominated television news programs as did the war in Vietnam. Yet analysis of the content of actual news broadcasts does not support the contention that nightly news programs were filled with pictures of battle, or the dead, dying and wounded.

Between 1965 and 1975, no single event so dominated television news as did the war in Vietnam. And only the domestic crisis precipitated by the Watergate affair was able to remove the Vietnam quagmire from the television screens of the nation for a sustained period of time.

Vietnam has been described as, among other things, the first war America ever lost; the most divisive American war since the Civil War; and as America's first television war. Michael Arlen called Vietnam history's "first living room war;" and David Halberstam has lent his support to that thesis.[1] It is even asserted that television "projected into the American home night after night not only pictures of American troops dead and dying and killing, but of the terrible destruction American might was wrecking on a peasant society. . . . As a result, the war, with all its 'horrors' was fought in everyone's living room."[2] And out of this graphic coverage, journalists and historians suggest, came an influence on American public opinion that far exceeds the actual events of the war itself.[3]

While there appears little doubt that American public opinion tended to polarize against the American involvement in Vietnam, systematic, objective analysis of the actual news broadcasts does not support the contention that nightly news programs were filled with pictures of "American troops dead and dying and killing." Even Michael Arlen, the critic who coined the phrase "living room war" has recently begun to question the generally accepted

---

Manuscript accepted for publication, April 1984.

[1]David Halberstam, *The Powers That Be: Process of Ruling Class Domination in America* (New York: Alfred A. Knopf, 1979), p. 514.

[2]Leonard Ziedenberg, "Vietnam and Electronic Journalism: Lessons of the Living Room War," *Broadcasting*, 19 May 1975, p. 36.

[3]"The Epilogue to Vietnam Proves Hard," *Broadcasting*, 5 May 1975, p. 36.

belief that nightly news accounts of Vietnam were filled with "killing and shooting."[4]

The emphasis of this study, therefore, was to investigate the content of nightly television news coverage of the Vietnam war. The analysis utilized the following questions as a basis for research: (1) Was coverage of the Vietnam war, in fact, a dominant portion of nightly news programs for the period under analysis? (2) Was television coverage of the Vietnam war an ongoing parade of film footage showing the American public not only battle, but also the dead, dying and wounded? (3) As the years passed, did television coverage of the Vietnam war vary in terms of number of stories aired and amount of graphic display of battle and of the dead, dying and wounded? And, (4) should the content prove to be less graphic than suggested, is there an alternative explanation for the public's recall of television coverage of the Vietnam war?

Method

For this study, a stratified random sample of television news programs drawn from the three major networks — ABC, CBS and NBC — was studied. The universe for the study was identified as being all regular evening television news programs broadcast by the three major networks between August 5, 1968 and August 15, 1973. Guidance in establishing an appropriate sample for analysis was obtained from Stempel[5] and Jones and Carter.[6] Stempel originally noted that, for a daily publication, increasing the sample size beyond 12 for a single year does not provide marked differences in the results. And Jones and Carter, replicating Stempel's study, stated that even though the data obtained from a random sample will never match exactly the true data, the estimate derived from the sample population using Stempel's sample size of 12 to represent one year's body of a daily publication compares closely enough as to make the sample statistically significant.

The sample analyzed was composed of 180 regular evening television news programs: 60 drawn from each of the three major networks. The sample was stratified into 12-month blocks, each block representing one year. This allowed for year by year trend analyses. Twelve programs were drawn for each year from each network. For this study, a year was defined as

[4]Michael Arlen, "The Falklands, Vietnam, and Our Collective Memory," *The New Yorker*, 16 August 1982, pp. 72–73.

[5]Guido H. Stemple III, "Sampling Size in Classifying Subject Matters in Dailies," *Journalism Quarterly* 29:333–334 (Summer 1952).

[6]Robert Jones and Robert Carter, "Some Procedures for Estimating 'News Hole' in Content Analysis," *Public Opinion Quarterly* 37:102–109 (Fall 1959).

beginning on August 5 and ending on August 4 except for the period 1972–1973. For this last period the ending date was extended to August 15. All programs analyzed were selected randomly by date with one program from each network being chosen for each individual date. This allows for comparison between networks across time.

The dates noted for the beginning and ending dates of the sample were imposed on the study for two reasons. First, the video tapes viewed in the analysis were obtained from the Vanderbilt Television News Archives which did not begin recording off the air until August 5, 1968.[7] And second, for this study, the Vietnam War was defined as ending on August 15, 1973. It was on this date that the last US bombing mission was flown over Cambodia.[8]

Once the sample was selected, the coding process began. Since the most common method of expressing content analysis data is through frequencies and percentages,[9,10] this study utilized a story count process based on the assumption that frequency of appearance is a reflection of implied importance, attention or emphasis. The sampling unit was the individual television news program and the recording unit was the individual story. Individual stories were delimited based on the referential unit definition given by Krippendorff.[11]

The basic goal of the analysis was to produce a study that was objective, systematic and replicable. To this end, the coding process involved several steps. First, the video tape of each program was viewed for familiarization. During this viewing information related to network identification, program date, program length and total number of stories was recorded. Each program was then viewed a second time during which information about individual stories was recorded. During this second viewing, the recording instrument consisted of a form with 48 major topical categories listed. Each story was recorded as belonging in one and only one of the categories. The 48 major topical categories identified and defined for this study ranged from "American Scene" to "U.S. Government" to "Weather." "Vietnam" was one of the

---

[7]Even though US Marines landed in Vietnam on March 8, 1965, the available television programs for this analysis begin on August 5, 1968. Prior to that date Department of Defense kinescopes were prepared, but they contain news items of interest specifically to the military and thus are edited versions of the broadcasts. Also, the kinescopes are now located in the National Archives and were not available for this study. The Vanderbilt archive, though beginning in 1968, was available.

[8]"Bombing in Cambodia Stopped, Marking Official U.S. End of Combat in Southeast Asia," *The New York Times,* 15 August 1973, p. 1.

[9]Bernard Berelson, *Content Analysis in Communication Research* (Glencoe, IL: Free Press, 1952), p. 18.

[10]Klaus Krippendorff, *Content Analysis: An Introduction to Its Methodology* (Beverly Hills, CA: Sage Publications, 1980), p. 11.

[11]*Ibid*, p. 21.

48 categories.[12] Guidelines in establishing the 48 categories were obtained from *Time* and *Newsweek* magazines and from discussions with colleagues.

A third viewing of each program was utilized to generate data about the stories coded under the category "Vietnam." Each story coded into the "Vietnam" category was further analyzed utilizing a coding instrument that provided for each story to be sorted into one or more of 45 content categories (a single story could be coded into more than one content category), six journalistic writing style categories and 10 presentational style categories.[13] The coding instrument utilized in this analysis was based on a previously reported study conducted by Bailey.[14] During this portion of the analysis emphasis was placed on the content of the story utilizing the 45 content codes with secondary emphasis being placed on journalistic or presentation style.

Reliability data was obtained by utilizing a second judge to analyze a total of 15 programs (one randomly selected program per network per year). Evaluation of the data utilized Scott's *pi* which corrects for number of categories in the set and probable frequency, and Holsti's composite reliability. For the 48 topics used, composite reliability was .94 and *pi* was .892. For the 45 content areas, composite reliability was .98 and *pi* was .882.

Analysis

The analysis of the sample of 180 regular evening television news programs provided 3502 individual stories. Of the 3502 stories, 847 or 24.2 percent were coded "Vietnam."

It appears rather obvious, then, from the small amount of data reported above that Vietnam was a dominant topic for the programs analyzed based upon the number of Vietnam-related stories aired. This dominance of television news by Vietnam-related stories, while relatively constant throughout the period under analysis, did vary to some degree from year to year. In fact, as the data in Table I indicate, network news programs in this sample devoted a larger percentage of their stories to Vietnam during the final year of American combat activity than during the period 1968–1969 when the war was at its height and US battlefield casualties most numerous.

Looking beyond total data certain trends of coverage appeared in this

[12]A complete list of the 48 content categories along with operational definitions is available from the author. Send a large, stamped, self-addressed envelope to: Oscar Patterson III, P.O. Box 42135, Fayetteville, NC 28309.

[13]A complete list of the 45 content codes, six journalistic writing styles and 10 presentation styles along with operational definitions is available from the author. See 12 above.

[14]George A. Bailey, "The Vietnam War According to Chet, David, Walter, Harry, Peter, Bob, Howard and Frank: A Content Analysis of Journalistic Performance (Ph.D. diss., The University of Wisconsin, 1973) pp. 102–331.

Table I
Percentage of Vietnam Related Stories Broadcast by Network and by Year

	Yearly Percentages and Total Percentages					
Source and Identity	1968-1969	1969-1970	1970-1971	1971-1972	1972-1973	Total
Total Stories Broadcast	714	758	712	676	642	3502
Percentage Vietnam-related	(20.7)	(27.3)	(27.0)	(21.5)	(24.1)	(24.2)
CBS Total Broadcast	248	276	241	228	187	1180
Percentage Vietnam-related	(18.6)	(30.1)	(29.1)	(21.1)	(22.5)	(24.5)
ABC Total Broadcast	233	230	206	208	209	1086
Percentage Vietnam-related	(25.3)	(27.8)	(32.5)	(21.2)	(24.9)	(26.3)
NBC Total Broadcast	233	252	265	240	246	1236
Percentage Vietnam-related	(18.5)	(23.8)	(20.8)	(22.1)	(24.8)	(22.0)

sample. Not only did CBS carry the most Vietnam-related stories, it also carried the most such stories in a single year — 83 in 1969–1970. ABC, on the other hand, carried the fewest total news stories, but the largest percentage of Vietnam-related stories — 26.3 percent. And NBC, which carried the most total stories, aired the smallest number and the smallest percentage of Vietnam-related stories.

When "Vietnam" was removed from the list of categories under analysis only two topics per network reached or exceeded a level of 5 percent of the total per-story coverage and no more than five topics covered by CBS and NBC, and four topics covered by ABC, achieved an arbitrarily established level of 50 stories per network. Of the categories most closely related to "Vietnam" in definition ("Terrorism" and "War — not Vietnam"), only ABC devoted sufficient coverage to either one to allow it to surpass the level of 50 stories per network.

While Vietnam-related stories may have dominated television news programs in this sample, the majority of the time none of the networks carried stories which included film or photographs of combat. As the data in Table II indicate, stories which carried such graphic coverage comprised only 4.2 percent of the total Vietnam-related stories aired on CBS; only 3.1 percent of that carried by ABC; and only 2.9 percent of the Vietnam-related stories carried by NBC. In addition, there were periods in the sample analyzed,

Table II
Percentage of Vietnam-Related Stories that Included Film or Photographs of Combat or the Dead or Wounded by Network and by Year

Source and Identity	Yearly Percentages and Total Percentages					
	1968–1969	1969–1970	1970–1971	1971–1972	1972–1973	Overall
CBS						
Combat	6.5	6.0	0.0	6.3	2.4	4.2
Dead or Wounded	2.2	2.4	1.4	10.4	0.0	3.1
ABC						
Combat	6.8	0.0	1.5	9.1	0.0	3.1
Dead or Wounded	1.7	4.7	0.0	0.0	1.9	1.7
NBC						
Combat	0.0	3.3	3.6	3.8	3.3	2.9
Dead or Wounded	0.0	0.0	0.0	5.7	3.3	1.8

during which no items appeared on an individual network containing film or photographs of combat. And at no point did any single network for the sample analyzed give Vietnam-related stories containing film or photographs of combat at a level in excess of 9.1 percent (ABC for 1971–1972) of its war-related coverage.

If network television coverage was not a daily pictorial account of battle in Vietnam, was it, then, a constant procession of the dead, dying and wounded? In answer, an emphatic "no" must be given based on the data analyzed in this study. In fact, there was little graphic (graphic defined as including film or photographs) coverage of the dead, dying or wounded found in the sample.

As the data in Table II indicate, utilization of stories that included film or photographs of the dead or wounded in the Vietnam war in this sample of network news programming was at an even lower rate than utilization of stories that included film or photographs of combat. CBS presented nine such items for an overall rating of 3.1 percent of its Vietnam-related coverage compared to 4.2 percent for its use of stories containing film or photos of combat. ABC and NBC both aired only five stories each that contained film or photographs of the dead, dying or wounded accounting for only 1.7 percent of ABC's Vietnam-related coverage, and only 1.8 percent of NBC's coverage of the war.

News stories that reported on the dead or wounded but did not include film or photographs were much more common than those which included graphic coverage: CBS aired 43 such items; ABC carried 23; and NBC reported on 29. Of course, the weekly "body count" was a part of the overall Vietnam experience. Generally reported in terms of total dead, wounded or missing for the preceding week, and total dead, wounded and missing to date, these reports became common fare in the media's coverage of the war.

404

However, they usually appeared only once a week — generally day — and did not include pictures. For the sample analyzed, CBS c such reports, ABC had 21 and NBC carried 10.

The data obtained in this analysis of a stratified random sample of re network television news programs indicate that for the period analyzed .e topic "Vietnam" dominated network television news to the extent that a plurality of the total stories carried was devoted to that topic. The data does not support the contention that television coverage of Vietnam was a daily parade of film footage showing the American public not only battle, but also the dead, dying and wounded. Finally, the data analyzed in this study does not provide a clear alternative to the popular belief that television news coverage of Vietnam was filled with pictures of battle and the dead, dying and wounded.

Conclusions and Discussion

As noted, there appears to be a generally held belief that "most Americans ... watched the fighting and dying in Vietnam on television" on a regular basis.[15] Lichty and Fromson suggested, however, that there were a few images of the war in Vietnam that are remembered by the public as symbols of that war: the Buddhist monk immolating himself; General Loan and the Viet Cong; the little girl accidently hit by napalm; and the Marine with the Zippo lighter.[16] Add to these the photographs carried in *Life* magazine that showed armored vehicles bringing wounded Marines from the citadel at Hue during the Tet offensive of 1968, and the cover of the same magazine for January 21, 1973 which carried the photograph of an American soldier and the headline "A weeks dead in Vietnam: the only boy who died," and a series of dramatic, striking, memorable impressions emerge. But these are not the stuff from which the daily media coverage of Vietnam was composed. They were the few highly dramatic events that occurred during a very long ten years.

This leads to the conclusion, then, based upon the data analyzed as well as upon the available literature, that a form of selective perception (and more importantly selective retention) on the part of the general public of certain highly dramatic events has led to the projection of those events as characteristic of television coverage of the Vietnam war to a far greater extent than was actually true. This study tends to suggest that the television audience possibly was more attracted by the unusual, the infrequent pictorial accounts of the

---

[15] "Fire From the Mountain: A Country Fiddler Scores With a City Boy's Tune," *Time*, 10 May 1982, p. 108.

[16] Lawrence Lichty and Murray Fromson, "Comparing Notes on Television's Coverage of the War," *Center Magazine*, May 1979, pp. 42–46.

more graphic types — actual film of battle or film or photos of the dead, dying and wounded — and thus have projected these infrequent episodes as common for all television news coverage.

It is not to be assumed, either, that the media have done nothing to aid in this selective recall/retention process. On May 25, 1982, Mort Cohen, General Manager of WLOS-TV in Asheville, North Carolina, stated: "During the Vietnam conflict, we saw the horrors and death and destruction of war nearly every night on national television."[17] And Lynne Shafer Gross in her introductory telecommunications text stated: "Filmed reports of battles appeared almost nightly on the evening news programs."[18] Even James Michener in his book *The Quality of Life* attempts to illustrate the content and power of the nightly television news reports by writing: "Abraham Lincoln would not have been able to prosecute the Civil War to a successful conclusion had television been flooding the contemporary scene with daily pictures . . . of the stark horror of Vicksburg."[19]

Based on the sample analyzed and the data obtained, it is concluded that television did not *show* us the dead, dying and wounded nearly every night on the nightly news, though it did report it. Nor did Americans *watch* the fighting and dying in Vietnam on a regular basis on regular network television news programs. Instead, we suggest, a few graphic, highly dramatic events appear to have so impinged on the public's — and the media's —consciousness as to drastically alter their recall of the daily television coverage of the Vietnam war and war-related events.

Oscar Patterson III is an Associate Professor in the Department of Communicative Arts, Pembroke State University. He received his Ph.D. degree from the University of Tennessee in 1982. His research interests are in media coverage of the Vietnam War and its influence on public opinion about the war and the warrior.

---

[17]Mort Cohen, "A Free Press," WLOS-TV, Asheville, North Carolina, May 25, 1982.

[18]Lynne S. Gross, *Telecommunications: An Introduction to Radio, Television and Developing Media* (Dubuque, IA: Wm. C. Brown Company, 1983), p. 96.

[19]James Michener, *The Quality of Life* (Philadelphia: J.B. Lippincott Company, 1970), p. 71.

"At the Cannon's Mouth": The American Press and the Vietnam War

by Clarence R. Wyatt

From the earliest days of the Vietnam War to the present, one of the most controversial aspects of America's involvement has been the role of the American press. In the early 1960s, United States military and government figures — with a number of editors and publishers in agreement — criticized many American reporters as being inexperienced, ill-informed and antagonistic.[1] As American military involvement grew, so did the press corps covering it. Also increased was the importance military and civilian officials in Saigon and Washington, D.C., attached to the public relations aspect of the war, as evidenced by the development of a sophisticated information administration in Vietnam.[2] Controversy and confrontation between reporters and officials, with charges of distortion, bias and lack of credibility hurled back and forth, continued throughout the war.

As Americans have, over the last decade, sorted through the aftermath of the war searching for explanations of the results, the role of the press has been a major issue. Vietnam has been called the first "television war," the "best reported but least understood"[3] war in our history. Indeed, for many people, the press, seemingly so pervasive and so controversial, came to be a decisive player in the war's outcome, with two images dominating discussion. The first of these images, especially prominent in the later years of the war and immediately afterward, casts the press as a challenger of the lies of government officials — a hero that, at least in part, helped to bring the war to an end. The second of these images, more widespread in recent years, portrays the press as having sapped, through its own distortions, misrepresentations and weaknesses, America's will to pursue a "noble cause" to victory.

How valid are these two images? Can we even speak of a single "role" for the press during Vietnam? This study of the coverage in six American newspapers of three major Vietnam War engagements suggests some preliminary answers to these questions.

The Current Debate

As early as 1967, Theodore Draper, a consistent critic of the Johnson administration's Vietnam policy, noted that

> One of the saving and most hopeful elements on the American scene throughout the Vietnamese war has been the relative independence and integrity of an important part of the American press. The wonder is not that much of the press was uncritical and covered up for official policy, but that a good part refused to do so.[4]

Paul Kattenburg, a member of the Johnson administration, called U.S. involvement in the war "an exercise in illusion which resulted in a tremendous loss of touch with reality on the part of U.S. policy-makers." But the deception, he said, "was bound sooner or later to catch up with them. It did, when the American public, well-nudged in that direction by

---

Clarence R. Wyatt is a PhD. candidate at the University of Kentucky, where he is working on his dissertation, a study of the American news media during the Vietnam War. He wishes to thank his dissertation adviser, George C. Herring Jr., for his help and encouragement in connection with this article.

104 Journalism History 13:3-4 Autumn-Winter 1986

the much more realistic media, ceased altogether to believe in the pronouncements of their leaders about the Indochina war."[5]

Walter Cronkite concluded the CBS News special on the fall of Saigon by declaring that "Our big lesson from Vietnam" is "the necessity for candor. We . . . cannot ever again allow ourselves to be misinformed, manipulated, and misled into disastrous foreign adventure."[6] Television critic Cleveland Amory felt that when Cronkite finally spoke out on Vietnam, "he not only brought down a presidency, but also, to all intents and purposes, ended a war."[7]

The second image of the press has both challenged this positive assessment of the press's role and reinforced the assumption of its independence and influence. This image has taken an extreme form in the views of such observers as former *Newsweek* Far Eastern correspondent Robert Elegant. "The South Vietnamese were, first and last, decisively defeated in Washington, New York, London, and Paris," Elegant argued. "Those media defeats made inevitable their subsequent defeat on the battlefield," for "the pen and the camera proved decisively mightier than the bayonet and ultra-modern weapons."[8]

A more restrained form of this idea is supported by Peter Braestrup's *Big Story*. This exhaustive study of the response of the three television networks, the New York *Times*, the Washington *Post*, *Time*, *Newsweek*, AP and UPI to the 1968 Tet Offensive concluded that the media over-reacted to and sensationalized the action, and conveyed a picture of American and South Vietnamese troops with their backs literally against the wall. By doing this, and by failing to follow up as dramatically on the American-South Vietnamese counter-offensive, said Braestrup, the news media made a psychological defeat out of what ultimately was a military victory, and contributed significantly to a sharp decline in support for the war at home.[9] This basic view has been adopted by many as a major lesson of the Vietnam experience. As Richard Neustadt, in considering the United States' ability to fight limited wars after Vietnam, said, "My guess is that the present administration will be keeping clearly in mind one lesson mentioned earlier — that is, how to keep television coverage under control."[10]

Military figures also have come to believe that the press contributed to America's defeat in Vietnam. General William Westmoreland gave many Vietnam reporters credit for bravery and for alerting him to problems in his command, but his overall assessment of the media was negative: "Reflecting the view of the war held by many in the United States and often contributing to it, the general tone of press and television comment was critical."[11] As a ressult, "the strategists in Hanoi indirectly manipulated our open society, and hence our political system."[12] Nor was this attitude confined to Westmoreland. Of those responding to Douglas Kinnard's survey of general officers who served in Vietnam, 89 percent rated the press's performance negatively, including 38 percent who said flatly that the press was "disruptive of United States efforts in Vietnam."[13]

This conception of the press has become an axiom for much of today's American military. As Drew Middleton wrote, "The armed forces emerged from the Vietnam War psychologically scarred. They were embittered by their failure to defeat the Vietnamese because of what they considered political manipulation in Washington and, above all, by the media's treatment."[14] Writing about press restrictions during the Grenada invasion, Middleton noted, "The majors and commanders of the Vietnam War who believed the media had worked against the American command there had become influential generals and admirals determined not to expose the Grenada operation to what they continue to view as a hostile adversary."[15]

These images of a powerful and antagonistic press have not gone unchallenged. Michael Mandelbaum, Lawrence Lichty, George Bailey and Michael Arlen, among others, have questioned the effect of television on public opinion.[16] Mandelbaum stated, "The United States lost the war in Vietnam because the American public was not willing to pay the cost of winning or avoid losing.[17] As Ted Koppel put it, "People don't need television to tell them a boy has gone to Southeast Asia and not come back."[18]

Others have expressed skepticism of these portrayals of the press. Peter Arnett, former AP correspondent in Vietnam, has questioned the consistency of Braestrup's investigation and conclusions in *Big Story*.[19] John Mueller's study of public opinion during the Korean and Vietnam wars points out that American opinion was moving significantly against the war well before the sudden shift supposedly caused by Tet coverage.[20] And Daniel Hallin's recent work has challenged what he calls "the myth of the adversary press."[21]

The most extreme indictments of the press have come under attack as well. Morley Safer responded sharply to Robert Elegant's article. Its strategy, he said, was to "meat-axe the critics of a policy by questioning their patriotism, by accusing them of being in the thrall of *petit bourgeois* ambition, generate enough smoke, and hope that no one examines the piece closely enough to notice that there are no facts, only scapegoats."[22] Charles Mohr, former *Time* and New York *Times* Vietnam correspondent, responded in much the same way. "I believe the performance of the news media during the Tet offensive — and indeed, throughout the entire course of the Vietnam War — is open to legitimate criticism," he explained. "It is also worthy of some praise. But let the criticism be legitimate. Some of the criticism of Vietnam War correspondents, it appears, has not been based on careful re-examination of the journalistic product."[23]

Methodology

Safer and Mohr are correct. Most of the discussion of the press and Vietnam, even the most thoughtful, has not been based on detailed, systematic analysis of "what the journalists *actually* said and wrote."[24] The only such examinations have been a series of articles by Lawrence Lichty and George Bailey dealing with television news and documentary reporting,[25] Braestrup's *Big Story* and Hallin's *The "Uncensored War,"* which looks at New York *Times* coverage from 1961 to 1965, and at random samples of network television evening news broadcasts from 1965 to 1973. All of these studies have limitations. For example, Braestrup's work focuses on only one, albeit important, incident in a long war. More importantly, these studies look only at national media, neglecting the regional and local outlets no comprehensive analysis should ignore.

The present study attempts to add to this short list of intensive analyses, and to avoid some of their problems. First, a sample of national, regional and local newspapers, representing a variety of market and circulation sizes, locations and political orientations, was selected. The papers were the Chicago *Tribune*, the New York *Times*, the St. Louis *Post-Dispatch*, the Minneapolis *Tribune*, the Nashville *Tennessean* and the Lexington *Herald*.

fire. Help finally reached the stricken unit on Tuesday the 21st, and the Americans took the hill on the following Thursday, Thanksgiving Day.[39]

The third engagement was *Lam Son* 719, the 1971 South Vietnamese assault against the Ho Chi Minh Trail in Laos,

NEWSPAPER SAMPLE[36]
(as of 1965)

Paper	Market Size/ Circulation	Politics	Editorial Stand on the War (Nov. '65)[37]
Chicago *Tribune*	3.67 mil. 836,702	Independent/ Republican	Supported escalation; said call for negotiations was an aid to Communists.
New York *Times*	7.81 mil. 652,135	Independent	Skeptical of escalation, called for negotiation.
St. Louis *Post-Dispatch*	830,168 342,882	Independent	Opposed escalation; called Vietnam a war of "anti-liberation."
Minneapolis *Tribune*	494,944 224,120	Independent	Supported war as effort to stop threat to SE Asia.
Nashville *Tennessean*	175,146 136,381	Democratic	Supported war, but mildly concerned about escalation.
Lexington *Herald*	66,013 50,954	Democratic	Supported escalation; called for "total victory."

Second, this study examined the coverage in these six papers of one battle from each of the three phases of American combat involvement. The first engagement, during the American build-up, was the Ia Drang Valley campaign in October and November 1965. This series of firefights in the central highlands of South Vietnam — the first major encounter between American troops and North Vietnamese regulars — began the night of October 19, when the 33rd North Vietnamese Regiment initiated a seige of the Plei Me Special Forces camp, and came to a climax November 14th through the 17th, in two vicious ambushes sprung by the North Vietnamese against the First Air Cavalry Division. Both sides suffered the heaviest casualties of the war up to that time.[38]

The second engagement, Dak To, came near the height of American combat strength, in the fall of 1967. Dak To began November 3, when a company of the Fourth Infantry Division tangled with a North Vietnamese unit in a brief but intense firefight. Over the next several days, the fighting settled into a pattern of American and South Vietnamese attempts to dislodge the North Vietnamese from positions around Dak To. On Sunday, November 19, a battalion of the 173rd Airborne Brigade began its asault on the last of the North Vietnamese redoubts on Hill 875, and for the next three days the battalion was cut off from resupply or reinforcement by a relentless stream of mortar and small arms

which was the first major test of Richard Nixon's "Vietnamization" program during the American withdrawal from Vietnam. On February 8 the cream of the South Vietnamese military, totalling some 22,000 Marine, paratroop and armored units, crossed the Laotian border headed for Sepone, a town sitting astride the junction of several major branches of the Trail some 25 miles inside Laos.[40]

The ARVN force met little resistance at first but, on February 18, the North Vietnamese struck with some 40,000 men, including armored units, stalling the South Vietnamese some seven miles from Sepone. Only by leap-frogging the North Vietnamese were the ARVN troops able to continue their progress toward Sepone, arriving on March 4 to find the town abandoned. Meanwhile, the North Vietnamese continued to push the South Vietnamese back, and only massive American air support saved the ARVN units. Even with this assistance, the South Vietnamese were sent reeling back across the border by the last week in March, having suffered casualties of at least 25, and possibly as high as 50, percent.[41]

This study examined coverage of these three battles by focusing on three main issues prevalent in the literature on the press and Vietnam produced by critics and supporters of the media alike. These issues are: (1) the incidence of distorted, uneven and inconsistent reporting of events; (2) the degree to which the press failed or succeeded in analyzing and placing events, especially combat, in perspective; and (3) the press's supposed independence from and skepticism of government information.[33]

Clarity of Coverage: Amount, Organization and Placement

One of the most persistent criticisms of the press's performance in Vietnam is that coverage often was distored and uneven, and that a key cause of such coverage was the way in which the news stories themselves were organized. Of the over 1,800 individual articles examined in this study, more than half were generated by wire services, predominantly AP and UPI. Obviously, the six papers had much source material in common. Indeed, the principal product of the wire services in Vietnam — the daily wrap-up — was the chief source of combat news for all but a handful of American papers. Yet, as close examination reveals, the amount and nature of the wire material used, the way in which it was organized and its placement varied widely from paper to paper. This significantly affected the clarity of an individual paper's coverage and, consequently, the picture of the war conveyed to its readers.

During Ia Drang, the dependence on wire summaries was especially heavy; such stories made up at least half of the total stories on the campaign in each of the newspapers studied except for the New York *Times*. Coverage of Ia Drang made evident the fact that the wire wrap-ups were often, as Braestrup charged, "too long, too disorganized, too jerky from many shifts in sphere of action and topics."[33] For example, 20 of the Lexington *Herald*'s 39 stories dealing with Ia Drang were wire summaries, and the November 2 wrap-up was typical. The story shifted from the action around Ia Drang to the bombing of the Bio Loi Forest northwest of Saigon, back to Ia Drang, to action around Qui Nhon, and back again to Ia Drang, all in nine paragraphs.[34]

Discovering this problem in a small-city newspaper, faced with limited space and a local orientation, is not too surprising. Finding choppy and unorganized stories in a major daily, though, is less expected. Nonetheless, the Chicago *Tribune* suffered from just such coverage. Of the *Tribune*'s 49 Ia Drang stories, 30 were wire summaries, and its use of these summaries resembled that of the *Herald*. The *Tribune*'s October 24 wrap-up led with the action around Ia Drang, moved to a discussion of the continued American build-up in Vietnam, turned to fighting just northwest of Saigon, and then came back to Ia Drang.[35]

The Minneapolis *Tribune* and the Nashville *Tennessean* also depended heavily on the wire summaries, and their coverage also was quite poorly organized. These two papers had another problem as well, for the war seemed to be a lower priority story for them than for the other papers surveyed. For example, November 18 was the climactic day of the Ia Drang campaign. Units of the First Air Cavalry Division, ambushed by the North Vietnamese, had endured the heaviest fighting and the highest casualties of the war. The Minneapolis *Tribune*, however, gave the day's action only 17 column-inches of an AP summary on its second page; the *Tenessean*'s story, also a wire summary, ran only 22 column-inches and was buried on page 18. The St. Louis *Post-Dispatch*, on the other hand, put the story on the front page, devoting some 43 column-inches of a UPI wrap-up to the bloody fighting.[36]

But dependence on wire service copy, even upon the war wrap-ups, did not necessarily doom a paper to incoherent reporting. Of the *Post-Dispatch*'s 55 stories dealing with Ia Drang, 31 were wire summaries. Seventeen of these, however, were labeled "combined wire," indicating that the paper's editor had reworked the wire material extensively, producing stories that, with only a few exceptions, were very clear. Typical of the quality of day-to-day coverage provided to St. Louis readers was the *Post-Dispatch*'s November 2 story, which devoted the first five of its 15 paragraphs to the sweep being carried out by the First Air Cavalry in the Ia Drang area. The story then told of a Vietcong attack near Qui Nhon, the rescue of an American pilot in the South China Sea, and finally of B-52 strikes in the Boi Loi Forest.[37]

The link between dependence on the daily wire summaries and the clarity of organization in a paper's reporting was not as pronounced during Dak To, and the stories of all the papers were generally focused and well-ordered. Brevity and paucity of detail, however, were still problems, especially for the *Tennessean* and the Minneapolis *Tribune*. From November 5 through November 12, the *Tribune* simply failed to relate a number of important developments and details. On November 8, for example, the wire summary in the *Post-Dispatch* reported fighting between the Fourth Infantry Division and the North Vietnamese around an NVA base area and added that the 173rd Airborne Brigade was also engaged in action nearby. The New York *Times*, in a story generated by its own staff, noted, in addition to these details, that 3,500 to 4,000 American reinforcements had been moved into the Dak To area. But the Minneapolis paper, in a UPI daily wrap-up, indicated only that "The Highlands fighting yesterday marked the second day of bitter battles where American commanders believe North Vietnamese regulars are planning a major dry-season offensive."[38]

Even when Dak To entered its final and most violent stage, the *Tribune* and the *Tennessean*'s coverage remained very limited. On November 15 two C-130 transport planes were destroyed, a third damaged and a huge stock of fuel and ammunition set on fire during a sustained mortar attack on the main Dak To camp. The *Times* devoted two stories — one from UPI, the other its own — on November 15 and 16 to the shelling. The attack story comprised the bulk of two Chicago *Tribune* war summaries on the 15th and 16th, the whole of a 54-column-inch article in the November 15 *Post-Dispatch*, as well as the entirety of the *Heald*'s war report on the 16th. Over the two days, the Minneapolis *Tribune* covered the story in a total of five paragraphs, while the *Tennessean* took seven, all buried in wire summaries.[39]

The same occurred as the final action of the Dak To campaign, the assault on Hill 875, began on November 19. The Minneapolis *Tribune* and the *Tennessean* did not report the attack until the 21st, a day later than the rest of the papers, and neither made much effort to catch up on two days of heavy fighting. The *Tribune* gave just six short paragraphs of a UPI story to its initial article on Hill 875, and the *Tennessean* printed only three paragraphs of an AP wrap-up.[40]

The organization of individual stories continued to improve in the years between Dak To and Lam Son 719. By the time of Lam Son in early 1971, the jumpy, disorganized stories seen in some of the reporting earlier in the war had, for the most part, been replaced by articles that were clearly focused and well-structured. Better organization and editing obviously accounted for some of this, but the fact that Lam Son overshadowed all other action also helped. The newspapers were less compelled to compress a number of incidents into one summary article, and were better able to focus on the one major operation, as was evidenced by the sharp decline in dependence on the war wrap-ups that had been the backbone of earlier coverage.

Perspective: Providing Context and Analysis

Despite these improvements in style and organization, confusion and self-contradiction were still present in the coverage of Lam Son. The worst incidents were caused by the newspapers' failure to place events in context and to analyze developments in the light of new information. For example, the South Vietnamese crossed the border into Laos on February 8, 1971. By February 11th or 12th, all of the papers, using wire sources, reported that the South Vietnamese had reached and occupied Sepone 25 miles inside Laos.[41] On the 13th, a *Times* story noted that the ARVN force was instead only 15 miles or so inside Laos, although the rest of the papers did not report this change until the 15th or 16th.[42] No paper, however, tried to explain this contradiction, either then or in early March, when the South Vietnamese actually entered the town. Where were the South Vietnamese? What kind of progress were they making? Could the readers of those papers believe any subsequent reports on the ARVN advance?

This lack of perspective, this "intentiveness on the moment,"[43] as I. F. Stone called it, was responsible for instances of poor reporting in Ia Drang as well. An article by UPI correspondent Eddie Adams in the October 23 Chicago *Tribune*, and in the October 24 editions of the *Post-Dispatch*, Minneapolis *Tribune* and *Tennessean*, is a good case in point. The story reported that the bodies of Vietcong maching gunners had been found chained to their weapons outside the Green Beret camp at Plei Me.[44] The Chicago *Tribune* carried the story on the 23rd with no qualification. The next day a UPI report in the *Tribune* and the *Post-Dispatch* noted that the story had not been confirmed but was being "double-checked."[45] Both papers used the story again within a few days, however, and neither made any reference to the earlier uncertainty surrounding it or to whether the story had ever been confirmed. The Minneapolis *Tribune* and the *Tennessean* never reported any doubt of the report's accuracy. Was it true? Were Americans facing such a foe? Readers in Chicago, Nashville, St. Louis and Minneapolis had no way of knowing.

This episodic quality also caused serious flaws in the reporting of Dak To. The November 17 headlines of the Chicago *Tribune* and the *Tennessean* trumpeted success for the United States in the Dak To campaign. "B-52s Blast Retreating Reds," the *Tribune* proclaimed; "U.S. Guns Force Reds To Flee From Dak To," announced the *Tennessean*. The wire stories running under these headlines were just as celebratory. The *Tribune* stated that "Giant B-52 jets today bombed North Vietnamese troops retreating from their smashing defeat in the battle of the central highlands." The *Tennessean* reported that American firepower had "forced North Vietnamese troops to pull back from the Dak To battlefield into Laos," and also noted "the apparent failure of the North Vietnamese dry season offensive in the highlands."[46] The other papers were much more restrained. For example, the *Times* report of the 17th stated that "A tense and uneasy mood gripped the American camp here today as mortar rounds sporadically struck the adjoining airstrip and thousands of soldiers scoured the jungle in search of an elusive and powerful enemy."[47] But neither the Chicago *Tribune* nor the *Tennessean* tried to reconcile its stories to the vicious fighting of the next few days. If the North Vietnamese had in fact retreated into Laos, who was cutting the troopers of the 173rd Airborne to pieces on the slopes of Hill 875? The editors of the *Tribune* and the *Tennessean* did not offer an answer.

Emphasis on day-to-day reporting and the lack of contextual coverage also apparently affected the papers' willingness and ability to analyze the three engagements and to judge their significance for the larger war. By late October 1965, for example, all six papers were reporting heavy fighting in the central highlands. By the first week in November, all six had reported North Vietnamese regulars in the Ia Drang Valley. At the time, however, only the *Post-Dispatch* recognized the significance of a large North Vietnamese presence in the highlands. It pointed out that "this first true Communist divisional operation of the war" supported "the growing belief that Hanoi appears to be determined to slug it out in South Viet Nam."[48]

Newspaper coverage of Dak To, November 1967.

Nor did the paper limit its analysis to the news columns. It was, in fact, the only paper surveyed that questioned the *ends*, not merely the means, of American policy in Vietnam as early as 1965. In its November 12 editorial, the *Post-Dispatch* argued that the United States should not allow itself to be manipulated into "a war of 'anti-liberation,' " while a November 17 editorial worried that the increase in American forces and the concommitant rise in the level of fighting would, ironically, create more instability in South Vietnam.[49]

The rest of the papers were not as quick to recognize the full significance of Ia Drang, nor were they as probing in their analysis. Only on November 16 and after did the others report — the *Times* in a Neil Sheehan article, the others in wire stories — that in the Ia Drang Valley the war had entered a new and more deadly phase.[50] While all five agreed on this point, they held different ideas on what that change meant. The *Times* had supported only hesitantly Johnson's increase in forces in July 1965, and by fall that hesitation had grown. Editorials in November called for a halt in the bombing of the North and for renewed efforts at negotiation, also criticizing those who called for a wider war.[51]

The Minneapolis *Tribune* and the *Tennessean* had also supported the American build-up and stated that Ia Drang represented a triumph of American arms, but each expressed some mild concern. Both papers carried a James Reston column which pointed out that the costs and aims of victory should be kept in balance,[52] and a *Tennessean* editorial hoped that North Vietnam might yet "come to its senses and listen to reason."[53] For the *Herald* and the Chicago *Tribune*, however, Ia Drang showed that the gloves were off, and they welcomed the increased fighting. "The Viet Cong must be crushed," stated the *Herald*. " 'Negotiation' is a magic word to pacifists and those who openly or covertly support the Communist cause," the *Tribune* proclaimed.[54]

A similar pattern emerged in the coverage of Dak To. For a number of analysts, the almost automatic explanation for any increase in enemy activity in the central highlands was that another attempt was being made to cut the South in two.[55] All of the papers reported this theory, but the *Post-Dispatch*, the *Times* and, to a lesser degree, the *Herald* presented alternatives, noting that the North Vietnamese might have been seeking "a propaganda and morale advantage" by inflicting heavy casualties on an isolated American unit, or that they were trying to lure American troops away from pacification duties along the coast.[56]

The Chicago *Tribune*, the *Tennessean* and the Minneapolis *Tribune* failed to present these possibilities, and they did even less to judge Dak To's significance after the battle. All three went little beyond repeating General Westmoreland's claim that Dak To was "the beginning of a great defeat for the enemy."[57] The *Herald* did only slightly better. Its only attempt at after-action analysis was AP correspondent Peter Arnett's November 26 articles pointing out that, far from the "beginning of a great defeat for the enemy," Dak To showed that the North Vietnamese still held the initiative in the field.[58]

The *Post-Dispatch* and the *Times* presented a much broader range of interpretations. The *Times* generated its own analysis, while the *Post-Dispatch* drew on Peter Arnett and *Times* material in addition to utilizing its own Washington correspondent, Richard Dudman. In a series of articles, both papers repeated the possibility that the North Vietnamese action was not "an essentially foolish" attempt to "show they're not losing the war," but rather was an effort to achieve a propaganda victory by punishing American troops and/or pulling troops from pacification duty. The *Post-Dispatch* and the *Times*, still the only papers among the six that opposed American policy editorially, were also the only two to go beyond merely repeating official characterizations of Dak To's results. Both concluded that if Dak To were indeed an American victory, it was an extremely costly one in which the North Vietnamese achieved at least part of their goals.[59]

By the time of Lam Son, most of the papers were doing a significantly better job in analyzing the operation's consequences. All six presented the Nixon administration's contention that a blow to the Ho Chi Minh Trail would reduce the enemy's capability at least temporarily and give Vietnamization time to work.[60] All of the papers also reported the official contentions of the invasion's success, and all except the Chicago *Tribune* — the only paper among the six still supporting American policy — presented alternative assessments that differed sharply with statements of South Vietnamese and American officials.

Richard Dudman wrote in the March 28 *Post-Dispatch* that heavy ARVN casualties made it increasingly doubtful "whether the South Vietnamese forces can 'hack it.' " Charles Bartlett reported in the April 11 Minneapolis *Tribune* that Nixon, at General Creighton Abrams' urging, scaled his intended 16,000-men per month withdrawal rate back to 14,300 per month because of the "setback in Laos." The AP's J. T. Woklerstorfer pointed out in the March 22 *Herald* that "at least half a dozen of South Vietnam's best battalions" had been decimated by the North Vietnamese. The *Times*' Gloria Emerson said in the March 28 editions of the *Times* and the *Tennessean* that "The morale of many soldiers in South Vietnam's finest military units, who fought the North Vietnamese in Laos, is shattered." But only once did the Chicago *Tribune* report any possibility that the operation was not proceeding as planned, quoting Senator Mike Mansfield, who said, "It appears that the withdrawal has been hastened. You can't arrive at a judgment until all the facts are in."[61]

As the cases discussed above illustrate, there did seem to be a connection between a paper's editorial stand on the war and its willingness to present a wide spectrum of analysis. All six papers had access to wire service material offering analyses both supporting and differing with official statements. Yet, in all three engagements, it was the papers that opposed American policy that, while presenting the official characterization of combat, most consistently presented alternate viewpoints to those assessments and attempted to place the events in some broader context. Once again, although these six papers shared wire material as a major source of coverage, the way in which that material was used and, consequently, the picture of the war presented to readers, varied greatly.

Independence from Official Sources

This does not mean, however, that the papers were as consistently independent of official information as both popular images of the press assume. In fact, at critical junctures in all three battles, the papers surveyed here failed to challenge official information, and these incidents suggest the high degree of control that the government military information system was able to exercise over the press.

A prime example is the handling of casualty figures. By late 1965, the American strategy of search-and-destroy and attrition, whose goal was to seek out and inflict heavy losses on the enemy, had emerged.[63] As a consequence, casualty figures, both Allied and enemy, became a significant measure of the war's progress, but the figures received a scrutiny that was inconsistent at best.

During Ia Drang, for example, the military did not release American casualty figures for individual actions, supplying the press only with general descriptions of "light, moderate and heavy." Despite the fact that this was the first major combat between American and North Vietnamese troops and by far the most intense action since the American escalation began, only the *Post-Dispatch* and the *Times* showed any skepticism about either American or enemy casualty figures, when their November 26th editions carried the sharpest questioning of estimates of enemy casualties produced during Ia Drang — Charles Mohr's "Misinformation" story. After citing several incidents of inflated casualty assessments, Mohr concluded: "So great is the pressure for body-count figures that soldiers . . . began to joke this week about Saigon's request for the 'WEG,' or 'wild-eyed guess.' "[64] Even these two papers, however, failed to follow through on these doubts. The day before running Mohr's "Misinformation" story, the *Times* carried the week's summary of casualties without any question, listing figures of 240 Americans and 2,262 enemy killed. The story was written by Charles Mohr.[64]

Having accepted the official criteria of progress, the papers, including the *Times* and the *Post-Dispatch*, could do little in the end but accept the official claim of victory in both Ia Drang and Dak To. During Lam Son this acceptance of government assessments and definitions produced perhaps the most striking example of official ability to manipulate information seen in any of the three battles. At this time the Nixon administration was able to change, almost without challenge, the previously stated objectives of the operation and create an illusion of victory to shroud a resounding defeat.

From the time when rumors of the invasion of Laos first began to circulate, all reports stated that its goal was to "cut" or "smash" or "plug" the Ho Chi Minh Trail at least until the end of the dry season in May, and perhaps longer.[65] President Nguyen Van Thieu of South Vietnam, in announcing the invasion of February 8, had stated that "This is an operation limited in time and in space with the clear and unique objective of *disrupting* [emphasis mine] the supply and infiltration network of the Communist North Vietnamese in Laos." Two days later, the *Times* quoted "Administration analysts" who "in private conversations . . . tried to shy away from such expressions as 'choking off' the trail." Still, for the next week or so at least, all six papers, including the *Times*, continued to describe Lam Son's aims in grander terms.[66]

The sources of this characterization were the officials responsible for the operation's planning and execution, along with their supporters. On February 8, Senate Minority Leader Hugh Scott, fresh from a briefing by National Security Advisor Henry Kissinger, said that the goal of the operation was to "pinch off the supply lines" and explained that "the South Vietnamese might have to stay there until May or June." For the next nine days, officials ranging from South Vietnamese Vice President Nguyen Cao Ky to Secretary of Defense Melvin Laird to Secretary of State William Rogers to President Nixon himself continued to speak of the operation's goal in terms of "cutting" the Trail.[67]

While the elite of the South Vietnamese military were fleeing from the North Vietnamese counterattack, Nixon stated, during a February 17th news conference, that the South Vietnamese did not want "to occupy any part of Laos.

Newspaper coverage of Lam Son 719, February and March 1971.

The South Vietnamese are not there to stay. They are there to *disrupt* [emphasis mine] the enemy's lines of communication, their supply lines, their infiltration routes and then get out."[68] After this, "disrupt" replaced "cut" as the goal of the operation. Administration officials and supporters, including General Abrams and California Governor Ronald Reagan, applauded ARVN's great achievement in "disrupting" the flow of supplies.[69]

Only after Senate Foreign Relations Chairman J. William Fulbright on March 30th disclosed that, in a secret briefing on February 9, Secretary Rogers and Director of the Joint Staff Lt. General John Vogt had declared Lam Son's most important objective to be the complete cutting-off of the Trail at least until the end of the dry season in May, did five of the papers begin to question the change in objectives and the fact that the operation had ended at least five weeks sooner than planned. Yet the Chicago *Tribune* did not even report Senator Fulbright's revelations, much less question the administration's claims of success.[70]

Conclusions

After studying over 1,800 articles and some 24 weeks worth of coverage, patterns emerge which challenge both popular images of the press in Vietnam. First, at least as represented by these six papers during these three battles, the press was not as independent as popularly conceived. In all three engagements examined, the government and military were able to control the flow of information from its source and the reporters' access to the combat areas, making the press dependent on official sources. In covering these three battles, the six papers relied mainly on official information and reported that information with only occasional qualification.

Nor was the press as monolithic as both images imply. There was a marked difference in the coverage presented by the papers of three distinct events. The clarity and breadth of coverage — as represented by the amount of coverage given, the organization of individual stories and their placement within the papers — varied greatly. The papers also differed in their efforts to place events in some sort of context of the larger war and to offer analysis of the actions' meanings.

There was at least a coincidental connection between a paper's coverage of the battles and its editorial stance on the war. For all three engagements, those papers most supportive of government policy were also those least likely to present challenges to official information, to provide analysis of the action, and to offer clear, extensive and prominently-placed coverage. The readers of these six publications not only received differing opinions of the war in their papers' editorial pages, but also significantly different pictures of the battles covered in their papers' news columns.

Narrowly focused through this study has been, its close examination of a sample of the "journalistic product" clearly casts doubt on the validity of the current dual images of an adversarial press. Indeed, such were the differences in coverage seen in these six papers, all drawing from the same basic pool of sources, that it is difficult to ascribe any one role — hero, villain or other — to the press during the Vietnam War.

NOTES

1. David Halberstam, "Getting the Story in Vietnam," *Commentary*, 39, No. 1, 1965, p. 34; Peter Braestrup, *Big Story: How the American Press and Television Reported and Interpreted the Crisis of Tet 1968 in Vietnam and Washington* (Garden City, NY: Anchor Books, 1978), p. 4; William C. Westmoreland, *A Soldier Reports* (Garden City, NY: Doubleday, 1976), p. 82.

2. Francis Faulkner, "Bao Chi" (Ph.D. dissertation, University of Massachusetts, 1981), p. 140; Edwin Emery, *The Press and America: An Interpretative History of the Mass Media*, 3rd edition (Englewood Cliffs, NJ: Prentice Hall, Inc., 1972), pp. 539-540.

3. Fred W. Friendly, "TV At the Turning Point," *Columbia Journalism Review* 9 (Winter 1970-71): 19.

4. Paul Kattenburg, *The Vietnam Trauma in American Foreign Policy, 1945-1975* (New Brunswick, N.J.: Transaction Books, 1980), p. 262.

5. Theodore Draper, *Abuse of Power* (New York: The Viking Press, 1967), p. 105.

6. Walter Cronkite quoted in Lawrence Lichty, "The Night At the End of the Tunnel," *Film Comment*, July-August 1975, p. 34.

7. Cleveland Amory, "What Walter Cronkite Misses Most," *Parade Magazine*, March 11, 1984, p. 4.

8. Robert Elegant, "How to Lose a War," *Encounter*, August 1981, pp. 88, 76; Keyes Beech, "Elegant's 'Viet Nam,'" *Encounter*, January 1983, p. 94; William F. Buckley Jr., "What's Happening to 'Civilised Discourse'?," *Encounter*, April 1982, p. 94; Norman Podhoretz, *Why We Were in Vietnam* (New York: Simon and Schuster, 1978), pp. 116-132.

9. Braestrup, pp. 508-529.

10. Richard Neustadt quoted in "Vietnam Reappraised," *International Security* 6 (Summer 1981): 22.

11. Westmoreland, p. 556.

12. Ibid., p. 558.

13. Douglas Kinnaird, *The War Managers* (Hanover, NH: The University Press of New England, 1977), p. 132.

14. Drew Middleton, "Barring Reporters from the Battlefield," *New York Times Magazine*, February 5, 1984, p. 69.

15. Ibid., p. 37.

16. Michael Mandelbaum, "Vietnam: The Television War," *Daedulus* III (Fall 1982); Lawrence Lichty, "The War We Watched on Television," *AFI Report* 4 (Winter 1973); George Bailey, "Television War: Trends in Network Coverage of Vietnam 1965-1970, *Journal of Broadcasting* 20 (Spring 1976); Michael Arlen, *The Living Room War* (New York: Penguin Books, 1982); see also a Harris survey for *Newsweek* in July 1967 which suggested that "TV has encouraged a decisive majority of viewers to support the war," "The Press: Room for Inprovement," *Newsweek*, July 10, 1967, p. 78.

17. Mandelbaum, p. 21.

18. Ted Koppel quoted in Tom Shales, "The War That Came in from the Tube," *Washington Post*, April 21, 1985, p. F4.

19. Peter Arnett, "Tet Coverage: A Debate Renewed," *Columbia Journalism Review* 16 (January-February, 1978): 44-47.

20. John E. Mueller, *War, Presidents, and Public Opinion* (New York: Wiley, 1973).

21. Daniel C. Hallin, "The Media, the War in Vietnam, and Political Support: A Critique of the Thesis of an Oppositional Media," *Journal of Politics* 46 (February, 1984): 2-24; Hallin, *The "Uncensored War"* (New York: Oxford University Press, 1986).

22. Morley Safer quoted in Perry Deane Young, "Revisionism Reconsidered," *The Quill*, May 1983, p. 7.

23. Charles Mohr, "Once Again — Did the Press Lose Vietnam?," *Columbia Journalism Review* 22 (November-December 1983): 51.

24. Mohr, p. 51.

25. George A. Bailey, "Interpretive Reporting of the Vietnam War By Anchormen," *Journalism Quarterly* 53 (Summer 1976): 319-324; George A. Bailey, "Television War: Trends in Network Coverage of Vietnam, 1965-1970," *Journal of Broadcasting* 20 (Spring 1976): 147-158; George A. Bailey and Lawrence Lichty, "Rough Justice on a Saigon Street: A Gatekeeper Study of NBC's Tet Execution Film," *Journalism Quarterly* 49 (Summer 1972): 221-229, 238; Lawrence W. Lichty, "The Night At The End of the Tunnel," *Film Comment*, July-August 1975, pp. 32-35; Lawrence W. Lichty, "Video Versus Print," *Wilson Quarterly*, Volume 6, No. 5 (special issue), 1982, pp. 48-57; Lawrence W. Lichty, "The War We Watched on Television," *AFI Report* 4 (Winter 1973): 29-37.

26. *Editor and Publisher International Yearbook, 1965* (New York: Editor and Publisher, 1965), pp. 96, 131-32, 162, 174, 198, 263.

27. Editorial stands were determined based on the following editorials: "That Magic World — 'Negotiation,' " *Chicago Tribune*, November 21, 1965, p. 4; "Vietnam Bombing Pause," *New York Times*, November 1, 1965, p. 40; "On 'People's War,' " *St. Louis Post-Dispatch*, November 12, 1965, p. 28; Leigh White, "We're in Viet Nam to Deny Big Area to Reds," *Minneapolis Tribune*, November 20, 1964, p. 4; "Full-Scale War in Area Seems a Little Closer," *Nashville Tennessean*, November 30, 1965, p. 10; "Vast Majority for Vietnam Policy," *Lexington Herald*, November 7, 1965.

28. George C. Herring, "Delusive Victory: The First Cavalry and the Ia Drang Valley," unpublished paper, 1982, pp. 17-32. Information concerning Ia Drang was also gathered from Colonel Harry G. Summers Jr., "The Bitter Triumph of Ia Drang," *American Heritage*, February-March 1984, pp. 50-59; Charles B. MacDonald, "A US Strategy to Stem the Communist Tide," in *The Vietnam War: The Illustrated History of the Conflict in Southeast Asia*, Ray Bonds, ed. (New York: Crown Publishers, Inc., 1979), pp. 96-105; and reports in the *Chicago Tribune*, the *St. Louis Post-Dispatch*, the *Minneapolis Tribune*, the *Nashville Tennessean*, the *Lexington Herald* and the *New York Times*.

29. Information concerning Dak To was taken from: Edward Doyle, Samuel Lipsman, *et al.*, *American Takes Over, 1965-67* (Boston: Boston Publishing Company, 1982); Charles B. MacDonald, "Communist Thrust — The Tet Offensive of 1968" and "The In-Country Enemy: Battle with the Viet Cong," in Bonds, ed., *The Vietnam War*; Robert Pisor, *The End of the Line: The Siege of Khe Sanh* (New York: Ballantine Books, 1983); and reports in the *Chicgo Tribune*, the *St. Louis Post-Dispatch*, the *Minneapolis Tribune*, the *Nashville Tennessean*, and *Lexington Herald* and the *New York Times*.

30. Information concerning Lam Son 719 was gathered from: Ronald H. Cole, "Southern Defeat on the Ho Chi Minh Trail" in Bonds, ed., *The Vietnam War*; Henry A. Kissinger, *The White House Years* (Boston: Little, Brown and Company, 1979); Richard M. Nixon, *RN: The Memoirs of Richard Nixon* (New York: Grosset and Dunlap, 1978); and reports in the *Chicago Tribune*, the *St. Louis Post-Dispatch*, the *Minneapolis Tribune*, the *Nashville Tennessean*, the *Lexington Herald* and the *New York Times*.

31. Ibid.

32. See, for example, Braestrup, pp. 30-31; John McLaughlin, "Saigon Newsgathering," *America*, November 2, 1968; Hanson W. Baldwin, "The Information War in Saigon," *The Reporter*, February 24, 1966; Emery, pp. 541-542; I.F. Stone, "Vietnam: An Exercise in Self-Delusion," *New York Review of Books*, April 22, 1965; "Reporting Vietnam: Eight Articles," *New Leader*, November 21, 1966; Michael Herr, *Dispatches* (New York: Avon Books, 1968); Richard West, "The Captive U.S Journalists," *Atlas*, December 1966; DeWayne B. Johnson, "Vietnam: Report Card on the Press Corps at War," *Journalism Quarterly* 46 (Spring 1969); Orville Schell, "Pop Me Some Drinks," *The New Republic*, January 30, 1970; Nathan B. Blumberg, "The Defaulting Press and Vietnam," *Commonweal*, July 12, 1968; "The Press: Room for Improvement," *Newsweek*, July 10, 1967, pp. 76-78; Westmoreland, *A Soldier Reports*, pp. 552-558; Jules Witcover, "Where Washington Reporting Failed," *Columbia Journalism Review* 9 (Winter 1970-71): 7-12; Philip Geyelin, "Vietnam and the Press" in Anthony Lake, ed., *The Vietnam Legacy: The War, American Society, and the Future of American Foreign Policy* (New York: New York University Press, 1976).

33. Braestrup, p. 31.

34. "Cavalry Troops Pound Commies," *Lexington Herald*, November 2, 1965, p. 1.

35. "Beat Back 2 Ambushes by Viet Rebels," *Chicago Tribune*, October 24, 1965, p. 1.

36. "Reds Ambush U.S. Unit, Losses High," *Minneapolis Tribune*, November 18, 1965, p. 2; "U.S. Unit of 600 Mauled in Ambush, Regroups to Move on Red Supply Base," *St. Louis Post-Dispatch*, November 18, 1965, p. 1. The *New York Times* ran a 32-inch story on page one, the *Chicago Tribune*, a front-page story 26 inches long, and the *Herald*'s page one story was 27 inches long. "VC Fought Off by Americans," *Nashville Tennessean*, November 18, 1965, p. 27; "Red Trap Backfires, 250 Guerillas Killed," *Nashville Tennessean*, October 25, 1965, p. 1; "Must Counter Foe's Buildup — McNamara," *Nashville Tennessean*, November 30, 1965, p. 1.

37. "92 Reds Killed, 26 Captured in Viet Nam, U.S. Troops Report," *St. Louis Post-Dispatch*, November 2, 1965, p. 1.

38. "Communists Open Attack In Highlands," *St. Louis Post-Dispatch*, November 8, 1967, p. 1; "G.I.'s in Highlands Battle a Large Enemy Force," *New York Times*, November 9, 1967, p. 4; "238 Viet Cong Killed as GIs Thwart Drives," *Minneapolis Tribne*, November 8, 1967, p. 3.

39. "2 Planes Set Afire By Enemy at Dakto," *New York Times*, November 15, 1967, p. 13; "Foe's Shells Set Dakto Base Ablaze," *New York Times*, November 16, 1967, p. 1; "Mortar Attack Destroys 2 U.S. Transport Planes," *Chicago Tribune*, November 15, 1967, p. 6; "Arms Dump Blown Up in Red Attack," *St. Louis Post-Dispatch*, November 15, 1967, p. 8; "Guns Destroy Two Planes at Dak To," *Minneapolis Tribune*, November 16, 1967, p. 4; "Dak To Atlck Destroys C130s," *Nashville Tennessean*, November 15, 1967, p. 1; "U.S. Camp Hit Near Saigon," *Nashville Tennessean*, November 16, 1967, p. 1.

40. "Reds Push Back U.S. Troops at Strategic Hill," *St. Louis Post-Dispatch*, November 20, 1967, p. 2; "40 Americans Die In Highland Fight," *New York Times*, November 20, 1967, p. 1; "40 GIs Die On Dak To Hill," *Chicago Tribune*, November 20, 1967, p. 1; "Tempo of War Picks Up On Ground, Over North," *Lexington Herald*, November 20, 1967, p. 12; "72 GIs Killed Trying to Take Hill at Dak To," *Minneapolis Tribune*, November 21, 1967, p. 2; "72 GIs Die In Hill Battle," *Nashville Tennessean*, November 21, 1967, p. 1.

41. "Post Marines Off Viet," *Chicago Tribune*, February 11, 1971, p. 1; "Paratroops Join Armor in Laos, Open Supply Line," *St. Louis Post-Dispatch*, February 11, 1971, p. 1; "U.S. Forces Reported Near DMZ Coast," *Minneapolis Tribune*, February 11, 1971, p. 1; "U.S. Reports 8 'Copters Lost in Laos Push," *Nashville Tennessean*, February 12, 1971, p. 1; "South Viets Seize Red Supply Base; Resistance Light," *Lexington Herald*, February 11, 1971, p. 4; "Airstrip Being Rebuilt," *New York Times*, February 11, 1971, p. 8.

42. "Yanks Err, Hit CIA Site," *Chicago Tribune*, February 15, 1971, p. 1; "South Vietnamese Drive in Laos Reported Slowed," *St. Louis Post-Dispatch*, February 16, 1971, p. 1; "U.S. Planes Bomb CIA Base In laos," *Minneapolis Tribune*, February 15, 1971, p. 1; "U.S. Errs, Bombs CIA Base?," *Nashville Tennessean*, February 15, 1971, p. 1; "Missile Site Hit by B52s," *Lexington Herald*, February 16, 1971, p. 1; "More Copters of U.S. Downed in Drive On Laos," *New York Times*, February 13, 1971, p. 1.

43. Stone, p. 5.

44. "Montagnards In Besieged Camp Blasted by Viet Cong for 4th Day," *Chicago Tribune*, October 23, 1965, p. 3; "Reds Ambush Troops Heading For Plei Me," *St. Louis Post-Dispatch*, October 24, 1965, p. 1; Eddie Adams, "Tiny-Force Holding Off Viet Cong," *Minneapolis Tribune*, October 24, 1965, p. 1; Eddie Adams, "Plei Me 'Blasted Wreck,' " *Nashville Tennessean*, October 24, 1965, p. 6.

45. "Beat Back . . .," *Chicago Tribune*, October 24, 1965, p. 1; "Reds Ambush . . .," *St. Louis Post-Dispatch*, October 24, 1965, p. 1.

46. "B-52s Blast Retreating Reds," *Chicago Tribune*, November 17, 1967, p. 6; "U.S. Guns Force Reds To Flee From Dak To," *Nashville Tennessean*, November 17, 1967, p. 1.

47. Bernard Weinraub, "Tense Dakto G.I.'s Hunt Elusive Foe," *New York Times*, November 17, 1967, p. 9; "G.I.s Capture Two Hills in Dak To Battle," *St. Louis Post-Dispatch*, November 17, 1967, p. 1; "67 Viet Cong Die Rushing GI Positions," *Minneapolis Tribune*, November 18, 1967, p. 2; "Yanks Drive North Viets From Two Dak To Hills," *Lexington Herald*, November 8, 1967, p. 1.

48. Raymong Coffey, "Aggressiveness Cited in Rise in U.S. Contact with Viet Cong," *St. Louis Post-Dispatch*, November 11, 1965, p. 1B; "Hanoi Troops' Dead Estimated at 1,200; G.I.s' Casualties High," *St. Louis Post-Dispatch*, November 16, 1965, p. 1; "U.S. Troops Rise Past 200,000 for Viet Nam Likely," *St. Louis Post-Dispatch*, November 18, 1965, p. 2; "Red Fire Stops Viet Nam Force Moving to Aid of Americans," *St. Louis Post-Dispatch*, November 19, 1965, p. 1; "What Viet Nam Objective Now?," *St. Louis Post-Dispatch*, October 31, 1965, p. 12; "On 'Peoples' War,' " *St. Louis Post-Dispatch*, November 12, 1965, p. 2C.

49. Ibid.

50. "3d Assault Is Raging; Count 465 Red Dead," *Chicago Tribune*, November 16, 1965, p. 1; "Ia Drang Battle Toll Heaviest of the War," *Minneapolis Tribune*, November 20, 1965, p. 1; Robin P. Mannock, "Vietnamese Paratroopers, Viet Cong Regulars Clash," *Lexington Herald*, November 20, 1965, p. 1; "Red Unit Regroups; 384 Dead in Valley," *Nashville Tennessean*, November 16, 1965, p. 1; Neil Sheehan, "G.I.'s Inflict Hevy Losses on North Vietnam Troops," *New York Times*, November 16, 1965, p. 1.

51. " 'This Is Really War,' " *New York Times*, July 29, 1965, p. 26; "Vietnam Bombing Pause," *New York Times*, November 1, 1965, p. 40; "The Irrepressible Mr. Nixon," *New York Times*, November 23, 1965, p. 44.

52. James Reston, "Balanced Reports Needed In Viet Nam," *Nashville Tennessean*, November 30, 1965, p. 10; James Reston, "Worry About Viet Nam Grows," *Minneapolis Tribune*, November 16, 1965, p. 4.

53. "Full-Scale War in Asia Seems a Little Closer," *Nashville Tennessean*, November 30, 1965, p. 10.

54. "Vast Majority for Vietnam Policy," *Lexington Herald*, November 7, 1965, p. 4; "That Magic Word — 'Negotiation,' " *Chicago Tribune*, November 21, 1965, p. 20.

55. "238 Viet Cong Killed . . .," *Minneapolis Tribune*, November 8, 1967, p. 3.

56. "B52's Smash Red Forces Near Dak To," *Lexington Herald*, November 13, 1967, p. 1; Edwin Q. White, "Yanks Beat Back 'Fierce' Charge By Communists," *Lexington Herald*, November 14, 1967, p. 1; "G.I.s Smash New Red Assault in Highlands," *St. Louis Post-Dispatch*, November 9, 1967, p. 2; "G.I.'s In Highlands Battle a Large Enemy Force," *New York Times*, November 9, 1967, p. 4; Peter Arnett, "Need To Shift Pacification Troops Feared," *St. Louis Post-Dispatch*, November 12, 1967, p. 21; "A Tough and Aggressive Enemy Again Moves to the Attack," *New York Times*, November 12, 1967, p. 1, Sec. IV.

57. "Westmoreland Sees Major Enemy Defeat," *Minneapolis Tribune*, November 23, 1967, p. 3; Fred Farrar, "Calls Dak To Start of Big Red Setback," *Chicago Tribune*, November 29, 1967, p. 3; "Optimism Over Vietnam Must Be Cautious Kind," *Nashville Tennessean*, November 24, 1967, p. 12; "U.S. Takes Key Vantage Point," *Nashville Tennessean*, November 25, 1967, p. 4; "Vietnam Reds May Be Using Cambodia Port," *Minneapolis Tribune*, November 24, 1967, p. 1.

58. Peter Arnett, "Dak To Was Costliest Battle of Vietnam War," *Sunday Herald-Leader*, November 26, 1967, p. 16.

59. Richard Dudman, "McNamara Resignation, Westmoreland Speech Point To A Bigger War," *St. Louis Post-Dispatch*, December 3, 1967, p. 3B; Hedrick Smith, "Some U.S. Officials Admit Hanoi Achieved Gains in Dak To Battles," *St. Louis Post-Dispatch*, November 29, 1967, p. 1B; Hedrick Smith, "U.S. Officials Say North Vietnam Also Gained At Dakto," *New York Times*, November 29, 1967, p. 2, Sec. IV; "Optimists Have Their Say," *New York Times*, November 26, 1967, p. 2, Sec.IV; "But at Dakto, the Going Is Very Rough," *New York Times*, November 26, 1967, p. 2, Sec. IV.

60. "Post U.S. Marines Off Viet," *Chicago Tribune*, February 11, 1971, p. 1; "Saigon Forces Seize Red Supplies in Laos," *St. Louis Post-Dispatch*, February 13, 1971, p. 1; "Red Arms Are Seized In Laos," *Minneapolis Tribune*, February 14, 1971, p. 1; "Allies Capture Sepone," *Nashville Tennessean*, March 7, 1971, p. 1; "1,000 U.S. Warplanes Support Allied Troops," *Lexington Herald*, March 8, 1971, p. 1; Alvin Shuster, "Saigon Forces Enter Tchepone, Key Goal In Laos," *New York Times*, March 7, 1971, p. 1; Alvin Shuster, "Foe Attacks G.I.'s Near Laos Border," *New York Times*, March 28, 1971, p. 1; Edwin Q. White, "U.S. Copters Begin Khe Sanh Pullout," *Chicago Tribune*, March 24, 1971, p. 1; "Last Base In Laos Abandoned By Saigon," *St. Louis Post-Dispatch*, March 24, 1971, p. 1; "Laos Operation Ends; Reds Continue Shelling," *Minneapolis Tribune*, March 25, 1971, p. 1; Edwin Q. White, "U.S. Copters Leaving Harassed Units Begin To Pull Out From Khe Sanh," *Lexington Herald*, March 24, 1971, p. 1; William Beecher, "Thieu Said to Have Curbed Offensive to Reduce Loss," *New York Times*, March 25, 1971, p. 1; Frank Staff, "Cites Traffic Cut on Supply Trail," *Chicago Tribune*, March 5, 1971, p. 1; James Deakin, "Laos Could Speed Pull-out, Nixon Says," *St. Louis Post-Dispatch*, March 5, 1971, p. 1; Charles W. Bailey, "Nixon Says Laos Invasion Assures GI Withdrawals," *Minneapolis Tribune*, March 5, 1971, p. 1; Walter R. Mears, "Nixon Says Laotion Drive Aids U.S. Exit," *Nashville Tenessean*, March 5, 1971, p. 1; Eugene V. Risher, "Nixon Strongly Defends Laotian Thrust," *Lexington Herald*, March 5, 1971, p. 1; Robert B. Semple, Jr., "President Says Laos Aids U.S. Pullout," *New York Times*, March 5, 1971, p. 1; "U.S. Bomb Drops Error Leaves 10 Allies Dead," *Nashville Tennessean*, March 15, 1971, p. 1; Holger Jensen, "Commander Says S. Viet Mission in Laos Fulfilled," *Lexington Herald*, March 15, 1971, p. 3; "Last South Viet Troops Quit Laos, Reds in Pursuit," *Chicago Tribune*, March 25, 1971, p. 2; William Beecher, "Thieu Curtailed Laos Offensive, Pentagon Says," *St. Louis Post-Dispatch*, March 25, 1971, p. 1E; "Laos Operation Ends; Reds Continue Shelling," *Minneapolis Tribune*, March 25, 1971, p. 1; "Red Drive Over Border Kills 22 Americans," *Nashville Tennessean*, March 25, 1971, p. 1; "Most Objectives held Attained," *New York Times*, March 25, 1971, p. 5; Fred Farrar, "Laird Explains Laos Pullout," *Chicago Tribune*, March 25, 1971, p. 2; Aldo Beckman, "100,000 More to Quit Viet," *Chicago Tribune*, April 8, 1971, p. 1; James Deakin, "Nixon To Step Up Troop Withdrawals, "*St. Louis Post-Dispatch*, April 8, 1971, p. 1; "Nixon to Withdraw 100,000 More GIs," *Minneapolis Tribune*, April 8, 1971, p. 1; Frank Cormier, "100,000 More Due Pullout," *Nashville Tennessean*, April 8, 1971, p. 1; Eugene V. Risher, "Nixon Reveals Plan to Withdraw Another 100,000 Troops By Dec. 1," *Lexington Herald*, April 8, 1971, p. 1; Max Frankel, "Nixon Promises Vietnam Pullout of 100,000 More GI's By December; Pledges To End U.S. Role In War," *New York Times*, April 8, 1971, p. 1.

61. Richard Dudman, "ARVN: Hacking Or Hacked?," *St. Louis Post-Dispatch*, March 28, 1971, p. 1B; J. T. Wolkerstorfer, "Officials Are Trying To Assess Effect of Laos Offensive," *Lexington Herald*, March 22, 1971, p. 5; Gloria Emerson, "Laos Shattered Allied Morale?," *Lexington Herald*, March 28, 1971, p. 1; Gloria Emerson, "Spirit of Saigon's Army Shaken In Laos," *New York Times*, March 28, 1971, p. 1; "Mansfield, Aiken Doubt Laos Gains," *Chicago Tribune*, March 22, 1971, p. 2.

62. George C. Herring, "Delusive Victory," p. 40; MacDonald in Bonds, *The Vietnam War*, p. 96; George C. Herring, *America's Longest War: The United States and Vietnam, 1950-1975* (New York: Wiley, 1979), p. 151.

63. Charles Mohr, "War and Misinformation," *New York Times*, November 26, 1965, p. 2; Mohr, "Misinformation on Viet Nam War Is Reaching American Public," *St. Louis Post-Dispatch*, November 26, 1965, p. 1B.

64. Charles Mohr, "G.I. Vietnam Toll is 240 For Week, Heaviest of War," *New York Times*, November 25, 1965, p. 1.

65. "2 Pronged Thrust at Reds," *Chicago Tribune*, February 5, 1971, p. 1; Richard Dudman, "Drive In Laos May Last 4 Months, Scott Says," *St. Louis Post-Dispatch*, February 8, 1971, p. 1; "S. Vietnamese Troops Launch Laos Invasion," *Minneapolis Tribune*, February 8, 1971, p. 1; "South Viets Mount Invasion of Laos With U.S. Support," *Lexington Herald*, February 8, 1971, p. 1; Alvin Shuster, "Saigon Viets Drive Into Laos To Strike Enemy Supply Line," *New York Times*, February 8, 1971, p. 1.

66. "Text of Thieu's Message on Laos Drive," *New York Times*, February 8, 1971, p. 14; William Beecher, "U.S. Aides Believe Thrust May Cost Foe Year or More," *New York Times*, February 10, 1971, p. 1.

67. Dudman, "Drive In Laos . . .," *St. Louis Post-Dispatch*, February 8, 1971, p. 1; "South Vietnam Troops Cut Branches of Red Supply Trail," *Minneapolis Tribune*, February 10, 1971, p. 4; "Laos Exit in May Eyed," *Nashville Tennessean*, February 17, 1971, p. 1; Terence Smith, "Laird Expecting 'Some Tough Days' In Laos Campaign," *New York Times*, February 17, 1971, p. 1; "Transcript of the President's News Conference on Foreign and Domestic Matters," *New York Times*, February 18, 1971, p. 14.

68. "Transcript of President's News Conference . . .," *New York Times*, February 18, 1971, p. 14.

69. Frank Starr, "Laird Expects Key Red-S. Viet Battle in Cambodia in 2 Weeks," *Chicago Tribune*, February 24, 1971, p. 1; Richard Dudman, "Nixon Rejects Plan for Faster Pull-Out," *St. Louis Post-Dispatch*, February 25, 1971, p. 1; "Red Tanks Hit S. Viet Post in Laos," *Chicago Tribune*, February 26, 1971, p. 7; Eugene V. Risher, "Nixon Strongly Defends Laotian Thrust," *Lexington Herald*, March 5, 1971, p. 1; "1,000 U.S. Warplanes Blast Reds," *Nashville Tennessean*, March 8, 1971, p. 1; Robert B. Semple, Jr., "U.S. Cities Gains in Laos Amid Reports of Setback," *New York Times*, March 19, 1971, p. 3; Alvin Shuster, "In the Laos Campaign: A Triumph or a Trap?," *New York Times*, March 21, 1971, p. 2, Sec. IV; Alvin Shuster, "The Campaign in Laos," *New York Times*, March 24, 1971, p. 4; "G.O.P. in St. Paul Hears Reagan and Goodell Divide Over Nixon," *New York Times*, March 28, 1971, p. 34; "Thieu Terms Laos Drive Saigon's 'Biggest Victory,' " *New York Times*, April 1, 1971, p. 1; "Big U.S. Loss in Laos Push Told," *Chicago Tribune*, April 5, 1971, p. 6' "End of the Tunnel," *Chicago Tribune*, April 9, 1971, p. 10; "Another Fierce Attack Repulsed, Saigon Says," *St. Louis Post-Dispatch*, April 4, 191, p. 1; "Nixon to Withdraw 100,000 More GIs," *Minneapolis Tribune*, April 5, 1971, p. 1.

70. John W. Finney, "Fulbright Plans Hearings On War," *New York Times*, March 31, 1971, p. 1; "House Democrats Propose Indochina Pull-Out By '73," *St. Louis Post-Dispatch*, March 31, 1971, p. 2; Charles W. Bailey, "Fulbright Doubts Success In Laos," *Minneapolis Tribune*, March 31, 1971, p. 1.

THE POW/MIA MYTH

BY H. BRUCE FRANKLIN

According to a Wall Street Journal*/NBC News poll, 69 percent of the American people believe that U.S. prisoners of war are still being held in Southeast Asia, nearly twenty years after the United States called its troops home. They hold this belief because of the cynical way the Nixon and subsequent administrations exploited the POW/MIA issue. And where Washington left off, Hollywood picked up, until fact and fantasy got hopelessly mingled in people's minds. Herewith the story of one of the most stubborn mass irrationalities of our times.*

★ ★ ★ ★ ★

ONLY ONE FLAG OTHER THAN THE STAR-SPANgled Banner has ever flown over the White House. There on one day every year since 1982 has fluttered the black-and-white POW/MIA flag, designed and distributed by the National League of Families of American Prisoners and Missing in Southeast Asia.

The endless flow of visitors to the rotunda of the nation's Capitol streams past an object that may seem somewhat incongruous beneath the epic paintings and amid the heroic statues: the POW/MIA flag, the only flag displayed in the Capitol, given this ongoing position of honor by vote of Congress in 1987. This banner thus displays to the world our nation's faith in the flag's central image, the silhouette of a handsome American prisoner of war, his head slightly bowed to reveal behind him the ominous shape of a guard tower. A strand of barbed wire cuts across just below his firm chin. Underneath runs the motto "YOU ARE NOT FORGOTTEN."

Each year since 1982 the U.S. government has officially declared it is operating "on the assumption that at least some Americans are still held captive." In 1983, ten years after the last official U.S. combat in Indochina, the President of the United States solemnly pledged that the fate of the POW/MIAs had become "the highest national priority." The following year Michael Dukakis, governor of a state that had been in the forefront of the movement against the Vietnam War, signed a decree authorizing that the POW/MIA flag fly above the statehouse lawn for a year. Today in Massachusetts every city and town must fly the POW/MIA flag over at least one municipal building and over all police and fire stations, while all state vehicles must display the POW/MIA logo. This policy is now typical of many states, and the flag is also a familiar sight at rest stops and toll plazas along state highways. Congress and the President every year enact legislation proclaiming National POW/MIA Recognition Day. By 1988 laws mandating observance of this day had been enacted by the legislatures and governors of forty-six states; the last four states fell into line by 1990. Last May, Secretary of Defense Dick Cheney sent a directive to the Secretary of each branch of the armed forces and to the Chairman of the Joint Chiefs of Staff reminding them of the preeminent importance of "the POW/MIA public awareness program" and specifying that every U.S. military installation should fly the flag, conduct Recognition Day ceremonies, and arrange for presentations from the National League of Families.

Official homage to the Americans still allegedly captive in Southeast Asia is no mere ritual. It is also a basis—at least an ostensible basis—for foreign policy. Last year the U.S. government boasted that it "has kept the live prisoner issue at the forefront of negotiations" with Vietnam and reiterated that "the POW/MIA issue is a matter of highest national priority," which can be resolved only after "the fullest possible accounting for the missing, the return of all Americans who may still be held in captivity, and the repatriation of all recoverable remains." Vietnam having signed the Cambodian peace accords in October, the main obstacle to normalizing U.S. relations with Vietnam is that nation's failure to meet these demands. Ever since 1982, under the Reagan Administration, the Department of Defense has issued annually a *POW-MIA Fact Book*, which states the official rationale for this policy. From 1984 through 1989 the key wording ran, "It would be irresponsible to rule out the possibility that live Americans are being held." In 1990, under the Bush Administration, the phrasing became less equivocal: "The U.S. Government's efforts are predicated on the assumption that some are still alive."

Devotion to American POWs in Indochina permeates the society, running especially strong in the working class. Throughout the nation, particularly in shopping malls and white working-class neighborhoods, the black-and-white flag often flies beneath or beside the Stars and Stripes. Bumper stickers, buttons, and T-shirts proclaim, AMERICAN POW/MIAS ARE ALIVE IN VIETNAM, ONLY HANOI KNOWS, RELEASE OUR POW/MIAS, and POWS NEVER HAVE A NICE DAY. A permanent vigil, staffed mainly by Vietnam veterans, is held at the Vietnam Veterans Memorial in Washington, D.C. Millions of Americans have worn POW/MIA bracelets, which are still sold by the thousands each year. The flag has waved over the General Motors parts-distribution center in Bensalem, Pennsylvania, ever since the United Auto Workers local there threatened to strike if it was not flown every day. Above the New York Stock Exchange, facing the visitors' gallery, hangs a large POW/MIA flag. Children of all ages play P.O.W.: Prisoners of War on Nintendo. A board game dedicated to the POW/MIAs "still alive and being held against their will" is played with 2,477 cards, each inscribed with a different serviceman's "name, rank, branch of service, casualty date, and country where lost or captured." Christmas trees are adorned with POW/MIA ornaments. This past September some 8,000 bikers staged the third annual Ride for Freedom, a motorcycle cavalcade that roared through New Jersey and Manhattan to demand the release of the American prisoners still held in Southeast Asia. The fate of the MIAs has become a vital concern of many Vietnam veterans, displacing their problems with unemployment, homelessness, Agent Orange, and inadequate medical care.

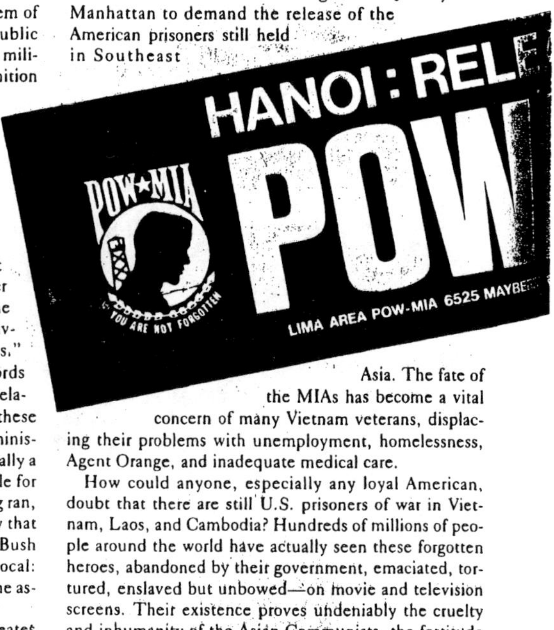

How could anyone, especially any loyal American, doubt that there are still U.S. prisoners of war in Vietnam, Laos, and Cambodia? Hundreds of millions of people around the world have actually seen these forgotten heroes, abandoned by their government, emaciated, tortured, enslaved but unbowed—on movie and television screens. Their existence proves undeniably the cruelty and inhumanity of the Asian Communists, the fortitude and heroism of the American fighting man, and the nobility of the cause for which the United States fought in Indochina. David Cline, who was wounded when his position was overrun in a battle at the same time and place as the one depicted toward the end of the movie *Platoon*, describes one aspect of this phenomenon succinctly: "Americans want to believe that we were the good guys and those rotten gooks are still making our boys grow rice."

The POW/MIA myth has had a profound political, cultural, and psychological influence on American society that continues to deepen, although the likelihood of finding any living POWs wanes with each passing year. Those not possessed by the faith may find it difficult to comprehend its power. There has yet to be any credible evidence that any prisoners were withheld in Indochina, and even if some were held, their number could not have b ·n more than a few dozen at the very most. The supposea ·ate of this conjectural small group might therefore seem to be almost incidental compared with the catastrophic effects of the war on the ruined nation of Vietnam, whose casualties ran into the millions and whose own MIAs still number more than 200,000, and also with the devastating effects of the war on the

United States itself—including the known fate of many tens of thousands of veterans. Indeed, for every missing man who the U.S. government at any time claimed might possibly have been a captive in Indochina after the war, there are now probably at least a thousand homeless Vietnam veterans on U.S. streets—to whom some people refer as "M.I.A: Missing in America." Gene Hackman, Chuck Norris, Sylvester Stallone, David Carradine, and the other saviors whom Hollywood has sent on quests to rescue imprisoned Vietnam veterans would have a more realistic chance of success in the United States, where hundreds of thousands are or have been incarcerated in jails and prisons.

Counting the Unaccounted-For

To keep one's bearings through the thickets that lie ahead, these facts will be helpful:

• A total of 2,273 Americans are still "unaccounted for" from the war in Indochina.

• Approximately half this total (1,101) were never considered to be either missing in action or prisoners of war. They were known at the time of their loss to have been killed in action; they are listed as "unaccounted for" only because their bodies have not been recovered.

• Today only one man is still officially listed as either missing in action or a prisoner of war, and he is known to have died about a quarter of a century ago.

In all major wars many combatants die without being identified or having their bodies recovered. Approximately 78,750 Americans are still unaccounted for from the Second World War, and approximately 8,170 are unaccounted for from the Korean War. So the number unaccounted for from the Vietnam War would seem surprisingly small, especially since about 80 percent of the missing were airmen lost over the sea, remote mountains, or tropical rain forest, often in planes that exploded at supersonic speeds, while most of the rest disappeared amid confused fighting in dense jungle. In fact, the proportion of unaccounted-for Americans to the total killed in action is far smaller for the Vietnam War than for any previous war in the nation's history—even though this was its longest war, included protracted "secret" wars in Laos and Cambodia whose very existence was denied by the U.S. government, and ended with every battlefield in the possession of the enemy. For the Second World War, after which the United States was free to explore every battlefield, the 78,750 still unaccounted for represent 19.4 percent of the total 405,399 killed. For the Korean War, more than 15 percent of the dead are still unaccounted for. In contrast, the unaccounted-for from the Vietnam War constitute less than four percent of the 58,152 killed.

What is the likelihood of finding and identifying aviators lost under combat conditions? A U.S. Navy study of all fatal non-combat accidents from 1969 to 1975 involving the type of combat aircraft flown in Vietnam showed that in 40 percent of the cases remains were insufficient for positive identification through autopsy, even though naval investigators arrived on the scene within hours of a crash and the identities of the airmen were already known. Bodies left in Indochina would additionally suffer the ravages of the tropical climate, with its monsoon rains, engulfing mud, and vegetative overgrowth, and would likely be torn apart and scattered by animals.

Speedy recovery even of those bodies that might eventually be found cannot reasonably be expected, given that despite extensive prior searches, the dead from much earlier wars are still turning up. Almost every year the remains of Americans killed in the Second World War are discovered in the European countryside, and the crews of at least two American bombers that crashed in New Guinea in the early 1940s were finally found in the 1980s. Although there was never any question as to the site of death, remains of soldiers killed in General Custer's 1876 Battle of the Little Bighorn were still being found in 1985. The skeletons of thirty-two Confederate soldiers killed in the Civil War Battle of Glorieta Pass were unearthed in New Mexico in 1987. That same year the remains of twenty-eight U.S. soldiers killed during the War of 1812 were discovered in Canada.

Such grim facts highlight a misconception basic to the

POW/MIA issue. The total of 2,273 unaccounted-for in Indochina is quite misleading, because it includes those 1,101 who are known to have been killed in action in circumstances where their bodies could not be recovered. Their official designation is KIA/BNR—"killed in action, body not recovered." Crews of airplanes that exploded in the air or crashed within sight of their aircraft carriers, soldiers machine-gunned to death before the eyes of comrades unable to retrieve their bodies, or men so thoroughly blown apart that there were no retrievable remains—all these are listed in the total of "unaccounted for." This KIA/BNR category was never included with the missing in action during the Vietnam War; it was lumped together with the POW/MIA category only after the 1973 Paris Peace Agreement was signed.

So of the 2,273 unaccounted-for, only 1,172 were ever actually listed as POW/MIA. But the category POW/MIA itself was an unprecedented invention designed to suggest that each and every missing person might be a prisoner of war, even though most of those missing in action were lost under circumstances that made capture impossible. Previously, the designation POW applied only to those known or believed to be prisoners. It was quite distinct from the MIA category. While lumping these two designations together in most public announcements, the Department of Defense internally kept them separate throughout the war and its aftermath. The Pentagon listed as a POW anyone reported as a possible prisoner anywhere in Vietnam, Laos, Cambodia, or China at any time from 1964 to 1973, whether or not there was credible evidence of capture and even if there was evidence of subsequent death. After the 1973 Peace Agreement all but fifty-six men on this internal list were either released or reported to have died in captivity. Over the next three years analysis of these remaining cases resolved all but a handful.

Architect of the Capitol

The POW exhibit in the U.S. Capitol, 1970

The category POW/MIA itself was an unprecedented invention designed to suggest that each and every missing person might be a prisoner of war, even though most of those missing in action were lost under circumstances that made capture impossible.

In the ensuing years exhaustive case-by-case investigation, together with the absence of contradictory evidence, has led the Department of Defense to make a presumptive finding of death for every single person on the combined POW/MIA list except one. This man is Air Force Captain (promoted after his loss to Colonel) Charles Shelton, who was shot down over Laos in April of 1965; according to the official U.S. position, Shelton is "listed as a prisoner of war as a symbolic gesture of the Administration's commitment to this issue." In discussing his case the Defense Department notes, "Shelton is the only American serviceman the U.S. Government still lists as a POW; this is for symbolic purposes as intelligence reports indicate that he . . . died in captivity in the mid-1960s." All other known or presumed prisoners of war have been either returned or determined to have died in captivity.

Every responsible investigation conducted since the end of the war has reached the same conclusion: there is no credible evidence that live Americans are being held against their will in Vietnam, Laos, Cambodia, or China. Most telling are those studies initiated from the opposing point of view.

In the immediate aftermath of the war, one of the principal figures in spreading the notion that Americans were still being held captive in Indochina was Gillespie "Sonny" Montgomery, a conservative representative from Mississippi, recognized at the time as being more outspoken about this belief "than any other member of Congress," according to *The Washington Post*. His fervor persuaded the House in 1975 to create the Select Committee on Missing Persons in Southeast Asia and to name him as its chair. After fifteen months of investigation, with access to every case file and all classified information, extensive hearings recorded in five volumes, and a fact-finding trip to Southeast Asia, the committee issued its final report in 1976, presenting the unequivocal conclusions that "no Americans are still being held alive as prisoners in Indochina, or elsewhere, as a result of the war in Indochina," and that "because of the nature and circumstances in which many Americans were lost in combat in Indochina, a total accounting by the Indochinese Governments is not possible and should not be expected." Confronted with overwhelming evidence, Montgomery ruefully confessed his now-shattered belief in live prisoners had been "based more on hope than fact and more on rumors than hard evidence," for "like so many others I wanted to believe they were alive, so I did."

Three years later the National Defense University published a book-length study of the POW/MIA issue and its history, written by Navy Captain Douglas L. Clarke, of the National War College. A veteran of 300 combat missions in Indochina, many flown as commander of a carrier-based attack-bomber squadron, Clarke had close friends among the missing in action and had served for eighteen months in the Navy's office of the Special Assistant for Prisoner of War Matters. Clarke found himself not only in agreement with the conclusions of the House Select Committee but also thoroughly convinced that the entire "matter of the missing men has worked against the best interests of the United States," the men, and their families, as he stated in his final paragraph.

> Whether there will ever be an adequate accounting of the men missing in Southeast Asia is extremely doubtful. There never was one in any previous conflict. The Government did the families—and therefore the lost men—a tragic disservice by encouraging the belief that there would be such an accounting in this war.

For eight years the Reagan Administration kept fomenting the issue of Americans supposedly held in captivity in Indochina. Yet its final report on the matter, jointly prepared by the Department of Defense and the Department of State and released just a few hours before Reagan left office (but never published by the Government Printing Office, listed as a government document, or made available to government-document depositories), was unable to cite any evidence of unrepatriated live POWs, despite intense scrutiny of "several million captured documents"; interrogation of "over one quarter of a million prisoners and defectors" during the war; thorough debriefing of all returning U.S. and allied prisoners; interrogation of thousands of refugees, including "defectors from Vietnam's security services, military and diplomatic corps"; the use of "national technical systems" (satellites, spy flights, and electronic monitoring); and "a special team deployed in Southeast Asia." The report was forced to state outright, "We have yet to find conclusive evidence of the existence of live prisoners, and returnees at Operation Homecoming in 1973 knew of no Americans who were left behind in captivity."

Full Accounting and Live POWs

THE MAIN DEMAND MADE BY THE U.S. GOVERNMENT on the governments of Vietnam, Laos, and Cambodia is that they provide "the fullest possible accounting" for all Americans missing in action during the many years of U.S. warfare in Indochina. The U.S. position, as stated in the lead headline of the 1990 *POW-MIA Fact Book*, is that "THE INDOCHINESE HOLD THE ANSWERS," and that because they refuse to tell the United States everything they know, the United States is justified in acting "on the assumption that at least some Americans are still held captive."

This logic confuses the issue of live POWs with the issue of accountability. The thorny question of what constitutes an adequate, acceptable, or "fullest possible" accounting is rife with debate and ambiguity. Many arguments—ethical, political, and legal—could be made on either side of the proposition that the governments of Vietnam, Laos, and Cambodia owe the government of the United States more information than they have provided. One's position on this question might very well be influenced by one's view of the history and justice of America's war against these nations. Laos and Vietnam have returned more than 300 sets of remains, and both countries have participated with the United States in a number of joint searches of crash sites. Vietnam has issued numerous diplomatic and public reports documenting what it argues are extraordinary efforts to determine the fate of the missing and to locate and return the remains of Americans who were killed. The United States aggressively disputes Vietnam's arguments. But, in any case, there is an enormous difference between retaining information and retaining prisoners.

The claim that "the Indochinese hold the answers" is at best disingenuous. How could they possibly know the circumstances of the loss of every missing American? The House Select Committee discovered hundreds of cases for which the United States was demanding an accounting although there was virtually no possibility whatsoever that the Indochinese governments could have any information. One of the many examples:

On February 2, 1968, a UH-1H helicopter with five U.S. Army men on board crashed into a mountain and exploded into flames while making a ground-controlled approach to Danang Air Base, according to airborne observers and those on the ground. A thoroughly trained Army crash-investigation team concluded that "everyone perished in the crash." The handful of charred and fractured bone fragments that they could collect were determined to be useless for identification by the Army mortuary, which therefore disposed of them by incineration. The five crewmen were classified as MIA, and the Vietnamese were asked to account for each of them.

The committee concluded that listing such cases, "for which no accounting can be expected," may have convinced "the Indochinese leaders that the United States has deliberately requested information which they cannot furnish in order to embarrass them or to prevent meaningful talks."

The Origin of the Issue

WHEN RICHARD NIXON ACCEPTED THE REPUBlican presidential nomination in 1968, he vowed, "If the war is not ended when the people choose in November. . . . I pledge to you tonight that the first-priority foreign-policy objective of our next Administration will be to bring an honorable end to the war in Vietnam." This pledge was vital to his winning the presidency in a nation that had come to consider the war at best futile and possibly catastrophic. How many people living in America in 1968 could have predicted that Richard Nixon would protract the Indochina war into 1973? Perhaps even fewer than those who remembered that back in 1954 he had been one of the key figures in engineering the events that led to the war. And who could possibly have predicted that President Nixon would rely on a brand-new issue—the fate of American prisoners of war and missing in action—to sustain the war that had defeated President Johnson and presidential candidate Hubert Humphrey?

Disturbing questions about prisoners in Vietnam had indeed already emerged, but these concerned mainly people captured by the United States and Saigon, not those held by Hanoi and the southern guerrillas. In fact, the fate of Saigon's prisoners had been one of the causes of the insurgency against the South Vietnamese government of Ngo Dinh Diem, whose infamous 1959 Law 10/59 branded members of the forces that had fought for independence against France as "Communists, traitors, and agents of Russia and China" and decreed a death sentence for any person actively resisting Diem's rule. The ensuing arrest, torture, and execution of hundreds of thousands of people, featuring portable guillotines and displays of victims' heads and intestines, helped lead to the outbreak in 1960 of organized armed struggle and the formation of the National Liberation Front of South Vietnam (NLF), contemptuously labeled the Viet Cong by Saigon and Washington. As the war developed, anyone even suspected of loyalty to the NLF, whether armed or unarmed, was subject to torture and summary execution. Only after Hanoi announced, in 1966, that it did not regard its captured U.S. fliers as prisoners of war and that it might try them as war criminals for bombing its schools and hospitals was any semblance of POW status conferred on captured insurgents in the South. Soon the American public began to learn something about their actual treatment. Among many disturbing books published in early 1968 were two that exposed the barbaric treatment of prisoners by the United States and the government it had set up in Saigon. Prominent U.S. clergymen published *In the Name of America*, a chronicle of U.S. war crimes in Vietnam, with several sections devoted to the torture, mutilation, and murder of combatant and civilian prisoners. Next came *Against the Crime of Silence*, the proceedings of the International War Crimes Tribunal held during 1967 in Stockholm and Copenhagen, with extended testimony by U.S. veterans about their participation in the systematic torture and execution of prisoners by both U.S. and Saigon soldiers and officials.

In February of 1968 the issue exploded into the consciousness of tens of millions of Americans, as they watched, in their own homes, the chief of the Saigon national police execute a manacled NLF prisoner. In a perfectly framed sequence Brigadier General Nguyen Ngoc

Loan unholstered a snub-nosed revolver and placed its muzzle to the prisoner's right temple. The prisoner's head jolted, a spurt of blood gushed out of his left temple, and he collapsed in death. A decade later this image, with roles reversed, would be transformed into the central metaphor of a Hollywood production crucial to re-imaging the history of the Vietnam War and its POWs: *The Deer Hunter*. And yet the original image remained so potent in the popular imagination that further efforts to reverse it continued at least through the 1980s.

With increasing horror, Americans soon witnessed even worse pictures and accounts of U.S. and Saigon soldiers torturing and slaughtering prisoners, not only combatants captured in battle but also civilians rounded up in sweeps through villages. As early as May of 1968 came the first published descriptions of the My Lai massacre of March, in which U.S. soldiers had killed hundreds of villagers after raping and sodomizing the young women and using babies for target practice. The full story, including horrifying photographs taken by one of the GIs, would not appear in the general U.S. media until late in 1969. The CIA's Phoenix program, designed to wipe out the insurgent infrastructure by rounding up, imprisoning, and assassinating tens of thousands of suspects, was launched in mid-1968. By the end of the year Nguyen Van Thieu, the head of the Saigon regime, boasted that Phoenix had already killed 18,393 people; U.S. intelligence officers attached to Phoenix later testified that they never saw any of its prisoners survive interrogation. Enemy soldiers captured by U.S. forces were, in violation of the 1949 Geneva Convention Relative to the Treatment of Prisoners of War, turned over to the Saigon government, whose appalling prison camps were gradually being exposed to American readers and viewers. The American public even saw photographs of the notorious tiger cages of Con Son Island, where the few survivors were almost all permanently disfigured and severely crippled by torture.

In this context the incoming Nixon Administration decided to make the American prisoners and missing a major issue. Five days after Richard Nixon's inauguration, his representative introduced it at the Paris peace talks. A month later the Defense and State departments began laying the groundwork for a tremendous campaign at home. Although one possible benefit of this new controversy might have been to neutralize some of the outrage about what was being done to Vietnamese prisoners, that was not its main purpose. Throughout Nixon's first term the issue of POWs and MIAs served mainly as an indispensable device for continuing the war, functioning on the domestic front as a potent counterforce to the anti-war movement and providing an ingenious tool for building insurmountable roadblocks within the peace talks. And then the issue would be transmuted into a major obstacle to normalized relations for more than eighteen years after the 1973 peace accords.

Domestically, the issue was a masterstroke. After all, how else could any deeply emotional support for the war be generated? Certainly not by holding out the old, discredited promises of military victory. Although in the early stages of the war sentiment could be aroused to defend the "democracy" of Ngo Dinh Diem, who would be willing to fight and die for the notoriously corrupt generals ruling Saigon? But supporting their own POWs and MIAs was something loyal Americans could not oppose. It also seemed easy to understand, requiring no knowledge of the history of Vietnam and the war. One measure of the campaign's success was the sale of more than 50 million POW/MIA bumper stickers over the next four years. And once infused with this intense domestic support, the issue could be presented as a purely "humanitarian" question, thus transforming the peace negotiations into a stage for displaying the inhuman features of the enemy.

The "Go Public" Campaign

THE NIXON ADMINISTRATION'S "GO PUBLIC" campaign, designed explicitly to marshal public support for the early release of all American prisoners of war, was initiated on March 1, 1969, and officially launched on May 19 in a press conference held by Defense Secretary Melvin Laird. It was immediately and enthusiastically promoted by the media, which, in the relatively restrained language of *The New York Times* editorial staff, denounced "the Communist side" as "inhuman," asserted that "at least half of the 1,300 Americans missing in action in Vietnam are believed to be alive," and insisted that "the prisoner-of-war question is a humanitarian, not a political issue."

By the fall the POW/MIA campaign was receiving media attention and exerting political influence far out of proportion to the small number of its participants, especially in comparison with the millions taking part in the anti-war movement. The campaign consisted of a medley of astute publicity schemes staged by the Nixon

White House, POW family organizations, Congress, and the Texas multimillionaire H. Ross Perot (a director of the Richard M. Nixon Foundation).

In September and October the media spotlighted three delegations of wives and parents of missing men who flew to Paris to demand meetings with the negotiators from the Democratic Republic of Vietnam (DRV) and the NLF. On November 5 and 6 Congress unanimously passed and President Nixon signed a bill declaring November 9 a national day of prayer for U.S. prisoners of war in Vietnam. On November 9 United We Stand, an organization formed and chaired by H. Ross Perot, ran full-page advertisements featuring a picture of two small children praying, "Bring our Daddy home safe, sound and soon." Headlined "THE MAJORITY SPEAKS: RELEASE THE PRISONERS," the ads demanded that the "North Vietnamese and Viet Cong . . . Release the prisoners now." On November 13 and 14 the House Subcommittee on National Security Policy and Scientific Developments of the Committee on Foreign Affairs held hearings to denounce "the ruthlessness and cruelty of North Vietnam" and to provide a pep rally for a congressional resolution demanding the release of American POWs; no one with a dissenting view testified. In mid-December the resolution, which had received unanimous endorsement from the Senate, passed the House by a vote of 405–0 and was immediately exploited by U.S. negotiators in Paris. A few days later Perot had 152 wives and children flown to Paris, while his own jetliner, laden with Christmas presents for the POWs and filled with reporters, was used to stage a major media event in Laos.

During the campaign's formative first few months, in 1969, Richard G. Capen, Laird's deputy assistant secretary of defense for public affairs, and other officials from the State and Defense departments had visited forty-five sites to conduct unpublicized meetings with families of the missing men, thus shrewdly building a foundation among those who could most readily win heartfelt support from the American people. "We brought them together for the first time," Capen later boasted of this whirlwind national trip to organize the families.

Five days after Richard Nixon's inauguration, his representative introduced the issue of American prisoners and missing at the Paris peace talks. A month later the Defense and State departments began laying the groundwork for a tremendous campaign at home.

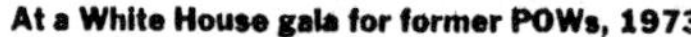

At a White House gala for former POWs, 1973

AP/Wide World

The most productive meeting was held at a naval officers' club on a base near San Diego, where on March 26 the State and Defense departments' representatives conferred with selected wives from the Los Angeles area and a San Diego–area group of wives organized by Sybil Stockdale, whose husband was the highest-ranking naval officer imprisoned in Vietnam and who herself had been working closely with naval intelligence since May of 1966. By June, Stockdale had made herself the national coordinator of an organization she christened the National League of Families of American Prisoners in Southeast Asia, linking groups of POW wives from various parts of the country. The following month she and several other selected POW family members met with Secretary of Defense Laird, and in December she and four other POW wives met with President Nixon, who pledged in their joint press conference that "this Government will do everything that it possibly can to separate out the prisoner issue and have it handled as it should be, as a separate issue on a humane basis."

In the spring of 1970 Sybil Stockdale received a phone call from Republican Senator Robert Dole, who asked whether she could "deliver 1,000 family members" to a POW/MIA "extravaganza" he was planning for May 1 in Constitution Hall if he were to help arrange government transportation for them. Dole pledged to orchestrate political support, putting Vice President Spiro Agnew and a bipartisan lineup of senators and representatives on the stage, and having Democratic Representative Clement Zablocki turn his Subcommittee on National

Security Policy and Scientific Developments into a publicity forum just prior to the event. Dole, Stockdale, and Perot collaborated in organizing the festivities, aided by a host of senators and representatives, including such prominent Democrats as Senate Majority Leader Mike Mansfield and Senator Edmund Muskie.

The day after the rally Stockdale presided in Washington over the meeting that transformed her network into the National League of Families of American Prisoners and Missing in Southeast Asia. Its incorporating bylaws seem to have been decided upon three days earlier by Stockdale, a handful of wives chosen by her, and Charles Havens, an attorney with whom she had worked when he was in the Office of International Security Affairs. Within three weeks of its incorporation the National League received its IRS tax-exempt status as a "nonpartisan, humanitarian" organization, free long-distance WATS telephone service provided by the White House, and office space donated by the Reserve Officers Association.

From then until now the National League of Families has played changing but always crucial roles in the dramatization and evolution of the POW/MIA issue. Almost all its principal organizers and activists were wives or parents of career officers, not draftees (mainly because the vast majority of missing and captured men were flight officers), and the politics of the organization were dominated by their outlook, especially during the war. Receiving in its early years direct and indirect material support from the White House, the Department of Defense, and the Republican National Committee, the League (as it is known to activists in the movement) would have dramatically shifting relations with the government until it became, in the 1980s, the main official liaison between the Department of Defense and the American public on all POW/MIA matters, a function it still serves today.

Promoting the National League of Families was not the only accomplishment of the Zablocki subcommittee. It gave Perot a podium from which to lecture the media on its duties in the POW/MIA campaign. Perot also issued marching orders to Congress about its role in the media campaign, instructions that the subcommittee obediently agreed to implement. Its immediate task, he explained, would be to set up as a display in the Capitol a POW exhibit that he had designed and would finance.

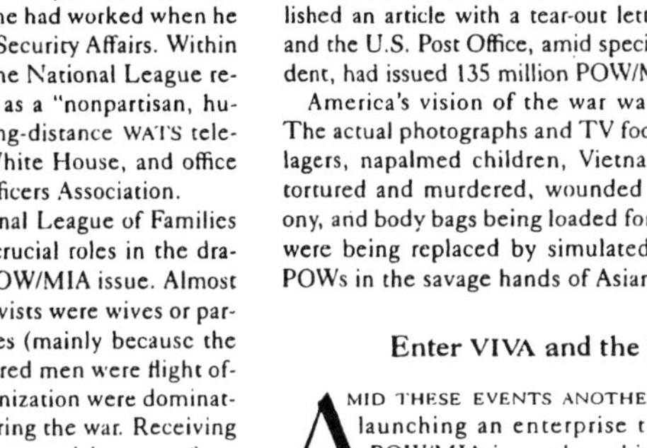

On June 4, 1970, House Speaker John McCormack was the featured speaker during the televised ceremony inaugurating this display. The exhibit was designed, according to *The New York Times*, "to arouse public opinion in behalf of the release of American prisoners of war" and "to encourage the thousands of tourists" who would see it each day to raise this demand "in letters to North Vietnamese leaders and members of Congress." At the center of the display were the figures of two American prisoners: "One sits in the corner of a bare cell, staring bleakly at an empty bowl and chopsticks on which a huge cockroach is perched. On the floor are other cockroaches and a large rat. The other figure lies in a bamboo cage, ankles shackled." By the end of the year this tableau was being set up in state capitols throughout the country, the *Steve Canyon* cartoon strip was featuring POW/MIA relatives in its daily sagas, ABC had presented a POW/MIA special, President Nixon had changed the official name of Veterans Day to Prisoner of War Day, the *Ladies' Home Journal* had published an article with a tear-out letter for readers to mail, and the U.S. Post Office, amid special fanfare by the President, had issued 135 million POW/MIA postage stamps.

America's vision of the war was being transformed. The actual photographs and TV footage of massacred villagers, napalmed children, Vietnamese prisoners being tortured and murdered, wounded GIs screaming in agony, and body bags being loaded for shipment back home were being replaced by simulated images of American POWs in the savage hands of Asian Communists.

Enter VIVA and the Bracelets

AMID THESE EVENTS ANOTHER ORGANIZATION WAS launching an enterprise that would make the POW/MIA issue the subject of intense passion among millions of Americans for decades. This was the Victory in Vietnam Association, or VIVA.

Back in the spring of 1966 Russell Kirk, in the *National Review*, had ballyhooed VIVA as a courageous new student-faculty group dedicated to counteracting the rising tide of anti-war feeling on American campuses. Kirk applauded VIVA members for counterdemonstrating against the "peaceniks" at the Oakland naval terminal in November of 1965 and at UCLA, where the group originated. He also lamented their "penniless" condition, displayed their address prominently, and noted that "as yet they have no financial angels."

By October, Gloria Coppin, wife of the Los Angeles industrialist Douglas Coppin, whose Hydro-Mill Company made airplane parts for major military contractors, was providing a headquarters for the organization and contacts with wealthy and influential members of southern California society. On March 9, 1967, the Victory in Vietnam Association received a state charter from California as an educational and service institution, and less than two months later the IRS granted it tax-exempt status as a "charitable and educational" organization. VIVA was then able to hold the first of its lucrative annual Salute to the Armed Forces balls, organized by its Ladies Auxiliary (made up of wives of wealthy business, military, and political leaders), and the guests—including Barry Goldwater, Alexander Haig, H. Ross Perot, Bob Hope, Los Angeles Mayor Sam Yorty, and California Governor Ronald Reagan—were able to receive tax deductions for their contributions. With brimming coffers, VIVA expanded rapidly and planned ever more ambitious campaigns to thwart the anti-war movement.

But by the time of the November, 1968, elections, "peace," not "victory," had become the catchword, as the nation bet on Nixon's secret peace plan. So in 1969 VIVA ceased to be the Victory in Vietnam Association and became Voices in Vital America.

A few months later members of VIVA and Robert Dornan—today a Republican representative from California and a leading proselytizer about live POWs, then a right-wing Los Angeles TV talk-show host and a friend of Gloria Coppin's—contrived the idea of selling bracelets engraved with the names of POWs and MIAs to promote and fund the POW/MIA campaign. In addition to Gloria Coppin, who chaired VIVA's board of directors from its founding until 1974, one of the prime movers in VIVA's bracelet manufacturing was Carol Bates, who was to take over the directorship of the National League of Families in 1976 and to become a coordinator of the POW/MIA issue for the Defense Intelligence Agency, a position she has held since 1984. Bracelets were produced just in time for the May 9, 1970, Salute to the Armed Forces ball, where Governor Reagan was the keynote speaker, Bob Hope and Martha Raye were made co-chairs of the bracelet campaign, H. Ross Perot was named Man of the Year, and Mrs. Perot accepted the first bracelet.

Later that month VIVA sold 1,200 bracelets at the National League of Families convention in Washington and ordered 5,000 more. The bracelet idea quickly mushroomed into a propaganda coup and financial bonanza for the POW/MIA campaign and especially for VIVA, which was soon wholesaling bracelets to the National League, Perot's United We Stand, and junior chambers of commerce across the country. Bracelets were prominently worn by such luminaries as Richard Nixon, General William Westmoreland, Billy Graham, George Wallace, Charlton Heston, Bill Cosby, Pat Boone, Cher and Sonny Bono, Fred Astaire, Johnny Cash, Steve Allen, Princess Grace of Monaco, and, of course, Bob Hope, who personally distributed more than a thousand.

By the time of the January, 1973, Paris Peace Agreement, from four million to ten million Americans were wearing POW/MIA bracelets. The influence on the national imagination cannot be calculated. Every person who wore a bracelet vowed not to remove it until his or her POW/MIA was either found to be dead or returned home. Millions of people thus developed profound emotional bonds with the men whose names were displayed all day on their wrists. Countless American schoolchildren went through some of their most formative years linked to these amulets. How could they not believe in the living existence of their POW/MIAs then—and perhaps today? And the bracelets themselves must still be potent amulets, because even now the National League of Families' official distributors and other organizations are reportedly selling hundreds daily.

The POWs in War and Peace

THE POW/MIA ISSUE SERVED TWO CRUCIAL FUNCtions in allowing Richard Nixon to continue the war for four years—and thus avoid the "loss" of Vietnam—even though he had assumed office almost a year after the nation had shown its desperate desire for peace. It was both a booby trap for the anti-war movement and a wrench to be thrown into the works of the Paris peace talks.

The Nixon Administration's four-year campaign to secure the release of American prisoners of war separate from U.S. withdrawal from Vietnam was doomed, along with its other war goals, by the peace accords signed in Paris on January 27, 1973. The agreement among the four parties—the United States, the Democratic Republic of Vietnam, the Republic of Vietnam, and the Provisional Revolutionary Government of South Vietnam—

called for the withdrawal from Vietnam of all "United States forces and those of the other foreign countries allied with the United States" within sixty days and the return of all prisoners of war to be "carried out simultaneously with and completed not later than the same day" as the U.S. troop withdrawal.

In conformity with the agreement, North Vietnam had already delivered to the United States and certified as complete a list of its prisoners of war and those who had died in captivity. Within the stipulated two months the living prisoners on the list, including all those who had been captured in Laos and South Vietnam, were repatriated. Their return was staged as Operation Homecoming, an event transformed by an awesome media blitz into a public-relations coup for President Nixon, who boasted at his formal White House dinner party for the ex-POWs that he had achieved "the return of all of our prisoners of war" as part of his successful conclusion of the war in Vietnam.

But the President's claims by no means satisfied many of those who had been agitating about the POW/MIA issue. They argued that there were "discrepancies" between the Vietnamese lists and American information. Some claimed that there were as many as fifty-six men "known" to have been captured for whom there was now no accounting. The myth of the forsaken POWs enslaved by the Asian Communists was about to emerge from the war to poison the peace.

The Pentagon's New Math

WAS THERE ANY BASIS FOR THE CLAIM THAT the DRV, the PRG, the Pathet Lao, and the Khmer Rouge were secretly keeping Americans as prisoners? As soon as the Paris agreements were signed, the Department of Defense started trying to make the American people think so. While the Administration was basking in glory for bringing home all the POWs, the Pentagon was issuing a series of conflicting statements evidently designed to create both suspicion and confusion. Readers of these statements—especially the families of the missing—could hardly avoid thinking that some men might be held captive someplace in Indochina. For in drafting its announcements the Defense Department was using ink as an octopus does, clouding the waters so as to obscure its own activity.

Here, for example, is what readers of *The New York Times* were encountering from day to day in early 1973:

"The [Defense] department presently lists 587 prisoners—473 in North Vietnam, 108 in South Vietnam and six in Laos—plus 1,335 more men missing in action. In addition, the State Department . . . believes that 51 American civilians have been captured in Indochina, principally in South Vietnam" (January 26).

"The list that the North Vietnamese turned over to American officials in Paris today named 27 American civilians as prisoners of the Vietcong, and listed seven other Americans as having died in captivity" (January 28).

"The Defense Department lists 1,334 men missing in action—519 in North Vietnam, 504 in South Vietnam and 311 in Laos" (January 29).

"Fifty-six Americans known to have been prisoners of war in Southeast Asia remain unaccounted for by North Vietnam, a Pentagon spokesman said today. . . . There were no clues to the whereabouts of 1,269 men now listed by the Pentagon as missing in Southeast Asia" (January 30).

"Fifty-four men . . . thought by American officials to be prisoners did not appear on the list of 562 confirmed P.O.W.'s held captive in North and South Vietnam and Laos. Nor were they listed as having died in captivity" (February 26).

Not having access to the mathematics of the Pentagon's computers, American citizens—not to mention the Vietnamese—would have to resort to simple arithmetic to try to understand what was being revealed, or obfuscated, by these shifting numbers.

Let us begin with the Defense and State departments' original figures, while bearing in mind that the Nixon Administration had been trying for more than three years to establish as high a total as possible of Americans believed to be prisoners. The Pentagon listed 587 servicemen it considered likely to be prisoners—473 in North Vietnam, 108 in South Vietnam, and six in Laos. Add to that the fifty-one American civilians that the State Department thought were captured throughout Indochina. The total is 638. How many did Vietnam and the Pathet Lao release or otherwise account for as having died in captivity? Here is the total:

Military prisoners from Vietnam released	555
Military prisoners from Laos released	7
Civilian prisoners from Vietnam released	27
Civilian prisoners from Laos released	2
Military prisoners died in captivity	55
Civilian prisoners died in captivity	7
Total prisoners released or died	*653*

So Vietnam and the Pathet Lao actually released or accounted for fifteen more prisoners than the Defense and State departments had listed as likely prisoners, even though both agencies, as revealed by their own documents, had attempted to inflate their figures. (Note also that the State Department's figure included civilians believed to have been captured in Cambodia.) The figures for Laos, due for a key role in the POW/MIA myth, were especially embarrassing for the Pentagon, which had listed six men thought to be prisoners there. Seven military prisoners were returned from Laos, and two of the supposed six Laotian military prisoners were actually in the hands of the Vietnamese; instead of the six on the Pentagon's list of Laotian POWs, it got back nine.

The Case of the Disappearing POWs

THE HOUSE SELECT COMMITTEE ON AMERICANS Missing in Southeast Asia, although it carefully reviewed the individual files of 200 other unresolved MIA cases, scrutinized most intensely the cases of unaccounted-for men actually listed by the various services as POWs. How many of these were there? It turns out that the number of cases classified as POWs was not fifty-six, fifty-four, or even fifty-three but thirty-six. Thirty-six was the number presented by the Defense Department. Thirty-six was the number accepted not only by the select committee but also by the chairman of the board of the National League of Families (which by this time was controlled by activists committed to the POW/MIA issue).

The committee conducted an exhaustive study of each of the thirty-six cases. This included a thorough analysis of the complete classified case file maintained by each man's own service, followed by an intensive cross-check with the classified intelligence file maintained by the Defense Intelligence Agency. For fifteen, the committee could find no evidence that the men had been taken alive. Eight of the rest could "possibly" have been captured alive, and eleven, twelve, or thirteen had been at one time "definitely" alive in enemy hands. Of crucial importance were the committee's findings about those eleven, twelve, or thirteen who were known to have been captured:

> In six cases, reports from indigenous sources indicate that the individual died in captivity. Another one was reported in 1973, both by the PRG and by returnees, as having died in captivity in 1967, but for technical reasons his case has not been reviewed. Still another defected to the Viet Cong in 1967, and he could still be alive in Vietnam. There is no evidence in the remaining four cases to suggest whether the individual is now dead or alive, but in no case did any of these four appear in a regular POW camp, and all have been missing for at least 6 years.

This handful of cases is the foundation on which the colossal structure of the POW/MIA myth has been built.

So there were not fifty-six or fifty-four or fifty-three unaccounted-for POWs. There were not even thirty-six or twenty-seven or twenty. At the most there were thirteen or twelve or eleven. Except for the defector, all but four of these had evidently died in captivity. None of the four had ever appeared in a regular POW camp, and there is no evidence that any survived later than 1970.

Crucifixion and Resurrection

IN THE LATE 1970S PRESIDENT JIMMY CARTER BEGAN to reverse course not just on possible relations with Vietnam but also on détente in general, which led, in the final two years of his Administration, to the restoration of draft registration, the removal of SALT II from consideration by the Senate, the embargo of grain sales to the Soviet Union, the boycott of the Olympics in Moscow, and the initiation of the biggest arms buildup in U.S. history.

Simultaneously there began a rewriting and re-imaging of the history of the Vietnam War which would restore the discredited vision of idealistic, courageous Americans heroically battling hordes of sadistic Asian Communists. On the academic front the charge was led by a brigade of revisionist historians who attempted to place the origins of the war and America's conduct of it in a more favorable light. Their task was formidable. Those who fought on the popular-culture front had a much easier job, for they could simply ignore the history and rely entirely on manipulative images. And no image had proved more powerful during the war than that of American prisoners.

By far the most influential work in this campaign was the movie *The Deer Hunter*, which in 1978 received four Academy Awards, including one for best picture, and was designated the best English-language film of the year by the New York Film Critics' Circle. *The Deer Hunter* succeeded not only in radically re-imaging the war but also in transforming POWs into crucial symbols of American manhood.

The re-imaging appears quite conscious, though most critics at the time seemed oblivious of it. The basic technique was to take images of the war that had become deeply embedded in America's consciousness and transform them into their opposite. For example, in the first scene in Vietnam a uniformed soldier throws a grenade into an underground shelter harboring village women and children, and then with his automatic assault rifle mows down a woman and her baby. Although the scene resembles *Life*'s pictures of the My Lai massacre, the soldier is not an American but a North Vietnamese. He is then killed by a lone guerrilla, who is not a Viet Cong but our Special Forces hero, Robert DeNiro.

When two men plummet from a helicopter, the images replicate a telephotographic sequence from the war showing an NLF prisoner being pushed from a helicopter to make other prisoners talk; but the falling men in the movie are American POWs attempting to escape from their murderous NLF captors. The central, structuring metaphor of the film is the Russian roulette that the sadistic Asian Communists force their prisoners to play. POW after POW is shown with a revolver at his right temple, framed to match with precision the sequence seen by tens of millions of Americans in which the chief of the Saigon police placed a revolver to the right temple of an

NLF prisoner and killed him with a single shot; even the blood spurting out of the temple is exactly replicated. There is no evidence that any such atrocity was ever committed against a single American prisoner of the NLF or North Vietnam.

The Deer Hunter's manipulation of images culminates in a long sequence in which DeNiro persuades Christopher Walken that their only hope of escape is to use the Russian-roulette revolver to kill their captors. The fiendish Vietnamese have placed them in a half-submerged tiger cage, behind which we see a single vertical and a single horizontal strand of barbed wire, which somehow frequently replace the bars of the tiger cage in the camera's field of vision. Whatever reason their captors may have had for this arrangement, it allows the camera to show only the heads and torsos of the two men, and the lighting is set up—by the director, not the Communists—so that throughout much of this sequence the heads and torsos are silhouetted in profile. Thus in frame after frame appears the logo, including the single strand of barbed wire, of the POW/MIA flag.

Intercut with this sequence are images of the POWs as crucified Christs, bloody headbands replacing the crown of thorns, with the hands of soldiers hauling them up to their torture and death. The religious and patriotic messages of *The Deer Hunter* are unified from the beginning, when a banner that proclaims SERVING GOD AND COUNTRY PROUDLY hangs over the wedding celebration, to the very end, when, just as at a National League of Families convention, everybody sings "God Bless America." And the unifying images are those of American white working-class men as crucified prisoners of the Vietnamese.

But for the POWs and MIAs to become an authentic myth gripping America's heart, less subtle visions had to be shaped by Hollywood. Who could resurrect those missing American fighting men who had been crucified by the Asian Communists and their domestic accomplices? This was a job for true heroes, led by one of VIVA's original boosters, Ronald Reagan.

Hollywood Heroes I: Bo Gritz and Ronald Reagan

THE STORY OF THE HEROIC AMERICAN PRISONers abandoned in Southeast Asia could not become a major American myth until the dream factory geared up its assembly line for mass production of the essential images. But Hollywood was actually involved in creating the historical raw materials that the POW rescue movies were later to fantasize.

The character central to the POW/MIA story as it attained its full mythic status in the 1980s was retired Special Forces Colonel James "Bo" Gritz, who organized raids into Laos to rescue men he already envisioned in images that would later be projected on movie and TV screens around the world. With devout faith in living POWs abandoned by their government to cruel Communist slavery, Gritz conceived of their rescue as a mission forced upon him by destiny. Why was he the chosen one? Because the only two other men capable of such intense "action," as he put it, were no longer around to do the job: "Both Teddy Roosevelt and John Wayne are dead."

But two other men of action were available at least to help finance the mission: Captain Kirk, of the starship *Enterprise*, and Dirty Harry. William Shatner put up $10,000 and received movie rights to the Gritz story. Clint Eastwood, who contributed $30,000, was assigned a far more crucial role in the adventure.

Ever since the Paris agreement of 1973 POW activists had been elaborating the theme of a conspiracy high in the government to

Those who fought on the popular-culture front had a much easier job, for they could simply ignore the history of the Vietnam War and rely entirely on manipulative images. And no image proved more powerful during the war than that of American prisoners.

POWs as depicted in *The Deer Hunter* (1978)

Movie Still Archives

deny the existence of American prisoners. The villains were government bureaucrats, CIA operatives, and liberal politicians, personified by President Carter himself. With the inauguration of Ronald Reagan in early 1981, the myth evolved with a new twist: the good President amid the evil officials. Ronald Reagan's heart yearned to save the POWs, but the President was surrounded and kept in ignorance by that claque of scheming bureaucrats and liberals now known as the doorkeepers or gatekeepers. Who could possibly get by the all-powerful evil gatekeepers and bring the truth to the good President?

The one man in America Colonel Gritz knew he could rely on for the job was Clint Eastwood. His plan hinged on two tête-à-têtes between Eastwood and the President. On the night of November 27, 1982, after receiving word that Gritz's team had crossed the Mekong River from Thailand into Laos, Eastwood was to fly from his California ranch to a prearranged meeting at Reagan's California ranch and inform the President about the raid. When the raiders had actually freed American POWs, they were to send a message by means of "nuclear fire plan boxes" ("state-of-the-art . . . Indirect Transmission Devices" furnished by Litton Industries) to their base in Thailand, which would relay the message to their "Angels West" base in Los Angeles, which would in turn relay the message to Eastwood, who would then once again fly to see his old friend Ronald Reagan, who would then have to do what he wanted to do all along: send U.S. forces to rescue the POWs. So crucial was Eastwood's first meeting with the President that Gritz led his men across the Mekong before most of their weapons had arrived, so that they would be in Laos by the night of the twenty-seventh, California time. Eastwood reportedly carried out his assignment—either flying from his Shasta ranch to Reagan's Santa Barbara ranch to meet with the President at the appointed time or, in a less theatrical version, informing the President about the raid by telephone. When the raiders returned from Laos to Thailand, on December 3, they found this message waiting for them from a team member in California:

CLINT AND I MET WITH PRESIDENT ON 27TH. PRESIDENT SAID: QUOTE, IF YOU BRING OUT ONE U.S. POW, I WILL START WORLD WAR III TO GET THE REST OUT. UNQUOTE.

Whether the President indeed said these words we don't know, but they would certainly be in character. After all, Ronald Reagan had been active in POW issues ever since he was himself a POW of Asian Communists during the Korean War—as the star of the 1954 movie *Prisoner of War.*

Gritz's raid, however, was not entirely a Hollywood production. Unlike all those heroes in the subsequent movies inspired by their adventure, the Americans did not ambush and wipe out hordes of Asian Communists. In fact, almost as soon as they arrived in Laos, they were ambushed, routed, and forced to flee back to Thailand—not by treacherous Communists, as they initially assumed, but by a rival anti-Communist Laotian group whom Gritz's men had offended in Thailand and to whom Gritz, ironically enough, reportedly had to pay a ransom of $17,500 to recover a captured American teammate. The raiders of course encountered no POWs.

In fact, neither this raid nor ones that Gritz claimed to have carried out deeper in Laos in the ensuing months yielded any tangible evidence of American POWs. Thirty rolls of photographs taken with high-tech cameras, which Gritz promised to give to a congressional subcommittee investigating his raids, never materialized. Alleged remains of two American POWs which Gritz brought back with him turned out to be bones from two Asians mixed with animal bones.

Yet Gritz was tremendously effective in achieving one of his principal goals: "We have heightened public awareness of the POW question." His escapades were to be vital to what the Reagan Administration was calling, in the same words used by Gritz, its "public awareness" campaign, initiated just as Gritz was preparing his raiders. As the *Final Interagency Report of the Reagan Administration on the POW/MIA Issue* phrased it, "From its inception in 1982, the public awareness campaign steadily gained momentum."

As it left office, in 1989, the Reagan Administration could truthfully exult that this "aggressive public awareness campaign," waged "in coordination with the National League of POW/MIA Families," had "raised domestic consciousness of this issue to the highest level

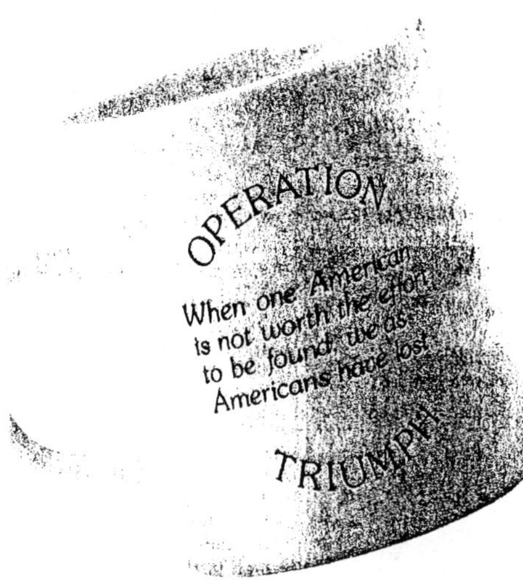

since the end of the war" while causing "media coverage" to increase "dramatically." A full "integration of the National League of Families into our efforts" meant that the League became even more thoroughly intertwined with the government than it had been with its creator, the Nixon Administration. The 1990 *POW-MIA Fact Book* states outright,

> United States Government policy regarding the POW/MIA issue is coordinated through the POW/MIA Interagency Group (IAG). Membership in the IAG includes the Defense Department, the White House National Security Council (NSC) staff, the State Department, the Joint Chiefs of Staff (JCS), the Defense Intelligence Agency (DIA) and the National League of POW/MIA Families.

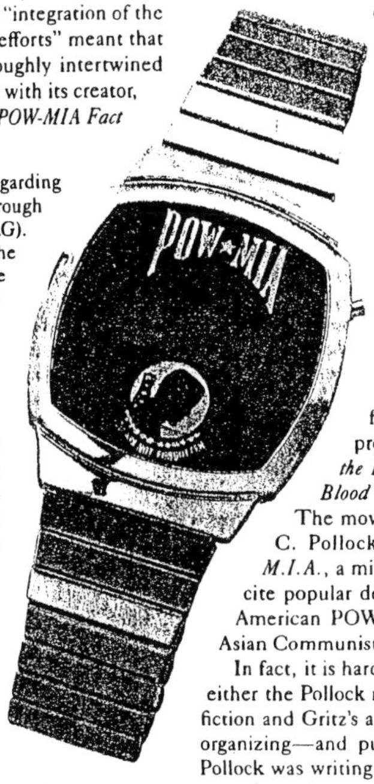

President Reagan vastly expanded the POW/MIA section of the Defense Intelligence Agency, more than tripling its staff and adding "a special team deployed in Southeast Asia" to solicit "refugee information." A key addition to the DIA staff was Carol Bates, who had been a co-founder of VIVA and its bracelet campaign and the executive director of the National League of Families during the period when it was transformed into the leading promoter of the belief in live postwar POWs.

Three days before news of Gritz's first raid burst upon the public, while Gritz was conducting his second raid, President Reagan, who had been kept closely informed, declared to a special meeting of the National League of Families that from now on "the government bureaucracy" would have to understand that the POW/MIA issue had assumed "the highest national priority" (a phrase echoing VIVA's "one of our nation's top priorities").

In the next few months Colonel Gritz became a star of magazines, newspapers, radio, and TV. But he was a fast-fading luminary, for the story of his raids was hardly a tale of spectacularly successful heroism. Hollywood would now have to show how the story was supposed to look.

Hollywood Heroes II: Gene Hackman and Chuck Norris

AMID THE MEDIA HOOPLA ABOUT THE GRITZ RAIDS, the first fantasized movie version began shooting. Starring Gene Hackman as a retired Marine colonel, *Uncommon Valor* made it to the screen in time for the Christmas season of 1983. The following year came *Missing in Action*, with Chuck Norris as retired Special Forces Colonel James Braddock, an even more thinly disguised impersonation of retired Special Forces Colonel Bo Gritz. And in 1985 the POW/MIA myth attained its apotheosis in *Rambo: First Blood Part II*, with Sylvester Stallone now incarnate as the true American superhero of our epoch.

The ideological agenda of *Uncommon Valor* is suggested by the identity of its co-producers: John Milius, whose vision is expressed most clearly in two films he directed during this period, *Conan the Barbarian* (1982) and *Red Dawn* (1984), and Buzz Feitshans, Milius's frequent collaborator, whose other productions include *First Blood, Conan the Barbarian, Red Dawn, Rambo: First Blood Part II, Rambo III*, and *Total Recall*. The movie also appears to draw heavily on J. C. Pollock's best-selling 1982 novel *Mission M.I.A.*, a militarist tract explicitly designed to incite popular demand for mercenary raids to rescue American POWs and to slaughter their subhuman Asian Communist captors.

In fact, it is hard to disentangle *Uncommon Valor* from either the Pollock novel or the actual raids, for Pollock's fiction and Gritz's adventures are intertwined. Gritz was organizing—and publicizing—his raids in 1981, while Pollock was writing *Mission M.I.A.*, and an extended excerpt from the novel appeared in the same issue of *Penthouse* (March, 1982) that printed a long interview with Gritz about his plans. So evidently Gritz and Pollock gave ideas to each other as well as to *Uncommon Valor*.

The film was labeled a mere "Okay grind actioner" by *Variety* and dismissed at first by most reviewers, whose reactions can be summed up by this headline: "COMIC-STRIP-LEVEL HEROISM MAKES UNCOMMON VALOR A COMMON BORE." But within a few weeks critics were trying to comprehend the startling audience response to what was turning out to be the "biggest movie surprise" of the 1983–1984 season. The best explanation seemed to come from "an ordinary moviegoer who said with satisfaction of the bloody ending in which dozens of the enemy are mowed down by the Americans, 'We get to win the Vietnam War.'"

Uncommon Valor's formula for such a revision of history was identified by the cultural critic Rob Edelman in terms that would soon also apply to its spectacular successors:

> The Vietnam war is not really over. . . and we—America—can still pass for a touchdown at Ho Chi Minh Stadium and eke out a last second victory in the Rice Paddy Bowl. Just send a few good boys back there, kick some Asian ass, liberate a few MIAs. The Laotians—or

> Cambodians, or Vietnamese, for they are really all alike—will fall like Indians in a John Wayne movie, and America will be proud and regain its honor.

This message would become explicit later in 1984, as full-page shoot-'em-up ads for *Missing in Action* proclaimed: "THE WAR'S NOT OVER UNTIL THE LAST MAN COMES HOME!"

Yet the revised history offered by *Uncommon Valor* was not quite as "mindless" as many critics labeled it, for they were ignoring a subtext based on the POW/MIA pseudohistory already widely diffused throughout sections of American society and accepted by many viewers as a true, even the essential, version of the Vietnam War.

The experience of Colonel Jason Rhodes (Hackman), whose son had been missing in action for a decade since the end of the war, helped to transform details of this pseudohistory into mythology that became part of the shared cultural inheritance of 1980s America. Like Colonel Gritz, Colonel Rhodes learned that there had been "over four hundred live sightings of men held against their will" and "there are compounds all over northern Laos." Why Laos? The case for live POWs in Vietnam was so untenable that true believers had been forced to shift the burden of their argument onto Laos. Colonel Gritz had testified to Congress, "Nearly 700 airmen were shot down over Laos during the Vietnam War. Not one has been returned." In fact, as previously discussed, more prisoners were returned from Laos than the Defense and State departments had listed as probable prisoners there; subsequent investigation demonstrated that no more than five others had ever been captive in Laos,

THE POW/MIA LOBBY

THE FEDERAL government is primarily responsible for the notion that U.S. prisoners of war languish in Indochina. However, several nonprofit organizations concern themselves with the issue, and their activities bolster its significance in the public mind. POW/MIA organizations have varying goals: some claim to have evidence of the whereabouts of prisoners and to be planning rescue missions; others, more modestly, seek to influence government policy. But each of the major groups has in its charter the goal of educating the public about the POW/MIA issue and raising its level of concern, mostly through direct-mail solicitations. The direct mail and speeches and videos that raise public concern thus also raise funds; the funds pay for more mail, which raises funds, which pay for mail.

Capsule descriptions of four of the major groups dealing with the POW/MIA issue appear below. Commenting on the first three of these groups in a 1987 report to Representative Stephen J. Solarz, the chairman of the House Subcommittee on Asian and Pacific Affairs, Brigadier General James W. Shufelt, of the Defense Intelligence Agency, wrote, "In closing, it is noteworthy that for all their 'proof' and the untold millions of dollars raised, none of these groups or individuals have yet to furnish even the slightest shred of evidence of PWs, much less secure the return of a living American captive."

American Defense Foundation and the *American Defense Institute:* Incorporated in 1983 by a retired Navy captain and former prisoner of war, Eugene B. "Red" McDaniel, the American Defense Foundation and its educational arm, the American Defense Institute, have been responsible for providing several of the photographs of alleged prisoners that have circulated in recent years. McDaniel's was the group that last summer publicized the now-familiar photograph of three "American prisoners" holding up a sign—a photograph that is widely regarded to be fake. In one fund-raising letter McDaniel writes, "I promise to tell all of our hostages, when they are finally freed, of the vital role you played in their release. I wish you would write a brief note on the enclosed donation card, which I will personally hand to the first man to regain his freedom." McDaniel's groups have interests wider than the POW/MIA issue. On the back of McDaniel's memoir of his life as a prisoner, *Scars & Stripes*, the American Defense Foundation is described as a nonprofit foundation that "promotes American moral and military strength as essential elements of world peace." The American Defense Institute supports continued government funding of the Strategic Defense Initiative and the B-2 Stealth bomber. In 1989 the ADI received $2.3 million in contributions. In that same year it spent $523,769 on publications, research, and public affairs, $223,369 on its speakers' bureau, $217,625 on internships for young people, $159,135 on seminars and videos, $325,648 on a drive to register members of the military and their eligible dependents to vote, $197,710 on POW awareness, and $422,753 on fund-raising.

Account For POW/MIA (also known as the *Skyhook II Project*): Incorporated in 1984 by John LeBoutillier, a one-term Republican congressman from Long Island, Account for POW/MIA describes its mission as "To secure humane treatment of, status information, and accountability and to promulgate concern for American Prisoners of War and Missing in Action in Southeast Asia in accordance with the Geneva Convention of 1949." Its appeals feature references to specific numbers of prisoners known to be held, detailed descriptions of the conditions under which prisoners live, and outlines of how prisoners might be rescued if the organization could raise the necessary money. "We are close to making contact with an American POW who has been alone since his fellow prisoner died of natural causes less than a year ago," one LeBoutillier letter reads. "That effort could fail for a lack of funds.

and all these had almost certainly died in the mid- or late 1960s. Yet by the time *Uncommon Valor* was screened, millions of Americans believed the Gritz version.

In a scene charged with a shock of recognition for viewers familiar with the widely accepted pseudohistory, Colonel Rhodes becomes convinced that his son is a prisoner in one of the Laotian camps. After ten years of being brushed off by government bureaucrats and victimized by con men in Thailand, Rhodes finally learns the truth from an active-duty Air Force colonel. Noting with a sigh, "I suppose someone could call this treason," the officer pulls from his briefcase a photograph taken from an SR-71 Blackbird high-altitude reconnaissance plane. "There's your proof," he declares. "It's a prison camp in Laos." Whatever the photograph's effect on most of the movie's reviewers, countless members of the audience were reminded of the famous "Fort Apache" photograph that inspired Colonel Gritz's raids, and were thrilled that the film anticipated their recognition.

The scene enshrines the Fort Apache photograph while wiping away its tarnished history. Word of such a photograph or photographs, taken either from an SR-71 flying at 80,000 feet and 2,000 miles per hour or from a spy satellite, began leaking out soon after Ronald Reagan assumed the presidency, in January of 1981. This was the interpretation of the photo: thirty men, who were in some kind of formation, cast shadows longer than Asians would; they seemed "posed in a secret body-language code taught to selected airmen facing a risk of capture"; tools were evident that were too big for Asians; one structure might be a guard tower; on one side of the camp there appeared to be a 5

Please be as generous as you can as soon as you can." LeBoutillier typically attributes his claims to reports from refugees, "secret information," or "sources," or gives no attribution.

In 1989 Account For POW/MIA raised $343,862 from direct mail and received $98,626 in unsolicited contributions. Of that money, $276,832 went for postage and mailing costs and $71,500 went to unspecified "program field expenses." It is difficult to determine how much of its money Account For POW/MIA spent on its aim of disseminating information and how much on fund-raising. The organization's financial statement makes the link between the two explicit: the expenses column includes the category "public information combined with fund raising."

Operation Rescue: Incorporated by a former fighter pilot, Jack Bailey, in 1981, Operation Rescue has produced photographs allegedly of missing servicemen, turned in bone fragments that it claimed were those of missing servicemen, and, both for humanitarian reasons and in the hope of getting information about POWs, sought to rescue Southeast Asian refugees from boats off the coast of Vietnam. One 1986 fund-raising letter reads, "Must raise $13,671.71 by Friday, October 31, or vital intelligence gathering missions may have to be stopped. Unless these missions continue, there is no hope for the return of POWs and MIAs captive in Vietnam. Again, if I cannot raise $13,671.71 by October 31, vital intelligence gathering cannot continue. And an American serviceman will die in the jungles of Vietnam." In 1989 Operation Rescue raised $228,005 in contributions. Of that money, $29,026 went to collecting intelligence on missing servicemen and aiding Southeast Asian refugees, $25,279 went to management expenses, and $163,298 went to fund-raising. From 1981 to 1989 Operation Rescue raised $3.3 million dollars. At no point from 1985 to 1989 did the amount of money that Operation Rescue spent on direct services rise above 16.6 percent of its total expenditures. The floor set by the Council of Better Business Bureaus for the portion of contributed money that a charitable group should spend on direct services is 50 percent.

National League of Families of American Prisoners and Missing in Southeast Asia: A copy of Brigadier General Shufelt's report is included in the information routinely provided to the public by the National League of Families. Incorporated in 1970, the League is the oldest and most respected POW/MIA organization. Membership is restricted to relatives of unaccounted-for servicemen. The league's executive director, Ann Mills Griffiths, is the only nongovernment representative on an interagency government panel that crafts policy positions on the POW/MIA issue. Griffiths travels with official delegations to Southeast Asia on missions concerning POW/MIAs. The league endorses the U.S. government's official position on POW/MIAs and, as its dissemination of the Shufelt report shows, is highly critical of the groups listed above.

If you call the National League's Washington, D.C., telephone number and request information, this is what you'll receive in the mail: statistics from the Defense Intelligence Agency on live-sighting reports and the number of servicemen unaccounted for, status reports on the POW/MIA issue and on the league's activities, answers to frequently asked questions about the league and the POW/MIA issue, and, on different-colored paper, a request for support. Among the suggested things you can do to support the league: participate in the adopt-a-missing-man program, at a cost of $5.00 a month; wear a POW/MIA pin, available for $3.00 each or two for $5.00; display a logo decal, available for $10.00 per hundred; fly the league flag, available for $35.00. In 1989 the National League brought in contributions of $932,344 and spent $193,884 for fund-raising and $843,188 on its programs. Among the program costs were $150,732 for printing and postage, $228,505 for public awareness, and $198,266 for salaries and employee benefits for the league's six employees. *—Ethan Seidman* and on the other side a 2, no doubt meant as either a call for help or a signal from the prisoners or both, referring to the number of men held in the camp or to the crew of a B-52 or to the number of hostages being held in Iran. The ostensible chronology of subsequent events is central to the POW/MIA myth.

Colonel Gritz, with considerable assistance from the Pentagon, immediately began training a team to rescue the prisoners from Fort Apache, a mission he dubbed Operation Velvet Hammer. But, according to his account,

> In mid-March 1981, at almost the precise moment that the 'VELVET HAMMER' team was preparing for overseas movement, I was informed that the new Reagan Administration had become fully persuaded of the existence of American POWs in Southeast Asia and had decided on an official rescue mission. . . . I was asked, therefore, to abandon the VELVET HAMMER Operation.

The official raid was to be carried out by Delta Force commandos. "In May 1981, the official rescue mission—the DELTA OPERATION—was also cancelled," Gritz testified. To him and to later true believers this was proof of government cowardice and betrayal.

One would never guess from the POW/MIA movies and writings and folklore that the U.S. government did in fact stage a raid into Laos, a raid that penetrated to the site of the alleged Fort Apache, only to discover that it was not a POW camp after all. This mission, by Laotian mercenaries trained, equipped, and paid by the CIA, was carried out in May of 1981; the failure of its on-site photographs to disclose any trace whatsoever of POWs was evidently the real reason that the Delta Force raid was called off. That raid, involving more than a hundred helicopters and transport planes, had been primed to go.

Nevertheless, government cowardice and betrayal could now be built into the mythological structure of *Uncommon Valor* and its successors. Hackman's efforts to recruit and train a team to rescue his son, which take up more than half the film, are constantly menaced by "the politicians" and omnipresent government agents equipped with high-tech spy mikes and phone taps. These sinister figures also try to intimidate the Texas oil tycoon who finances the raiders' training camp (he, too, has an MIA son)—by threatening an IRS audit of his corporation. Just as Hackman and his team are about to launch their mission from Thailand into Laos, U.S. agents have them apprehended by Thai authorities, who confiscate their weapons, forcing them to rely on a Bangkok gun dealer and an aged Laotian drug runner.

To recruit his team of rescuers, Hackman first had to rescue each man from the corrupting and emasculating bonds of civilian life in America, including the domestic bondage imposed by women. Only then could these all-American heroes slaughter hordes of puny little Asians, rescue their enslaved comrades, give the Vietnam War a noble ending, and redeem America.

The image of a nation run by "bureaucrats," "politicians," and shadowy secret agents in business suits who revile and betray its true warrior-heroes forms part of the tableau that gives the POW/MIA myth such potency. For the myth rejects and repudiates not only the history of the Vietnam War but also what, according to the myth, is the quintessence of everyday life in post-Vietnam America. The idealism, virility, and heroism of men who dedicate their lives to rescuing their abandoned comrades, sons, and fathers are presented as the alternative to a weak, decadent America subjugated by materialism, hedonism, and feminism.

Hollywood Heroes III: Rambo

THE TRANSFORMATION OF THE POW/MIA STORY into genuine myth was consummated in a fantasy whose hero's name would soon become a term in the political discourse and everyday vocabulary not only of the nation but of the world. Without this movie (or some equally sensational dramatization) the POW/MIA issue could hardly have assumed its mythic role in the lives of tens of millions of Americans, for essential to their personal faith was some powerful visual display of the key elements of the myth.

Six weeks after the opening of *Rambo: First Blood Part II*, President Reagan projected himself into its star role—while symbiotically hyping the film with a presidential plug—as he declared (ostensibly as a microphone test before his national address on the release of U.S. hostages in Beirut): "Boy, I saw *Rambo* last night. Now I know what to do the next time this happens." Later that month members of Congress "signaled a new tough-minded attitude" on foreign relations by invoking the image of Rambo a dozen times in debating a foreign-aid bill. Rambo's political repercussions have continued to be heard around the world. Late last year, for example, President Saddam Hussein of Iraq defiantly responded to the U.S. threat of war with his own bluster in the guise of cultural criticism: "The Americans are still influenced by Rambo movies, but this is not a Rambo movie."

As *Rambo* packed theaters with audiences who howled with pleasure and wildly cheered every slaying of a Vietnamese or Russian by its invulnerable hero, the nation was flooded with Rambo "action dolls," watches, walkie-talkies, water guns, bubble gum, pinball machines, sportswear for all ages, and even "Rambo-Grams," messages delivered by headbanded musclemen sporting bandoliers across their bare chests. A TV cartoon serial transformed Rambo into "liberty's champion," a Superman-like figure engaged in global struggles against evil; designed by Family Home Entertainment "for ages 5-12," it began its extended run in 1986.

Movie Still Archives

A scene from *Rambo: First Blood Part II* (1985)

The transformation of the POW/MIA story into genuine myth was consummated in a fantasy whose hero's name would soon become a term in the political discourse and everyday vocabulary not only of the nation but of the world.

This new American hero was constructed in Hollywood through highly sophisticated manipulation of recycled cultural materials. Rambo's roots tap into the very foundation of American self-identity: the myth of the frontier. As Richard Slotkin has shown, the frontier's corollary "myth of regeneration through violence became the structuring metaphor of the American experience." Rambo perpetuates the wartime vision of Vietnam as "Injun country." But Rambo is not just the Indian-fighter, recognized as the first national hero of the American state; he is also the Indian. For as the myth of the frontier continued to evolve, its hero metamorphosed from being just the captive or destroyer of Indians into a figure coalescing with the Indian and the wilderness. John Rambo, we are told, is of "Indian-German descent"—"a hell of a combination." "What you choose to call hell, he calls home."

But the main models for Rambo come much more directly out of American popular culture, a genesis that helps account for his tremendous impact on audiences. Perhaps once the most popular author in America, Edgar Rice Burroughs created two of Rambo's forebears: a martial-arts expert and veteran of a defeated American army who fights for good causes in alien lands against seemingly insurmountable odds (John Carter), and a bare-chested, muscular he-man who merges completely with the tropical jungle to carry out spectacular deeds of heroism (Tarzan). And Rambo draws much of his psychological power from one of America's most distinctive cultural products, the comic-book hero who may seem to be an ordinary human being but really possesses superhuman powers that allow him to fight, like Superman, for "truth, justice, and the American way" and to personify national fantasies, like Captain America.

In *Uncommon Valor* and *Missing in Action*, the imprisonment to which American society subjects its Vietnam veterans is mostly domestic and metaphorical. But when we first see Rambo in *First Blood Part II*, he is performing slave labor, breaking rocks in a desolate prison as punishment for his rebellion against the brutal lawmen of *First Blood* (1982); so he suffers the same fate in America that his buddies, abandoned by America, suffer in Vietnam. When his former commanding officer, Green Beret Lieutenant Colonel Trautman, offers him freedom in exchange for undertaking the mission in Vietnam, Rambo makes his famous reply: "Do we get to win this time?" Resonating in the question are years of rewritten and re-imaged history which have taught the 1985 audience that we could have won the war if only the politicians, the media, the liberal establishment, bureaucrats, draft-dodging college students and their pinko professors, hippies, wimps, bleeding-heart housewives, and Jane Fonda hadn't tied our boys' hands and stabbed them in the back.

The real enemy is personified as the archetypal bureaucrat, the perfidious, gutless, but seemingly omnipotent Marshall Murdock. Accused of being "a stinking bureaucrat that's trying to cover his ass," Murdock, who explicitly represents "Washington," replies, "Not just mine . . . a nation's." Trautman advises Rambo, "Let technology do most of the work," referring to Murdock's wondrous computer complex and high-tech weaponry. But Murdock uses his machines and underlings to sabotage the mission. The climax of *First Blood Part II* comes after Rambo returns with the POWs he has rescued, when he proceeds to blast Murdock's computers with automatic-weapon fire and then uses his gigantic knife to subjugate the whining, quivering, wimpy traitor.

The Plots Thicken

THE CULTURAL PRODUCTS THAT DISSEMINATE the MIA mythology and help to give it potent forms in the popular imagination have tended increasingly to project a vast government cover-up and conspiracy. *Vietnam Journal*, for example, last year ran a three-part series titled "Is the U.S. Hiding the Truth About Missing Soldiers?" (The answer, of course, was yes.) In the 1989 TV movie *The Forgotten*, starring Keith Carradine and Stacy Keach, high government officials actually conspire to psychologically torture and assassinate POWs previously held by Vietnam so that they won't reveal that these officials had colluded with North Vietnam to sabotage a POW rescue mission. The hero of Jack Buchanan's sixteen M.I.A. Hunter novels constantly battles against "Washington" and its sinister operatives; in *M.I.A. Hunter: Cambodian Hellhole* he can pursue his quest only "after demolishing a C.I.A. hit team sent to arrest him."

Meanwhile, however, Rambo was having an influence on the government itself. No postwar White House spokesperson actually claimed that American prisoners were still being held in Vietnam until October of 1985, when *Rambo*, released in May, was still packing the theaters. The assertion that "there have to be live Americans there" was made by none other than Robert C. McFarlane, President Reagan's National Security Adviser, to a forum for business executives and political consultants sponsored by the syndicated columnists Rowland Evans and Robert Novak.

But just as in the movie, Rambo proved difficult for the government to control once he was unleashed and empowered. Within weeks of the release of the film its messages were being taken too literally by a group of POW/MIA activists that came to be known as the Rambo faction. At the July convention of the National League of Families a speech declaring that the government had "attempted to track down every lead, and respond to every allegation, and we will continue to do so" was interrupted by belligerent chants of "Rambo! Rambo!"

In December, *60 Minutes* aired a segment on the POW issue titled "Dead or Alive." Its producer, Monika Jensen-Stevenson, claimed that the show was designed to present the "two sides" of the issue. One side was the official position of the Reagan Administration: there might be live POWs in Southeast Asia; when and if their existence was proved, the government would use all necessary means to recover them. And what was the other side? That live POWs were merely a myth that had become a distinctive feature of American culture? No, the other side was the position of the Rambo faction: the government itself was engaged in a vast conspiracy to conceal its own certain knowledge of the existence of dozens if not hundreds of live POWs.

Jensen-Stevenson, soon aided by her husband, William Stevenson, the author of *A Man Called Intrepid* and *Ninety Minutes at Entebbe*, spent the next five years building a case for this enormous conspiracy by the State Department, the Defense Department, the CIA, and other branches of government under the Reagan Administration. But before the couple published *Kiss the Boys Goodbye: How the United States Betrayed Its Own POWs in Vietnam*, in the fall of last year, an even more radical attack on the government appeared in a volume titled *A Nation Betrayed*, by none other than Colonel Bo Gritz.

In 1987 Gritz made his second trip to a remote region of Burma that forms part of the Golden Triangle, one of the world's major sources of heroin, to interview the drug lord and warlord General Khun Sa about American POWs in Laos. But the interview, which Gritz videotaped, evidently consisted mainly of detailed allegations by Khun Sa about his drug dealings with U.S. government agents, including officials high in the Reagan and Bush Administrations, who were using facilities in Bangkok not to resolve the POW/MIA question but mainly as a cover for their own drug deals and illicit cloak-and-dagger activities. The following year Gritz published *A Nation Betrayed*, an astonishing document whose thesis is that "a parallel government has existed for decades, which led us into a war that cost more than 58,000 lives and infused our nation with drugs," that this "shadow government has used drug and arms trafficking to fund illegal covert operations," and that the agents of this "cancerous bureaucracy," realizing that the discovery of American POWs would lead to the unmasking of their own sinister activities in Indochina, have systematically sabotaged every effort to find and rescue the prisoners.

Kiss the Boys Goodbye considerably elaborates Gritz's argument, incorporating it into a wider thesis: "America's wars in Southeast Asia had not ended with the fall of Saigon," and the "rogue secret wars in Asia," conducted by "a really deep-cover privatized CIA" and other covert agencies, were financed by a "trillion-dollar drug trade." The Stevensons thus explain not only why Vietnam, Laos, and Cambodia would continue to hold American POWs but also why officials and agencies of the U.S. government would conspire to conceal the existence of the POWs, even resorting to assassinations of those who knew too much: the Indochinese governments keep prisoners because wars are still being waged on them, and the U.S. officials are afraid that discovery of the POWs will expose the connection between their covert wars and

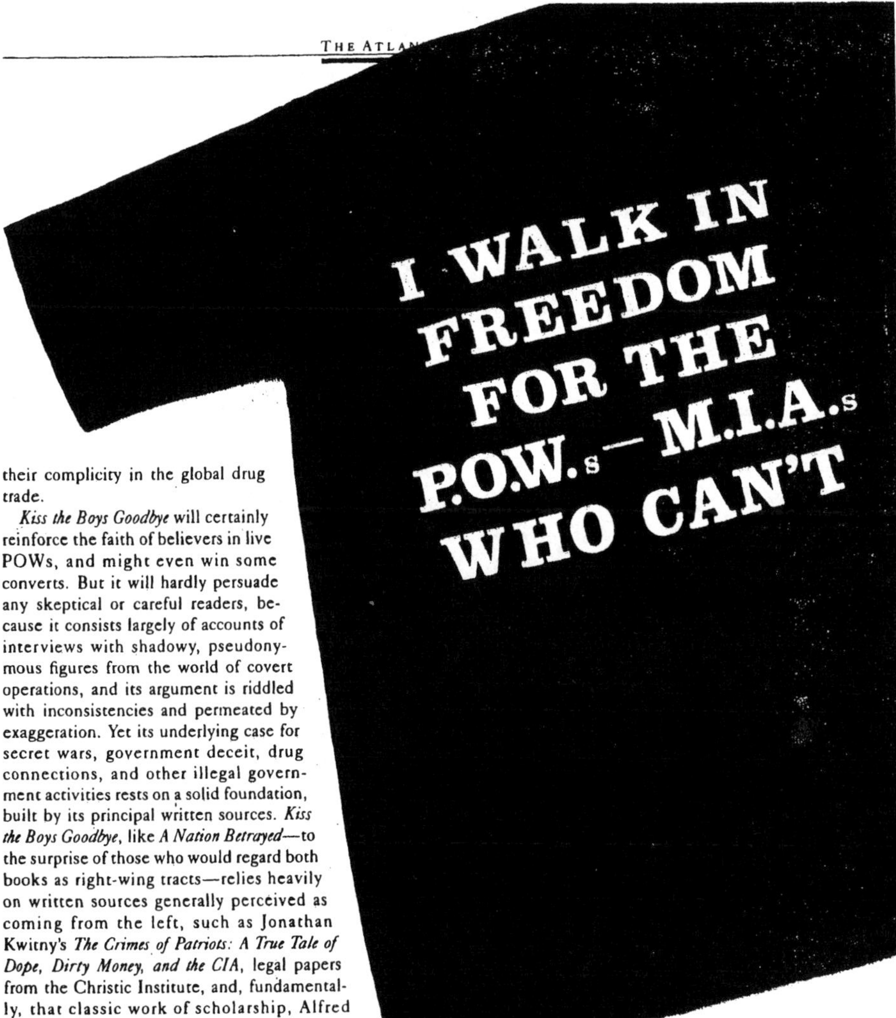

their complicity in the global drug trade.

Kiss the Boys Goodbye will certainly reinforce the faith of believers in live POWs, and might even win some converts. But it will hardly persuade any skeptical or careful readers, because it consists largely of accounts of interviews with shadowy, pseudonymous figures from the world of covert operations, and its argument is riddled with inconsistencies and permeated by exaggeration. Yet its underlying case for secret wars, government deceit, drug connections, and other illegal government activities rests on a solid foundation, built by its principal written sources. *Kiss the Boys Goodbye*, like *A Nation Betrayed*—to the surprise of those who would regard both books as right-wing tracts—relies heavily on written sources generally perceived as coming from the left, such as Jonathan Kwitny's *The Crimes of Patriots: A True Tale of Dope, Dirty Money, and the CIA*, legal papers from the Christic Institute, and, fundamentally, that classic work of scholarship, Alfred McCoy's *The Politics of Heroin in Southeast Asia* (whose discrediting by the CIA the newer book documents). Though it fails to demonstrate how the reality of covert, illegal government activities proves the existence of live POWs, *Kiss the Boys Goodbye* does succeed in suggesting why the people engaged in these activities might desperately want to keep unrestrained POW/MIA investigators from mucking around in Southeast Asia. And the main effect of the book may be to introduce people who believe in live prisoners of war to the scholarship demonstrating that the Vietnam War itself was one of those "murky foreign wars" conducted for aims shrouded by U.S. government duplicity and waged by "disposable soldiers."

So as the final decade of the twentieth century dawned, the POW/MIA myth, which had already assumed a life of its own, was beginning to resemble a Frankenstein's monster for the forces that had fabricated it out of spare parts from older myths. Whether it can be disposed of, once it has fulfilled the varying purposes that it has been serving since 1969, remains to be seen. □

The Myth of the Troubled and Scorned Vietnam Veteran

ERIC T. DEAN, JR.

In the United States since the conclusion of the Vietnam War, the Vietnam veteran has become known as a neglected, troubled, and even scorned individual.[1] According to this view, the Vietnam veteran's problems began in Vietnam where he was forced to participate in a brutal and disturbing war in which he was under fire twenty-four hours a day. The enemy, the wily and tenacious Vietcong and North Vietnamese regulars, were not always clearly defined nor were they above hiding behind or using civilians, leading to the unintentional – and sometimes intentional – killing by American forces of noncombatants, including women and children. Due to the military's policy of limiting the tour of duty in the war zone to one year, combat groups lacked cohesion and suffered from low morale, resulting in the excessive use of marijuana and heroin and an eventual breakdown of discipline, leading to the "fragging" of officers who attempted to reimpose order.

Sent home quickly without counseling, the Vietvet was either totally ignored by the civilian population, or worse, spat upon and blamed for losing the unpopular war.[2] He was given no parade or welcome home as were veterans of previous US wars, received inadequate GI Bill benefits,

Eric T. Dean, Jr., formerly practiced law and is currently a Ph.D. student with the Department of History, Yale University, New Haven, CT 06520, USA.

[1] For one of the first complete presentations on the television news of the image of the Vietnam veteran as a neglected and scorned individual, see "Vietnam Veterans' Dilemma, Part 1," which aired on the CBS Evening News on 4 April 1973. The report contained the elements: (a) unemployment, (b) inadequate GI Bill, (c) betrayed by US government, (d) psychological problems, (e) no welcome from civilians, (f) war fought by the poor.

[2] See ABC Evening News, 30 April 1985, in which one veteran, reflecting on the hostile homecoming he received, said that a World War II veteran accused him of losing the war. Another veteran said that the first girl he saw spat on him, and a third Vietvet related: "I feel betrayed, let down." In "Heroes Without Honor Face the Battle at Home," *Time*, 23 April 1979, 31, Vietvet Alan Fitzgerald is quoted: "'When I came back and landed at San Francisco airport with 200 others, we were spit on and kicked at.'"

Journal of American Studies **26** (1992), 1, 59–74 *Printed in Great Britain*

3 AMS 26

and, as a result, suffered from a number of readjustment problems, including high unemployment, drug addiction, divorce, suicide, crime, homelessness, ill health due to exposure to Agent Orange, and lingering psychological problems (post-traumatic stress disorder) which manifested themselves in the form of flashbacks, nightmares, guilt over atrocities and dead buddies who did not come back, and "psychic numbing."[3]

By the 1980s it became common in the United States to view the Vietnam veteran as beset by a wide range of problems and betrayed by his fellow citizens and government. The Vietvet was seen as *unique* amongst veterans of all American wars in receiving this ungrateful, if not outright hostile treatment. As a result, the Vietnam veteran has acquired an almost mythic stature, where he is seen as the "survivor-as-hero," who fought under insane conditions in Vietnam and then rebuilt his life in ungrateful America;[4] some critics even see the Vietnam veteran – because he lost the most, because he did it seemingly for nothing – as the most romanticized war hero in American history.

Contrary to this view, the evidence indicates that the Vietnam veteran has not, in comparison with veterans of prior American wars or his civilian contemporaries, been unusually neglected, scorned, or disadvantaged. This paper will demonstrate that: (1) the Vietnam veteran has, in fact, readjusted to civilian life quite well, (2) his problems have been grossly exaggerated in the popular media by a number of groups and factions in the United States for a variety of reasons, and (3) far from being *unique*, the Vietnam veteran is *typica* in many respects of the veteran throughout American history. What *is* unusual about the Vietnam veteran is the fact that many of the old problems and images would seem to linger in the midst of widespread readjustment benefits.[5]

[3] Matthew J. Friedman, M.D., Ph.D., "Post-Vietnam Syndrome: Recognition and Management," *Psychosomatics*, **22**, 11 (1981), 931–43; Peter G. Bourne, "The Viet Nam Veteran: Psychosocial Casualties," *Psychiatry in Medicine*, 3, 1 (1972), 23–27.

[4] "The War and the Arts; There Has Been a Cultural Turnaround on the Subject of Vietnam," *New York Times Magazine*, 31 March 1985, 51.

[5] The media programs or articles analyzed by this paper are as follows: (a) all articles on Vietnam veterans appearing in the *Reader's Guide to Periodical Literature* from 1963 to May of 1988 (220+ articles); (b) all articles from the *New York Times* relating to Vietnam veterans from 1963 to August of 1988 (156+ articles); (c) selected articles on Vietnam veterans appearing in the *Washington Post*, the *Chicago Tribune*, and the *Los Angeles Times* from 1965 to 1988; (d) all programs on Vietnam veterans in the Vanderbilt Television News Abstracts from the beginning of this series (which covers the television news on ABC, CBS, and NBC) in August, 1968 to September, 1988 (381 programs). In addition, I viewed approximately 75 of these television news programs at the Vanderbilt Television News Archives in Nashville, TN, to check the accuracy of the abstracts (which I found to be quite accurate).

II

During the height of American participation in the Vietnam War in the 1960s, most accounts of the Vietnam veteran returning from the war zone presented him as readjusting quite well to civilian life. The *New York Times* noted in 1968 that returning servicemen were finding jobs faster than at any time in the past 10 years, and some were even worried that the Vietnam veterans would not utilize the GI Bill for education since jobs were so easy to find.[6] The first American troops to be withdrawn from Vietnam (in 1969) were greeted by a parade in Seattle at which the crowd yelled "Thank you! Thank you!" and "flags waved, ticker tape showered down on the troopers, and pretty girls pressed red roses into the men's hands."[7] Comparisons with the veterans of previous American wars tended to favor the Vietnam veteran who was described as "knowing exactly what he wants" compared to the veterans of the Korean War who were characterized as "quiet, apathetic young men who shuffled aimlessly about," with a "glassy faraway look... staring nowhere."[8] However, by 1971, the Vietnam veteran had begun to acquire a new image as unappreciated, troubled, and unique in being rejected and blamed for the war. Four factors contributed to this increasingly prevalent view.

First, the domestic opposition to the war significantly shaped the image of the Vietnam veteran. Particularly after the Tet Offensive of early 1968 and the revelation of the Mylai Massacre of 1969, the Vietvet came to symbolize everything that was wrong with the war. On the one hand, he seemed to be an instrument of mass destruction; on the other hand, he seemed to be a victim himself, perverted by a strange war. The idea that American soldiers could commit atrocities shocked and disappointed the American public which opposed the Vietnam War itself in increasing numbers.[9] By pointing to the Vietvet as a corrupted, tarnished, and ruined innocent, critics of the Vietnam War could condemn the war, demand full American withdrawal, and pursue a related agenda of reform, which

[6] "Veterans Find Jobs Faster," *New York Times*, 3 May 1968, 35: 7; "The Re-Entry Problem of the Vietvets," *New York Times*, 7 May 1967, VI, 23: "But the Vietnam veteran may be lured instead into the labor force; even in an economy which has softened somewhat, he is *much sought after by business and industry*... since he cannot be drafted!" (emphasis added).

[7] "Joy in Seattle; Troops Withdrawn from Viet Nam," *Time*, 18 July 1969, 15 A.

[8] "Invisible Veterans," *Nation*, 3 June 1968, 723–26.

[9] Phillip Knightley, *The First Casualty* (New York: Harcourt, Brace, and Jovanovich, 1975), 393, notes that an outcry in the United States followed the Mylai revelations: *Time* called it "an American tragedy," and *Newsweek* ran a headline "A Single Incident in a Brutal War Shocks the American Conscience."

3 2

included (after disengagement from Vietnam) an attempt to change military and foreign policy, achieve greater access to health care, and secure equal rights at home.[10]

Second, the massive demobilization of 1970 to 1972 created a short-term crisis and the *perception* of a serious continuing problem. With the withdrawal of American forces from Vietnam, approximately one million soldiers were released from military service in 1970; this coincided with President Nixon's effort to "cool down" the economy. As a result, unemployment increased at the exact time that the greatest number of Vietvets were entering the job market. Though the concern in the 1960s had been that few Vietvets would use the GI Bill since they were being actively pursued by employers, attention suddenly shifted to a disproportionately high unemployment rate for Vietvets. *Business Week* concluded that: "Back home, [the Vietvet] is primarily a job problem."[11] Numerous magazine and newspaper articles trumpeted the fact that 12·4 percent of Vietvets in the 20–24 years age group were unemployed, compared to a national unemployment rate of 6 percent; television news programs emphasized jobless Vietvets, and highlighted protests by disgruntled Vietvets.[12] By 1973, the returning Vietvets had been reabsorbed into the economy and their unemployment rate was essentially the same as that for the general civilian population,[13] but the indelible impression had been created that Vietnam veterans were unemployed or even unemployable.

Third, there had been a "Heroin Epidemic" in Vietnam from 1970–72, in which as many as 50 percent of the American forces used heroin,[14] and television news in particular highlighted these drug problems of both the

[10] Jim Castelli, "Society and the Vietnam Veteran," *Catholic World*, Jan. 1971, 188.

[11] "Returning Heroes Get the Cold Shoulder," *Business Week*, 31 July 1971, 46–48.

[12] "Home from the War," *New Republic*, 30 Jan. 1971, 11; "Why Vietnam Veterans Feel Like Forgotten Men," *U.S. News and World Report*, 29 March 1971, 42 44; "Job Placement Lags for Vietnam Vets," *U.S. News and World Report*, 11 Oct. 1971, 102; "The Plight of Viet Nam Era Vets," *Time*, 27 Dec. 1971, 57; "The Vietnam Vet: 'No One Gives a Damn,'" *Newsweek*, 29 March 1971, 27–28+. See NBC, 6 Nov. 1970, noting 80,000 jobless blacks in Chicago; and NBC, 9 May 1972, which reported that "thousands of jobless Vietnam War vets" attended a job fair which was condemned as a publicity stunt.

[13] "Jobless Problem for Ex-GI's Eases," *New York Times*, 15 Jan. 1973, 61, citing the fact that the unemployment rate of Vietvets in the 20–29 years age group had dropped from 11% in 1971 to 5·5% in 1973, comparable to the 5·2% rate of all civilians.

[14] "Veterans Still Fight Vietnam Drug Habits; Heroin Use, Stressed by U.S., Is Only Part of the Problem Plaguing Ex-G.I.'s," *New York Times*, 2 June 1974, section I:4, 46. See also Special Action Office for Drug Abuse Prevention, *The Vietnam Drug User Returns* (Washington, D.C.: U.S. Government Printing Office, 1973), 29, vii, which determined heroin use at 34% amongst a sample of returning American soldiers in 1971, and estimated general narcotics use amongst Army enlisted men in this group at 45%.

soldiers in Vietnam as well as returning Vietnam veterans. Though studies showed that returned Vietvets were not primarily using heroin, that their usage of drugs was similar to that of civilians, and that their drug use had dropped to pre-Vietnam rates or lower,[15] the "drug addict" component of the "troubled Vietnam veteran" became embedded in the national conscience.

Fourth, with the return of the Vietnam POWs in 1973 to parades and national hoopla, the myth-making process was complete as Vietvets were described as "The Forgotten Veterans"[16] who, despite their sacrifices in Vietnam, had never received "their parade" or any recognition or appreciation from their society.

In sum, media reports of the early 1970s commonly described Vietnam veterans as the newest "minority." Mere teenagers, they had been forced by their government to fight in an unpopular war where they had committed atrocities, and came home psychologically disturbed and addicted to drugs, facing future unemployment and neglect. Articles such as "Will Somebody Please Welcome This Hero Home?", "The Vietnam Vet: 'No One Gives a Damn'," and "Vietnam Veterans: A Shocking Report on Their Damaged Lives"[17] became typical. Vietvets were called "unheralded, even unwanted," and "the most alienated generation of trained killers in American history."[18]

III

In response to the perceived crisis of the Vietnam veteran in the early 1970s, the military developed drug screening and treatment programs, Congress raised the level of GI Bill benefits, the head of the Veterans' Administration, Donald Johnson (who was supposedly responsible for red tape and delays), was sacked,[19] and efforts were made to "welcome

[15] *Legacies of Vietnam: Comparative Adjustment of Veterans and Their Peers* (Washington, D.C.: A study prepared for the Veterans' Administration submitted to the Committee on Veterans' Affairs U.S. House of Representatives, 1981), 371, notes: "Nonveterans, era veterans, and Vietnam veterans, whether exposed to combat or not, consume drugs at virtually identical rates when compared to men of similar social background living in the same area." See also *The Vietnam Drug User Returns*, viii.

[16] James Reston, "The Forgotten Veterans," *New York Times*, 2 June 1974, section IV, 21.

[17] *Today's Health*, June 1971, 54–56+; *Newsweek*, 29 March 1971, 27–28+; and *Redbook*, May 1973, 94–95+.

[18] "As Johnny Comes Marching Home," *Time*, 11 Jan. 1971, 58–59; and "When Johnnie Comes Marching Home," *America*, 24 March 1973, 255–56.

[19] Regarding drug programs, see "What the U.S. Is Doing For Ex-GI Addicts," *U.S. News and World Report*, 27 March 1972, 81, which pointed out that the VA had launched

home" the Vietnam veteran. President Nixon proclaimed a "Vietnam Veterans Day" for 29 March 1974, and President Ford's Veterans' Day Speech in 1974 centered on the Vietnam veteran, whom he described as "the forgotten hero."[20]

Veteran unemployment, which had stood at 4·5 percent in 1969 and increased to 11 percent in 1971, returned to 4·4 percent in 1973. By 1977, over 64 percent of Vietvets had used the GI Bill (compared to 55 percent by World War II veterans and 43·4 percent by Korean War veterans) and a greater percentage of these Vietvets used the GI Bill to pursue a higher education than ever before (60 percent, compared to 51 percent of Korean veterans utilizing the bill and 30 percent of World War II veterans).[21] Since the major problems of the Vietnam veteran had apparently been solved, there were few articles or programs in the print or television media in 1975 and 1976 on the Vietvet. President Ford declared an end to the Vietnam era and developed programs of clemency and amnesty to Vietnam-era draft-dodgers and deserters.

In 1977, however, the Vietnam veteran suddenly became a focus of renewed interest in the media. Newspapers and magazines again routinely described the treatment of the Vietnam veteran as a "national disgrace,"[22] and, as had been the case with the 1973 repatriation of the American POWs from Indochina, the return of the Iranian hostages to national exultation in 1981 strengthened the perception that Vietnam veterans were being neglected.[23] The *New Republic* noted in 1981: "Few topics

---

the largest drug-treatment program the nation had ever seen; for increases in the GI bill, see "Nixon Seeks 8% Increase in School Aid to Veterans; Congress Leaders Say Proposed Rise Is Too Small – President Also Calls for Higher Pensions for Ex-G.I.'s" *New York Times*, 29 Jan. 1974, 14. Regarding the Johnson matter, see NBC news on 22 April 1974.

[20] NBC, 26 Feb. 1974; CBS, 28 Oct. 1974.

[21] "Jobless Viet Vets: Anger Clouds Facts," *Chicago Tribune*, 6 Nov. 1977, section I, 18. See also "Hearings on Employment Programs for Veterans," (Hearings Before the Subcommittee on Education, Training and Employment of the Committee on Veterans' Affairs, House of Representatives; Washington, D.C.: U.S. Government Printing Office, 1979); and "GI Bill Improvement Act of 1977," (Hearings Before the Subcommittee on Health and Readjustment of the Committee on Veterans' Affairs, United States Senate; Washington, D.C.: U.S. Government Printing Office, 1977), and "Vietnam Veterans' Readjustment," (Hearings Before the Committee on Veterans' Affairs, United States Senate; Washington D.C.: U.S. Government Printing Office, 1980).

[22] The March issue of the *Atlantic* in 1978 was entitled "Soldiers of Misfortune; The Treatment of Vietnam Veterans Is a National Disgrace."

[23] "Wounded Vietnam Vet on Hostage Adulation: 'It's Damned Unfair,'" *Washington Post*, 31 Jan. 1981, A-6-6.

have received as much anguished attention lately as our national inattention toward Vietnam veterans."[24]

This renewed interest in the Vietnam veteran focussed less on concrete problems of unemployment or the GI Bill (though these topics were rarely excluded from a discussion of the Vietnam veteran), but shifted to new issues such as "delayed stress syndrome" (later to become "post-traumatic stress disorder" – PTSD), Agent Orange, and a supposedly high rate of suicide in Vietnam veterans. Common to all three issues was an inability to quantify exactly the magnitude of the problem, but with a steady barrage of media stories and recriminations from Vietvets, the *impression* emerged that Vietnam veterans were in a *crisis*, and that the government was largely to blame, for sending them to Vietnam to start with and for ignoring them upon their return.

Most of these problems related to the supposed fact that the Vietvet had never been properly welcomed home (the "forgotten veteran" component); hence, a national obsession to "welcome home" the Vietvet developed in the late 1970s, and manifested itself primarily in various declarations, lavish parades for the Vietnam veterans, and the construction of the Monument to the Vietnam War Dead in Washington, D.C. President Carter followed the example of Presidents Nixon and Ford of honoring the Vietvets by declaring a Vietnam Veterans Week. In addition, Veterans' Day on 11 November 1979, was dedicated to the Vietnam veterans, and Congress declared 26 April 1981 to be "Vietnam Veteran Recognition Day."[25]

On 7 May 1985, 25,000 Vietnam veterans marched in a New York City ticker-tape parade attended by one million people, many of whom held signs saying: "You're Our Heroes, Vietnam Vets."[26] Similar parades followed in Chicago, Houston, and elsewhere. An oddity associated with these repeated welcomes and parades was that with each new one, some veteran would inevitably be quoted as saying that the Vietnam veterans had never received such recognition before and were "finally being welcomed home."

Another central landmark in the 1980s "Welcome Home, Vietnam Vets" phenomenon was the Vietnam Memorial constructed in Washington, D.C. The dedication ceremony in 1982 drew a crowd of 150,000, and on 10 November 1982, a four-day tribute to the Vietnam veterans commenced during which the names of all 57,939 servicemen who died in

[24] "The Vet Offensive," *New Republic*, 1–8 Aug. 1981, 23–25.
[25] NBC, 28 May 1979; ABC, 11 Nov. 1979; and CBS, 26 April 1981.
[26] "New Yorkers Roar Thanks to Veterans," *New York Times*, 8 May 1985, section I, 1.

Vietnam were read at the Washington Cathedral.[27] Television coverage focussed on weeping veterans and survivors at the monument itself, interviews with veterans who still claimed they had been betrayed and rejected by society, or interviews with family members who commented that the war was a waste and that the men (and women) had died for no good reason. However, by the end of the 1980s, in spite of continuing effusive welcomes, stories in the media of troubled Vietvets continued, and the Vietnam veteran was still viewed as one who had suffered more than veterans of other American wars, and one who had received less attention than he deserved.[28]

IV

Despite the presentation throughout the 1970s and 1980s of a "troubled and scorned" Vietnam veteran, the Vietvet has actually readjusted to civilian life successfully compared with both contemporary civilians and with veterans of past American wars. Studies have demonstrated that Vietnam veterans have a *higher* median income than their civilian peers (a 1977 study showed the median weekly wage of the Vietnam veteran to be $24 higher than that for the nonveteran)[29] and are the best educated veterans in American history. For Vietnam veterans themselves, pride rather than shame is the most common characteristic, and seventy-seven percent of Vietnam era veterans felt they received a "very friendly" reception from family and close friends upon their return from the service;[30] some veterans even viewed their experience in the war zone as the most exciting and meaningful time in their lives.[31] For those Vietvets who have *not* readjusted well, predisposition and an earlier troubled life were often contributing factors in the development of problems.[32]

[27] "Diverse Crowd is Unanimous in Homage to Vietnam Veterans," *Washington Post*, 14 Nov. 1982, A 18 a; ABC, 10 Nov. 1982.

[28] "'Just Don't Fit'; Stalking the Elusive 'Tripwire Veteran,'" *Harpers*, April 1985, 55–63.

[29] *Legacies of Vietnam*, 186.

[30] *Myths and Realities: A Study of Attitudes Toward Vietnam Era Veterans* (Report completed by Lou Harris for the Veterans' Administration and submitted to the Committee on Veterans' Affairs, U.S. House of Representatives; Washington, D.C.: U.S. Government Printing Office, 1980), xxxix, 39.

[31] Fred Reed in the December issue of *Harpers* in 1980, wrote (p. 44): "To many of us there, the war was the best time of our lives, almost the only time. We loved it because in those days we were alive, life was intense, the pungent hours passed fast over the central event of the age and the howling jets appeased the terrible boredom of existence."

[32] William Goldsmith, M.D., and Constantine Cretekos, M.D., "Unhappy Odysseys; Psychiatric Hospitalizations Among Vietnam Returnees," *Archives of General Psychiatry*, 20 (1969), 82; John E. Helzer et al., "Depressive Disorders in Vietnam Returnees," *Journal of Nervous and Mental Diseases*, 163, 3 (1976), 180; F. S. Sierles et al.,

Despite a great deal of angry rhetoric and a class action lawsuit settled for $180 million, it is still unclear if Agent Orange really damaged Vietnam veterans. The Centers for Disease Control have concluded that children born to Vietnam veterans are *not* suffering from birth defects attributable to Agent Orange.[33]

Although Vietnam veteran advocates have tended to paint an idyllic readjustment for American veterans of past wars, in actuality soldiers in the field in most wars become alienated from the civilian population at home, and sometimes even begin to view the enemy in sympathetic terms as a fellow sufferer. Upon returning home after the war is concluded, the veteran will shun parades, feeling that the civilians who are making such a fuss do not have the slightest idea what war is actually about.[34] He often carries a lingering bitterness, and feels that civilians who have profited from the war at his expense now fear and distrust him. Some veterans from all past wars have demonstrated a continuing inability to readjust to civilian life due to shell-shock, psychoneurosis, or outright insanity caused by war,[35] and problems of unemployment, crime, and suicide – whether associated with psychological problems or not – have also been recurring problems in the veteran population. Often returning veterans have found it difficult to "settle down," either because of disturbing wartime experiences or simply because they have "seen the world" and are

---

"Posttraumatic Stress Disorder and Concurrent Psychiatric Illness: a Preliminary Report," *American Journal of Psychiatry* (hereafter *AJP*), **140** (1983), 1177–79; D. Behar, "Configuration of Concurrent Illnesses in Posttraumatic Stress Disorder [letter]," *AJP*, **141** (1984), 1310–11.

[33] Michael Gouch, *Dioxin, Agent Orange: The Facts* (New York: Plenum Press, 1986), 108–10, citing the CDC study: J. D. Erickson, J. Mulinare, P. W. McClain, et al., "Vietnam Veterans' Risks for Fathering Babies with Birth Defects," *Journal of the American Medical Association*, **252** (1984), 903–12.

[34] Dixon Wecter, *When Johnny Comes Marching Home* (Westport, Conn.: Greenwood Press, 1944), 129, 144, 317; and Willard W. Waller, *The Veteran Comes Back* (New York: Dryden Press, 1944), 105.

[35] Willard Waller states (at 51): "War is full of horrors. Many soldiers carry with them into life after the war the memory of these jumbled emotions of fear and horror. For some, at least, these emotions are complicated by feelings of guilt." For reports on World War II veterans, see R. R. Grinker, "Psychiatric Disorders in Combat Crews Overseas and in Returnees," *Medical Clinics of North America*, **29** (1945), 729–39; Norman Q. Brill, M.D., and Gilbert W. Beebe, M.D., "Follow-Up Study of Psychoneuroses; Preliminary Report," *AJP*, **108** (1951), 417–25; Herbert C. Archibald, M.D., and Read D. Tuddenham, Ph.D., "Persistent Stress Reaction After Combat," *Archives of General Psychiatry*, **12** (1965), 475–81; D. Dobbs, M.D., and W. P. Wilson, M.D., "Observations on Persistence of War Neurosis," *Diseases of the Nervous System*, **21** (1960), 686–91; and Samuel Futterman, M.D., and Eugene Pumpian-Mindlin, M.D., "Traumatic War Neuroses Five Years Later," *AJP*, **108** (1951), 401–08.

dissatisfied with narrow horizons. Veterans of World Wars I and II were presented in motion pictures, on occasion, as troubled or dangerous.[36]

The lavish parades which veterans of past wars supposedly received are often more a myth than reality. Few World War II units were welcomed home as a group, and, in the past, by the time the soldiers who did the actual fighting returned, the civilian enthusiasm for parades and ticker tape had often waned.[37] Hence, it is by no means obvious that the Vietnam veteran has had a more difficult period of readjustment that veterans of prior American wars. Much evidence points to just the opposite conclusion.

V

Why then did the myth of the "unique" Vietnam veteran emerge in the 1970s and 1980s?

First, the Vietnam veteran has been a powerful tool for those who wish to shape American society or influence the course of American politics. The original image of the troubled and scorned Vietvet was born in the days of the anti-Vietnam War movement from 1969 to 1973 when critics of the war attempted to show that the war was doing psychological damage to the American troops, who were supposedly haunted by guilt from war experiences (from seeing friends die to the commission of atrocities). Obviously, the portrayal of the Vietvet as well-adjusted and untroubled by the war would have undermined the anti-war agenda; hence, critics such as Robert Jay Lifton probably exaggerated the problems of the returning Vietvets. In the 1980s, those on the Right of the political spectrum began to see the Vietnam veteran not as the victim of an immoral war, but as a frustrated patriot, betrayed by his own country which would not "let him win." Pursuant to this trend, the image of the Vietvet was modified from that of a victim of war's madness (the paraplegic and POW) to that of the "survivor-hero" in the 1980s.[38]

[36] For World War I, see "Heroes For Sale" (1933), and "They Gave Him a Gun" (1937), the latter portraying a veteran turned into a killer by the war experience. For World War II, see Foster Hirsch, *The Dark Side of the Screen: Film Noir* (New York: A. S. Barnes, 1981), 21, noting the portrayal of veterans as "disoriented, shell-shocked, and violent."

[37] Regarding World War II, see Robert H. Fleming, "Post Vietnam Syndrome: Neurosis or Sociosis?" *Psychiatry*, 48 (1985), 124, noting that there was only one major unit Victory Parade in World War II. Waller and Wecter note that most soldiers come home individually or in small groups and that the most satisfying reunion, often the only one that has real meaning for the veteran, is that with his *immediate family*.

[38] "The War and the Arts; There Has Been a Cultural Turnaround on the Subject of Vietnam," *New York Times Magazine*, 31 March 1985, 51, 55; Kevin Phillips, *Post-*

Beyond proponents of specific political points of view, some Vietnam veterans themselves have used the image of the "troubled and scorned Vietvet" to obtain a number of benefits from the Federal government. Statements frequently made by Vietvets to the effect that "billions are spent on defense but only pennies, by comparison, for providing fully staffed hospitals"[39] belie the fact that veterans in the United States have become a privileged class, and that it is difficult for any politician to say "no" to the veterans' lobby. The Veterans Administration is one of the largest federal agencies with a budget of over $28 billion (FY 1989), a work force of 240,000, and a hospital system which includes 172 hospitals, 226 outpatient clinics, and 106 nursing home centers.[40] For every American War since the Civil War, at least as much (and usually a great deal more) money has been spent on the veterans as on the conduct of the war itself, and before all the veterans of World War II, Korea, and Vietnam have died, these wars will follow the same pattern.[41] Based on prior experience, one can predict that veterans' benefits will be paid to Vietvets and their families through the year 2100.[42]

A particularly important factor in the creation of the image of the "troubled and scorned Vietnam veteran" has been the movement for

---

Conservative America: People, Politics and Ideology in a Time of Crisis (New York: Random House, 1982), 165; and Lisa M. Heilbronn, "Coming Home a Hero; The Changing Image of the Vietnam Vet on Prime Time Television," *Journal of Popular Film and Television*, 13 (1985), 1, 25–30.

39 "The Vietnam-Veteran Blues," *New York Times*, 29 March 1974, 35.

40 Veterans Administration, *Annual Report, 1984* (Washington, D.C.: U.S. GPO, 1985), xvi, 13; Hearing Before the Committee on Veterans' Affairs, *Fiscal Year 1989 Budget for Veterans' Programs and S. 2049, The Veterans' Home Loan Program Improvements Act of 1988*, U.S. Senate, 100th Cong., 2nd sess. (Washington, D.C.: U.S. GPO, 1988), 559; and Sar A. Levitan and Karen A. Cleary, *Old Wars Remain Unfinished: The Veteran Benefits System* (Baltimore: Johns Hopkins, 1973).

41 See Series Y 849–55, "Estimates of Total Cost of U.S. Wars," U.S. Bureau of the Census, *Historical Statistics of the United States, Colonial Times to 1970*, Part 2 (Washington, D.C.: U.S. GPO, 1975), 1140; No. 546, "Estimates of Total Dollar Costs of American Wars", and No. 569, "Veterans' Benefits – Expenditures From Appropriated Funds, By War: Total and 1940 to 1988," in U.S. Bureau of the Census, *Statistical Abstract of the United States, 1990*, (Washington, D.C.: U.S. GPO, 1990), 336, 345; and the statement of James L. Clayton, University of Utah, at Hearings before the Subcommittee on Economy in Government, U.S. Congress, Joint Economic Committee, *The Military Budget and National Economic Priorities*, part I, 91st Cong., 1st sess. (Washington, D.C.: U.S. GPO, 1969), 143–50.

42 The last veteran of the Revolutionary War, Daniel F. Bakeman, died on 5 April 1869, and the last Revolutionary War widow, Esther S. Damon, died on 11 Nov. 1906. William H. Glasson, *Federal Military Pensions in the United States* (New York: Oxford University Press, 1918), 93; Clayton statement, 146–47.

psychiatric reform during the 1970s which culminated in 1980 when the American Psychiatric Association recognized PTSD as a mental illness. In the late 1960s and early 1970s, Robert Jay Lifton met with Vietvets in "rap groups" to discuss their experiences and feelings, but these veterans tended to have antiwar convictions (Lifton apparently made no effort to obtain a "scientific sample" of veterans). In addition, Lifton's use of the "rap group" constituted an innovation in psychiatry[43] and employed antiwar politics in which the Vietnam War was viewed as an "atrocity-producing situation" in which "survivor guilt" functioned as "animating guilt" to propel one toward connection, integrity, and movement. The "vet centers," established by the federal government in the 1980s to treat Vietvets with PTSD, rejected traditional psychiatry and followed instead the "rap group" model and functioned along the lines of an alcoholics anonymous meeting.[44] According to this model of therapy, the Vietnam veteran was by definition guilty and disturbed, and needed to participate in these "rap groups" to come to terms with his guilt. The overall effect of this method of treatment was to exaggerate the problems of Vietvets, and ignore the well-adjusted Vietnam veteran, who was not paralyzed by guilt. Guenter Lewy in *America in Vietnam*[45] noted that Vietnam veterans in the 1970s often claimed to have participated in atrocities, when the evidence suggested no such thing had occurred; Lewy concluded that some Vietvets achieved a feeling of importance and solidarity with the antiwar movement by calling attention to themselves in this way. Charles C. Moskos has suggested that atrocity stories out of Vietnam were the functional equivalent of heroic war stories out of World War II in that both gave the soldiers' participation in these wars a meaning which could resonate with certain elements of the public back home.[46] The work of George Rosen raises the possibility that PTSD and other abnormal behavior was *embraced* by certain Vietnam veterans for a variety of reasons.[47]

Moreover, the creation of PTSD as a new medical category in 1980 marked an extension of psychiatry. Historians such as David Rothman and Andrew Scull have argued that "mental illness" is not a neutral term

[43] See Don Browning, "Psychiatry and Pastoral Counseling: Moral Context or Moral Vacuum?" *Christian Century*, 6 Feb. 1974, 158.

[44] "Vietnam – Will There Be a Collective Healing?" *Center Magazine*, July/Aug. 1981, 15.

[45] New York: Oxford University Press, 1978.

[46] Ibid., 321.

[47] George Rosen, *Madness in Society: Chapters in the Historical Sociology of Mental Illness* (Chicago: The University of Chicago Press, 1968); Robert H. Fleming, "Post Vietnam Syndrome" notes that the borrowing of embellished "war stories" is regularly practiced.

and that psychiatry is not driven purely by scientific principles.[48] Rather, there is the "psychiatric model" of human behavior which analyzes human behavior as a psychiatric problem calling for "professional help"; some would call this approach the "therapeutic state" or "psychiatric imperialism." Hence, social rather than medical forces have often influenced reforms in mental health concepts. While the impression emerged that Vietnam was unique since large numbers of veterans from that war suddenly seemed to be mentally ill, the truth of the matter was that an expanding category of disease was including more and more people who would have been considered "normal" in the past.

The Vietnam War also marked the predominance of a new type of military history which tends to emphasize the experience of the common soldier. John Keegan in *The Face of Battle* notes that military history has primarily consisted in the past of the study of generals and generalship,[49] and advocates instead a new approach to investigate the experience of the common soldier. However, there are dangers to this type of military history: first, to the common soldier in all eras, war has seemed a chaotic and terrifying business, so the greater purpose and flow of the war is rarely evident on the level of the small unit; second, as S. L. A. Marshall has demonstrated, even in a war such as World War II, the infantryman is motivated primarily by loyalty to his immediate unit and seeks mainly to survive, so, again, the overall purpose and meaning of the war may not be evident at this level.

In the portrayal of American participation in the Vietnam War, the primary focus has been on the experience of the individual soldier. Hence, the public has been bombarded by images of chaos, destruction, and meaningless death, and the larger questions of military and political strategy are essentially ignored as war in general is condemned as wasteful and immoral. This skewed presentation has revealed the Vietvet as a victim and survivor, and as little else.

Fifth, the image of the Vietnam veteran as a troubled and scorned individual, specifically as a *victim*, can be attributed in part to rising expectations and an attendant obsession with risk in the United States in

[48] See David J. Rothman, *The Discovery of the Asylum: Social Order and Disorder in the New Republic* (New York: Little, Brown, and Co., 1971); Andrew Scull, "From Madness to Mental Illness: Medical Men as Moral Entrepreneurs," *European Journal of Sociology*, 16 (1975), 219–61; S. P. Fullinwider, "Neurasthenia: The Genteel Caste's Journey Inward," *Rocky Mountain Social Science Journal*, 11, 2 (1974), 1–9; and Barbara Sicherman, "The Uses of a Diagnosis: Doctors, Patients, and Neurasthenia," *Journal of the History of Medicine and Allied Sciences*, 32, 4 (1977), 33–54.

[49] New York: Dorset Press, 1976, 27.

the past twenty years.[50] One might ascribe this development of rising expectations to greater demands on technological performance and solutions, or, alternatively, to *cultural factors* such as institutionalized mistrust (e.g. of corporations) which have triggered a new view of liability.[51] The Vietnam veteran movement can be seen as a manifestation of the growing trend of blaming available governmental entities or corporations for harm and incurred risk. The risk at issue here has been the risk associated with war, most notably exposure to Agent Orange, but through PTSD, exposure to all facets of life in the war zone which would tend to affect a person adversely. One might view the entire Vietnam veteran movement as a sort of multi-year, multi-million dollar class-action lawsuit against the United States government.

Last of all, the role of the media must be considered. Once the Vietnam veteran had become a national concern, television coverage in particular may have been critical in reinforcing and embellishing emerging stereotypes in that television news, as opposed to the print media, carried very few *dissenting* views on the Vietnam veteran issue, and tended instead to dramatize and simplify the issues.[52] Such a tendency to present the news for dramatic impact alone, without alternative viewpoints or historical analysis, may be the result of what Neil Postman has described as the descent of television into triviality as it becomes *entertainment* and little more.[53]

[50] George L. Priest, "The Invention of Enterprise Liability: A Critical History of the Intellectual Foundations of Modern Tort Law," *The Journal of Legal Studies*, 14, 3 (1985), 461–528.

[51] Mary Douglas and Aaron Wildavsky, *Risk and Culture: An Essay on the Selection of Technical and Environmental Dangers* (Berkeley: University of California Press, 1982).

[52] The usual television coverage showed a Vietnam veteran in agony: "I started flashing back; I was in the Nam...; I burned a village to the ground and everyone in it... I need help" (CBS, 30 May 1979); "We were made into weapons of war and then discarded" (CBS, 11 Jan. 1984); "I'm living the war just like I was there yesterday, I can't shake it" (ABC, 29 Sept. 1987); "They fought and struggled and came home to a public that didn't care..." (CBS, 12 May 1988). In the print media, however, dissenting views have been somewhat common, if not predominant. For instance, see Anne Keegan, "GI's Vietnam Was Bittersweet Plum," *Chicago Tribune*, 31 Jan. 1983, a, 15 C: 1 (story of a Vietvet who was not assigned to combat and had a good time in Vietnam); "Victims of Our Noble Cause," *Progressive*, Feb. 1983 (calls the Vietvet obsession a "freak show"); and Fred Reed, "Jello Writers," *Harper's*, Dec. 1980 (recounts the excitement of the war zone, and ridicules the writers who couldn't begin to understand or put the experience in perspective).

[53] Neil Postman, *Amusing Ourselves to Death: Public Discourse in the Age of Show Business* (New York: Penguin Books, 1985).

VI

Davis R. B. Ross, in *Preparing for Ulysses; Politics and Veterans During World War II*,[54] maintains that the World War II veteran was the *exception*, not the *rule* in the history of American veterans. With the World War II veteran, for the first time, broad readjustment benefits were made available to *all* returning veterans, not just those who could prove a disability. Prior to World War II, the *usual pattern* for American veterans was a period of neglect after the conclusion of a war; veterans often felt spurned and frustrated, and from these feelings emerged a separate veteran identity, and often hostility or bitterness towards the civilian population.

Hence, to the extent that some Vietnam veterans experienced readjustment problems and felt rejection and bitterness towards civilian society, they were *typical* of veterans throughout American history, and far from unique. What is unusual about the Vietnam veteran is the development of this actual or imagined hostility and bitterness even in the face of World War II-type readjustment benefits. The fact that the Vietnam veteran could readjust to civilian life so well in objective terms and yet either feel or be portrayed as feeling bitter and betrayed indicates, first, that the image of the veteran is potent and will always be subject to use by different factions in society to achieve their agenda; this has been true from the "bloody shirt" of Reconstruction to the "betrayal" theme of Weimar Germany. Second, expectations have increased to the point where *all* veterans, even the *eighty-six percent* of Vietnam veterans who were not assigned to combat,[55] have a claim not just for "readjustment" benefits (which would mark their transition to the status of "civilian"), but for sympathy and exclusive eligibility for continuing veterans' benefits, which at times may seem completely out of proportion to the actual detriment (if any) incurred.

Franklin D. Roosevelt, in addressing the American Legion in 1933, maintained that able-bodied veterans, simply because they had worn the uniform, should not be viewed as a privileged class entitled to benefits to which civilians were not entitled.[56] In the wake of the Vietnam War, the myth of the troubled and scorned Vietnam veteran has made this type of

[54] Davis R. B. Boss, *Preparing for Ulysses: Politics and Veterans During World War II* (New York: Columbia University Press, 1969).

[55] Loren Baritz, *Backfire: A History of How American Culture Led Us into Vietnam and Made Us Fight the Way We Did* (New York: Ballantine Books, 1985), 297.

[56] Ross, *Preparing for Ulysses*, 18.

critical thinking impossible, for in the current climate of opinion in the United States, one simply tends to *assume* that veterans as a class should be entitled to special consideration and remuneration. In spite of the rhetoric of "sacrifice," the legacy of the Vietnam veteran may actually be the demise of the concept of military service.

Vietnam Veterans And the Agent Orange Controversy

JAMES B. JACOBS
New York University

DENNIS McNAMARA
University of Texas

From 1965 to 1971 American military forces sprayed more than 11 million gallon of Agent Orange (and other herbicides) over the South Vietnamese landscape to defoliate jungle terrain and destroy enemy crop cultivation.[1] The herbicides were applied to approximately 10.3 percent of inland forests, 36.1 percent of mangroves, and 3 percent of cultivated areas[2]—in all, covering between 8 percent and 10 percent of the total land area of South Vietnam.[3]

In the mid-1970s, Vietnam veterans began charging that Agent Orange contamination had caused them a wide range of health problems, including genetic damage. They sought treatment and compensation from the Veterans Administration, as well as compensatory and punitive damages from the chemical companies that manufactured the herbicide. These claims and charges generated controversy in the VA, Congress, and especially the courts; they may well prove to be the major veterans' issue spawned by the Vietnam War.

A case study of the Agent Orange controversy should contain much of interest to students of civil/military relations. The outcome is important in its own right because it affects veterans' morale and their ability to cope financially and psychologically with the larger society. It demonstrates the contemporary status and potential political power of American veterans and their capacity through litigation to mobilize into

ARMED FORCES & SOCIETY, Vol. 13 No. 1, Fall 1986 57-80

a special-interest movement. It also demonstrates the gap, in terms of legal rights, between military personnel and veterans on the one hand and civilians on the other; it forces us to ask whether the special legal norms that define the status of military personnel in a democratic society can be maintained in the face of dramatic legal and social changes in the larger society.

Agent Orange: The Chemical and Its Threat to Human Health

Agent Orange (so-called because of the identifying strip on its container) is a mixture of two phenoxy herbicides: 2,4-D and 2,4,5-T. One by-product of the manufacture of 2,4,5-T is TCDD, commonly known as dioxin. In high concentrations this compound is extremely toxic, harmful to both animals and humans; in low concentrations its effect is unknown. In 1969, a National Institutes of Health report found that heavy 2,4,5-T exposure caused stillbirths and birth defects in mice.[4] These and other medical findings led the military to limit Agent Orange spraying to remote areas of Vietnam. Meanwhile, on 15 April 1970, the U.S. Department of Agriculture suspended the domestic use of 2,4,5-T; that same day, the Department of Defense suspended military use of Agent Orange in Vietnam.[5] Several months later, DoD instructed the Air Force to dispose of all remaining stocks of the defoliant.[6]

Congressional activity concerning Agent Orange began later that year. The Armed Forces Appropriations Act directed DoD to contract with the National Academy of Sciences to study the ecological and physiological effects of herbicide use in Vietnam.[7] The NAS report, published in 1974, found no identifiable health problems related to 2,4,5-T use. But it cautioned that the politico-military situation in Vietnam limited the study and urged further research.[8] Although several studies had demonstrated dioxin's ability to produce adverse health effects in animals, little "hard evidence" connected such health effects with low-level human exposure to TCDD.[9]

Top officials of the Environmental Protection Agency's Environmental Research Center became convinced during the early 1970s that laboratory experiments on dioxin exposure were not clearly applicable in the real world, where pesticides are sprayed over wide areas and where, because of trees and other foliage, much of the small amount of dioxin in the pesticides does not reach the ground. The low possibility of direct human exposure and lack of evidence confirming toxic effects from low levels of 2,4,5-T convinced EPA it "could no longer sustain the finding that there was a substantial question of safety in its use."

Nevertheless, in subsequent years, the agency vacillated on the need for a complete ban on 2,4,5-T pesticides; and eventually, the manufacturer withdrew it from the market.

Emergence of a Sociopolitical Movement

Vietnam veterans did not initially connect their postservice medical problems with herbicide exposure. However, in 1978 a VA benefits counselor, investigating a claim made by a veteran terminally ill with cancer, queried VA scientists concerning any possible connection between Agent Blue and the veteran's illness. The scientists ruled out a connection but told the counselor, Maude De Victor, that the effects of Agent Orange were less well understood and could not be as readily dismissed.[10]

De Victor, convinced that Agent Orange was responsible for a wide range of veterans' medical problems, took her information and hypotheses to Chicago television journalist Bill Kurtis, who, in March 1978, produced a special report entitled "Agent Orange: Vietnam Veterans Deadly Fog." It attracted national attention. The dramatic presentation suggested a clear causal link between Agent Orange and the veterans' health problems, which now included a wide variety of medical, neurological, and psychiatric disorders (e.g., rashes, sexual dysfunctions, cancers, miscarriages by wives, and birth defects in children). Agent Orange claims to the VA increased from less than ten a month[11] to hundreds. After two additional segments of Kurtis' TV documentary were aired (in March 1980), claims escalated to several thousand a month.[12] The media's portrayal of Agent Orange as the cause of veterans' ailments had triggered a sociopolitical movement.

While the news and broadcast media created nationwide awareness of Agent Orange, several Vietnam veterans' groups sought to organize social, political, and legal action. Foremost among the organizers was Paul Reutershan, an Air Force veteran struggling with terminal abdominal cancer. Along with several of his fellow Vietnam veterans, he founded Agent Orange Victims International (AOVI)—to seek justice for Agent Orange victims. And he worked tirelessly until his death in search of a lawyer willing to mount a class action on the veterans' behalf. Finally, his successor, Frank McCarthy, was able to convince Long Island lawyer Paul Yannacone to file the class action. Over the next several years, Yannacone's appearances at veterans' rallies all over the country served to raise veterans' consciousness about Agent Orange and to fuel the movement.[13]

It is easy to see why Agent Orange hit a responsive chord for Vietnam veterans suffering from various genetic, physiological, and mental illnesses. Because Agent Orange contamination was not associated with any particular illness, veterans could ascribe almost any health problem to it. No veteran could be certain that he or she had not been exposed by drinking water, touching plants and trees, or just breathing the air. Understandably, many veterans, especially those who were suffering physically or psychologically, feared the worst. (It is likely that along with many veterans, other individuals in advanced industrial societies harbor morbid fears of being poisoned by invisible chemicals.)[14] That the chemicals had been dropped on them by their own government confirmed the anger and alienation of many veterans, who also felt they had been sacrificed in a pointless war. Many veterans expressed such feelings at the hearings, in 1984, on the proposed settlement of the Agent Orange litigation. One Marine Corps veteran told the court:

> As we walked through the rice paddies and the jungle and the marshlands to locate, to close and engage the enemy, we were aware of the risks to our life and limb, but at no time did we feel that our own country would care so little about our welfare that they would spray down from the skies... poison.[15]

Assistance for the victims of Agent Orange became a rallying cry for the Vietnam veterans and their organizations. Eventually the largest and best-established veterans' organization, the American Legion, joined the movement.

Struggle with the Veterans Administration

Not surprisingly, as awareness of Agent Orange grew among veterans, more and more sought treatment at VA hospitals for what they believed or feared to be Agent Orange-related illnesses. The VA, which is responsible for treating veterans for service-related injuries and illnesses, held that there was no basis for believing that Agent Orange had caused service personnel any medical problems other than chloracne, a rare skin disease.[16] The refusal to recognize their complaints and provide medical assistance confirmed many Vietnam veterans' negative view of the VA; it also fed the disillusion of those who felt unappreciated and rejected by their country.[17]

Lobbying Efforts

War veterans, especially those who have been injured defending their country, receive a great deal of sympathy. Throughout American history, their demands have proved difficult to deny. On account of their vast numbers alone, they are a formidable political force.[18] The Agent Orange veterans achieved a major victory in 1981 when, despite opposition from the VA and some veterans' groups, Congress gave the VA discretionary authority to provide hospital and nursing home care for "Agent Orange-type illnesses," regardless of insufficient scientific evidence on causality.[19] Under the law, a veteran needs to show only that *he could have been exposed* in order to receive treatment.

Service in Vietnam during the period of Agent Orange spraying creates a presumption that any plausibly connected illness was caused by the herbicide and entitles the veteran to free medical treatment. The presumption can only be overcome if the VA is sure that the illness or injury could not have been contracted or caused in Vietnam. During FY 1983, this law accounted for 10,900 inpatient admissions and 434,000 outpatient visits.[20] The legislation also provides that any veteran claiming an Agent Orange illness be given a physical examination and that his complaints be logged onto an Agent Orange registry. By October 1983, 125,649 veterans had received the initial physical examination.[21] Congress also provided for a massive study of the health impact of Agent Orange to be conducted by the Center for Disease Control; the CDC study is due to come out in the late 1980s.[22]

Although this federal legislation represented a substantial victory, the veterans were not appeased. The VA steadfastly rejected the disability claims of veterans allegedly suffering from all Agent Orange-related health problems, except chloracne. By October 1983, there were more than 18,500 claims. The Agent Orange veterans, supported by most Vietnam veterans' organizations—and eventually the American Legion—lobbied aggressively for social welfare benefits. Members of Congress responded by introducing a variety of benefit packages.

In a 1984 compromise, Congress passed the Agent Orange and Atomic Veterans Relief Act, authorizing temporary disability payments to Vietnam veterans suffering from soft tissue sarcomas, porphia cutanea, and chloracne, unless it could be shown that those diseases had been contracted by causes other than Agent Orange exposure during military service.[23] While a victory of sorts, this relief was limited: only a very small percentage of the Agent Orange veterans suffer from these illnesses.[24] Thus, the lobbying continues. Vietnam veterans seek to extend the service-related presumption to a multitude of medical problems associated with Agent Orange. The Reagan administration refuses to support this position. Providing disability pensions to tens of thousands of Vietnam veterans claiming Agent Orange-related diseases and health defects would be enormously costly and perhaps encourage more veterans' demands.

The Agent Orange Litigation

In Re Agent Orange Litigation[25] developed as one of the most complex and extraordinary lawsuits in American history. Ultimately, the court certified a plaintiff class comprised of "all persons who were in the United States, New Zealand or Australian Armed Forces at any time from 1962 to 1971 who were injured in or near Vietnam by exposure to Agent Orange or other phenoxy herbicides.... The class also includes spouses, parents and children of veterans born before January 1, 1984, directly or derivatively injured as a result of the exposure."[26] The exact size of the "class" is unknown; named plaintiffs number some 15,000, with nearly 2.5 million potential class members. The plaintiffs—charging negligence and strict products liability[27]—sought billions of dollars of compensatory and punitive damage from 15 chemical companies (later reduced to 7), which they claimed injured them and their families by the manufacture of herbicides containing dioxin.

Plaintiffs' lawyers, for tactical reasons, did not sue the U.S. government: making the government a defendant would have severely increased litigation costs, which were already a crushing problem for their lawyers. In limiting the suit to the chemical companies, plaintiffs could obtain the government's cooperation in discovery, particularly with respect to the relationship between the government and the chemical companies. This was a crucial question: the companies' "government contractor defense" depended upon their having supplied Agent Orange according to government specifications, rather than their own.[28]

Another reason not to join the United States as a defendant was the doctrinal roadblock posed by *Feres v. United States* (1950),[29] which established governmental immunity for tortious acts arising out of military service. While certain legal arguments were available for an end-run around *Feres* or even for a head-on assault,[30] the prospect of success was slight. It would have been disastrous to have incurred the enormous expense of suing the government—only to have had it dismissed as a defendant later on in the litigation.

Unlike the plaintiffs, the defendants had every reason to bring the government into the case. The chemical companies denied all liability on grounds there was no causal evidence to connect Agent Orange to the melange of veterans' health problems. Their fall-back position was that in the event a causal connection was found, the United States should be held liable rather than the companies, because it specified the product and, indeed, compelled its manufacture and sale under the Defense Production Act.[31] While the chemical companies brought the United States into the case as a third-party defendant, ultimately, the latter obtained dismissal from the suit. The district court held that the United States could not be liable to the defendants since that would, in effect, violate *Feres* by allowing former servicemen to recover in tort against the government—albeit by using war contractors as a kind of intermediary.[32]

Problems in the Veterans' Suit

From the outset, the plaintiffs faced enormous obstacles in proving general and specific causation. Scientific evidence had not demonstrated that human exposure to low levels of dioxin resulted in the kinds of illnesses from which plaintiffs suffered. In February 1982, the U.S. Air Force released a study of the "Ranch Hand" group—those veterans who had conducted spraying missions over Vietnam and who had therefore been highly exposed to Agent Orange.[33] The Air Force found no statistically significant differences between the Ranch Hand veterans and a control group. Several months later, the CDC published its own study, concluding there was "strong evidence" that Vietnam veterans did not suffer from an increased risk of conceiving children with birth defects.[34] These two reports, together with other available evidence, led the court to conclude that the plaintiffs' position on causation was "at best open" and probably too weak to justify tort recovery.[35]

Even if the plaintiffs could prove that dioxin *could cause* some of their illnesses, they faced the further challenge of proving that any particular plaintiff actually *contracted* his illness through Agent Orange exposure. All the alleged Agent Orange-related diseases are also acquired by *nonveterans* in the general population. Moreover, even if it could be shown that Vietnam veterans suffered disproportionately from particular illnesses, how could it be shown that Agent Orange was the cause, rather than some other environmental or health factors indigenous to South Vietnam, or to wartime stress?

Another problem was the defendants' contention that the various companies produced Agent Orange with varied amounts of dioxin. How could the plaintiffs show which defendants (companies) had injured them? Finally, the defendants claimed that if, ultimately, they were held liable, they should be exonerated, since they had been operating as war contractors following government specifications. Plaintiffs developed imaginative solutions to all these problems, but the possibility of a victory that would stand up on appeal was small.

The Settlement

After Chief Judge Jack Weinstein took over the case from Judge George Pratt, he pushed it aggressively toward trial, while at the same time urging the parties to discuss settlement terms. As the trial date approached, he appointed Washington lawyer Kenneth Feinberg as a special master to assist in mediation.[36] The tenuousness of the plaintiffs' case, as well as the financial strain on their lawyers who were funding the litigation, clearly gave the plaintiffs a strong incentive to settle. The defendants, whose resources (including insurance) and prospects for success were much greater, might have had more reason to go to trial, perhaps hoping that a victory would deter future class-action, toxic tort suits. However, there was always a possibility, albeit small, that a jury moved by the veterans' suffering and the defendants' wealth would bring in a stunning multibillion dollar verdict for the plaintiffs. Thus, on the eve of trial—7 May 1984—the parties settled for $180 million. The chemical companies, however, explicitly denied any liability.

In a complex class action, with thousands of named plaintiffs who have never met their lawyers or had any direct contact regarding their case, the judge must independently determine that the settlement is fair, reasonable, and in the interest of the class, rather than a sweetheart deal for the plaintiffs' lawyers or for a small number of named plaintiffs. While a large aggregate sum, $180 million would necessarily leave many class members uncompensated; it seemed unlikely that any plaintiff would receive more than 10 or 15 thousand dollars.[37]

Chief Judge Weinstein, believing it important to get veterans' thinking regarding the settlement, ordered notice of the agreement sent to class members and also scheduled unprecedented "fairness hearings" around the country. Hundreds of veterans testified; hundreds of others wrote personal letters. Many disgruntled Agent Orange veterans wanted to go to trial; having their day in court after so many years of struggle and frustration was more important than the possibility of modest compensation. For them, *In Re Agent Orange* was about vindication, not compensation. They wanted to publicize their suffering and sacrifice and the villainy of the chemical companies in a public forum. As one Agent Orange Army veteran told the court:

> I have come here to plead with you not to accept this [settlement] offer, to give us our day in court. I have heard some say this settlement is fair and I ask them, would any amount of money help correct the problems with our children? Would all the money in the world be worth having a child born without a hand, without a foot, severely brain damaged, deformed grossly or dead? What price do you put on my suffering? We started this lawsuit to bring those responsible to trial and find them guilty. We can't stop now.

A combat veteran, who spent 13 months in a hospital after Vietnam, told the court:

> I think we should have some sort of resolution made from this courtroom where we can sue the United States government, let them be accountable. And let them say that they did wrong. They owe us something. I don't care whether it's a nickel or a dime, I want them to say, "I was wrong." I want justice from my country who I stood for, who I fought for, who I loved and who I gave everything I could in my life.

Some class members felt that the trial would bring to light valuable information about the toxicity of dioxin.

Another group of veterans opposed the settlement on the ground that $180 million was inadequate to provide significant compensation to the hundreds of thousands of present and potential claimants. They predicted there would be tens of thousands of claims by veterans and their families who needed costly medical treatment, and that allocating the limited funds among so many deserving claimants would necessarily become a matter of triage. In his opinion approving the settlement, Judge Weinstein noted that the majority of veterans who communicated with the court opposed the settlement.

Class members who favored the settlement emphasized the importance of immediate medical assistance for veterans and their families, especially those with birth-defective children. In their view, the settlement could provide some measure of immediate relief. The alternative, they said, would be years of litigation that might possibly result in no relief at all. A third group of veterans would not approve or disapprove the settlement without knowing how it would be distributed, and how much their attorneys would be paid.[38]

In his 7 January 1985 order approving settlement, Chief Judge Weinstein stressed the benefits both for the parties and the public. For the plaintiffs, chances of recovering anything at trial were very slim. A decisive defeat for them might jeopardize their efforts to obtain assistance from Congress and the VA. Trial and appeals would place intolerable strain on the plaintiffs' lawyers, and would postpone or possibly eliminate the assistance that so many class members needed immediately. Weinstein also concluded that the settlement was reasonable for the defendants, who would incur tens of millions of dollars in costs if litigation proceeded. Putting an end to the case would free employees and executives for more productive work, demonstrate the companies' compassion and respect for the plight of the Vietnam veteran, and set an example for the government and the citizenry. The court also emphasized that the settlement would free judges, magistrates, and other court personnel to adjudicate other cases pending on the civil and criminal dockets.[39]

Settlement Plan

Although Weinstein gave final approval to the settlement in early January 1985, four months elapsed before he adopted Special Master Feinberg's plan to distribute the settlement fund.[40] The plan subdivided the settlement fund into three parts. *First*, $150 million will be devoted to a cash payment program for totally disabled veterans and survivors of deceased veterans. The court likened this subfund to "an insurance policy for death and disability during the period from 1970 to 1995."[41] To receive a cash award, a totally disabled veteran must merely show that he was exposed to Agent Orange; a survivor of a deceased veteran must only show that death was not "predominantly caused by trauma."[42]

Judge Weinstein stressed that limiting the cash payment program to nontraumatic death and total disability would provide the most equitable allocation of a fund "not sufficient to satisfy the claimed losses of every class member."[43] Not only would this program provide a meaningful cash award to those who suffered the most severe injuries, it would also compensate claimants who had the "greatest likelihood of ultimate success."[44] By requiring only a "showing" of exposure, the plan would avoid the troublesome causation issue and thus reduce the possibility that administrative costs would eat up the fund.[45]

The initial Feinberg plan assumed there would be about 50,000 potential claimants; however, by May 1985, 245,000 claims had been filed. Although the court had originally anticipated maximum payouts of approximately $12,800, the flood of claims may reduce the size of the individual awards, possibly triggering a new round of criticism of the settlement by veterans. No action will be taken until the Second Circuit Court of Appeals resolves the appeal of the settlement brought by various disgruntled class members and other veterans who had opted out of the class and who had their cases dismissed.[46]

While admitting that the cash payment program would not provide an award to each exposed veteran, the court stressed that the *second* part of the plan, the class assistance foundation, would be designed "to help meet the needs of the entire class."[47] The foundation would receive $45 million to provide medical, social, and legal services to class members. Veterans would be allowed to play a significant role in disbursing settlement funds, and they would be provided with "an opportunity to mobilize themselves and others to deal with the enormous problems of the class." Reacting to the views expressed by class members at the fairness hearings, the court ordered the foundation to provide priority medical service to children with birth defects. To ensure efficient use of the fund and to promote public and private contributions, the court ordered that the foundation be organized as a nonprofit, tax-exempt entity. The court emphasized that the foundation should expend its resources on existing groups; it should not create its own bureaucracy.

Third, the plan assigns 2 percent of the funds to a trust for New Zealand and Australian class members. The 2 percent figure represents the proportion of total class members from those countries. (The court initially favored implementation of a trust so that a distribution plan tailored to these veterans could be developed.)[48]

The Agent Orange Controversy and Civil/Military Relations

It is beyond the scope of this article to analyze all the complex procedural and tort issues raised by *In Re Agent Orange*. For students of civil/military relations, two issues are of particular importance.

The Feres/Stencel Doctrine

While the Federal Tort Claims Act allows suits against the U.S. government, it carves out an exception for military personnel whose injuries arise from wartime combat. In *Feres v. United States*,[49] the

U.S. Supreme Court was asked to consider the torts claims of three servicemen, two alleging medical malpractice and the third, negligence in the maintenance of a barracks that had caught fire. The Court rejected all three suits, extending the Tort Claims Act's exemption to all injuries arising out of active military service. The Court pointed to the Veterans' Benefits Act as the congressionally mandated means for providing disability compensation to injured service personnel.

Further, it expressed concern for military discipline. If service personnel could sue the government, the courts would be required to second-guess military commanders' decisions. Lower- and higher-ranking personnel would have to testify against one another at trials. The Court found this specter highly disturbing.

A quarter-century later, the Supreme Court took a second look at the same issue. An Air Force pilot had been permanently disabled because the ejection seat of his plane had malfunctioned. The pilot sought to recover a large sum from both the contractor and the federal government. The former argued that if it were liable, it should be indemnified by the United States, which, it claimed, was more at fault because of its poor maintenance of the equipment. In *Stencel Aero Engineering Corp. v. United States (1977)*,[50] the Court rejected the claim. To require the United States to indemnify a supplier of ordnance for tort awards in favor of injured military personnel would thwart the purpose of the Veterans' Benefits Act and undermine military discipline. It would also undermine *Feres*: injured service personnel—prohibited from suing the government directly—would, in effect, be allowed to reach into its pocket by using the contractor as an intermediary.[51]

In their efforts to bring the United States into the case, the defendant chemical companies attempted to distinguish the government's possible liability in *In Re Agent Orange* from the Supreme Court precedents. They argued that the government should be held liable for failing to warn the plaintiffs of the health risks of Agent Orange *after* they had returned to civilian status. Moreover, the companies argued that nothing in *Feres/Stencel* barred veterans' wives' and children's suits (for miscarriages and birth defects). They are not covered by the Veterans' Benefits Act, and permitting their claims would not undermine military organization and discipline.[52] Judge Pratt (whose elevation to the Court of Appeals resulted in reassignment of the case to Chief Judge Weinstein) granted the government's motion to dismiss the complaints, describing the postdischarge failure-to-warn theory as "artful pleading."

> Plaintiffs' complaints here neither allege nor support a conclusion that the post-discharge failure to warn was sufficiently separate and distinct from the underlying "incident to service" tort claims. Moreover, the *Feres* doctrine bars claims that are not only "incident to service" but also those which, like these, "arise out of" military service. The injuries here alleged are "inseparably intertwined with, and directly related to, plaintiffs' military service [citations omitted]. The important and well established principle of the *Feres* doctrine cannot be circumvented by inventive pleadings presentation or artful pleading which attempts to create an actionable post-discharge claim out of what is in reality a claim of continuing neglect.[53]

Judge Pratt also dismissed the family members' suits, stating that "although Agent Orange may ultimately be found to have caused injuries in subsequently conceived children, those injuries, nevertheless, arose out of and were incident to the service of the parent." Later, Chief Judge Weinstein reconsidered and reversed the court's position, letting it go into the discovery phase.[54] This necessarily left intact the chemical companies' third-party complaints against the government for indemnity for any payments they might ultimately make to wives and children. After the settlement, however, Weinstein dismissed these third-parties' suits. He also rejected similar claims brought (after the settlement) by the plaintiffs themselves. He allowed the veterans' birth-defective children to voluntarily withdraw their suits, however, so they would not be barred from renewing their suit if new evidence emerges to sustain their theory that Agent Orange had damaged their fathers' sperm cells.[55]

The result of these *In Re Agent Orange Litigation* rulings is that in an age of revolutionary developments in tort law, especially products liability, the U.S. government remains immune to suits arising from injuries sustained by military personnel. Congress and the courts have defined the relationship of a citizen to the armed forces as special, governed by its own specific laws and norms. The judicial view is that to permit military personnel to sue for their injuries might bring about a degree of adversariness and litigiousness that would undermine military discipline and esprit.

There is much to this view, although the impact on military discipline of permitting veterans to sue for injuries arising from defective equipment and products would be very different from suits regarding tactics and strategy. A suit about the safety of a pesticide or a weapon pits an injured or former serviceman against the Pentagon or the federal government, not against his present or former commander. A finding in favor of the serviceman would permit recovery similar to what a civilian would be entitled and would merely create a claim on the public coffers. Moreover, if for reasons of military necessity such suits cannot be allowed, it might be thought that a reasonable quid pro quo should be commensurable or, at least, generous VA compensation. While VA medical care and disability benefits are reasonably good, they cannot approach the windfall recoveries some civilian litigants are fortunate enough to obtain. This may be an insolvable dilemma. Our society is becoming used to huge recoveries in tort suits (although few plaintiffs actually recover enormous amounts). Claims consciousness will necessarily extend to citizen/soldiers, who will inevitably be disappointed when learning that the veterans' benefits system precludes such windfalls.

The Government Contractor Defense

In dealings between the armed forces and contractors, it would not be desirable for suppliers to question the military's needs, specifications, or timetables. Thus, the government contractor defense holds such suppliers free from liability if their injury-causing product was designed according to government specifications.[56] Nevertheless, some courts have held that government contractors have at least an obligation to inform the government of any health or other risks in their designs so the latter can make a fully informed choice as to whether to go ahead with the order.

The Agent Orange plaintiffs and the U.S. government argued that the chemical companies should not be protected by the government contractor defense because they knew of dioxin's dangers and had a responsibility to reveal those dangers to the government to allow an informed decision. The defendants contended that their product was supplied pursuant to government specifications; and, in any event, that the government was just as informed as they about the possible health hazards of Agent Orange. The defendants also argued that even if the government's knowledge had been inferior, it would have contracted for the pesticides in any event, even if it had been informed by the companies of dioxin's risks; if so, the companies should be free from liability. The court initially accepted this position.

Chief Judge Weinstein ruled that the contractors would be entitled to a judgment dismissing all claims if they could show:

- The government established the specifications for Agent Orange;

• The Agent Orange manufactured by the defendant met the government's specifications in all material respects; and

• The government knew as much as or more than the defendant about the hazards to people that accompanied use of Agent Orange.[57]

He later modified his position in response to the plaintiffs' argument that the policy behind the government contractor defense was not furthered by protecting suppliers of "shelf products." Unlike suppliers who create a new product to fill a government order, suppliers of "shelf products" simply provide the government with a product that they have long been selling in the civilian market. According to the plaintiffs, since under such circumstances, suppliers can purchase insurance and pass its costs along to consumers, they should be under an obligation to share their knowledge with the government.

Chief Judge Weinstein, partly persuaded by this argument, modified the third leg of his previous government contractor formulation as follows:

> A plaintiff would be required to prove, along with the other elements of his cause of action, that the hazards to him that accompanied use of Agent Orange were, or reasonably should have been, known to the defendant. The burden would then shift to each individual defendant to prove (1) that the government knew as much as or more than that defendant knew or reasonably should have known about the dangers of Agent Orange, or (2) even if the government had been given as much knowledge as that defendant should have had, it would have ordered production of Agent Orange in any event and would not have taken steps to reduce or eliminate the hazard.[58]

The parties undertook a great deal of discovery to determine how much the "government" knew about the possible toxicity of the herbicides it sprayed in Vietnam. The plaintiffs tried desperately to overcome the government contractor defense, arguing that even if many low-ranking persons in various government agencies knew as much as the chemical company executives, such knowledge could not be imputed to the government; and, therefore, the companies had failed to fulfill their duty to inform. In finding the settlement reasonable, Chief Judge Weinstein expressed the view that lower-ranking government officials' knowledge did constitute "knowledge by the government," and, therefore, that the defendants would have been able to establish a prima facie case that the government knew as much as the chemical companies about the health hazards of Agent Orange. Since the defendants chose to settle the suit, we do not know whether they could have sustained this defense before a jury.

If Judge Weinstein's ultimate formulation of the government contractor defense achieves wide acceptance, that defense would be weakened. It would not be as easy for a contractor to avoid liability for a defective product by pointing to the government's contract specifications. An injured victim might still be able to demonstrate the contractor's superior knowledge and failure to fully inform the government of risks.

Sociopolitical Implications

The efforts of the Vietnam veterans to obtain recognition and benefits continue a long tradition of veterans' activism in American history. It took Revolutionary War veterans half a century to obtain their pensions. While the World War I bonus army lost its dramatic Washington campaign, eventually the veterans did achieve many of their goals.

Since World War II, however, American veterans have achieved a special status. The Veterans Administration's budget requests are usually well received in Congress. For example, despite various proposals to abolish or trim the VA hospital system, there is almost no possibility of this special medical network being dismantled. Vietnam veterans have been recipients of numerous new programs and entitlements. Despite frequent assertions to the contrary, they have utilized the VA as actively as their predecessors.[59] That successes have failed to extinguish criticisms of the VA and charges of societal insensitivity is entirely consistent with historical experience. As David Ross points out, "From 1919 to the outbreak of war in 1941, veterans demanded that society repay them for their wartime sacrifices. Each successful demand seemed to increase, not decrease, their sense of unredeemed sacrifice."[60]

American veterans remain an extremely powerful political force, and they are likely to become more so. By 1990, more than *half* the U.S. male population over 65 years of age will be veterans. While they are hardly a homogenous group, most can be rallied around bread-and-butter benefit issues. A democratic state is extremely hesitant to put a brake on veterans' demands. As a special interest group, veterans are well organized and numerous. They strongly believe that they have earned a right to special governmental benefits and prerogatives. Veterans' programs, for the most part, are politically popular.

The Agent Orange controversy demonstrates the veterans' political power. The United States has properly assumed the responsibility of providing medical care to veterans with service-related injuries and illnesses, but it has not committed itself to free lifetime medical, hospital, and nursing care for anyone who has served in the armed forces. Yet the extension of full medical benefits to the Agent Orange claimants moves the country further in this direction. Hundreds of thousands of veterans have claimed that their medical problems are Agent Orange related and thereby have obtained free treatment. There is no denying that these claimants are suffering, but it is not clear why taxpayers should pay for their medical care and not for that of other members of the society who are suffering, unless, of course, medical evidence someday shows that the veterans are suffering because they were poisoned by herbicides sprayed by American military forces in South Vietnam.

It is certain that the Agent Orange veterans will continue to lobby Congress for disability benefits and for aid and compensation for the birth defects of their children. Admittedly, children born with birth defects are among society's most sympathetic candidates for assistance. Between 1 percent and 2 percent of all babies are born with serious birth defects; the rates are the same for Vietnam veterans (or for Agent Orange veterans) as for the general population.[61] If assistance is to be extended to these children and their families, there would seem to be no justification for extending it to only veterans' children and families. Nevertheless, the momentum and politics of the Agent Orange movement may eventually lead to federal assistance for veterans' families.

Since the Vietnam War many veterans groups have sought—indeed some have been formed expressly—to vindicate veterans' legal rights. The Agent Orange case, however, marks the first instance of a large-scale legal action. While many veterans may not regard the settlement as an unconditional victory, the capacity to have mounted such litigation will serve as a reminder to all veterans that an alternative, or at least a supplement, to traditional veterans' lobbying forums exists at the courthouse.

The Agent Orange litigation is a consequence of the extraordinary rights consciousness and litigiousness of the times. The courts are now open to all sorts of personal injury and products liability claims that would not have been cognizable even a decade ago. We are moving rapidly toward a popular perception that when a person is injured, the injurer should pay (and pay generously) regardless of fault. The *Feres/Stencel* doctrine and the government contractor defense are inconsistent with evolving law and popular perceptions of tort justice. Nevertheless, because the precedents are very strong, it is unlikely the courts will tear down these barriers to tort claims by injured service personnel; whether Congress might do so is another matter.[62]

The expanding opportunities for accident victims to obtain compensation from accident "causers" create a gulf between civilians and military personnel. While the sociopolitical and legal status of armed forces personnel has always been distinct, and the product of military necessity, it has evolved throughout our history in response to developments in the larger society. Lawyers, academic commentators, and service personnel themselves have already begun to ask whether the bars on tort suits for injuries arising out of military service are really necessary to support national defense interests. Bringing these issues into focus is one of the major legacies of the Agent Orange movement.

Notes

1. Comptroller General Report to the Congress, "Health Effects on Individuals Exposed to Herbicide Agent Orange in South Vietnam" 250, 16 August 1978. The herbicides consisted of Agent Blue, Agent White, Agent Purple, Agent Green, Agent Pink, and Agent Orange. The names were derived from the particular color stripe on the barrel storing each herbicide.
2. A. L. Young et al., *The Toxicology, Environmental Fate, and Human Risk of Herbicide Orange and Its Associated Dioxin*, USAF OEHL Technical Report (October 1978), pp. I-11.
3. *In Re Agent Orange Product Liability Litigation*, 557 F. Supp. 740, 777 (E.D.N.Y. 1984) (hereinafter *In Re Agent Orange*).
4. *New York Times*, 8 February 1970, p. 29.
5. Ibid., 16 April 1970, p. 29.
6. Although the administration's official response dealt with the increasing concern of 2,4,5-T's health effects, some military officials believed the herbicide program's termination was primarily motivated by a desire to defuse antiwar activity in the United States. See Herbicide Agent Orange: *Hearings Before the Subcommittee on Medical Facilities and Benefits of the House Committee on Veterans Affairs*, 96th Cong. 2d sess. (1978) p. 15. Testifying before the subcommittee, USAF General Dettinger stated, "This was one of the programs we felt should be removed to decrease the opposition to our involvement there."
7. *Armed Forces Appropriations Act, FY 1971*, Public Law no. 91-441, 84 Stat. 905 (1970).
8. *Agent Orange Update Hearings: Hearings Before the Subcommittee on Medical Facilities and Benefits of the Senate Committee on Veterans Affairs*, 96th Cong., 2d sess. 799 (1980) (Department of Defense Herbicide Orange Status Report I). p. 802.

9. One study by a North Vietnamese medical school suggested such a connection, attributing an abnormal increase in liver cancer among Vietnamese citizens to dioxin contamination; many U.S. officials discounted the study as politically motivated. *Pesticide Oversight: Hearings Before the Subcommittee on Environment of the Senate Committee on Commerce*, 93d Cong., 2d sess. 20 (1974) (statement of Dr. Elizabeth Courtney, EPA), p. 22.

10. Interview with Col. Al Young, a member of the president's Science Advisory Council, 16 December 1985.

11. Ibid.

12. Ibid.

13. For more information concerning Reutershan, McCarthy, and the founding of AOVI, see Peter Schuck, *The Chemical and the Court: the Agent Orange Case and Mass Toxic Disasters* (forthcoming, Harvard University Press), chap. 2. Professor Schuck provides fascinating insights into the personalities behind the litigation. The plaintiffs' lawyers were badly divided throughout the years of litigation. The charismatic Yannacone was replaced as lead counsel in 1983. On the eve of trial, none of the lawyers who had been involved in recruiting veterans as clients (and in working with them) were any longer involved in the key decision making. The case had been taken over by toxic tort and class-action specialists.

14. See Dorothy Nelkin and Michael Brown, *Workers at Risk* (University of Chicago Press, 1984); Paul Slovick et al., "Perceived Risk: Psychological Factors and Social Implications," *Proceedings of the Royal Society*, A376 (1981), pp. 17-34.

15. *In Re Agent Orange Litigation*, 597 F. Supp. 740, 769. (E.D.N.Y. 1984).

16. *Veterans Exposure to Agent Orange: Hearings Before the Senate Committee on Veterans Affairs*, 98th Cong., 1st sess., (1983), pp. 250-257.

17. See Charles R. Figley and Seymour Levantman, eds., *Strangers at Home: Vietnam Veterans Since the War* (New York: Praeger, 1980); Paul Starr, *The Discarded Army: Veterans After Vietnam* (Charterhouse, 1973).

18. Sar Levitan and Karen Alderman, *Old Wars Remain Unfinished: The Veterans Benefits System* (Johns Hopkins University Press, 1973).

19. *Veterans Health Care, Training and Small Business Loan Act of 1981*, Public Law no. 97-72, 95 Stat. 1047 (codified in pertinent part at 38 U.S.C. section 610: authorizing the VA to provide hospital, nursing-home, or outpatient care to veterans who may have been exposed to toxic herbicides).

20. The corresponding numbers for FY 1984 were 3,800 inpatient admissions and 342,000 outpatient visits; in FY 1985 there were 1,400 inpatient admissions and 102,000 outpatient visits. The quality of care is another and disputed matter. Vietnam veterans have been extremely critical of the VA system, charging it with incompetence and insensitivity: see Starr, *The Discarded Army*; but other observers believe these charges are unfair and inaccurate, e.g., Levitan and Alderman, *Old Wars Remain Unfinished*; see also 557 F. Supp. 740, 766 (E.D.N.Y. 1984): "[I]t seems highly unlikely that service to veterans is as uniformly bad as was suggested at the Fairness Hearings."

21. Government Accounting Office, "V.A.'s Agent Orange Experimentation Program: Action Needed to More Efficiently Address Veterans Health Concerns"

(Washington, D.C.: GPO, 1983). (As of April 1986, that number had risen to 211,482; additionally, disability claims had risen to 28,556.)

22. *Veterans Health Programs Extension and Improvement Act of 1979*, Public Law no. 96-151, 93 Stat. 1092 (1979). Apparently the study is mired in conflict and its future in doubt. See Iver Petersen, "Study of Effects of Agent Orange on Veterans is Stalled in Dispute," *New York Times*, 19 May 1986, p. 1.

23. *Veterans' Dioxin and Radiation Exposure Compensation Standards Act of 1984*, Public Law no. 98-542, 98 Stat. 2725 (1984).

24. The VA's implementary *Rules and Regulations* state: "No other diseases will be considered service connected," because "sound medical evidence does not establish a cause and effect relationship between dioxin exposure and [any other disease]," 38 C.F.R. 3311 (A)(4)(d).

25. *In Re Agent Orange*. There are dozens of opinions on various issues and motions. The most important opinions are listed:
506 F. Supp. 762 (E.D.N.Y. 1980)
534 F. Supp. 1046 (E.D.N.Y. 1982)
565 F. Supp. 1263 (E.D.N.Y. 1983)
580 F. Supp. 690 (E.D.N.Y. 1984)
580 F. Supp. 1242 (E.D.N.Y. 1984)
597 F. Supp. 740 (E.D.N.Y. 1984)
603 F. Supp. 239 (E.D.N.Y. 1985)
611 F. Supp. 1396 (E.D.N.Y. 1985)

26. See *In Re Agent Orange*, 506 F. Supp. 762 (E.D.N.Y. 1980), *modified*, 100 F.R.D. 718 (E.D.N.Y. 1983), *denied* 725 F. 2d 858 (2d Cir.), cert. *denied* 465 U.S. 1067, 104 S. Ct. 1417, 79 L. Ed. 2d 743 (1984).

27. The initial complaint asked for damages "in the range of 40 billion dollars," Schuck, *The Chemical and the Court*, chap. 3, p. 15.

28. See note, "The Essense of the Agent Orange Litigation: The Government Contract Defense," 12 *Hofstra Law Review* 983 (1984). The defense traces back to the Supreme Court's 1940 decision in *Yearsley v. Ross Construction Company*, 309 U.S. 18 (1940), where the Court held that if a government contractor carried out its plan in strict compliance with the government contract and the contract was deemed faultless, the contractor would be shielded from liability.

29. 340 U.S. 135 (1950).

30. See "From Feres to Stencel: Should Military Personnel Have Access to FTCA Recovery?" 77 *Michigan Law Review* 1100 (1979).

31. 50 U.S.C. app. sections 2061-2166 (1966).

32. The Supreme Court had explicitly rejected just this type of indemnification of war contractors by the government in *Stencel Aero Engineering Corp. v. United States*, 431 U.S. 666 (1977).

33. W. Buckingham, *Operation Ranch Hand, the Air Force, and Herbicides in Southeast Asia 1961-1971* (1982). See also George D. Lathrop et al., *An Epidemiological Investigation of Health Effects in Air Force Personnel Following Exposure to Herbicides: Baseline Mortality Results*, Initial Annual Report, 30 June 1983, Defense Technical Information Agency AD A 130793; Lathrop et al., *An Epidemiological Investigation of Health Effects in Air Force Personnel, Results*,

Interim 1979–1982 Report, 24 February 1984, Defense Technical Information Agency AD A 138340.

34. *In Re Agent Orange*, 597 F. Supp. 740, 782 (E.D.N.Y. 1984).

35. Ibid., 795.

36. The government steadfastly refused to take part in the settlement negotiations, holding that "any settlement of this case that calls for contribution by the United States is not warranted." Ibid., 879.

37. *In Re Agent Orange*, 611 F. Supp. 1418 (E.D.N.Y. 1985).

38. The plaintiffs' lawyers had sought fees in excess of $34 million. The court, seeking to preserve as much of the fund as possible to help the class, awarded $9.3 million in fees, noting that this amount could be paid out of interest on the fund. *In Re Agent Orange*, 611 F. Supp. 1296 (E.D.N.Y. 1985), *modified* 18 June 1985 (unpublished order).

39. *In Re Agent Orange*, 597 F. Supp. 740, 799 (E.D.N.Y. 1984).

40. The court's apparently unprecedented action put each plaintiff in the difficult position of having to react to the "fairness and reasonableness" without knowing how the settlement would affect each plaintiff. Several factors, including the creation of a 29-member advisory board, ostensibly representing a cross-section of the plaintiff class, to help draft the distribution plan as well as the court's desire to facilitate an early start of the appeals process, militated in favor of such an approach. However, the court's action clearly contravened existing law on class action procedure. In the leading case to address this issue, *In Re Chicken Antitrust Litigation* 669 F. 2d 228 (5th Cir. 1982), the court found that a final judgment order could not have been entered before a distribution plan had been approved. The court stated, "This, of course, reflects the fact that no overall settlement can be adjudged fair or unfair unless the allocation scheme is also examined."

    Moreover, the court stated that so long as the elements of the distribution plan remain at issue, "an order will not be considered final regardless of its characterization, and there may be no intrusion by appeal." The Agent Orange court, by taking action proscribed by *Chicken Antitrust*, appeared to step outside of established law and created a situation whereby an appellate court might refuse to approve the parties' settlement. To avoid such a situation, Chief Judge Weinstein entered a "final" order and judgment in the case, thus allowing it to appear that no final order had been entered until after a settlement plan was approved. The court's action obviates the need to vacate the settlement on procedural grounds and increases the likelihood the settlement will be approved on appeal. This approval would allow the distribution plan to be put into immediate operation. *In Re Agent Orange*, 611 F. Supp. 1396 (E.D.N.Y. 1985).

41. *In Re Agent Orange*, 611 F. Supp. 1396, 1400 (E.D.N.Y. 1985).

42. Ibid., at 1400-1401.

43. Ibid., at 1411.

44. Ibid., at 1418, 1421.

45. The original plan proposed that only 50 percent of the veterans most highly exposed to Agent Orange receive benefits from the cash award program. This would have allowed a maximum disability payment of $25,000 to those veterans severely injured in Vietnam. Reiterating that causality was "too speculative a basis for distribu-

tion," Weinstein eliminated the 50 percent proposal. By doing so, however, the court reduced the potential maximum disability award to $12,800 and the corresponding maximum death award to $3,400.

46. At the time this article went to press, the Second Circuit Court of Appeals had not confirmed the settlement agreement.

47. *In Re Agent Orange*, 611 F. Supp. at 1411 (1985).

48. In August 1985, Special Master Feinberg reported that the Australian and New Zealand governments had agreed to oversee the creation of distribution mechanisms in their respective countries. Feinberg proposed that the funds be placed in private trusts to act as a repository from which the foreign governments could distribute the funds. On 11 September 1985, the court adopted the special master's proposals. *In Re Agent Orange*, 618 F. Supp. 625 (E.D.N.Y. 1985) (order at 9/11/85).

49. 340 U.S. 135 (1950); see also *Brown v. United States*, 348 U.S. 110, (1954): allowing tort suit by ex-serviceman for negligent treatment at VA hospital of a knee injury that occurred *after* separation from service.

50. 431 U.S. 666 (1977).

51. See comment, "Stencel Aero Engineering v. United States: An Expansion of the Feres Doctrine to Include Military Contractors, Subcontractors and Suppliers", 29 *Hastings Law Journal* 1217 (1978).

52. See note, "Agent Orange as a Problem of Law and Policy," 77 N.W.U.L. Rev. 48 (1982); Seidelson, "The Feres Exception to the Federal Tort Claims Act: New Insights into an Old Problem," 11 *Hofstra Law Review* 629 (1983); comment, "Expansion of the Feres Doctrine," 32 *Emory Law Journal*, pp. 237-271.

53. *In Re Agent Orange* 506 F. Supp. 762, 779 (E.D.N.Y. 1980).

54. *In Re Agent Orange*, 580 F. Supp. 1242 (E.D.N.Y. 1984).

55. *In Re Agent Orange*, 603 F. Supp. 239 (E.D.N.Y. 1985). For a vigorous attack on the application of the *Feres-Stencel* doctrine to servicemen's children, see note, "Pushing the Feres Doctrine a Generation Too Far: Recovery for Genetic Damage to the Children of Servicemembers," 32 *American University Law Review*, 1039-1085 (1983).

56. The government contractor defense does not extend to products which are défectively produced or which are not designed according to government specifications. In other words, if a manufacturer provides the government with a cracked airplane engine, it will be liable for injuries to the plane's crew. See note, "The Essense of the Agent Orange Litigation: The Government Contract Defense," 12 *Michigan Law Review* 983 (1984); Jules F. Miller, "Liability and Relief of Government Contractors for Injuries to Service Members," 104 *Military Law Review* (1984), pp. 1-108.

57. *In Re Agent Orange*, 554 F. Supp. 1046 (1982).

58. *In Re Agent Orange*, 597 F. Supp. 740, 849 (E.D.N.Y. 1984).

59. Levitan and Alderman, *Old Wars Remain Unfinished*; Center for Policy Research. *Legacies of Vietnam: Comparative Adjustment of Veterans and Their Peers: A Study Proposed for the Veterans Administration* (Washington, D.C.: GPO, 1981).

60. David R. Ross, *Preparing for Ulysses: Politics and Veterans* (New York: Columbia University Press, 1969).

61. J. D. Erickson, "Vietnam Veterans' Risks for Fathering Babies with Birth Defects," *Journal of the American Medical Association* 252 (1984): pp. 903-912.

62. On 7 October 1985, the House passed H.R. 3174 to allow active duty military personnel to sue the federal government for medical or dental malpractice in government facilities. Rep. Barney Frank (D-Mass.) stated, "What we say is that members of the armed forces now have the same right as civilians. . . ." See *Congressional Quarterly*, 12 October 1985, p. 2067.

AUTHORS' NOTE: *The authors wish to express thanks to Peter Schuck for allowing them to read a draft of his book,* The Chemical and the Court: The Agent Orange Case and Mass Toxic Disasters. *Professor Jacobs acknowledges with appreciation the generous support of the Filomen D'Agostino and Max E. Greenberg Research Fund of the New York University School of Law.*

JAMES B. JACOBS is professor of law and director, Center for Research in Crime and Justice, New York University School of Law. He holds both an LL.D. and a Ph.D. (in sociology) from the University of Chicago, where from 1973 to 1975 he studied with Morris Janowitz. Professor Jacobs wrote *The Socio-Legal Foundations of Civil Military Relations*, published by Transaction Press in 1986.

DENNIS McNAMARA, a third-year law student at the University of Texas School of Law, received his B.A. from Cornell University. He coauthored with Professor Jacobs "Selective Service Without a Draft" (the dilemmas and symbolic politics of draft registration), which appeared in the Spring 1984 issue of this Journal.

rately, the lack of a welcome home, the veterans received when they returned.

Those who attribute postwar troubles to the unique character of the war dwell on its brutality, its lack of established lines, and its confusions over who was friend and who was foe. They also point to the soldiers' youth and pattern of service. Almost seven years younger on average than his World War II predecessor, the Vietnam soldier found himself suddenly delivered, alone, into the war zone where he served a one-year tour, and then, just as abruptly and still alone, he returned to the United States. While not necessarily disputing assumptions about uniqueness, other observers argue that the veterans' problems lay in the outcome of the war. Theologian W. Taylor Stevenson, for example, contends that the veteran suffers from a sense of defilement—a belief that he was dishonored and symbolically dirtied by breaking the taboos that protect Americans' sense of innocence and powerfulness. Still others argue that by 1968 Americans neither supported the war nor expected to win it. Consequently at the time, veterans serving after 1967, and in retrospect all veterans, regarded their service as purposeless—"It don't mean nothing," in the refrain of the Vietnam soldiers in the recent movie *Hamburger Hill.* Surveys do show that veterans most likely to undergo postwar stress had served after 1967, when the war had become increasingly unpopular and, for many, its purpose increasingly unclear.

Despite the partial validity of these arguments, whether combat in Vietnam was unique remains very much an open question. Certainly the one-year rotation, a policy adopted in no other conflict save Korea, created many difficulties, but other aspects of the Vietnam War may not have differed as radically from those in previous conflicts as some accounts assume. The destruction of villages and murder of civilians may not have been as frequent or as cold-blooded as movies like *Platoon* and memoirs like *A Rumor of War* make them seem, and clearly similar atrocities have occurred in earlier wars. In World War II and Korea, according to one historian, civilian casualties probably equalled or exceeded those in Vietnam; and, as James Reston, Jr.'s *Sherman's March and Vietnam* serves to remind, even when Americans fought other Americans they did not always spare civilians or towns. Nor were other aspects of the Vietnam War totally different from the Civil War. The Confederate soldiers, no older than their Vietnam War counterparts, also faced horrifying brutality and suffering in an age of mass casualties but rudimentary medicine that could do little to heal them or ease their pain. Their war, a fight to overthrow their own government and to preserve slavery, could have led to a sense of defilement as readily as did the Vietnam War. Significant anti-war agitation occurred in the South toward the end of the war, and the Confederate soldiers, like the Vietnam vets, endured the conflicting emotions of a frustrated and defeated army. Yet little evidence of post-traumatic stress disorder appears in the postwar letters, diaries, and reminiscences of Confederate veterans. Though scarred by defeat, they seem to have suffered far less difficulty adjusting after the war than the Vietnam veterans have. The nature of combat in the two wars may help explain that difference, but of greater importance may be the way veterans of the two wars perceived their return from battle.

The treatment of returning Vietnam soldiers has itself become an issue central to the third Vietnam war. Popular lore tells of returning soldiers who were harassed by anti-war civilians, but these accounts should not be accepted until systematic investigation confirms them. Clearly, however, veterans believe themselves to have been the victims of civilian hostility. Many talk of trying to hide their service; others who did not or could not because of injury, recount sad tales of harassment by angry or scornful fellow citizens. "Did you kill any babies?" they say people asked them. They tell of a passerby looking at their empty sleeve and hissing, "Serves you right" or of anti-war protestors spitting on them. The image of being spit on by civilians—whether fact or myth—aptly symbolizes what the veterans feel—a sense of defilement, a sense that society condemned their actions and rejected them as unclean.

Confederate soldiers, too, worried about whether defeat dishonored them, but few recounted tales of scorn. They talked instead of how Southerners warmly embraced them. A one-armed veteran likely met not a hostile comment but a bevy of adoring females. Towns throughout the South staged picnics and celebrations to welcome their soldiers. More important, in the 10 to 15 years after the Confederate surrender, Southerners built Confederate cemeteries, erected funereal monuments, and held yearly memorial celebrations in honor of the dead and the veterans. These celebrations and memorials, though avoiding the issues and passions of the war, publicly, ritualistically testified to the honor of the Confederate soldier; they signaled to the soldier that his society did not consider him defiled by war or defeat.

Exactly this sort of ritual of acceptance and honor was denied Vietnam veterans when first they came home or even once the war ended. The one-year tour and the soldiers' return as individuals and not in units made organizing a triumphant parade unlikely, if not impossible. More important, some Americans were appalled by the war and others frustrated by defeat; both groups shunned the Vietnam War's soldiers and avoided discussion of the conflict. For a time, Americans almost succumbed to a sort of collective amnesia. This initial failure to accept the returning Vietnam warriors, so very much in contrast to the South's reception of its armies after Appomattox, contributed significantly to the vets' adjustment problems.

War, as Vietnam veteran William Broyles, Jr., and others point out, sets up conflicting emotions within soldiers: it both horrifies and fascinates. It demands that soldiers kill and destroy, actions that they have been taught to consider wrong in other situations, and at the same time generates tremendous excitement since it is, in Broyles' analogy, the greatest of all games. Taught the standards and values of the game in basic training, what Robert Jay Lifton calls a rite of passage into another world, few Vietnam soldiers questioned the morality of killing the enemy or resorting to extreme violence. The ethics of war justified and the need to survive demanded them. But what was logical and moral in "Indian country," to use the significant slang of the soldiers, the veterans feared might not be seen as such "back in the world." To ease their fears, soldiers may well need another rite of passage—a ritual welcome home, be it a grand parade, memorial day, or monument unveiling—to facilitate their return to the "world." Such a public, symbolic act helps the soldiers resubmit themselves to normal social values. And it allows society to welcome them back, allows it both to acknowledge its role in and acceptance of their temporary violation of moral dictates and to admit the nobility of the soldiers' sacrifice and the legitimacy of what has so fascinated them. Veterans of any war need such acceptance, but those who fought in a controversial, defeated cause, which brings with it feelings of failure and purposelessness, need it even more. The returning Confederates received such ritualistic welcome; the returning Vietnam vets at first did not—a difference that helps explain why so many more Vietnam than Confederate veterans had a difficult time putting the war behind them. In the absence of a ritualistic acceptance, the psychological tensions and moral anxieties some veterans felt remained unresolved and unratified by society. As a result, some veterans felt defiled, in theologian Stevenson's term, or spat upon, in the image of popular accounts. But their feeling of uncleanness resulted less from the specific evils of Vietnam, less from some special brutality or violation of American innocence and powerfulness, than from the absence of the usual postwar ritual of restoration and cleansing.

The welcome came later, and the veterans' enthusiastic, emotional response showed their need for ritual acceptance. In the late 1970's, two movies, *Coming Home* and *The Deer Hunter*, despite differing views of the war, won popular and critical acclaim, marking new, intense interest in Vietnam veterans and their war. Early treatments still stressed the vet's problems, and in some ways harkened back to the older anti-war spirit, but soon his image began to be rehabilitated. An early favorable presentation appeared on television as a new American frontier hero, a not-quite-so-innocent American Adam on that not-quite-so-innocent last American frontier, Hawaii. There, "Thomas Magnum, P.I.," battled for truth and justice, between swims, volleyball, love affairs, and, in his early seasons, flashbacks to Vietnam. "Magnum" never really confronted the issues of the war but rather celebrated a noble, model veteran who took pride in having fought in Vietnam and cherished—indeed, with sidekicks T.C. and Rick, still enjoyed—the camaraderie of battle. The brief flashbacks not only advanced the plot but offered viewers a sense of the experience of combat in Vietnam and of its after effects. A few years later veteran Oliver Stone's *Platoon* put a vivid, bloody vision of this experience on the big screen. On one level, Stone's movie re-created the brutality and morality of "Indian country," of the war in Vietnam, in order to ask the civilians "back in the world" to understand what the vets had endured and done. The tremendous acclaim for *Platoon* seemed at last to signal society's acceptance of that behavior and to spur an emotional catharsis.

As this interest in Vietnam grew, Americans finally offered the veterans the ritualistic reassurance so long denied them. By 1986, 143 monuments to the Vietnam veterans had been planned or constructed in 45 states at a cost of $20 million in privately raised funds. In 1982 the nation dedicated the most important of these monuments, the Vietnam Memorial, located on the Mall, not far from the Lincoln Memorial, in the nation's capital. It resulted from private fund-raising efforts led by veterans who sought to separate the government's war from the warrior, who sought reconciliation and acceptance, and who therefore strove to keep the project free from politics or ideology. In avoiding wartime issues and passions, their efforts resembled early Confederate memorial activities, and so, too, did the memorial's design. Conceived by a Yale University student, Maya Ying Lin, the monument was not, in her words, "meant to be cheerful or happy, but to bring out in people the realization of loss and a cathartic healing process." A grand review, the welcome home parade denied the veterans, marked its dedication, and soon thereafter this monument of mourning and purification drew four million visitors a year, making it the biggest attraction in Washington save for the Air and Space Museum.

V-shaped, constructed of black marble panels, sunk slightly into the ground so that visitors faced the some 58,000 names of the men and women who died in Vietnam, names etched in the seemingly endless order in which they died, the monument evokes, almost commands, mourning. "Nothing I had heard or written had prepared me for the moment," columnist James J. Kilpatrick wrote of his visit to the memorial. "I could not speak. I wept. . . . This memorial has a pile driver's impact. No politics. No recriminations. Nothing of vainglory or glory either." Or, as one of the judges who selected the design put it in imagery also used to describe Confederate Memorial Day, it "Looks back to death and forward to life." The tourists who flocked to it searched for names they knew, made rubbings of names of friends and relatives, left flags, flowers, medals, or some personal token of love and respect. More than any single thing, the memorial on the mall and its ceremony of dedication offered the ritualistic acceptance so long denied the Vietnam veterans.

Americans, then, have begun to recover from their collective amnesia. Hostility toward veterans has cooled, and the nation has at last formally offered welcome and cleansing. This memorial activity by stressing mourning resembles the South's treatment of its veterans. The South's adjustment to defeat, however, rested not only in its memorialization of its soldiers, but in its interpretation of the war and its reconciliation with the North. The three developments proved interrelated because as reunion proceeded, the North joined in the homage to the veterans, and a shared, heroic interpretation of the war developed, thereby helping ensure that the veterans' sacrifice had purpose and meaning. The continued celebration of the Vietnam veterans may well also depend on whether and how the nation achieves reconciliation and reinterprets the war.

III

The reconciliation of the foes in the war over Vietnam, the "hawks" and "doves" in the lingo of the sixties, has not kept pace with acceptance of the veterans. Some combatants have tried to bridge their differences, but as Myra MacPherson detailed in *Long Time Passing*, hostilities between soldiers of the war and protestors against it continue. James Fallows has perceptively argued that preexisting class differences between the mostly poor and disadvantaged who volunteered or were drafted and the comparatively rich and well-connected who avoided the draft help explain these persisting resentments. But estrangement results not just from class conflict, as a comparison with what happened after the Civil War suggests. The reconciliation of North and South occurred slowly and only as the passions of the war dissipated and veterans on both sides deemphasized the issues of the war, slavery and secession, and focused instead on their common wartime experience, the camaraderie and excitement of battle. Vietnam veterans, though, share such memories with the Vietnamese, as revealed in William Broyles' *Brothers in Arms*, a Marine veteran's account of his return to Vietnam. In passages that resemble reflections by Civil War veterans, Broyles describes visits to former battlefields and with former foes and concludes that confrontation in battle created bonds with his one-time enemy. For the foes in the war over Vietnam, the warriors and anti-warriors, no such shared experience exists on which to build reconciliation. Indeed, as Fallows and others have pointed out, the two groups have starkly different memories of the war: one of the army and combat, the other of college and protest. These differences make a second feature of the post-Civil War reconciliation of Blue and Gray, a willingness by each side to celebrate the other's heroism and motives, even more important in the reconciliation of the two sides in the war over Vietnam. That willingness, though, may ultimately depend on how Americans interpret the war in Vietnam, just as it did on how the North and South came to view the Civil War.

The South, after a brief period of examination and debate, developed an interpretation of defeat that facilitated acceptance of the veterans and reconciliation with the North, but hindered any learning of lessons or gaining of wisdom. Southerners rejected any notion that defeat constituted a judgment upon their cause; instead, they concluded that they had fought the war over valid constitutional principles and therefore had acted morally and legally. God had allowed their defeat not because He judged their cause evil, but because He planned to use them for some greater purpose. Certainly defeat had not resulted from any failing of the South or, more specifically, any shortcomings of Confederate soldiers. This interpretation helped Confederate veterans cope with defeat by telling them that, even though they lost, they had acted nobly and heroically and by reassuring them that their sacrifice had been part of a divine plan. It also meant that by the time of national reconciliation during the Spanish-American War most Southerners accepted national myths of divine mission and powerfulness, just as most Northerners did. The North had always assumed that God directed its cause and that it had acted heroically and nobly in saving the Union and freeing the slaves. Robert Penn Warren labeled this moral self-satisfaction the North's "Treasury of Virtue," a treasury that provided moral capital to underwrite the corruption and materialism of the subsequent Gilded Age. By the early 20th century, Northerners not only believed that they had acted rightly but had also come to share the Southerners' assessment of Confederate soldiers. With both sides celebrating their role and seeing themselves as part of God's plan for the nation, the Civil War had been rendered a battle in which everyone had been right and everyone had fought heroically—a war, in other words, that on some level everyone had won. Hence neither side perceived the conflict's tragic dimensions but instead interpreted the war as a vindication leading to a reaffirmation of God's mission for the United States in the world.

No such simple, creative consensus about Vietnam has come to dominate public thinking as the third Vietnam War for the historical hearts and minds of the American public escalates. The divisions of the war years persist: both the proponents and opponents of the war continue to consider their side to have been right and to refight the war pretty much along old lines. Thus Stone's *Platoon*, though "new" in its vivid and sympathetic recreation of the experience of combat in Vietnam (which may explain its popularity), still takes a traditional anti-war approach by dividing American attitudes toward the war between good and evil and by portraying the United States role as one of almost unrelieved brutality, violence, frustration, and failure. Two recent histories of the war, Loren Baritz's *Backfire* and Gabriel Kolko's *Anatomy of a War*, each in its own way echoes anti-war arguments of the sixties, the former in its condemnation of America's bureaucratic, technological society and the latter in its romanticization of the Viet Cong and North Vietnamese.

Many doves, of course, do not perceive any need to rethink the war or their role in it because, they believe, they rightly opposed American involvement and won the battle at home over Vietnam. Some even seem to suffer from their own "Treasury of Virtue"; they know they were right about the war all along, that therefore they have built up a treasury of moral capital for a new gilded age of BMW's and Rolexes. Events in Indochina since 1973 and new evidence about the North Vietnamese war effort, however, indicate that some doves do need to reconsider their simplistic conception of a peace-loving peasantry attacked by a brutal imperialistic America or to revise their belief that only American intransigence prolonged the war. The anti-warriors might even question whether the shrillness of some protestors dangerously escalated the war at home or consider whether an absence of will among the anti-warriors actually helped prolong the war. James Fallows and Myra MacPherson have argued that if the anti-war movement had been willing to pay a heavier price, if its partisans had gone noisily to prison rather than quietly avoiding the draft and marching noisily on the Pentagon, the war might have ended sooner.

Although their "Treasury of Virtue" has made it easy for the doves to avoid hard questions about their role in the Vietnam wars, defeat logically should have forced the hawks to rethink their position. But they have proved even less ready to do so than have most doves. For a time hawks ignored the war or argued that its uniqueness precluded drawing any lessons from it. Beginning in the late 1970's, though, and with greater visibility in the 1980's, a few scholars, politicians, and polemicists took the offensive in the third Vietnam War. In 1978 Guenter Lewy published *America in Vietnam*, one of the first, and still one of the best, of such interpretations. It scathingly attacks the way the United States fought the war between 1965 and 1968 but still defends the legality and morality of the war and contends that the United States could have won. Public figures prove less critical and cautious than Lewy in championing this view of the war. Journalist Norman Podhoretz flails the anti-war movement and proclaims America's role in Vietnam an "act of imprudent idealism whose moral soundness" has been vindicated. In 1980 Ronald Reagan complained that Americans dishonor "the memory of 50,000 young Americans who died" in Vietnam "when we give way to feelings of guilt as if we were doing something shameful. Well, it's time," he argued, that "we recognize that ours was, in truth, a noble cause." Similarly, H. Ross Perot and other conservative critics of the Vietnam Memorial condemned Maya Lin's design for dishonoring the cause and its defenders, demanded a more heroic statue to the soldiers, and succeeded in securing an addition to the wall, a group of three representative soldiers placed to one side and to the front of the V-shaped memorial.

IV

For those who continue to believe the Vietnam War could have and should have been won, explaining defeat becomes crucial. No real consensus, though, has emerged on why the United States lost; the confusion that characterized the war still haunts its historiography. But most postwar critics of American policy have stressed two interrelated themes. The first, with antecedents in the debates of the 1960's, blames defeat on the policy of phased escalation: awesome force did not succeed because it was applied piecemeal rather than in one decisive blow. Lyndon Johnson and his civilian advisors, according to this argument, hesitated to approve bombing targets and to commit sufficient troops, thereby tying the military's hands and allowing the other side to match American force. The second attributes defeat to a failure of public will to win. Leslie H. Gelb, in one of the best analyses of the decision to escalate the war, perhaps unintentionally gives aid and comfort to the proponents of this view when he stresses that the leaders of the Kennedy and Johnson administrations never really expected victory or dedicated enough resources to achieve it. Military analysts Harry G. Summers, Jr. and Bruce Palmer, Jr. catalogue many American errors but still blame defeat in large measure on a loss of will among the politicians and public. Summers claims that President Johnson never fully developed the national consensus essential to the war effort. Palmer, too, criticizes the civilian leaders for failing to sustain public support and identifies two crucial points at which it was lost: in the wake of the Tet Offensive and during Watergate. Many critics join Palmer in arguing that during the Tet Offensive, a massive enemy attack in early 1968, the Americans and their South Vietnam allies won a decisive victory that irresponsible reporters and panicky politicians transformed into a defeat. Others, too, agree that Watergate kept President Nixon from fulfilling his promise of additional aid and air support for South Vietnam after the American withdrawal, thereby leaving South Vietnam unable to repel the North's final offensive. In his *No More Vietnams* Nixon himself flatly asserts that in "a spasm of . . . irresponsibility," Congress in 1973 threw away everything that had been "achieved in twelve years of fighting."

Together, both explanations, the failure of phased escalation and of will, support an even more simplistic interpretation of defeat. Politicians declare that American soldiers should never again be sent to fight a war that their nation is not willing to win. The movie *Rambo* presents a cartoon-like but nonetheless prototypical American hero, with glistening and glorious biceps, skilled with both the bow and modern weapons, who could have won the war by himself—if only he had not been betrayed by the wimps of the bureaucracy. Though they differ in many ways, *Rambo*, the politicians' pleas, and even Palmer's and Nixon's books share a common theme: the failure of will at home, to some extent the creation of craven journalists, disloyal protestors, and timid politicians, robbed the soldiers of victory. Such explanations resemble the "stab-in-the-back thesis" used in Germany in the 1920's and 1930's to explain defeat in World War I. The American version, however, emphasizes popular failure rather than a conspiracy by a few dastardly individuals.

Moreover, American proponents of a "stab-in-the-back thesis," unlike their German counterparts who used theirs to nurse bitterness over the loss of World War I, employ it to explain away American defeat. In that regard, the emerging defense of America's role in Vietnam resembles the South's interpretation of defeat in the Civil War. The South, too, insisted upon the morality, nobility, and heroism of its cause and so celebrated its efforts in the war that Southerners came to perceive their defeat almost as military victory. The same thing appears to be happening to Americans' views of Vietnam. Building from key points developed in the failure of will argument, political scientist Timothy J. Lomperis, who served in Vietnam, maintains that in some ways the United States did win in Vietnam. He even entitled his book *The War Everyone Lost—and Won*, a title that one can easily imagine for an early 20th-century address before a Blue-Gray reunion. The complex argument in the text acknowledges that the United States lost the war to preserve South Vietnam, but also contends that its destruction of the Viet Cong during the 1968 Tet Offensive and its subsequent effort over the next five years left the South sufficiently strong to defend itself. The United States had, in effect, defeated the attempt through a people's war to overthrow the government of South Vietnam and thereby denied legitimacy to the Communist government established after the North's conquest of the South in 1975. Everyone won; everyone lost. Former President Nixon went even further in turning defeat into victory. "When we signed the Paris peace agreements in 1973, we had won the war. We then proceeded to lose the peace." In 1985 President Reagan expressed virtually the same sentiment as he blamed the fall of South Vietnam on Congress' refusal to supply aid to South Vietnam. "Well," he said, "the truth of the matter is that we did have victory. We continue to talk about losing that war. We didn't lose that war. We won virtually every engagement."

Interpreting American involvement in Vietnam as a justified, moral, and noble crusade, one all but won militarily only to be lost because of timidity and a failure of will at home, constitutes a major, new offensive in the third Vietnam War—a frontal assault on the doves who condemn the American war effort as both hopeless and wrong. Many leaders of the charge come from the ranks of the right, and it clearly supports conservative political and foreign policy objectives. Yet this interpretation has an appeal beyond its utility to conservatives. Proclaiming the nobility of the war, blaming defeat on a failure of will, and assuming the nearness of victory support efforts to rehabilitate the reputation of the veterans. Moreover, as the South's experience suggests, defeated Americans may well find such explanations not just appealing but believable.

Deciding exactly what the American public believes about any issue is difficult, especially so in this case because polls often seem contradictory. One taken in 1985 showed that almost three quarters of the American people considered the United States involvement in Vietnam to have been wrong, though this total may include many who believed in the morality and wisdom of the war but opposed the way it was fought. This same poll, however, suggests that the hawks may be succeeding in convincing Americans of the war's nobility. The proposition that Vietnam was a noble crusade received its highest levels of support among 18- to 22-year-olds, the group with no personal memory of the war. Americans also seem quite receptive to the failure of will explanation for defeat. In 1980 47 percent of Americans strongly agreed and another 26 percent somewhat agreed with the statement: "The trouble in Vietnam was that our troops were asked to fight a war which our political leaders in Washington would not let them win." That the majority of Americans accepted the validity of this statement and that Vietnam veterans and, again, the young with no memory of the war concurred most readily of all, suggests attitudes exist on which the proponents of a positive view of the war may build.

Despite its growing popularity, though, this interpretation makes coming to terms with defeat difficult. It portrays irresolute leaders and domestic opponents of the war as villains who cost the nation victory. Already, surveys show tremendous resentment toward those who refused to serve and reveal far less support for those who protested than for those who fought. But just as veterans want and need public acceptance of their actions during the war in Vietnam, protestors want and need public approval for their role in the war at home over Vietnam. To withhold it or, worse, to blame defeat on the anti-warriors can only hinder reconciliation of the former foes in the war over Vietnam; reconciliation must rest on mutual respect and acceptance of each side's position in the conflict—as the South's post-Civil War reunion with the North suggests. Similarly, the South's experience after the Civil War indicates that an interpretation of defeat that simply reaffirms the righteousness of the cause and the heroism of the armies, without wrestling with the implications of failure, leads only to a trivialization of the memory of the war and to a failure to derive any special insight from it.

The tendency toward trivialization also emerges in a second recent offensive in the third Vietnam War, one that does not frontally assault older, anti-war positions but rather outflanks them by focusing on the Vietnam combat experience. "Magnum," *Platoon*, and similar portrayals of the war in popular culture attempt to explain what the war was like to those who never fought there, a healthy, necessary corrective to the early tendency to ignore the war and its warriors. But very easily explanation becomes glorification. The movie *Hamburger Hill*, for example, answers its own refrain—"It don't mean nothing"—by celebrating the camaraderie, courage and sacrifice of the warriors which, the film implies, gave meaning and purpose to the war. Therein lies the danger of the new emphasis on the experience of combat: it makes the soldiers' heroism sufficient justification for the cause. The South and the North did much the same thing following the Civil War, which made sectional reconciliation possible since it ignored the divisive issues and celebrated common experiences, but it ultimately trivialized the meaning of the war. In the case of Vietnam, the emphasis on the camaraderie and excitement of combat does not foster reconciliation but rather further divides the warriors and anti-warriors. In *Hamburger Hill*, the anti-warriors almost become the enemy, and the movie comes close to saying they had no right even to comment on the war. The emphasis on the Vietnam combat experience may thus further polarize the nation. It also ignores and thereby trivializes the war's issues and its meaning—or worse, renders Vietnam only another setting for popular culture adventure stories, perhaps the ultimate trivialization.

Neither of the two offensives, the reinterpretation of the war nor the glorification of combat, appears likely to yield a victory in the third Vietnam War, to lead Americans successfully to come to terms with defeat. Nor, for that matter, do the continued attacks of the doves, who, secure in their virtue, still slug it out along old fronts. Few on either side seem to have found a way out of the difficulties inherent in the third Vietnam War. Just as the first came to be considered a "no-win situation," so may the attempt to come to terms with the meaning of Vietnam. An interpretation of the war that depicts the veterans' service as a purely noble, heroic undertaking renders the protestors' actions disloyal, thereby making reconciliation difficult. But the reverse is also true: making the anti-warriors into the force of light encourages casting the warriors as the force of darkness. And declaring both sides right or focusing only on the experience of combat trivializes the hard moral choices of the 1960's and may well prevent the nation from gaining insights from defeat.

The way out of the quagmire of the third Vietnam War, the strategy that will allow the United States to "win," necessitates that both opponents and proponents of the war be willing to take new positions. They must seek and accept new information; in studying contemporary history, those who lived through it too easily assume they know what happened and too readily reject evidence that challenges old beliefs. They must also develop a new appreciation for complexity and an openness to the views of the other side. In short, they must fight the third Vietnam War with a subtlety, with a consciousness of political and moral ambiguity rarely displayed in the first two Vietnam wars and uncharacteristic of politics and popular culture. A "new Vietnam scholarship," as journalist Fox Butterfield put it, has already challenged "some of the most cherished beliefs of both the right and the left" and presented "a war that was more complex, more morally ambiguous, than either the doves or the hawks had maintained." But it has certainly not won the field from either the hawks or the doves. Nor has it begun to uncover all the facts or even ask all the pertinent questions. Much remains to be learned about the war itself, particularly about whether or not combat in Vietnam was unique, and more needs to be understood about the veterans' postwar adjustment.

Even as scholars begin to develop these and other points, Americans need some framework for understanding the war's meaning. Unless further evidence suggests another, Americans can probably do no better than to view the Vietnam War as Robert Penn Warren suggested they interpret the Civil War—as a tragedy. As with the Civil War, American participation in the Vietnam War can not be blamed on any one group or person but on the policies and assumptions accepted by most Americans at the time. And no one group came out of the wars in and over Vietnam with a "Treasury of Virtue"; the fight besmirched both warrior and anti-warrior alike. Neither should be held up as model "heroes," but both can claim heroism in the midst of tragedy, a shared experience that might serve as a basis for reconciliation. Historians and the public alike can find inspiration for the task of reinterpreting the war as tragedy in the Vietnam Memorial on the mall. The wall evokes mourning but also demands reflection. For as the nation looks at those haunting black marble panels, looking through the names of those who died at its behest, it sees ultimately its own reflection. The memory of the Vietnam War should serve the same function, should force the nation not to bask in that reflection, but to consider and reconsider it—to analyze, not glorify, the war.

HISTORIOGRAPHY

Vietnam Reconsidered*

ROBERT A. DIVINE

A curious pattern runs through the literature of American diplomatic history in the twentieth century. For each major conflict there is a cycle of historical analysis that runs from contemporary support through a critical revision and finally culminates in a synthesis that incorporates elements of both earlier views. Thus for the issue of American entry into World War I, early writers like Charles Seymour defended Woodrow Wilson's policy on grounds of meeting the challenge of German submarine warfare. Only in the 1930s did a different view emerge, when such revisionists as Charles Tansill and Walter Millis suggested that deliberately unneutral policies and economic ties to the Allies fatally warped U.S. policy and led to an unnecessary war. After World War II a synthesis emerged as historians, notably Ernest May and Arthur Link, broadened Seymour's narrow focus on the submarine to justify Wilson's defense of legitimate American interests, including economic ones.[1]

A similar pattern can be discerned for World War II. The initial view, especially the two volumes by William L. Langer and S. Everett Gleason, defended Franklin D. Roosevelt's policy of all-out aid to Britain and eventual entry into the conflict. Shortly after the war, however, revisionists, led again by Charles Tansill but joined now by Charles A. Beard, accused FDR of deceiving the American people by promising peace while leading the country toward war. Roosevelt, they charged, invited the Japanese attack on Pearl

---

*This paper originally was presented at a conference in Yokohama in September 1986 sponsored by the Japan Association of International Relations. The author wishes to thank the JAIR for many kindnesses, including permission to publish this paper in the United States.

[1]Charles Seymour, *American Neutrality, 1914–1917: Essays on the Causes of American Intervention in the World War* (New Haven, CT, 1935); Charles C. Tansill, *America Goes to War* (Boston, 1938); Walter Millis, *Road to War, 1914–1917* (Boston, 1938); Ernest R. May, *The World War and American Isolationism, 1914–1917* (Cambridge, MA, 1959); Arthur S. Link, *Wilson the Diplomatist* (Baltimore, 1957).

Harbor by deliberately exposing the American fleet. Few responsible historians have accepted this extreme revisionist view. But more reasonable criticism, such as that leveled by Paul Schroeder and Bruce Russett, has led to a more balanced view of American policy, as embodied in my own work and the fine account by David Reynolds.[2] The synthesis that now prevails, while generally endorsing American involvement in World War II, does not excuse FDR for his often deceptive policies nor skip over the real differences between the United States and Great Britain in the 1930s.

The origin of the Cold War has been the most recent, and heated, topic of debate among American diplomatic historians. The initial view, promulgated by Herbert Feis above all, argued that the breakup of the wartime alliance was entirely the fault of an aggressive and expanding Soviet Union. Only in the 1960s did such scholars as Gar Alperovitz and Gabriel Kolko, encouraged by the dissent over the Vietnam War, begin to overturn the postwar consensus. They argued that the United States had provoked the Soviet Union by refusing to grant postwar economic assistance and maintaining a monopoly over the atomic bomb. Finally, in the 1970s, historians began to forge a synthesis which portrayed the Cold War as beyond individual or national responsibility, seeing it instead as an unfortunate but virtually inevitable consequence of World War II. Today this postrevisionist interpretation associated with John Lewis Gaddis and Daniel Yergin prevails.[3]

Given this pattern of contemporary support, later revisionist challenge, and ultimate synthesis, it would not be surprising to find the cycle repeated for the Vietnam conflict. But what is striking is the reversal that has occurred. The initial interpretation was anything but supportive of American policy; to a greater or lesser degree, nearly all the early writers on Vietnam were highly critical of American intervention. As a result, when revisionism began in the later 1970s and early 1980s it came in the form of a belated justification for U.S. policy, rather than the usual critique. The synthesis has not yet fully

[2]William L. Langer and S. Everett Gleason, *The Challenge to Isolation, 1937–1940* (New York, 1952) and *The Undeclared War, 1940–1941* (New York, 1953); Charles C. Tansill, *Back Door to War* (Chicago, 1952); Charles A. Beard, *American Foreign Policy in the Making, 1932–1940* (New Haven, CT, 1946) and *President Roosevelt and the Coming of War, 1941* (New Haven, CT, 1948); Paul W. Schroeder, *The Axis Alliance and Japanese-American Relations, 1941* (Ithaca, NY, 1958); Bruce M. Russett, *No Clear and Present Danger: A Skeptical View of the United States Entry into World War II* (New York, 1972); Robert A. Divine, *The Reluctant Belligerent: American Entry into World War II* (New York, 1965) and *Roosevelt and World War II* (Baltimore, 1969); David Reynolds, *The Creation of the Anglo-American Alliance, 1937–41: A Study in Competitive Cooperation* (Chapel Hill, 1982).

[3]Herbert Feis, *Between War and Peace: The Potsdam Conference* (Princeton, NJ, 1960) and *From Trust to Terror: The Onset of the Cold War, 1945–1950* (New York, 1970); Gar Alperovitz, *Atomic Diplomacy: Hiroshima and Potsdam, the Use of the Atomic Bomb, and the American Confrontation with Soviet Power* (New York, 1965); Joyce and Gabriel Kolko, *The Limits of Power: The World and United States Foreign Policy, 1945–1954* (New York, 1972); John Lewis Gaddis, *The United States and the Origins of the Cold War, 1941–1947* (New York, 1972); Daniel Yergin, *Shattered Peace: The Origins of the Cold War and the National Security State* (Boston, 1977).

developed, but the early signs point to a position much closer to the original criticism of American policy than the revisionist defense.

Virtually all contemporary historical analysts of the Vietnam War shared a strong distaste for American intervention and a fervent belief that U.S. policy was seriously mistaken. Yet within this broad consensus, there were three distinct views of why the United States had become involved in such a hopeless situation. The first interpretation can be labeled the liberal internationalist perspective, and its chief advocate was the distinguished historian and adviser to President Kennedy, Arthur Schlesinger, Jr. Writing while the war was at its height, Schlesinger expressed the widely held view of American liberals that Vietnam was a quagmire. American leaders from Truman to Johnson had undertaken a series of incremental steps in Indochina which ended in disastrous U.S. involvement. This came about by chance, not design, and if any of the presidents had known where his policies were leading the nation, he never would have approved them. In a famous passage in his 1967 book, *Bitter Heritage*, Schlesinger observed that

> the policy of "one more step" lured the United States deeper and deeper into the morass. In retrospect, Vietnam is a triumph of the politics of inadvertence. We have achieved our present entanglement, not after due and deliberate consideration, but through a series of small decisions. It is not only idle but unfair to seek out guilty men. . . . Each step in the deepening of the American commitment was reasonably regarded at the time as the last step that would be necessary. Yet, in retrospect, each step led only to the next, until we find ourselves entrapped today in that nightmare of American strategists, a land war in Asia—a war in which no President, including President Johnson, desired or intended. The Vietnam story is a tragedy without villains.[4]

Schlesinger's quagmire thesis, while condemning American involvement, nevertheless excused American leaders of any real responsibility. It was all an accident, a tragic series of mistakes, but not one that called for a reconsideration of America's Cold War policies or for a searching reappraisal of men and decisions. David Halberstam, in a somewhat later account, *The Best and the Brightest*, took essentially the same position. Although he stressed the arrogance of such presidential advisers as McGeorge Bundy, Robert McNamara, and Maxwell Taylor, he did not accuse them of deliberately leading the nation astray. Instead, with the best intentions in the world, these paragons had proved to be all too mortal, making mistakes like ordinary humans.[5]

A second contemporary interpretation consciously rejected the quagmire thesis as false, and instead offered a "stalemate" concept in its place. According to this view, offered by civilian strategists involved in the compilation of the Pentagon Papers, American presidents had taken a series of steps with

---

[4]Arthur M. Schlesinger, Jr., *The Bitter Heritage: Vietnam and American Democracy, 1941–1966* (Boston, 1967), 31–32.

[5]David Halberstam, *The Best and the Brightest* (New York, 1972).

full knowledge that none was likely to achieve the desired result. This view tends to excuse the advisers, who supposedly gave sound advice, and blames the presidents, who decided on dubious actions for political reasons. The result was a stalemate in Vietnam, but one deliberately achieved as a foreseeable consequence of American policy.

Leslie Gelb and Richard Betts offered the clearest statement of the stalemate concept in their book *The Irony of Vietnam: The System Worked.* The startling subtitle reflects their claim that "virtually all important decisions were made without illusions about the odds of success." The dominant consideration, according to this view, was the perceived danger of losing Vietnam to communism. To prevent this from happening American presidents were willing to take a series of steps, none of which promised victory or peace. Lower ranking officials in the CIA and the State Department were fully aware of the limitations of American policy but could not exert influence in the White House, where advisers were willing to risk deeper entanglement knowing full well that the outcome was likely to be failure. Thus McGeorge Bundy, in recommending to LBJ the policy of reprisal bombing of North Vietnam in February 1965, argued that "even if it fails to turn the tide—as it may—the value of the effort seems to us to exceed its cost." This contention, according to Gelb and Betts, is the "good doctor" analogy: Even though the patient, South Vietnam, is likely to expire, the world would see the United States as the good doctor who did everything possible to prevent this calamity.[6]

The most provocative statement of the stalemate concept came from Daniel Ellsberg, the civilian Defense Department analyst who leaked the Pentagon Papers. In direct contrast to Schlesinger, Ellsberg blames the presidents, from Truman through Johnson, for allowing domestic political considerations to override the cautions and suggestions of their advisers. Thus Ellsberg accuses Kennedy in 1961 of suppressing Maxwell Taylor's recommendation for introducing combat troops, yet giving the public the impression that he was implementing Taylor's advice. This presidential deception, which reached its climax with Lyndon Johnson, but began with Eisenhower and Kennedy, leads Ellsberg to refute Schlesinger's claim that Vietnam was "a tragedy without villains," calling this "a process of immaculate deception" in which there are "war crimes without war criminals, lies without liars."[7]

The true explanation, according to Ellsberg, is the traumatic impact of the loss of China to communism in 1949 and the devastating effect of that event on the Democratic party. Neither Kennedy nor Johnson ever wanted to risk repeating that experience, and so anything was preferable to defeat in Vietnam, even a deliberate stalemate. Ellsberg describes the dilemma of American presidents in terms of the card game "Old Maid." Just as players did not want to be caught with the queen of spades in their hands, so no American president wanted to be held responsible for the loss of Vietnam to

[6]Leslie H. Gelb and Richard K. Betts, *The Irony of Vietnam: The System Worked* (Washington, DC, 1979), 2, 25–26, 238–43.

[7]Daniel Ellsberg, *Papers on the War* (New York, 1972), 64, 129.

the Communists. But in observing rule one of this game, each president was in danger of violating rule two: "Do not commit U.S. ground troops to a land war in Asia." Truman, Eisenhower, and Kennedy all played the game successfully, undertaking limited measures to save South Vietnam while knowing that their policies had little chance of long-run success. It was Lyndon Johnson who got caught with the Old Maid—in order not to lose Vietnam to the Communists, he got involved in a land war in Asia that could not be won.[8]

The stalemate concept offers considerable insight into why American policy led only to deeper involvement, not victory, in Vietnam. But focusing on the political process and shifting blame to the presidents has the self-serving purpose of absolving civilian advisers such as Leslie Gelb and Daniel Ellsberg from any degree of responsibility for the Vietnam disaster. More importantly, this explanation ignores the question of why the United States placed such a high value on preserving Vietnam from the Communists.

A third contemporary explanation is more satisfactory in this regard. This view, expressed in several variations, claims not only that the system did not work, but that the system, defined as the entire postwar containment policy, was fatally flawed. This view thus makes George Kennan, not Lyndon Johnson, the scapegoat by portraying Vietnam as the logical culmination of the Cold War effort to contain communism.

Gabriel Kolko offered a radical version of the containment thesis in his 1969 book, *The Roots of American Foreign Policy*. He saw the intervention in Vietnam as revealing the bankruptcy of a policy that had been relentlessly pursued since the end of World War II:

> Ultimately, the United States has fought in Vietnam with increasing intensity to extend its hegemony over the world community and to stop every form of revolutionary movement which refuses to accept the predominant role of the United States in the direction of the affairs of its nation or region.[9]

Nearly twenty years later, in a much more detailed and more fully documented account of America's failure in Vietnam, Kolko restated the same basic explanation:

> The Vietnam War was for the United States the culmination of its frustrating postwar effort to merge its arms and politics to halt and reverse the emergence of states and social systems opposed to the international order Washington sought to establish. It was not the first serious trial of either its military power or its political strategy, only the most disastrous. Despite America's many real successes in imposing its hegemony elsewhere, Vietnam exposed the ultimate constraints on its power in the modern era.[10]

---

[8]Ibid., 80–82, 102–3.

[9]Gabriel Kolko, *The Roots of American Foreign Policy: An Analysis of Power and Purpose* (Boston, 1969), 132.

[10]Gabriel Kolko, *Anatomy of a War: Vietnam, the United States, and the Modern Historical Experience* (New York, 1985), 547.

Other writers saw the fundamental mistake of American policy in less ideological terms. John Donovan, for example, blamed Vietnam on the American foreign-policy elite. Despite changes in administration, the same small band of lawyers, academics, and bankers, operating on the same shared assumptions, presided over American foreign policy throughout the Cold War. Never questioning the key belief that Vietnam was vital to American security until it was too late, these foreign-policy experts allowed the mandate of containment to lead them into disaster in Vietnam.[11]

The most balanced statement of the containment thesis comes from George Herring, who wrote a concise history of American involvement in Vietnam in 1979. The containment policy which Truman had used so effectively in Europe in the 1940s, he wrote, was simply not applicable to Asia in the 1960s.

> The United States' involvement in Vietnam was not primarily a result of errors of judgment or of the personality quirks of the policymakers, although these things existed in abundance. It was a logical, if not inevitable outgrowth of a world view and a policy, the policy of containment, which Americans in and out of government accepted without serious question for more than two decades. The commitment in Vietnam expanded as the containment policy itself grew. In time, it outlived the conditions that had given rise to that policy. More than anything else, America's failure in Vietnam calls into question the basic premises of that policy and suggests the urgent need for a searching reappraisal of American attitudes toward the world and their place in it.[12]

Thus Herring, like Kolko and Donovan, thinks the system itself was at fault, not the presidents or their advisers. In his view, which was widely shared by the end of the 1970s, the lesson of Vietnam was clear. Containment was a bad policy which led to a global involvement that endangered rather than protected the best interests of the United States.

Vietnam revisionism, which began in the late 1970s and reached its peak in the early 1980s, reflected a growing conservative mood in the United States, symbolized by the election of Ronald Reagan in 1980, and a belated national effort to come to grips with the Vietnam experience, as indicated by the popularity of three remarkable motion pictures of the late 1970s—*Coming Home*, *The Deer Hunter*, and *Apocalypse Now*. Rejecting the prevailing view that the Vietnam War was an unmitigated evil, revisionists defended and justified American involvement. While few saw the Vietnam War as an unmixed blessing, they did feel compelled to correct what they considered a one-sided and unfair indictment of American policy. There is still considerable disagreement among these writers on many points, but they share a common desire to treat the American effort in Vietnam more sympathetically than

---

[11]John C. Donovan, *The Cold Warriors: A Policy-Making Elite* (Lexington, MA, 1974).

[12]George C. Herring, *America's Longest War: The United States and Vietnam, 1950–1975* (New York, 1979), x.

earlier historians. The revisionists include academic political scientists, notably Guenter Lewy and Timothy Lomperis, military strategists such as Bruce Palmer and Harry Summers, and political advocates like journalist Norman Podhoretz and former president Richard Nixon.[13] Rather than discuss their work individually, I will focus on some of the common themes in the revisionist interpretation of the Vietnam experience.

A central point in revisionist accounts is the contention that the war could have been won. Richard Nixon goes even further, arguing that he had achieved victory by 1973 only to have Congress throw it away by refusing to aid South Vietnam two years later. "In the end, Vietnam was lost on the political front in the United States," he writes, "not on the battlefield in Southeast Asia."[14] Other revisionists, notably the military strategists, admit that the United States lost the war on the battlefield, but contend that defeat was not inevitable. Instead they argue that if the war had been fought differently, the United States could have prevailed.

Harry Summers offers two explanations for the American defeat. First, the United States tied its own hands by not making a maximum effort at victory. The nation did not declare war against North Vietnam, nor did it make the kind of sacrifices at home that had ensured victory in World War II. Instead, LBJ tried for guns and butter at the same time, and lost both. According to Summers, Johnson's "conscious political decision not to mobilize the American people for war" was a "fundamental mistake" that prevented the country from focusing its "full attention" on the war. He cites former Secretary of State Dean Rusk's admission that "we never made any effort to create a war psychology in the United States during the Vietnam affair. . . . We tried to do in cold blood perhaps what can only be done in hot blood." Summers blames not only Johnson for this "failure to invoke the national will" but also the Joint Chiefs of Staff, whom he thinks should have insisted on an all-out effort in Vietnam and then backed up their demands by threatening to resign if the president did not act.[15]

Summers's second contention is that the United States lost in Vietnam because the military waged a counterinsurgency campaign against the Viet Cong instead of a conventional war against North Vietnam's main forces. The search-and-destroy tactics employed by General William Westmoreland, according to Summers, were bound to fail. The real enemy was the invading army from North Vietnam, which he contends could have been defeated by

---

[13]Guenter Lewy, *America in Vietnam* (New York, 1978); Timothy J. Lomperis, *The War Everyone Lost—And Won: America's Intervention in Viet Nam's Twin Struggles* (Baton Rouge, LA, 1984); Bruce Palmer, Jr., *The 25-Year War: America's Military Role in Vietnam* (Lexington, KY, 1984); Harry G. Summers, Jr., *On Strategy: A Critical Analysis of the Vietnam War* (New York, 1984); Norman Podhoretz, *Why We Were in Vietnam* (New York, 1982); Richard Nixon, *No More Vietnams* (New York, 1985).

[14]Nixon, *No More Vietnams*, 15.

[15]Harry G. Summers, Jr., "Lessons: A Soldier's View," in *Vietnam as History: Ten Years after the Paris Peace Accords*, ed. Peter Braestrup (Washington, DC, 1984), 109, 111; Summers, *On Strategy*, 43, 168.

the same tactics the United States used successfully in Korea and in World War II. Bruce Palmer agrees, offering a specific two-part strategy of concentrating American forces along the Demilitarized Zone to cut off North Vietnamese infiltration into the south and force fixed battles in which superior American firepower would prevail, together with a naval blockade of North Vietnam. "The U.S. resources were there—what was missing was a bold decision, admittedly involving some risk, and an imaginative concept that would have allowed the United States and its allies to turn the strategic tables on Hanoi." Such a conventional war, Palmer concedes, might not have produced outright victory, but could at least have provided "a better foundation for negotiations undertaken to end the war."[16]

Not all revisionists agree that the use of conventional military tactics could have avoided defeat in Vietnam. Guenter Lewy, for example, argues that the American military relied too heavily on traditional military concepts that were inappropriate for a guerrilla war that was essentially political in nature. Lewy believes that a greater effort on pacification, especially in the later stages of the conflict, might well have led to a stable and secure South Vietnam.[17]

There is one point in regard to military strategy on which all the revisionists agree. The Tet offensive of 1968, portrayed by the media and accepted by the American people as a great defeat, was in reality a major military victory. The Communists failed to take a single South Vietnamese city and they lost over 50,000 men in their futile attacks. Most important, they failed to achieve their main objective, which was to mobilize the population of South Vietnam in a true people's war. Timothy Lomperis stresses the failure of these revolutionary tactics in his provocative book, *The War Everyone Lost—and Won*:

> Tet was supposed to be the culmination of the people's war strategy, but the offensive was beaten back. More than just a military defeat, the Tet offensive shattered the revolutionary strategy. After some groping, the Communists thereafter essentially abandoned people's war and took another road.

The ultimate irony, as Lomperis and other revisionists point out, is that the Communists achieved their final victory through conventional warfare. The successful North Vietnamese invasion and conquest of the South in 1975 was a traditional military action similar to those of World War II and Korea.[18]

In addition to claiming that the United States might have won in Vietnam with different tactics, revisionists also challenge the view that the American war effort was immoral. While they admit that the use of chemical defoliants, the free-fire zones, and the heavy air bombardments killed many civilians, they claim that this war was no worse in that respect than other twentieth-century conflicts. Guenter Lewy is particularly persuasive on this point. In

---

[16]Summers, *On Strategy*, 122, 127–31; Palmer, *25-Year War*, 182–84, 187–88.
[17]Lewy, *America in Vietnam*, 162–67.
[18]Lomperis, *The War Everyone Won*, 165; Summers, *On Strategy*, 157–61.

his 1978 book, *America in Vietnam*, which was the first and in many ways the most impressive of the revisionist accounts, Lewy uses United Nations figures to rebut charges by antiwar activists that the United States engaged in acts of genocide in Vietnam. The civilian population of South Vietnam, far from being wiped out, increased from just over 16 million in 1965 to almost 20 million in 1973, while the population of North Vietnam went from just under 19 million to over 22 million in the same period. "This fact," he comments, "makes the charge of genocide a bit grotesque." He also finds that the percentage of civilian deaths in the overall toll of the Vietnam War was 28 percent, lower than the 40 percent in World War II and much less than the 70 percent in the Korean War.[19]

Norman Podhoretz is much more strident on the moral issue. He claims that those who opposed the Vietnam War acted immorally by giving aid and encouragement to the enemy, ignoring the totalitarian nature of the North Vietnamese government, and exaggerating the damage done by American raids on North Vietnam. On this last point he notes that the American media compared the Christmas bombing of Hanoi in 1972 to Dresden and the 1945 incendiary raids on Tokyo, when in fact between 1,300 and 1,500 died in the Christmas bombings, compared to 35,000 at Dresden and over 80,000 in the Tokyo raids. More importantly, Podhoretz sees the American commitment to defend South Vietnam as a moral act. In contrast to Herring, Podhoretz believes in containment and thinks the United States was acting morally by trying to halt the expansion of communism. Thus he contends that

> the United States went into Vietnam for the sake not of its own direct interests in the ordinary sense but for the sake of an ideal. The intervention was the product of the Wilsonian side of the American character—the side that went to war in 1917 to "make the world safe for democracy." . . . Why, then, were we in Vietnam? To say it once again: because we were trying to save the Southern half of that country from the evils of Communism.[20]

The most striking difference between the revisionists and the earlier writers on Vietnam lies in the lessons they draw from this experience. Refusing to see American intervention as a tragic mistake, the revisionists are not willing to embrace the traditional conclusion that the United States should be very careful "never again" to become involved militarily in the Third World, a view best summed up by Earl Ravenal in his 1978 book, *Never Again*.[21] On the contrary, they warn against the danger of transforming Vietnam into a symbol like Munich. For thirty years after Chamberlain and Daladier gave in to Hitler at Munich in 1938, appeasement was viewed as the cardinal sin of diplomacy, giving any form of diplomatic negotiation a bad name. Instead

---

[19]Lewy, *America in Vietnam*, 301, 451.

[20]Podhoretz, *Why We Were in Vietnam*, 121–22, 197.

[21]Earl C. Ravenal, *Never Again: Learning from America's Foreign Policy Failures* (Philadelphia, 1978).

of focusing on the weak performance of the negotiators at Munich, the revisionists point out, people tended to equate diplomacy with appeasement and thus opted for military measures instead. Thus one reason the United States ended up fighting in Vietnam was precisely because of this fear of another Munich. It would be equally mistaken, according to Podhoretz, to make "No More Vietnams" the guiding principle of American foreign policy for another generation.[22]

Timothy Lomperis makes the strongest case about being careful not to draw the wrong conclusions from the Vietnam experience. There was much that was contradictory in Vietnam, he argues, and little that has universal application:

> For most Americans, the memory of Viet Nam festers as a haunting nightmare of failure. Far from being a simple and abject failure, though, the American intervention in Viet Nam was one of rich variegation. As in the case of Mark Twain's cat drawing the wrong conclusion from sitting on a hot stove and therefore unquestioningly assuming that stoves are at all times and places hot, the burners of Viet Nam were hot and cold from time to time and place to place. . . . Thus, in losing a people's war, the Communists went on to win the war itself. But in adopting a conventional war strategy, they won by a means they should have lost. The United States, on the other hand, won a war it thought it lost, and lost by default what it could have won.[23]

It is Harry Summers who draws the most surprising lesson from the Vietnam War. He sees the key difficulty as the artificial restraints that the United States placed on its war effort. When he says "never again," he means something very different from Earl Ravenal:

> Never again must the president commit American men to combat without first fully defining the nation's war aims and then rallying Congress and the nation for war. Otherwise, the courageous Americans who fought and died in the defense of South Vietnam will truly have done so in vain.[24]

Richard Nixon is even more outspoken in refuting what he calls the battle cry of the new isolationists, "No more Vietnams." Calling Vietnam only "a temporary setback," he continues, "it is vital that we learn the right lessons from that defeat. In Vietnam, we tried and failed in a just cause. 'No more Vietnams' can mean that we will not *try* again. It *should* mean that we will not *fail* again."[25]

This attempt to learn the lessons of Vietnam indicates once again the great difficulty in trying to draw a simple guide for future conduct from complex historical events. Throughout the twentieth century, Americans have kept making the same mistake. After World War I, Congress adopted the

[22]Podhoretz, *Why We Were in Vietnam*, 11–13.
[23]Lomperis, *The War Everyone Won*, 176.
[24]Summers, "Lessons," 114.
[25]Nixon, *No More Vietnams*, 237.

neutrality legislation on the theory that the sales of arms to England and France from 1914 to 1917 got us into war. Yet the first thing the nation did when World War II broke out in 1939 was to repeal the arms embargo so that the United States could become what Franklin Roosevelt described so aptly as "the arsenal of democracy." At the end of the Second World War the United States took the lead in founding the United Nations in the belief that American refusal to join the League of Nations had destroyed Wilson's dream of a lasting peace. But only nine days after the Senate ratified the United Nations Charter, the United States dropped the atomic bomb on Hiroshima, ushering in a nuclear age in which this global forum proved largely irrelevant. And in the ensuing Cold War, Americans took the lesson of Munich so much to heart that time after time the nation chose confrontation rather than negotiation, insuring a deepening of the conflict with the Soviet Union and the escalation of the nuclear arms race.

There are no simple lessons to be drawn from the Vietnam experience. But by challenging the superficial idea of "never again," the revisionists have provided a useful reminder of how complex the Vietnam War really was and the wide variety of possible guidelines for the future that can be drawn from this episode. If nothing else, the revisionists have forced scholars to do what American policymakers failed so conspicuously to do over Vietnam—reexamine basic premises and not take anything for granted.

The third phase of historical analysis, postrevisionism or synthesis, is just beginning for the Vietnam War. The early signs point to a view that is still highly critical of American intervention, but one which is more sympathetic, or at least understanding, of the dilemmas faced by American policymakers. The presidents and their advisers are no longer seen as villains, but as victims of ignorance and of circumstances beyond their control.

The first works of synthesis began to appear in the early 1980s and were marked by a much more dispassionate and scholarly tone than either the traditional or the revisionist books. Larry Berman began the trend with his careful analysis of Lyndon Johnson's 1965 decision to send American ground forces to Vietnam and Kathleen Turner added to it with her detached assessment of LBJ's credibility gap over the war. By far the most significant work of synthesis yet to appear is the 1986 study by George Kahin, *Intervention*. A political scientist who specializes in the governments of Southeast Asia, Kahin combined a comprehensive understanding of the culture and politics of South Vietnam with massive research in previously classified American government documents. The result is a richly detailed survey of U.S. policy in Vietnam from the end of World War II through the 1965 escalation, one which offers many new insights and interpretations. Finally, the 1985 book by radical historian Gabriel Kolko, while repeating his earlier critique of American policy and thus hardly qualifying as a work of synthesis, provides both a much fuller statement of Kolko's views and some surprising areas of agreement with Kahin's more balanced interpretation.[26]

---

[26]Larry Berman, *Planning a Tragedy: The Americanization of the War in Vietnam* (New York, 1982); Kathleen J. Turner, *Lyndon Johnson's Dual War: Vietnam and the Press* (Chicago,

Two issues stand out in the recent histories. The first is a revised assessment of the role of Lyndon Johnson. He no longer is portrayed as the thoughtless hawk who blundered into Vietnam; instead he is seen more sympathetically as a figure caught up in a difficult situation. Berman was the first to take a more neutral view of Johnson. As a political scientist concerned with the relationship between the president and his advisers, Berman used the extensive documentation at the LBJ Library to examine how Johnson arrived at his July 1965 decision to commit combat troops to Vietnam on a large scale. He concluded that Johnson carefully orchestrated the advisory process to "legitimize a previously selected option." Such manipulation by a politician with a legendary reputation for building a consensus was hardly surprising. But what Berman discovered was that Johnson used his considerable powers of persuasion to choose a middle road between the doves, notably George Ball, who urged disengagement, and his military advisers, who wanted to call up the reserves and go all out for victory in Vietnam. The result was disastrous. "The president committed the United States to fight a limited war against an enemy totally committed to revolutionary war."[27]

Berman's interpretation sustains the original stalemate concept pioneered by Gelb and Betts and by Ellsberg, portraying LBJ as ignoring the warnings of his advisers that the steps he is taking are not enough to bring about victory. But Berman offers a different explanation of why Johnson chose a cautious middle road. Rather than fear of the political consequences of losing Vietnam to the Communists, the author thinks LBJ was motivated by an intense desire to preserve his Great Society program, which was moving through Congress just when the situation in Vietnam became most critical. He insisted on limiting American military involvement in order to avoid asking Congress to put the nation on a war footing, which he feared would doom measures such as Medicare, federal aid to education, and civil rights legislation. As a consequence, he eventually lost both in Vietnam and at home, as the Great Society became overshadowed by the military venture abroad. "Lyndon Johnson's greatest fault as a leader," Berman concludes sympathetically, "was that *he chose* not to choose between the Great Society and the war in Vietnam."[28]

Kathleen Turner focuses on the consequences of Johnson's refusal to choose between reform at home and war abroad. He was caught in a "double bind—an inability to convince a large enough portion of the population that America was doing enough for Vietnam with an inability to convince another large element that America was not doing too much." The result was the credibility gap. Reporters thought the president was deliberately holding back on the extent of American involvement in Vietnam, when in fact he was trying to restrain public opinion to avoid a call for an all-out military effort. Vetoing a suggestion for a national television speech on the July 1965 troop

1985); George McT. Kahin, *Intervention: How America Became Involved in Vietnam* (New York, 1986); Kolko, *Anatomy*.

[27]Berman, *Planning*, 93, 112.

[28]Ibid., 145–50.

decision. Johnson told his aides that he thought he could secure public support "without having to be too provocative and warlike." As Turner points out, this policy led only to confusion and dissent. "The United States was engaged in military conflict," she writes, "but hadn't declared war," a policy that "simply didn't make sense to a growing proportion of the population."[29]

This postrevisionist analysis offers an interesting contrast to the revisionist argument that Johnson should have declared war in Vietnam and rallied the nation behind him. Summers and other military strategists ignore the domestic scene and especially Johnson's genuine commitment to the cause of reform. And even though this refusal to make a choice between Vietnam and the Great Society would be his ultimate undoing, it offers a far more appealing portrait of LBJ as a leader caught in a genuine dilemma rather than as a political manipulator deceiving the American people.

George Kahin goes farthest in rehabilitating Johnson on Vietnam. In part he does so by putting more of the blame for the failure of American policy on his predecessors, especially on Eisenhower for committing the United States to the Diem regime in the mid-1950s and on Kennedy for deepening the commitment in 1961. But Kahin's most surprising point is to charge Johnson's advisers, not the president himself, with responsibility for the decision to escalate. Unlike writers of the stalemate school who blame the president and excuse the bureaucrats, Kahin sees LBJ as the last dove in the administration and accuses his advisers, especially McGeorge Bundy, Robert McNamara, and Maxwell Taylor, of misleading him. Despite Johnson's repeated requests, these men refused to present him with alternatives other than escalation or withdrawal, usually labeled as "bugging out." Kahin even accuses these advisers of deliberate deception, such as holding back the true facts of the Gulf of Tonkin incident and not giving the president George Ball's initial proposal for a negotiated withdrawal from Vietnam. He suggests that the advisers may well have confused what was best for the United States with what was best for their own careers. "It was usually not difficult for these men," Kahin notes, "to equate the U.S. national interest with their own reputations."[30]

Instead of the bloodthirsty hawk of legend, Johnson emerges as a prudent and cautious leader who has grave doubts about escalation. Told that it is necessary to bomb North Vietnam to save a tottering government in the South, Johnson objects, telling the chairman of the Joint Chiefs of Staff that he "did not wish to enter the patient in a 10-round bout, when he was in no shape to hold out for one round." And in the July 1965 debate over troop commitment, it was the president, not his advisers, who kept raising the critical questions, asking at one point, "Are we starting something that in two or three years we simply can't finish?"[31]

---

[29]Turner, *Johnson's Dual War*, 6, 150, 164–65.
[30]Kahin, *Intervention*, 66, 126, 191, 216, 245.
[31]Ibid., 239, 383.

The second theme which runs through the postrevisionist books is the fatal American ignorance of the force and vitality of Vietnamese nationalism. In contrast to the revisionists, who keep wondering if the war could have been won, these scholars answer with a resounding "No!" Kahin is particularly effective on this point, stressing throughout the strength of nationalist sentiment in Vietnam and the folly of trying to create a separate state in the South. The Diem regime was doomed from the outset, he argues, because it owed its existence to a foreign power and was not an expression of indigenous nationalism.[32]

Gabriel Kolko agrees that the American cause was lost from the beginning, but he differs from Kahin by identifying the Communist Party in Vietnam as the dominant factor, rather than a vaguer form of nationalism. Where Kahin sees the National Liberation Front as a genuine expression of Vietnamese nationalism, Kolko is convinced that it is controlled by the leadership of the Communist Party in Hanoi all along. Thus Kolko refuses to accept Kahin's contention that the conflict began as a civil war rather than as a clear-cut case of aggression from the north, as the United States claimed. For Kolko, the fight was simply a continuation of the long struggle begun by Ho Chi Minh to deliver his nation from the grasp of foreign imperialists, whether French or American.[33]

Despite their differences, Kahin and Kolko reach similar conclusions. Whether perceived as a civil war or as a struggle against imperialism, the Vietnam conflict was bound to end in an American defeat. Nothing the United States might have done, short of nuclear destruction, would have altered the outcome. And both writers note the ultimate irony of the impact of massive American military intervention on the society and government of South Vietnam. The free-fire zones and search-and-destroy missions uprooted millions of people, destroyed the agricultural base of South Vietnam, and led to a massive influx of refugees into the cities. This social disruption eroded any chance a government in Saigon had of achieving legitimacy and popular support.[34] As a result, the harder the United States tried to determine the outcome in Vietnam, the more remote became the likelihood of victory. In that sense, the original Schlesinger analogy to a quagmire was even more apt than he realized.

It is still far too early to offer more than a tentative judgment on the American experience in Vietnam. But historians are already beginning to move beyond the early condemnation of a wicked policy to search for an understanding of how a great nation could go so wrong. And as they continue this quest, Vietnam is likely to be seen more and more as a national tragedy. The most striking finding so far is the degree of foreknowledge. The stalemate writers are correct in rejecting the original quagmire thesis—both the Pentagon Papers and recently opened government documents show that Johnson and

[32]Ibid., 103, 323.

[33]Ibid., 115–16; Kolko, *Anatomy*, 107, 460.

[34]Kahin, *Intervention*, 403–12; Kolko, *Anatomy*, 238–46.

his advisers had a realistic understanding of the difficulties they faced in Vietnam. They chose to escalate on a limited basis, knowing full well that the measures they took would not bring about a satisfactory conclusion. Domestic considerations, not just the political consequences of losing Vietnam to the Communists but the cost of all-out war in Southeast Asia to the Great Society program, placed very real limits on American policy. The result was, as Berman notes, that "President Johnson defined the situation in a way which severely constrained his military options and ultimately undid his political base."[35]

Thus the key to understanding American policy lies in domestic politics. At the present time Charles Chatfield is completing the late Charles DeBenedetti's study of the antiwar movement and its impact on the Johnson administration, while Terry Anderson is conducting research on student protests against the Vietnam War. And George Herring is studying the equally important issue of how Lyndon Johnson attempted to honor the commitment he had inherited in Southeast Asia without abandoning his reform program at home. When these books appear, we should have a much better understanding of the way in which political considerations shaped the course of American policy in Vietnam. Until then, we can at least be grateful that American historians have moved beyond the early, and often simplistic, analyses of the Vietnam War, to begin acquiring a more sophisticated and scholarly appreciation of the nature of this great national tragedy.

---

[35]Berman, *Planning*, 143.

HISTORIOGRAPHY

The Unending Debate: Historians and the Vietnam War

GARY R. HESS*

The burgeoning literature on the Vietnam War testifies to its status as a defining event in American history. The early availability of a considerable body of documentation on U.S. policymaking in Washington and warmaking in Vietnam, together with the intensity of controversies stirred by the war, help to account for this extensive writing. The duration of the war and its antecedents—a thirty-year process between Ho Chi Minh's 1945 assertion of independence in the name of the Democratic Republic of Vietnam and the Ho Chi Minh campaign of 1975 that reunified the country—make this a lengthy story and one being told more in fragments than in its entirety. Hence, while much early scholarship was devoted to American policy and actions in World War II and the early Cold War, the more recent focus has moved to subsequent developments, with considerable attention to the administrations of Dwight D. Eisenhower and Lyndon B. Johnson. Most scholarship has been devoted to the American side, but the emerging literature includes a number of important efforts to see the conflict from Vietnamese perspectives and to set it in an international context. This essay explores the development of the principal interpretive issues in an emerging Vietnam War historiography with a focus on the literature that has appeared in the last dozen years.[1]

---

*I would like to thank Brian Cassity of the University of Hawaii for research assistance.

[1] There are numerous assessments of the literature on Vietnam. Among the more recent are: David L. Anderson, "Why Vietnam? Postrevisionist Answers and a Neorealist Suggestion," *Diplomatic History* 13 (Summer 1989): 419–29; Warren I. Cohen, "Vietnam: New Light on the Nature of the War?" *International History Review* 9 (February 1987): 108–16; Robert A. Divine, "Vietnam Reconsidered," *Diplomatic History* 12 (Winter 1988): 79–93; John M. Gates, "Vietnam: The Debate Goes On," *Parameters* 14 (Spring 1984): 15–24; George C. Herring, "America and Vietnam: The Debate Continues," *American Historical Review* 92 (April 1987): 350–62; idem, "Vietnam Remembered," *Journal of American History* 73 (June 1986): 152–64; Gary R. Hess, "The Military Perspective on Strategy in Vietnam [Review of Harry G. Summers's *On Strategy* and Bruce Palmer's *The 25-Year War*]," *Diplomatic History* 10 (Winter 1986): 91–106; Thomas G. Paterson, "Historical Memory and Illusive Victories: Vietnam and Central America," *Diplomatic History* 12 (Winter 1988): 1–18; and Geoffrey S. Smith, "Light at the End

At one time, the Vietnam War seemed easily understandable. While it was being waged, the predominant (orthodox) interpretation saw the United States, driven by a mindless anticommunism and with disregard for Vietnamese politics and culture, being drawn into a conflict that it could not win. The titles of representative orthodox books convey the sense of misguided, if not arrogant, idealism leading to a tragic military intervention: *The Making of a Quagmire*; *Washington Plans an Aggressive War*; *The Abuse of Power*; *The Arrogance of Power*; *The Bitter Heritage*; *The Lost Crusade*.[2]

Just as the administration of Richard M. Nixon was ending U.S. involvement in 1972, the orthodox critique was given its fullest expression in two influential and highly praised books: David Halberstam's *The Best and the Brightest* and Frances FitzGerald's *Fire in the Lake*. Together these works explained the tragedy that Vietnam had by then come to symbolize: Halberstam's devastating portraits of the men brought to power by John F. Kennedy, who embodied the "historical sense of inevitable victory"; and FitzGerald's contention that the war they waged was irrelevant given the forces of Vietnamese history, which assured the triumph of the Communist revolution.[3]

As Halberstam and FitzGerald were providing what seemed to be definitive explanations of the war, the scholarly impact of what quickly became known as the Pentagon Papers was changing the terms of thinking about Vietnam. The controversial publication in 1971 of the massive Department of Defense study of policymaking from 1945 to 1967 gave Americans an unprecedented opportunity to read classified documents about a war while it was still being waged. But it also challenged orthodox assumptions and provided the opening scholarly wedge of revisionism. In early interpretations of the Pentagon Papers, the project's documents and narrative were seen as stripping the veneer of innocence from U.S. policymaking by showing that officials recognized the likelihood that escalatory steps would fail as well as the deceit they engaged in by publicly promising "progress." To Daniel Ellsberg, who had helped to compile the study and then to leak it to the press, the story of the Pentagon Papers was simple: Each president had done the minimum necessary to avoid defeat in Vietnam.[4]

---

of the Tunnel? New Perspectives on the Vietnam War," *Canadian Journal of History* 26 (April 1991): 67–86.

[2]David Halberstam, *The Making of a Quagmire: America and Vietnam during the Kennedy Era* (New York, 1964); Ralph L. Stavins, Richard J. Barnet, and Marcus G. Raskin, *Washington Plans an Aggressive War* (New York, 1971); Theodore Draper, *The Abuse of Power* (New York, 1966); Chester Cooper, *The Lost Crusade: America in Vietnam* (Fawcett, CT, 1970); J. William Fulbright, *The Arrogance of Power* (New York, 1966); and Arthur M. Schlesinger, Jr., *The Bitter Heritage: Vietnam and American Democracy*, rev. ed. (Greenwich, CT, 1968). The most scholarly of the orthodox works was George McT. Kahin and John W. Lewis, *The United States in Vietnam* (New York, 1967).

Other early works stressed an imperialist imperative leading to the war in Vietnam; these included: Richard J. Barnet, *Roots of War: The Men and Institutions behind U.S. Foreign Policy* (New York, 1972); and Gabriel Kolko, *The Roots of American Foreign Policy* (Boston, 1969). For contemporary apologies of U.S. policy see: Chester A. Bain, *Vietnam: The Roots of Conflict* (Englewood Cliffs, 1967); and Robert Scigliano, *South Vietnam, Nation under Stress* (Boston, 1963).

[3]David Halberstam, *The Best and the Brightest* (New York, 1972), 123; Frances FitzGerald, *Fire in the Lake: The Vietnamese and the Americans in Vietnam* (Boston, 1972).

[4]Daniel Ellsberg, *Papers on the War* (New York, 1972).

After publication of the Pentagon Papers, a spate of revisionist-oriented works quickly appeared, principal among them four books published in 1978 and 1979—*The Irony of Vietnam*, by Leslie Gelb with Richard Betts; *Summons of the Trumpet*, by Dave Richard Palmer; *Strategy for Defeat*, by U. S. Grant Sharp; and *America in Vietnam*, by Guenter Lewy.

In *The Irony of Vietnam: The System Worked*, Gelb, who had directed the Pentagon Papers project, collaborated with Betts in countering the conventional view that America had blundered into Vietnam. The bureaucratic system "worked" in that policymakers: (1) were consistently aware of the obstacles to U.S. objectives; (2) did the minimum necessary to avoid defeat at each escalatory step; and (3) were successful until losing "the essential domino"—American public support. The Gelb and Betts emphasis on a designed stalemate reinforced the wave of military revisionism that began in earnest with Sharp's *Strategy for Defeat* and Palmer's *Summons of the Trumpet*. These works, and several that followed, reflect the military leadership's long-standing resentment of civilian direction of the war. Sharp, a retired admiral who was Commander in Chief Pacific from 1964 to 1968, and Palmer, a general who served in various command positions in Vietnam, were the first of several high-ranking officers to write revisionist accounts of the war in which they served.

Finally, Lewy's *America in Vietnam*, based in large part on special access to classified documents, offers a scholarly apology for the U.S. effort, stressing the morality of the objective of defending South Vietnam and of the military means employed toward that end. The United States, Lewy asserts, failed to do enough: It should have taken direct control of the South Vietnamese government, incorporated the Army of the Republic of Vietnam (ARVN) into the U.S. command structure, and enforced the reforms necessary to win peasant support.[5]

In the years following this initial wave of revisionist literature, three main groups of revisionists have emerged: the Clausewitzians, the "hearts-and-minders," and the "legitimacists." Although there are elements of "if only" history in all of these works, it is a central tool for the Clausewitzians, who promise a retrospective prescription for victory. The hearts-and-minders and the legitimacists tend to be more scholarly and less certain that the American effort could have attained its objectives.

The most explicit and best known Clausewitzian statement is provided by Harry Summers's *On Strategy*, which cleverly contrasts U.S. conduct of the war with the classic strategic doctrines set forth in Karl von Clausewitz's *On War*. Summers contends that American political leaders were principally responsible for a strategy that was deficient on every count. Other officers of the Vietnam War have argued along similar lines; their works include *The 25-Year War: America's Military Role in Vietnam*, by Bruce Palmer; *The Rise and Fall of an American Army: U.S. Ground Forces in Vietnam, 1965–1973*,

---

[5]Leslie H. Gelb, with Richard K. Betts, *The Irony of Vietnam: The System Worked* (Washington, 1978); Dave Richard Palmer, *Summons of the Trumpet: U.S.-Vietnam in Perspective* (Novato, CA, 1978); U. S. Grant Sharp, *Strategy for Defeat: Vietnam in Retrospect* (San Rafael, CA, 1978); Guenter Lewy, *America in Vietnam* (New York, 1978).

by Shelby Stanton; and two works by Phillip B. Davidson, *Vietnam at War: The History, 1946–1975*, and *Secrets of the Vietnam War*.[6]

With varying degrees of intensity and emphasis, Clausewitzian revisionists argue that civilian leaders misunderstood the Vietnam conflict and sent the military off to wage the wrong kind of war. Had Washington recognized Vietnam as a war of aggression from the North and not as an insurgency supported by the North, had U.S. power been used fully against the North, and had Johnson enlisted popular support and a national commitment, the war could have been won quickly and decisively. Instead, a protracted war played into the hands of the enemy and contributed to disillusionment at home, a factor aggravated by the antiwar protests and biased reporting in the media. Even in the mistaken war of search-and-destroy, the United States had its opportunities to win, but the military was restrained by civilian leaders: It could not bomb vital targets in the North; it could not pursue the enemy into Cambodian and Laotian "sanctuaries"; it could not exploit its "victory" in the Tet Offensive. When Nixon removed many restrictions, some revisionists argue, U.S. air power demonstrated its ability to force concessions. Generally, Vietnamization succeeded, but the South Vietnamese were let down by a spineless Congress and were overwhelmed by the North's 1975 invasion.

Although the Clausewitzian revisionists focus their criticism on civilian leadership, they are mindful of many shortcomings in the military's command structure and in its conduct of the war. Some accounts are critical of Westmoreland's leadership, while others see him as forced by circumstances into a futile war of attrition.

Such revisionism has a familiar tone. Just as revisionist writings on American intervention in the two world wars found America victimized by conspirators or, at the least, by incompetent civilian leaders, so too do Clausewitzians see fools and knaves undermining the Vietnam War effort. Beyond criticism of Johnson's conduct of the war, revisionists maintain that the media and the antiwar protest movement misled and divided the country. Elevating Vietnam into the mythology of a lost cause, some revisionist writing thus explains defeat implicitly in "stab-in-the-back" terms.[7]

While the Clausewitzians criticize Johnson and other civilian leaders for misinterpreting the conflict and restraining the military, the hearts-and-minds revisionists argue that too much attention was devoted to conventional warfare to the detriment of effective pacification. While the Clausewitzians blame

---

[6]Harry G. Summers, *On Strategy: A Critical Analysis of the Vietnam War* (Novato, CA, 1982); Bruce Palmer, Jr., *The 25-Year War: America's Military Role in Vietnam* (Lexington, KY, 1984); Phillip B. Davidson, *Vietnam at War: The History, 1946–1975* (Novato, CA, 1988); idem, *Secrets of the Vietnam War* (Novato, CA, 1990); Shelby L. Stanton, *The Rise and Fall of an American Army: U.S. Ground Forces in Vietnam, 1965–1973* (New York, 1985).

Among other expressions are: William C. Westmoreland, *A Soldier Reports* (Garden City, 1976); Richard M. Nixon, *No More Vietnams* (New York, 1985); General William E. DePuy, "What We Might Have Done and Why We Didn't Do It," *Army* 36 (February 1986): 23–40; and Robert F. Turner, "Myths and Realities in the Vietnam Debate," *World Politics* 149 (Summer 1986): 35–47.

For the thinking of military officers who opposed the war on political, strategic, and moral grounds see Bob Buzzanco, "The American Military's Rationale against the Vietnam War," *Political Science Quarterly* 101:4 (1986): 559–76.

[7]Jeffrey P. Kimball, "The Stab-in-the-Back Legend and the Vietnam War," *Armed Forces and Society* 14 (Spring 1988): 433–58.

civilian officials for failure, the hearts-and-minders fault the army leadership for both resisting and misapplying counterinsurgency doctrine. The "search-and-destroy" campaign was actually waged in far too conventional a manner, resulting in insufficient attention to pacification.

To many participants in the war, this issue still stirs deep emotions. For instance, in *About Face*, David Hackworth, renowned for his battlefield achievements in Vietnam, indicts the search-and-destroy strategy, the shortcomings of which were evident to the American command early in the war. General William Westmoreland had "enough troops and charts and graphs and formulas to do everything but win and solve the conflict," Hackworth writes. But he failed to understand guerrilla warfare—"an almost criminal shortcoming."[8]

Andrew Krepinevich and Larry Cable share Hackworth's assessment of the U.S. military leadership but offer more measured and fuller expressions of the hearts-and-minds argument. In *The Army and Vietnam*, Krepinevich criticizes the army's dismissal of counterinsurgency as a "fad" of the New Frontier and its insistence on waging it "American-style" through an air mobile "high-cost low-payoff strategy" that minimized the "other war" of pacification. Securing the countryside would have been difficult, but according to Krepinevich, who served as an army officer in Vietnam, it would have been less costly in human and financial terms and "would have placed the Army in a position to sustain its efforts in a conflict environment certain to produce a protracted war."[9]

In both *Conflict of Myths* and *Unholy Grail*, Cable faults the army's misapplication of counterinsurgency doctrine. In fact, he turns the Clausewitzian argument on its head and says that the United States actually (but incorrectly) fought a conventional war against the North. Insisting that the Vietcong insurgency exemplified partisan warfare in which a guerrilla movement depended on external support, the army incorrectly saw North Vietnam as the enemy and fought a conventional war with Clausewitzian emphasis on massive destruction. Only the Marines, with their experience in the Banana Wars of the early twentieth century, understood and dealt with the indigenous origins of insurgency. American military strategy consistently played into the hands of North Vietnam, giving it greater influence in the South: Rolling Thunder provided the impetus for increased infiltration of the South; and the mindless ground war disrupted Southern society and undermined the Vietcong. "In an attempt to solve a problem that did not exist," Cable writes, "[the United States] created a problem that could not be solved."[10]

Complementing the Clausewitzians and the hearts-and-minders are the legitimacists, who emphasize the moral and political necessity of U.S. involvement in terms of national security and the viability and progress of the

---

[8]Colonel David H. Hackworth and Julie Sherman, *About Face* (New York, 1989), 556, 613–14.

[9]Andrew F. Krepinevich, *The Army and Vietnam* (Baltimore, 1986), 233.

[10]Larry E. Cable, *Conflict of Myths: The Development of Counterinsurgency Doctrine and the Vietnam War* (New York, 1988), 225; idem, *Unholy Grail: The US and the Wars in Vietnam, 1965–1968* (London, 1991).

South Vietnamese government. Also emphasizing the "aggression" of North Vietnam, the legitimacists help reinforce the Clausewitzian contention of a conventional war. Legitimacists see the United States as headed in the right direction in the late 1950s and argue that it should have stood by Ngo Dinh Diem, who, as subsequent events would demonstrate, was the South's most effective leader. His overthrow led only to the political instability that eventually necessitated U.S. military intervention. In an early expression of this viewpoint, Norman Podhoretz's strident *Why We Were in Vietnam* stresses the moral and political imperatives of U.S. policy, the strength of anticommunism in the South, and the shallowness of the war's critics.[11]

The legitimacist argument is being presented most fully in R. B. Smith's multivolume *An International History of the Vietnam War*. In his first two volumes—*Revolution versus Containment* and *The Kennedy Strategy*—Smith advances a view of the emerging conflict that emphasizes the Chinese and Soviet interest in Vietnam. As the Soviet Union pursued coexistence with the West in the late 1950s, Hanoi feared isolation and dependence on China. But by taking advantage of Southern insurgent demands for support, Ho Chi Minh forced the Chinese and the Soviets into backing the nationalist cause. By the time that John F. Kennedy became president, Vietnam had become a major problem "for reasons more to do with the global strategies of the Soviet Union and China, and with American vulnerability, than with the exercise of options on the part of the United States." The symbolic value was real: "In both the American and the Marxist-Leninist context, South Vietnam—an agrarian country of fewer than fifteen million people—thus acquired an international significance out of all proportion to its size." The demise of Ngo Dinh Diem played into the hands of the North Vietnamese who exploited and infiltrated a Buddhist protest movement that attracted widespread notoriety in the reports of gullible Western journalists. Contrary to the conventional view that the political deterioration of South Vietnam began in the summer of 1963, Smith believes that "there can be little doubt that the principal factor in the deterioration (which certainly occurred by mid-December) was the coup itself and its political consequences." Buoyed by the weaknesses of the South and the assurances of external support, Hanoi forced the military showdown with the Americans in February 1965. To the Americans and the Chinese, the ultimate prize was Indonesia. Hence, U.S. intervention "bought time" for "democracy" in the region.[12]

Ellen Hammer and Patrick Hatcher concur with Smith that the "crisis" leading to Diem's overthrow was more of American than Vietnamese origin and that the United States erred in replacing him. This judgment essentially restates the Defense Department's 1963 position as it opposed State Department and Central Intelligence Agency (CIA) maneuvering against Diem. To his contemporary and retrospective supporters, Diem's strong-willed nationalism was the best hope for South Vietnam. In *A Death in November*, Hammer suggests that Diem, despite his considerable faults, had a

[11] Norman Podhoretz, *Why We Were in Vietnam* (New York, 1982).

[12] R. B. Smith, *An International History of the Vietnam War*, Vol. 1, *Revolution versus Containment, 1955–1961* (New York, 1983), 261; Vol. 2, *The Kennedy Strategy* (New York, 1985), 1, 190.

better sense of South Vietnam's interests than other indigenous leaders and certainly than the Americans. Resentful of American manipulation, Diem refused to play the puppet and was prepared to lessen his dependence on Washington by pursuing a neutral course. As a result, the CIA engaged in intrigue with South Vietnamese dissidents that led to Diem's assassination. In their frustrations with a situation that defied American expectations, correspondents Neil Sheehan, Malcolm Brown, David Halberstam, and others found a scapegoat in Diem and blithely assumed that his overthrow would bring stability and progress.

In *The Suicide of an Elite: American Internationalists and Vietnam*, Hatcher cites evidence of rural and urban economic growth during the Diem era. He contends that the failure to stand by Diem deprived the South of the only leader capable of upholding Vietnamese pride in the face of the technical superiority of the growing American presence, which "denied authenticity to the Vietnamese character of Saigon's intervention."[13]

The conviction that Diem was America's best hope was shared by the legendary hard-nosed CIA operative Edward Lansdale and is implicitly embraced by Cecil B. Currey in his admiring biography, *Edward Lansdale: The Unquiet American*. Convinced that lessons from his renowned work in the Philippines could be applied in Vietnam, Lansdale pressed Americans and Diem to recognize the centrality of pacification and preparation for counter-insurgency. Despite their close friendship, Lansdale could not persuade Diem to pursue rural reform or to broaden his political base. Yet he strongly criticized the coup, believing that only Diem could bring orderly constitutional development to South Vietnam.[14]

The subsequent Americanization of the war is treated in R. B. Smith's third volume, *The Making of a Limited War, 1965–66*, where he argues that the international challenge posed by the situation in Vietnam justified Johnson's decision for war. Given the Soviet and Chinese support of Hanoi, the instability of Southeast Asia, and "a very real Chinese campaign to eliminate United States power and influence not just from South Vietnam but from the East and Southeast Asian region," Vietnam was by 1965 "part of a global power struggle which President Johnson could not easily have ignored." By the end of 1966, however, Johnson was forced by circumstances to accept Secretary of Defense Robert S. McNamara's prescription for "stabilization," which meant to gird for a longer war. "Limiting the scope of the war was now more vital to the interests of the United States," Smith writes, "than going all out to win it."[15]

In *The War Everyone Lost—and Won*, Timothy J. Lomperis carries the legitimacy argument to the end of the war, contending that the United States "lost while winning" and betrayed South Vietnam in the process. Lomperis characterizes the struggle between the North and the South as one to attain

---

[13]Ellen Hammer, *A Death in November: America in Vietnam, 1963* (New York, 1987); Patrick Lloyd Hatcher, *The Suicide of an Elite: American Internationalists and Vietnam* (Stanford, 1990).

[14]Cecil B. Currey, *Edward Lansdale: The Unquiet American* (Boston, 1988).

[15]R. B. Smith, *An International History of the Vietnam War*, Vol. 3, *The Making of a Limited War, 1965–66* (New York, 1991), 3, 18, 417.

legitimacy. The Communists failed to demonstrate the legitimacy of people's war and, after defeat in the Tet Offensive, they resorted to conventional warfare. By 1973, the Saigon government "found the tide . . . decidedly in its favor," but it had gained only a "passive legitimacy" and never had the opportunity to build an "active legitimacy." When the critical test came in the North Vietnamese attack of 1975, the United States abandoned South Vietnam. In the end, Hanoi may have unified the country, but the lack of revolutionary legitimacy has plagued its governance.[16]

Paralleling the wave of revisionism has been refinement of the orthodox criticism of U.S. involvement, with most of this neo-orthodox scholarship focusing on the 1954–1968 period.[17] As revisionism was taking hold, George Herring's *America's Longest War* and Paul Kattenburg's *The Vietnam Trauma in American Foreign Policy*, published in 1979 and 1980, respectively, cast the war in the context of a Cold War-driven quarter century's effort to assure the establishment of a non-Communist state in Vietnam. Suggesting a more complex policymaking than that described by Gelb and Betts, Herring and Kattenburg contend that a misreading of U.S. interests and Vietnamese realities led to a doomed effort to build an independent South Vietnam and ultimately to an unwinnable military intervention.[18] This "flawed containment" interpretation is central to much subsequent neo-orthodox scholarship. These works have moved beyond analysis of decision making in Washington to examine the impact of the war protests and media on the home front and the conduct of the war itself. Although most of the recent writing has an American emphasis, some scholars have tried to understand the various Vietnamese "sides" of the story, including the struggle for control of the South Vietnamese countryside and the strategies of the North Vietnamese and Vietcong. In the process, these works help to join the debate with revisionism, for their

[16]Timothy J. Lomperis, *The War Everyone Lost—And Won: America's Intervention in Viet Nam's Twin Struggles* (Baton Rouge, 1984), 173.

[17]On the earlier involvement dating from World War II, much work has been done that is being augmented by recent notable efforts that promise to recast developments in Vietnam during World War II and the early Cold War within an international history context. These include at least two dissertations in progress—Mark Bradley, Harvard University, "Making Cold War: Vietnam and the United States, 1941–1955," and Patricia Lane, University of Hawaii, "U.S.-Vietnam-France Relations, 1940–1945: The View from the Field." Already completed is Stein Tonnesson, *The Vietnamese Revolution of 1945: Roosevelt, Ho Chi Minh, and de Gaulle in a World at War* (Oslo, 1991), which stresses the importance of the Japanese coup of March 1945 in the Vietminh's bid for power. Tonnesson argues that the United States fostered the coup. Roosevelt, clinging to his objective of eliminating the French administration as essential to realization of his trusteeship plan, deceived the Japanese into anticipating a U.S. attack and thus encouraged the coup.

The geopolitical interests behind the U.S. reconsideration of its Southeast Asian policy in 1949–50 that led to the initial diplomatic and material support of the French has been explored in a number of works, including William S. Borden, *The Pacific Alliance: United States Foreign Economic Policy and Japanese Trade Recovery, 1947–1955* (Madison, 1984); Gary R. Hess, *The United States' Emergence as a Southeast Asian Power, 1940–1950* (New York, 1987); Andrew J. Rotter, *The Path to Vietnam: Origins of the American Commitment in Southeast Asia* (Ithaca, 1987); and Michael Schaller, *The American Occupation of Japan: The Origins of the Cold War in Asia* (New York, 1985). For a useful survey of the literature see Robert J. McMahon, "The Cold War in Asia: Toward a New Synthesis?" *Diplomatic History* 12 (Summer 1988): 307–27.

[18]George C. Herring, *America's Longest War: The United States and Vietnam, 1950–1975* (New York, 1979); Paul M. Kattenburg, *The Vietnam Trauma in American Foreign Policy, 1945–1975* (New Brunswick, 1980).

findings provide insight into the viability of certain revisionist arguments and "if only" scenarios.

A few scholars endeavor to relate the war to cultural imperatives. To Loren Baritz and James William Gibson, American involvement reflected a technological culture run amuck. Both Baritz, a social historian, and Gibson, a sociologist, stress an expansionist and militarist technology. Their works are assuredly not dispassionate, and perhaps ought to be dismissed as more polemic than scholarship. Yet each of their books offers certain insights. In *Backfire: A History of How American Culture Led Us into the Vietnam War and Made Us Fight the Way We Did*, Baritz contends that a "national myth showed us that we were good, [that] our technology made us strong, and [that] our bureaucracy gave us standard operating procedures. It was not a winning combination." Ethnocentric American leaders "invented" South Vietnam and relied on a technologically based capacity to kill to achieve a vision of Pax Americana.[19]

In a similar argument, Gibson, in *The Perfect War: The War We Couldn't Lose and How We Did*, characterizes American society as enthralled by the "logic of Technowar," which rendered unthinkable any outcome other than that the "largest, fastest, most technologically advanced system [would] win." Although filled with abstraction and jargon, *The Perfect War* nonetheless includes useful information on how war managers' obliviousness to Vietnamese political realities and faith in quantitative data led to consistent miscalculations and an inept military strategy.[20]

With the opening of British and American archives as well as the personal papers of key figures, scholars have reexamined the 1954 crisis that began with the siege of Dien Bien Phu and continued through the Geneva and Manila conferences partitioning Vietnam and establishing the Southeast Asia Treaty Organization (SEATO), respectively. In a careful study of Eisenhower's leadership, *Decision against War*, Melanie Billings-Yun follows the Eisenhower revisionist interpretation of a decisive leader shrewdly and indirectly achieving his goal of keeping the United States out of war. As Billings-Yun demonstrates, the conventional view of a president restrained by British and congressional opposition to intervention was an astute misrepresentation designed by Eisenhower, who had decided early in the crisis that the use of U.S. force was not worth the resultant damage to American stature and, above all, the risk of a war. Restating a more conventional view is James Arnold's *The First Domino*. Arnold contends that only political considerations held back a hawkish Eisenhower in 1954, but that his critical decisions in the "watershed year" 1955 forged inexorable links to the subsequent Americanization of the struggle.[21]

---

[19]Loren Baritz, *Backfire: A History of How American Culture Led Us into the Vietnam War and Made Us Fight the Way We Did* (New York, 1985), 27, 40.

[20]James William Gibson, *The Perfect War: The War We Couldn't Lose and How We Did* (Boston, 1986), 16–17, 23.

[21]Melanie Billings-Yun, *Decision against War: Eisenhower and Dien Bien Phu, 1954* (New York, 1988); James R. Arnold, *The First Domino: Eisenhower, the Military, and America's Intervention in Vietnam* (New York, 1991).

In *Approaching Vietnam*, Lloyd Gardner casts U.S. policy within the context of the "liberal empire's" post-World War II objective of "liberation," which by 1954 centered on freeing Indochina from French mistakes. Gardner stresses the role of the peripatetic John Foster Dulles in forging a British-French-American commitment to the partition of Vietnam at Geneva and the subsequent reaffirmation of that outcome through SEATO. The resultant support of a "liberated" Vietnam ultimately revealed the "contradictions in nation building . . . [derived from] the conviction, shared before [Dulles] by people all the way back to Roosevelt with his plan for a trusteeship, that America had a special talent for liberating colonized peoples."[22]

Like Gardner, Anthony Short criticizes U.S. policy in 1954 as being shortsighted and leading to warfare a decade later. In Short's judgment, however, the U.S. failure was not so much in misguided nation-building but in missing what was in its grasp: international commitment to permanent partition. The principal contribution of Short's *The Origins of the Vietnam War*, a work notable for its even-handed criticism of all of the governments involved in leading Vietnam to war in 1965, is a detailed reexamination of the 1954 crisis. Short questions whether America's determined effort to be "in but not of" the Geneva settlement served its interests. The failure of the United States to approve the Geneva Accords, Short argues, undermined its very interest in partition. "By refusing to join in any guarantees with the communist states," Short contends, "one has to ask whether Dulles rejected a finite end to the first Vietnam War and, in so doing, doomed the United States to participate in the second."[23]

Scholars are also reexamining America's relationship with the government headed by Ngo Dinh Diem. Chief among them is David L. Anderson, whose *Trapped by Success* describes U.S. support for Diem during the Eisenhower administration as "buying time but also buying trouble." American policy was the "creator and [the] captive of an illusion in Vietnam." Dismissing any idea of a "stalemate" thesis, Anderson shows how officials believed that time was in their favor, that progress was occurring, and that North Vietnam was not a serious threat. The mission of J. Lawton Collins in 1955 constituted the "point of no return," for Collins alone among high officials recognized Diem's shortcomings. Nevertheless, spurred by Dulles's enthusiasm for Diem, American policy embraced a partnership with his

---

[22]Lloyd C. Gardner, *Approaching Vietnam: From World War II through Dienbienphu, 1941–1954* (New York, 1988), 354.

[23]Anthony Short, *The Origins of the Vietnam War* (London, 1989), 328–29. In addition to the monographs regarding the United States and the 1954 crisis, a number of articles—notably the work of Richard H. Immerman—add significantly to the story: George C. Herring and Richard H. Immerman, "Eisenhower, Dulles, and Dienbienphu: 'The Day We Didn't Go to War' Revisited," *Journal of American History* 71 (September 1984): 343–63; Richard H. Immerman, "Between the Unattainable and the Unacceptable: Eisenhower and Dienbienphu," in *Reevaluating Eisenhower: American Foreign Policy in the Fifties*, ed. Richard A. Melanson and David Mayers (Urbana, 1987), 120–54; and idem, "The United States and the Geneva Conference of 1954: A New Look," *Diplomatic History* 14 (Winter 1990): 43–66. Immerman finds Eisenhower's diplomacy to be reasonably effective in responding to the Dien Bien Phu crisis but questions the soundness of the U.S. approach to the Geneva settlement.

government. Ignorance and indifference resulted in a "commitment to the survival of [America's] own counterfeit creation."[24]

The analyses of Ronald Spector on the early military assistance program and of D. Michael Shafer on pacification reinforce Anderson's conclusions. In *Advice and Support*, Spector describes the first flawed effort at Vietnamization. Trained by Americans to resist Korea-type aggression from the North, ARVN was ill-prepared for counterinsurgency. More important, it suffered from the moral, structural, and political problems that were endemic to the Diem regime.

In his *Deadly Paradigms: The Failure of U.S. Counterinsurgency Policy*, Shafer challenges the retrospective "might have beens" about "winning" the countryside through pacification by pointing out the flaws in American thinking and programs. He faults American doctrine for linking insurgency to external sources, based in part on inappropriate "lessons" of Greece and Turkey. In both cases, U.S. efforts were irrelevant, as leaders of threatened regimes used aid to reinforce their strength but without confronting the basis of the insurgency. Hence, contrary to the thinking of people like Edward Lansdale, the United States had no useful experience to bring to the Vietnam conflict. Focusing on counterinsurgency during the Diem regime, Shafer finds an uncoordinated U.S. program compounded by Diem's resistance to U.S. suggestions and Washington's reluctance to employ its leverage.[25]

The opening of documentation on Johnson's decisions to Americanize the war in 1965 has led to several notable studies, with the president's role a point of historiographical debate. Whether writing critically or sympathetically of Johnson's situation, scholars generally stress the influence of "guns-and-butter" thinking on his 1965 decisions and see a flaw in his penchant for compromise.

Larry Berman's *Planning a Tragedy* characterizes Johnson as driven by a domestic political agenda that would "merit nothing less than Mount Rushmore" and therefore as determined to resolve the Vietnam problem quickly and quietly. Fearful that the loss of Vietnam would trigger the kind of partisan debate that followed the Chinese civil war, Johnson used the decision-making process from February through July 1965 in ways that ignored any

---

[24]David L. Anderson, *Trapped by Success: The Eisenhower Administration and Vietnam, 1953–1961* (New York, 1991), 227, 304, 409.

[25]Ronald H. Spector, *Advice and Support: The Early Years of the U.S. Army in Vietnam, 1941–1960* (New York, 1985); D. Michael Shafer, *Deadly Paradigms: The Failure of U.S. Counterinsurgency Policy* (Princeton, 1988).

There are two books on Kennedy's Vietnam policy: William J. Rust, *Kennedy in Vietnam: American Foreign Policy, 1960–1963* (New York, 1985); and John M. Newman, *JFK and Vietnam: Deception, Intrigue, and the Struggle for Power* (New York, 1992). Newman's book, which accompanied the release of Oliver Stone's motion picture *JFK*, pieces together documents that purportedly demonstrate a conspiracy against a Kennedy commitment to withdraw from Vietnam; immediately after Kennedy's assassination, Johnson, duped into thinking he was carrying on Kennedy's policy, actually reversed it and took the measures that led to U.S. military involvement. The Rust work summarizes Kennedy's involvement and, like Newman's (although without any hint of conspiracies), sees Kennedy disengaging from Vietnam. For more critical appraisals of Kennedy's policy see Lawrence Bassett and Stephen Pelz, "The Failed Search for Victory: Vietnam and the Politics of War," in *Kennedy's Quest for Victory: American Foreign Policy, 1961–1963*, ed. Thomas G. Paterson (New York, 1989), 223–52; and Gary R. Hess, "Commitment in the Age of Counter-Insurgency: Kennedy and Vietnam," in *Shadow on the White House: Presidents and the Vietnam War*, ed. David L. Anderson (Lawrence, 1993).

examination of the assumptions about the commitment to South Vietnam and that placed the burden of proof on dovish, not hawkish, advisers. With scant regard for the magnitude of his decisions, Johnson went to war out of fear that "losing Vietnam in the summer of 1965 would wreck his plans for a truly Great Society."[26]

The inadequacy of decision making in the Johnson White House is also stressed in *How Presidents Test Reality: Decisions on Vietnam 1954 and 1965* by John P. Burke and Fred I. Greenstein (with the assistance of Berman and Richard H. Immerman). Comparing Johnson's decision-making process with that of Eisenhower, Burke and Greenstein suggest that Johnson could have learned something from Eisenhower's more formal, open advocacy advisory system. In the incoherent policy review leading to the 28 July 1965 troop commitment, it seemed that "a great swirl of policy recommendations and analyses . . . simply floated past the President."[27]

In Brian Van De Mark's *Into the Quagmire*, Johnson and his advisers are seen as more reluctant warriors. "Like figures in a Greek tragedy," Van De Mark writes, "pride compelled these supremely confident men further into disaster." In this largely sympathetic appraisal of a president confronting intractable problems, Johnson emerges as soliciting advice from dovish as well as hawkish advisers. While Van De Mark portrays a more open minded Johnson than Berman and Burke and Greenstein, his work also underlines the fact that debate was limited by the failure to examine basic assumptions of U.S. interest in Southeast Asia and the fears of right-wing backlash if Johnson appeared irresolute.[28]

According to Yuen Foong Khong, these conventional accounts of the decision for war minimize the significance of historical analogies—in this case, the lessons of the Korean War—on the reasoning of policymakers. In *Analogies at War: Korea, Munich, Dien Bien Phu, and the Vietnam Decisions of 1965*, Khong offers a provocative interpretation of the mindset that both exaggerated Vietnam's importance and minimized the obstacles to American objectives. Employing cognitive psychology research and techniques, he examines policymakers' reasoning through historical analogies. Earlier scholars have acknowledged the references to "lessons of the past" in policy debates and in public justifications for intervention, but often this has been to show how poorly history is used and without substantive analysis of the extent to which lessons actually influenced decisions or provided rationales for choices made on other grounds. Khong contends that schemas and analogies are fundamental to apprehending reality, interpreting problems, and determining policy options. After analyzing how policymakers used the Munich, Korean, and Dien Bien Phu analogies, Khong concludes that the lessons of the Korean War (a successful limited war in which the only major

---

[26] Larry Berman, *Planning a Tragedy: The Americanization of the War in Vietnam* (New York, 1982), 147.

[27] John P. Burke and Fred I. Greenstein, *How Presidents Test Reality: Decisions on Vietnam 1954 and 1965* (New York, 1991), 261.

[28] Brian Van De Mark, *Into the Quagmire: Lyndon Johnson and the Escalation of the Vietnam War* (New York, 1991), 219.

mistake was the provocation of China) defined the terms of intervention in Vietnam.[29]

In contrast to the centrality of Washington in most accounts of the 1965 decisions, the culmination of George Kahin's notable binational study, *Intervention*, is both the decision for war and its effects on the Vietnamese. American indifference toward Vietnamese history and politics is central to Kahin's careful analysis of U.S.-Vietnamese interaction beginning in 1946. In the South, American actions after 1954 blunted the emergence of a viable "third force" centering around the Buddhist leadership. By 1964–65, Johnson weighed his options in a deteriorating situation. Recognizing that the Saigon government would likely seek negotiations with the National Liberation Front (NLF), that the Chinese had a strong interest in Vietnam, and that America's allies did not support escalation, Johnson searched for answers to an intractable problem. A negotiated settlement risked South Vietnam's survival and hence political support for his Great Society. When Johnson intervened, it was done cautiously, rejecting calls for an invasion or all-out bombing of the North. Intervention, however, had a devastating effect on South Vietnam as it buttressed U.S. support of the government headed by Generals Nguyen Cao Ky and Nguyen Van Thieu and thus destroyed whatever prospects existed for the Buddhist third force between the NLF and the Saigon military. The "rigid polarization" left the South Vietnamese without the option of compromise, "permitting only two active choices—supporting the NLF or a Saigon regime shaped by and dependent upon the United States." Hence, U.S. intervention meant an ever-widening divergence of American objectives from indigenous political forces.[30]

Johnson's determined consensus building, which hindered effective decision making in 1965, continued, in the judgment of most scholars, to limit his effectiveness as a wartime president. In *When Governments Collide*, Wallace Thies finds that Johnson's determination to control the conduct of the war actually led to a loss of control. Thies's focus is the futile search for a means of negotiation. The doctrine that orchestrating diplomacy with fine-tuned military coercion could bring the North Vietnamese to the negotiating table failed in practice. Johnson was largely to blame: His consistent search for consensus within his administration, rather than control of the U.S. war, "provides an almost perfect lesson in how *not* to engage in coercion." As Johnson compromised between the advice of the hawks and the doves, which always meant increased warfare, he left leaders in Hanoi seeing only hypocrisy and deceit. Whether the two sides could have reached an agreement on the issue of South Vietnam's political status is problematic, but mismanagement of U.S. diplomacy and warfare meant that "errors and misunderstandings *did* exist, and their effect was to make an already difficult problem virtually insoluble."[31]

---

[29] Yuen Foong Khong, *Analogies at War: Korea, Munich, Dien Bien Phu, and the Vietnam Decisions of 1965* (Princeton, 1992).

[30] George McT. Kahin, *Intervention: How America Became Involved in Vietnam* (New York, 1986), 432.

[31] Wallace J. Thies, *When Governments Collide: Coercion and Diplomacy in the Vietnam Conflict, 1964–1968* (Berkeley, 1980), 373–74 (emphasis in original).

Johnson's leadership at home, according to Kathleen J. Turner and Larry Berman, suffered from similar flaws. Turner, in *Lyndon Johnson's Dual War: Vietnam and the Press*, analyzes the public dimension of the futile effort to appease both hawks and doves by demonstrating that the United States was doing "enough" but not "too much." Turner examines in detail the Johns Hopkins University address of April 1965—in which Johnson blended a strident defense of the American position with a proposal for American-financed cooperative development of the Mekong Delta—as an early illustration of Johnson's frustrations in rationalizing Southeast Asian policy.[32]

In *Lyndon Johnson's War*, Berman extends such analysis into a portrayal of Johnson as becoming a tragic figure whose ultimate demise resulted from flaws of leadership. The "tragedy in the making" in Berman's earlier book thus gained national and personal dimensions. Berman writes of a president who took the country to war without calling for national commitment and who publicly embraced a strategy that he privately questioned. Unable to resolve the dilemma of maintaining the independence of South Vietnam without destroying North Vietnam, Johnson by 1967 faced the imperfect alternatives of sending another three hundred thousand troops or stabilizing the commitment at five hundred thousand. With a presidential campaign on the horizon, Johnson avoided difficult choices and indulged in wishful thinking that the war was actually being won. He thus orchestrated the "big sell" of "progress" in Vietnam and unwittingly contributed to the popular disillusionment that came with the Tet Offensive.[33]

Besides paying considerable attention to Johnson's leadership, historians have also been reassessing the roles of other key figures in Vietnam policymaking. As the war went sour, the reputations of the "best and the brightest" were tarnished and "doves" moved into the ascendancy. Scholarship thus far completed suggests that the war left mostly "losers."

Dean Rusk may be doing as well as any. In retrospect, Rusk looks much as he did in the 1960s: the uncomplicated Cold Warrior unswervingly loyal to Kennedy and Johnson and committed to U.S. objectives. In Warren I. Cohen's close analysis of Rusk's years as secretary of state and in Thomas J. Schoenbaum's biography of Rusk—both sympathetic accounts—and in Rusk's own quasi-memoir, told largely in response to his son's questions, Rusk emerges as skeptical of U.S. military strategy and Saigon's viability and perplexed by the dedication of the enemy and the war weariness of the American public. Only domestic political necessity forced his acceptance of negotiations and deescalation.[34]

Although now somewhat dated, Robert L. Gallucci, *Neither Peace Nor Honor: The Politics of American Military Policy in Viet-Nam* (Baltimore, 1975), provides a still useful comparative analysis of Kennedy and Johnson policymaking within a bureaucratic politics framework. As the war escalated from 1965 to 1967, a pattern of compromise continued, but without benefit of sufficient nonmilitary input—a conclusion that challenges revisionist contentions about a lack of military influence.

[32]Kathleen Turner, *Lyndon Johnson's Dual War: Vietnam and the Press* (Chicago, 1985).

[33]Larry Berman, *Lyndon Johnson's War: The Road to Stalemate* (New York, 1989).

[34]Warren I. Cohen, *Dean Rusk* (Totowa, NJ, 1980); Thomas J. Schoenbam, *Waging Peace and War: Dean Rusk in the Truman, Kennedy, and Johnson Years* (New York, 1988); Dean Rusk, as told to Richard Rusk, *As I Saw It*, ed. Daniel S. Papp (New York, 1990).

Rusk's self-effacing style contrasts sharply with that of the visible and energetic Robert McNamara, the subject of Deborah Shapley's insightful and unflattering biography. *Promise and Power: The Life and Times of Robert McNamara* is strongest in its effort to come to terms with McNamara's mind and character. Shapley describes an arrogant, number-crunching, emotionally and intellectually flawed Cold Warrior who believed that "applied intelligence, organization, and resources could mold reality to suit his will." McNamara's quantitative measures in Vietnam led to arbitrary decisions and premature evaluations of success. Moreover, as the good manager, McNamara determined what superiors wanted and acted accordingly. Yet he was unable to accept a flawed outcome. The emotional strain of his growing realization that the war was unwinnable brought him nearly to the breaking point, and going to the World Bank in 1967 provided an opportunity to atone for the suffering that he helped to inflict on Vietnam. McNamara agreed to be interviewed by Shapley, who finds his recollections on Vietnam to be self-serving and disingenuous. Yet Shapley gives McNamara a hearing, allowing him to emphasize that as early as 1965 he doubted whether the military could achieve U.S. objectives and that he thus sought to keep open the negotiating channels even as intervention went forward. Had his calls for extended bombing pauses been accepted, he argues, the war could have ended earlier.[35]

Among the Kennedy advisers on Vietnam none carried greater initial prestige than Maxwell Taylor. Yet as Douglas Kinnard illustrates in *The Certain Trumpet*, Taylor—as Kennedy adviser, chairman of the Joint Chiefs of Staff, ambassador to South Vietnam, and consultant to Johnson—underestimated the problems facing the United States and exhibited a lack of character. The Taylor-Rostow report, Kinnard correctly notes, is often remembered for the eight thousand troop recommendation that Kennedy rejected, but more important was the open-ended increase of advisers and resources it portended. In 1963, Taylor declined to "stand up and be counted when in the minority," putting aside his reservations about U.S. complicity in the plotting against Diem and about promises that American personnel could be withdrawn within two years. As ambassador in 1965, Taylor supported the bombing of North Vietnam and just as strongly opposed the introduction of ground forces. After losing on that issue, however, he characteristically stated that ground forces should have been committed earlier. In sum, Taylor's shortcoming in Vietnam policy "was not in what he did, but what he failed to do."[36]

Critics of the war were not necessarily more knowledgeable about Vietnam nor more honorable under pressure. The renowned dissent of resident dove Undersecretary of State George Ball is analyzed fully by David L. DiLeo in *George Ball, Vietnam, and the Rethinking of Containment.* Ball emerges as a complex, ambitious man whose opposition to escalation and advocacy of negotiation reflected a Europe-centered worldview. Disdain, with a trace of racism, characterized his thinking on the Third World. Ball's refusal to make

[35]Deborah Shapley, *Promise and Power: The Life and Times of Robert McNamara* (Boston, 1993), 559.

[36]Douglas Kinnard, *The Certain Trumpet: Maxwell Taylor and the American Experience in Vietnam* (Washington, 1991), 216, 219.

his December 1966 resignation a matter of principle reflected more than loyalty to those he served. It also stemmed from Ball's reluctance to sabotage whatever prospects there were of Johnson turning to him to replace Rusk as secretary of state. According to DiLeo, Ball was too concerned with preserving his status to vigorously criticize American conduct of the war.[37]

Then there was John Paul Vann, who was never modest about "understanding" the Vietnamese and whom Neil Sheehan calls "the one compelling figure [in the] war without heroes." Sheehan was part of the small Saigon press corps in the early 1960s that Vann transformed "into a band of reporters propounding the John Vann view of the war." In *A Bright Shining Lie: John Paul Vann and America in Vietnam*, he argues that Vann's "accumulated expertise and aptitude for this war made him the one irreplacable American." Yet the subsequent analysis of Vann's military and advisory career in Vietnam sustains Vann as more "compelling" than "irreplacable." Losing his life in a helicopter accident in 1972, Vann "died believing he had won this war." The "lie" in all of this was Vann's nonheroic side. He was an amoral, selfish, deceitful, compulsive man whose duality of character exemplified the American role in Vietnam. Vann emerges as a tragic figure in a doomed enterprise: "He was much that was wrong about the war . . . but he could never bring himself to conclude that the war itself was wrong and unwinnable." In the end, Americans were betrayed by Vann and the U.S. government, for both became a "bright shining lie." Whether the career of Vann or any figure can be a metaphor for the American experience, Sheehan's work yields insight into the remarkable arrogance of the American intervention.[38]

The paucity of documents on the administration of Richard M. Nixon has limited research on its Vietnam policy. The fullest account is Arnold R. Isaacs's *Without Honor*. Isaacs acknowledges the problems and accomplishments of the approach taken by Nixon and Henry Kissinger. They came to power recognizing that the war could not be won and seeking an exit that would be tolerable to the American public and that would preserve American credibility. The 1973 agreement they brokered was more favorable to American and South Vietnamese interests than what could have been negotiated at the beginning of Nixon's term. Yet the flaw in the Nixon-Kissinger approach was that the two realists failed to focus on the objective of an honorable exit. They could not understand that the North's suspicion of negotiations derived from frustrating experiences in 1946 and 1954. In "the single act by which the Nixon administration closed the trap on itself," they senselessly expanded the fighting into Cambodia with devastating consequences for both that country and the United States. Before and especially after the 1973 agreement, they allowed the South Vietnamese government to expect long-term American aid and thus "nourished [Thieu's] fantasies of support in pursuit of an unattainable victory." And they shamelessly blamed

[37]David L. DiLeo, *George Ball, Vietnam, and the Rethinking of Containment* (Chapel Hill, 1991).

[38]Neil Sheehan, *A Bright Shining Lie: John Paul Vann and America in Vietnam* (New York, 1988).

Congress and antiwar protesters for undermining their efforts and South Vietnam's capacity to survive.[39]

Finger pointing accompanied the end of the war, as Kissinger and President Gerald Ford blamed Congress for the U.S. defeat. P. Edward Haley's *Congress and the Fall of South Vietnam and Cambodia* sees this criticism as disingenuous and contradictory. The White House kept secret its promises to save the Thieu government because it knew Congress would disapprove, and then in 1975 acted as if Congress should approve. Despite the realization that the commitments were meaningless and that the war was lost, congressional inaction brought Kissinger's "frustrations out, and he dressed them in cataclysm and the decline of the West."[40]

As Gelb and Betts write, the home front was "the last domino," and recent scholarship suggests a more complex domestic scene than that depicted by revisionists, who emphasize biased media coverage of the war and unpatriotic antiwar protesters as undermining public support and contributing to defeat. Two complementary studies—*An American Ordeal*, by Charles DeBenedetti and Charles Chatfield, and *The Debate over Vietnam*, by David Levy—yield insight into the controversies generated by the war. DeBenedetti and Chatfield examine the many and shifting expressions of the antiwar "movement of movements" and capture the spontaneity and disjointed nature of protest. They contend that the major role of the antiwar movement was in "keeping open the prospect of defeat as a national option. Never a popular position, disengagement—and even policy failure—was discussed in public from the start." The public always mistrusted the protesters, even as it gravitated toward the antiwar contention that Vietnam was not related to U.S. security.[41]

Levy's work looks at the arguments dividing hawks and doves and at the way the war affected various subcommunities, including minorities, intellectuals, religious groups, organized labor, political parties, and higher education. Unlike DeBenedetti and Chatfield, Levy largely eschews judgments on the meaning of the debate that he chronicles, but he does observe, as have scholars of public opinion, that war weariness augmented by the surprise of the Tet Offensive, rather than the force of argumentation, led to popular disaffection.[42]

---

[39]Arnold R. Isaacs, *Without Honor: Defeat in Vietnam and Cambodia* (Baltimore, 1983), 493, 505.

Two early appraisals of the Paris agreement—Gareth Porter, *A Peace Denied: The United States, Vietnam, and the Paris Agreement* (Bloomington, 1975); and Allan E. Goodman, *The Lost Peace: America's Search for a Negotiated Settlement of the Vietnam War* (Stanford, 1978)—stress the futility of negotiating where fundamental issues defied compromise. Porter is the more critical of the American negotiating position, seeing the commitment to the preservation of an independent South Vietnam as delaying a settlement, precluding its implementation, and preventing adaptation to political-military changes in 1973–1975. Goodman is more apologetic for the American position, faulting Johnson's strategy of escalation mixed with conciliatory gestures for sending the wrong message to Hanoi. Yet Goodman is also skeptical of the viability of the Saigon government and concurs with Porter that the Paris agreement was fundamentally flawed.

[40]P. Edward Haley, *Congress and the Fall of South Vietnam and Cambodia* (Rutherford, NJ, 1982), 154.

[41]Charles DeBenedetti, assisted by Charles Chatfield, *An American Ordeal: The Antiwar Movement of the Vietnam Era* (Syracuse, 1990), 407.

[42]David W. Levy, *The Debate over Vietnam* (Baltimore, 1991).

In *Johnson, Nixon, and the Doves*, Melvin Small undertakes the difficult task of tracing the antiwar movement's influence on two presidents, each of whom professed indifference to protest. Small's cautious conclusions are plausible, as he finds a largely indirect but significant impact. Together with the force of events, protest informed the thinking of the intellectual and opinion-making communities, whose support is vital to any president, and thus helped to force Johnson and Nixon into deescalatory steps. Moreover, both presidents shaped policy partly on the calculation that Hanoi considered popular opposition in America as a factor in its favor.[43]

The role of J. William Fulbright (D-AR) who, as chairman of the Senate Foreign Relations Committee emerged as the leading congressional critic of the war, has been most fully analyzed by William C. Berman. Presenting Fulbright's opposition within the framework of his realist approach to foreign policy, Berman details his tireless role, both through his writings and through the Foreign Relations Committee, to educate Americans about the folly of the war and, more generally, about mindless militant anticommunism. It took longer than Fulbright and other doves had anticipated to reassert congressional prerogatives, but in 1973 the curtailment of the Cambodian campaign and the passage of the War Powers Resolution constituted important victories.[44]

The conclusions reached by Daniel Hallin in *The "Uncensored War"* and by William Hammond in *The Military and the Media* refute revisionist claims regarding biased reporting. Hallin's analysis of selected newspaper and television coverage finds that the media as an establishment institution represented, rather than determined, public opinion. Coverage of the war in the *New York Times* and on network news supported the U.S. effort through 1967; afterward, stories became more skeptical, but by that time the war was a topic of legitimate controversy. Hammond's study, a volume in the army's history of the war that stresses the dilemmas facing the military's information officers, criticizes coverage for a lack of depth but also emphasizes the accuracy of the media, especially when contrasted with the Johnson administration's record of concealments and circumlocutions. Most television coverage was banal and stylized, and Hammond questions its impact on public opinion.[45]

---

[43]Melvin Small, *Johnson, Nixon, and the Doves* (New Brunswick, 1988).

[44]Preceding Berman's work were studies by Eugene Brown, who also integrates Fulbright's ideas and actions and reaches similar conclusions, and by Lee Riley Powell, who highlights the contents of the Fulbright committee's hearings on Asian policy. William C. Berman, *William Fulbright and the Vietnam War: The Dissent of a Political Realist* (Kent, OH, 1988); Eugene Brown, *J. William Fulbright: Advice and Dissent* (Iowa City, 1985); Lee Riley Powell, *J. William Fulbright and America's Lost Crusade: Fulbright's Opposition to the Vietnam War* (Little Rock, 1984).

Congress and the war has received little attention. The role of Republicans, especially their congressional leaders, in the debate over Vietnam policy has been studied by Terry Dietz. The war strained the party's commitment to bipartisanship and caused divisions within its ranks, thus preventing it from playing an effective opposition role. As House minority leader, Gerald Ford was an exception; his probing of Johnson's policy contrasted sharply to the deference shown Johnson by his friend, Senate minority leader Everett Dirksen. Terry Dietz, *Republicans and Vietnam, 1961–1968* (Westport, 1986).

[45]Daniel C. Hallin, *The "Uncensored War": The Media and Vietnam* (New York, 1986); William M. Hammond, *Public Affairs: The Military and the Media, 1962–1968* (Washington, 1988).

Besides the attention to events in the United States, scholars have also focused on Vietnam—the nature of warfare, the struggle for the South Vietnamese countryside, and the conflict from the "other side." Perhaps the best account of a single battle is Harold Moore and Joseph Galloway's *We Were Soldiers Once . . . and Young*, which recounts the Ia Drang Valley campaign of November 1965 in which American and North Vietnamese regular units met for the first time and from which both sides drew "lessons" that guided subsequent warfare. Moore and Galloway base their compelling narrative on interviews with American and North Vietnamese veterans. They conclude their account of the brutal combat with a final chapter outlining the "lessons" each side took from the encounter. While the North Vietnamese learned that they could withstand mobile air power, the American command read the twelve-to-one casualty ratio and incorrectly deduced that "they could bleed the enemy to death over the long haul, with a war of attrition." Alone among civilian officials, McNamara recognized that the war had changed as the stalemate at Ia Drang signaled a long and costly war.[46]

A number of notable studies have analyzed the ensuing air and ground war. In *The Limits of Air Power: The American Bombing of North Vietnam*, Mark Clodfelter challenges the air force's central historical "lesson," that "airpower can be strategically decisive if its application is intense, continuous, and focused on the enemy's vital systems." Clodfelter's argument rests on two main points: (1) The ineffectiveness of Operation Rolling Thunder reflected inherent limitations on strategic bombing and the ineptitude of military, as much as civilian, leaders; (2) The Linebacker campaign is an inappropriate model of what air power could have achieved earlier, since it "worked" because Nixon had the limited objective of facilitating U.S. withdrawal and because the North Vietnamese had shifted to conventional warfare. On the politics of the bombing, Clodfelter's work complements James Clay Thompson's earlier study, *Rolling Thunder*, which employs organizational theory to explain the air force's resistance to evidence of the bombing campaign's failure.[47]

The air war in the South has been analyzed in John Schlight's *Years of the Offensive*, a volume in the air force history, and in Donald J. Mrozek's *Air Power and the Ground War in Vietnam*. Both find that the air force handled its tactical mission effectively and innovatively. But Mrozek, in the more critical analysis, concludes that although the air war enabled the United States to wage the ground conflict with fewer troops, at most it helped to avoid defeat rather than to bring victory. An especially controversial aspect of the air war was Operation Ranch Hand, which between 1962 and 1971 sprayed some eighteen million gallons of chemicals in the South. William Buckingham's *Operation Ranch Hand*, another volume in the air force history, explains the

---

[46]Harold G. Moore and Joseph L. Galloway, *We Were Soldiers Once . . . and Young: Ia Drang—The Battle That Changed the War in Vietnam* (New York, 1992), 339. Moore does not limit his criticism to Westmoreland. Instead, like almost all other commanders in Vietnam, he questions the limitations placed on military operations that allowed the retreating North Vietnamese to take sanctuary in Cambodia.

[47]Mark Clodfelter, *The Limits of Air Power: The American Bombing of North Vietnam* (New York, 1989), 209; James Clay Thompson, *Rolling Thunder: Understanding Policy and Program Failure* (Chapel Hill, 1980).

expansion of the defoliation campaign as a function of escalation as well as the controversy surrounding the political, military, and ecological effects of the defoliants themselves. Richard L. Stevens is outspoken on the ecological issue and the futility of bombing. His study, *The Trail: A History of the Ho Chi Minh Trail and the Role of Nature in the War in Viet Nam*, asserts that bombing was doomed to fail, for the North Vietnamese had the advantage of nature and were able to change the trail to meet their needs. The Americans gained only a tragic "victory" over nature through the bombing's massive ecological damage.[48]

Ronald Spector's *After Tet* offers analysis not only of the neglected bloodshed of the year after the Tet Offensive but of the entire nature of the ground war. In many ways, this book is the most comprehensive integration of the conflict's political and military dimensions. Nineteen sixty-eight began and ended in stalemate, suggesting a repetition on the battlefield and in military thinking more akin to World War I than other modern wars. Each side was convinced that the other was about to capitulate and that victory would result from maintaining the offensive. Hence, the North Vietnamese undertook three subsequent offensives in the year after Tet and suffered enormous losses. Meanwhile, the United States continued inconclusive operations that reflected "the lack of any systematic attempt to pass on lessons or develop doctrine." Moreover, the South Vietnamese army had learned "how to rule, but not how to fight." In Spector's assessment, the "battles of 1968 were decisive . . . because they were so indecisive," for the stalemate benefited North Vietnam. Hence, the American position steadily eroded, as military morale declined in a morass of drug abuse and racial tensions and as the Communists rebuilt their forces and shadow governments in the countryside.[49]

Jeffrey Clarke's study of Vietnamization, a volume in the Department of the Army's history, reinforces Spector's findings. Clarke's study of the army's advisory role sees Vietnamization as clarifying U.S. objectives for ARVN and fostering American-ARVN operational cooperation. Evidence of military progress, however, was offset by ARVN's continuing lack of mobility and by its dependence on U.S. air and sea power. The ultimate failure was that no one believed ARVN could withstand an assault from the North on its own. Thus, Vietnamization, like earlier advisory phases, reflected an effort that may have been "hopeless from the start . . . [for] it was beyond the capacity of one power to reform and reshape the society of another." Vietnamization could equip ARVN, but it could not buy a will to fight.[50]

All sides in the conflict believed that what was happening in South Vietnam's villages was vital to the war's outcome. Several efforts have been made to examine political developments in rural areas, but the body of such

---

[48]John Schlight, *The United States Air Force in Southeast Asia: The War in South Vietnam: The Years of the Offensive, 1965–1968* (Washington, 1988); Donald J. Mrozek, *Air Power and the Ground War in Vietnam: Ideas and Actions* (Washington, 1989); William Buckingham, *Operation Ranch Hand: The Air Force and Herbicides in Southeast Asia, 1961–1971* (Washington, 1981); Richard L. Stevens, *The Trail: A History of the Ho Chi Minh Trail and the Role of Nature in the War in Viet Nam* (New York, 1993).

[49]Ronald H. Spector, *After Tet: The Bloodiest Year in Vietnam* (New York, 1993), 116, 313.

[50]Jeffrey J. Clarke, *United States Army in Vietnam. Advice and Support: The Final Years, 1965–1973* (Washington, 1988), 521.

work, by definition, remains fragmented and limited by the scant availability of documentation. The few studies thus far completed suggest that the NLF had greater strength than the Saigon government and that American-South Vietnamese pacification programs, often flawed in their basic assumptions, had little effect. Vietnamization, it also seems, may have weakened the insurgency, but it did not necessarily bring attendant gains for the Saigon government.

In *The Endless War*, James Harrison traces the resiliency of Vietnamese communism and attributes its ultimate success to a program of determined organization in the South during the 1950s and 1960s. Examining village level work in three Mekong Delta provinces, Harrison argues that the entrenched Communists managed to survive Diem's anti-Communist campaign.[51] Among the provinces included in Harrison's study is Long An, and, for that part of his work, Harrison draws on Jeffrey Race's pioneering 1972 study, *War Comes to Long An*, which documents the insurgency's success in virtually eliminating the South Vietnamese government's presence by 1965 and how subsequent American and South Vietnamese military operations and reform efforts only further alienated the peasantry.[52]

Race completed his work in 1968, just as pacification was gaining renewed emphasis, and subsequent studies suggest that such efforts had negligible impact. Adjacent to Long An was the province of Hau Nghia, the locale Eric Bergerud studies in *The Dynamics of Defeat*. Detailing the various efforts of Americans and South Vietnamese in Hau Nghia from 1963 to 1973, Bergerud finds that the "difficulties [the Americans] faced were virtually beyond solution." Nothing could overcome the Saigon government's lack of legitimacy, which meant that while the NLF was weakened by the Phoenix campaign of 1969–1973, the Saigon government could not replace it. The rural population generally, and especially the "best and the brightest" among young people, supported the NLF, which derived its strength from its legacy of struggle and its promise of a better future. Finally, the Americans and the South Vietnamese were caught in the contradictions of the use of military force; it was the only means of attacking NLF strongholds, but it caused great suffering and destruction, which the NLF turned to its advantage.[53]

James Trullinger's *Village at War*, based on research in a different part of South Vietnam and at a later time, yields similar findings. Conducting interviews in a village near Hue from 1974 until overwhelmed by events in 1975, Trullinger stresses Communist resiliency. My Thuy Phuong was atypical in that the U.S. Army in 1968 had established an airmobile base there that brought ten thousand Americans into a village normally populated by seventy-six hundred Vietnamese. Reconstructing the history of the struggle in this village, Trullinger finds that most of the village's inhabitants were disdainful of ARVN, sympathized with the activities of the insurgents, identified with

---

51 James P. Harrison, *The Endless War: Fifty Years of Struggle for Independence in Vietnam* (New York, 1989).

52 Jeffrey Race, *War Comes to Long An: Revolutionary Conflict in a Vietnamese Province* (Berkeley, 1972).

53 Eric M. Bergerud, *The Dynamics of Defeat: The Vietnam War in Hau Nghia Province* (Boulder, 1991), 3.

their bold strikes in the Tet Offensive, and saw during the 1972 Easter offensive ARVN's continued dependency on the United States.[54]

The pacification efforts of the Marine Corps, which had a tradition of such operations, have been cited by some of the hearts-and-minds revisionists as a model that should have been applied widely in Vietnam. Michael E. Peterson concurs, but with reservations. In *The Combined Action Platoons: The U.S. Marines' Other War in Vietnam*, Peterson, a veteran of such operations in Vietnam, asserts that Westmoreland's application of the traditional army emphasis on warfare against "partisans" who are seen as dependent on an external country misinterpreted Vietnamese insurgency. The search-and-destroy strategy "declared war against peasant society [and] . . . the United States irretrievably lost that war." Peterson goes on to criticize the Marine Corps leadership for failing to devote greater manpower to the pacification and to document a record of success disproportionate to the limited commitment. Yet he also concludes that a nationwide program would not have been successful; at best, firepower "with an eye to protecting—rather than disrupting—the hamlets [meant that] we would not have lost the war so terribly as we did."[55]

Robert Chandler's study of U.S. propaganda programs, *War of Ideas*, likewise suggests the enormity, if not the impossibility, of the American challenge in the countryside. In 1965 the Joint United States Public Affairs Office (JUSPAO) effectively became the information agency of the Saigon government and managed a prodigious outpouring of printed communications (at the rate of fifteen hundred for every Vietnamese) as well as radio and television programming to all parts of the country. Most JUSPAO propaganda was directed toward enlisting Southern support for the Saigon government and undermining the morale and credibility of the Vietcong. The results were disappointing, in part because JUSPAO's personnel were poorly trained and culturally insensitive, in part because its propaganda was not targeted to specific groups. In a larger sense, the propaganda campaign failed precisely because it was an American, not a Vietnamese, program.[56]

The most systematic, and controversial, pacification effort was the Phoenix program, which became a cornerstone of Vietnamization. Criticized as amounting to a program of political assassination and defended by officials led by William Colby and Robert Komer as a model that ought to have been employed earlier, the program has received reasonably balanced appraisals from Stuart Herrington and Dale Andrade. Both see it as making significant inroads against the Vietcong but also as limited by the long-standing hostility between the South Vietnamese government and the rural population. In *Silence Was a Weapon*, Herrington, who served in 1971–72 as a Phoenix program officer in Hau Nghia Province west of Saigon, contends that the Phoenix operation was generally discriminating and successful in terms of

---

[54]James Walker Trullinger, *Village at War: An Account of Revolution in Vietnam* (New York, 1980).

[55]Michael E. Peterson, *The Combined Action Platoons: The U.S. Marines' Other War in Vietnam* (Westport, 1989), 19, 125.

[56]Robert W. Chandler, *War of Ideas: The U.S. Propaganda Campaign in Vietnam* (Boulder, 1981).

eliminating the Vietcong infrastructure, but it was undermined by the resistance and corruption of South Vietnamese officials and the resultant cynicism of the peasantry toward the Saigon government. Andrade's *Ashes to Ashes* details several Phoenix operations between 1968 and 1971 and finds that they decimated the Vietcong infrastructure at the village level, only to be limited by the hostility of South Vietnamese provincial officials' hostility to it and by the shift toward conventional warfare, which made pacification less relevant.[57]

The Land-to-the-Tiller program constituted another belated effort at securing Saigon's rural base of support. Charles Callison's field-research based study of the program from 1971 to 1974 in relatively secure, pro-government Mekong Delta villages concludes that it brought social and economic changes that enhanced political stability.[58]

If there is one thing on which virtually all accounts agree it is that the United States faced a determined enemy. Although documentation is limited, several works have made use of existing materials to examine Hanoi's strategy and its implementation. In compiling *Portrait of the Enemy*, David Chanoff and Doan Van Toai interviewed Vietnamese refugees, including Vietcong and North Vietnamese army veterans, and drew upon recorded interrogations of prisoners. In a book in which participants in the war do most of the talking, Chanoff and Toai conclude that although the Communist leadership engaged in "utter ruthlessness and massive social manipulation," it succeeded because of "the nature of the human material it had to work with" and its compelling patriotic vision. Hundreds of thousands displayed a "quixotic disregard for the impossible ... throw[ing] themselves into the perils, accepting the terrible risks in exchange for a very distant glimpse of something better."[59] Drawing principally upon RAND Corporation interviews with prisoners of war and defectors, Michael Lanning and Dan Cragg, in *Inside the VC and the NVA*, similarly underscore the effectiveness of North Vietnam's tactics, logistics, recruitment, and organization. Attention to the military basics resulted in a mobile, committed, disciplined, and well-equipped fighting force.[60]

---

[57]Stuart A. Herrington, *Silence Was a Weapon: The Vietnam War in the Villages, A Personal Perspective* (Novato, CA, 1982); Dale Andrade, *Ashes to Ashes: The Phoenix Program and the Vietnam War* (Lexington, MA, 1990). For recent criticisms of the Phoenix program see Zolin Grant, *Facing the Phoenix: The CIA and the Political Defeat of the United States in Vietnam* (New York, 1991); and Douglas Valentine, *The Phoenix Program* (New York, 1990).

In *Lost Victory* and *The Bureaucracy at Work*, Colby and Komer, respectively, argue that the Phoenix program illustrated how the war could have been won earlier and at greatly reduced costs. Had the United States given priority to pacification during the 1955–1963 period and had it not betrayed the South's most effective leader, Ngo Dinh Diem, the Vietcong would not have been able to build their considerable strength in the rural areas. Defending the Phoenix program that he directed against charges that it amounted to little more than a campaign of terrorism and political assassination, Colby sees the ends justifying the means. The CIA and the South Vietnamese accomplished what the army's search-and-destroy ignored: the need to confront the Communist insurgents on their own terms. Robert W. Komer, *Bureaucracy at War: U.S. Performance in the Vietnam Conflict* (Boulder, 1986); William E. Colby, *Lost Victory: A First Hand Account of America's Sixteen Year Involvement in Vietnam* (Chicago, 1989).

[58]Charles Stuart Callison, *Land-to-the-Tiller in the Mekong Delta: Economic, Social and Political Effects of Land Reform in Four Villages of South Vietnam* (Lanham, MD, 1983).

[59]David Chanoff and Doan Van Toai, *Portrait of the Enemy* (New York, 1986), 209.

[60]Michael Lee Lanning and Dan Cragg, *Inside the VC and the NVA: The Real Story of North Vietnam's Armed Forces* (New York, 1992).

Several works trace the reason for the Communist success to an effective integration of political and military strategy that built on a nationalist tradition. The principal contribution of Gabriel Kolko's massive *Anatomy of a War: Vietnam, the United States, and the Modern Historical Experience* is its analysis of "the Revolution's" political-military strategy against an American intervention that was driven by the need to control revolutionary regimes in the Third World. Kolko contrasts America's imprecise objectives and mindless warfare and the attendant shallowness of the South Vietnamese regime with the North's dedicated and disciplined cadres and the mass mobilization that characterized Northern society. If the North's victory was inevitable, it was facilitated by the limits placed on the use of American power, a fact plainly evident in how the war's devastating effect on the U.S. economy forced deescalation. The Tet Offensive, while costing the Communist forces heavily, guaranteed that they would not be defeated.[61]

William Duiker's *The Communist Road to Power in Vietnam* offers a similar, but more even handed, appraisal of Hanoi's response to American warfare and ultimate victory. The groundwork was laid by the Communist party's ability to organize and direct an insurgency that exploited "the pervasive sense of malaise through[out] South Vietnamese society, the legacy of a generation of failure by successive governments to build the foundations of a viable non-Communist state." The ultimate success of the Communist party resulted from its commitment to a comprehensive strategy of people's war that linked nationalism with social reform and built on the leadership of Ho Chi Minh—"an unusual composite of moral leader and organizational genius, half Gandhi, half Lenin."[62]

Douglas Pike, although decidedly not sympathetic to the Communists, also writes respectfully of their success in unconventional warfare, which he attributes to a capacity to exploit the enemy's weakness and to integrate political-military strategy. The latter, labeled Dau Tranh, a "strategy for which there is no known counterstrategy," eliminated distinctions between combatants and civilians and prolonged the struggle to dishearten the enemy. But despite the cogency of the strategy, Pike, unlike Kolko, rejects any suggestion that it assured victory. He embraces instead a revisionist perspective, similar to that of Lomperis in *The War Everyone Lost—and Won*, that the war was more "lost" by Americans than "won" by the North Vietnamese. The Americans and South Vietnamese, he argues, won the armed struggle because ARVN was still intact by 1975, but the "political dau tranh gauntlet was never actually picked up; no comprehensive counterstrategy was ever developed, and the effort that was made failed."[63]

Dismissing Pike's work as a "not very promising venture into Vietnamese metaphysics" and contending that Western scholars generally have paid insufficient attention to the People's Army, Greg Lockhart, in *Nation in Arms*, traces the simultaneous evolution of the political and military arms of Vietnamese nationalism from 1940 to 1954. In a situation where struggle was

[61]Gabriel Kolko, *Anatomy of a War: Vietnam, the United States, and the Modern Historical Experience* (New York, 1985).

[62]William J. Duiker, *The Communist Road to Power in Vietnam* (Boulder, 1981), 319, 323.

[63]Douglas Pike, *PAVN: People's Army of Vietnam* (Novato, CA, 1986), 55, 127, 251.

the only way to attain nationhood, the army played a central role in defining the power of the state. Detailing the history of the army from its origins in the World War II guerrilla bases and the August revolution to its integrative role in the subsequent struggle against the French culminating at Dien Bien Phu, Lockhart finds that not only did the People's Army "[grow] as a manifestation as well as an instrument of the *legitimate* power of the Vietnamese nation-state" but that it was also "the central reason for the outcome of the Vietnam War."[64]

Ken Post's multivolume *Revolution, Socialism and Nationalism in Viet Nam*, although written with certain acknowledged biases, offers a remarkably comprehensive overview of the revolution, which was a struggle for both liberation and social transformation and which the United States sought to contain. Offering what he describes as "an independent Marxist viewpoint," Post criticizes most other Western analyses of Vietnamese nationalism for being unsympathetic toward communism and contends that R. B. Smith's international history minimizes the internal forces that led to conflict. While stressing the development of the Vietnamese Communist party, Post also emphasizes its relationship to China and the Soviet Union, which provided political and material support and, equally important, ideological guidance. Indeed, the ideological connection is central to Post's view of the Vietnamese revolution's significance. "The Hanoi leaders['] . . . skill in combining Marxist-Leninist internationalism with . . . Vietnamese patriotism," he argues, "made theirs the quintessential national liberation movement of the twentieth century."[65]

Post's fourth volume, *The Failure of Counter-Insurgency, 1961–1965*, is the only one devoted principally to U.S. involvement. Predictably, Post foresees U.S. efforts as effectively futile. Like some revisionists, Post faults the American military leadership's emphasis on the military, and not on the economic, component of counterinsurgency and argues that the overthrow of the Diem regime was a major mistake in terms of U.S. interests. Yet the American ability to influence the situation was limited, for historical developments were working to the advantage of the Communist revolution. Despite his bias and Marxist fondness for an endless sequence of "contradictions," Post offers a substantial analysis of Hanoi's worldview and its response to changes inside and beyond Vietnam.[66]

With the opening of more documents and the coming of more reflective scholarship, the literature on the Vietnam War will refine some of the contentions dividing the neo-orthodox and revisionist views, and eventually a fuller synthesis will emerge. The more conspiratorial and "if only" aspects of revisionism traditionally are relegated to the fringes of scholarship, and that will likely be true in the case of the writing on the Vietnam War. The

---

[64]Greg Lockhart, *Nation in Arms: The Origins of the People's Army of Vietnam* (Wellington, Australia, 1991), 1, 11 (emphasis in original).

[65]Ken Post, *Revolution, Socialism and Nationalism in Viet Nam*, Vol. 1, *An Interrupted Revolution* (Aldershot, England, 1989), xiii; Vol. 4, *The Failure of Counter-Insurgency in the South, 1961–1965* (Aldershot, England, 1990), 324.

[66]Post, *Revolution, Socialism and Nationalism in Viet Nam*, Vol. 2, *Viet Nam Divided* (Aldershot, England, 1989); Vol. 3, *Socialism in Half a Country* (Aldershot, England, 1989).

Clausewitzians' prescription for retrospective victory has been criticized for minimizing the Vietnamese and international politics of the war, but their attention to a variety of command, logistical, and bureaucratic problems is likely to remain a part of the military histories. Likely also to have a lasting impact is the hearts-and-minders' indictment of the military leadership's approach to the war and of the flawed approach to pacification. The legitimacists should force fuller attention to the range of competing international interests at stake in Vietnam (which rarely receives much attention in neo-orthodox accounts) and to the "better side" of the Diem government, but whether they will convince future scholars to embrace the conclusions that the international situation demanded U.S. military intervention or that Diem deserved unswerving U.S. support is more problematic. The useful work done thus far on the Vietnamese "sides" speaks to the need for more research on the wide range of social, political, economic, and military issues that helped to define and shape the struggle. Such scholarship will underscore that the conflict was a "long war . . . a trauma . . . an ordeal . . . a tragedy" even more for Vietnamese than for Americans. Only then can historians approach a genuine synthesis that addresses one of the major events of the twentieth century in its Vietnamese, American, and international dimensions.

Review Article

America and Vietnam: The Debate Continues

GEORGE C. HERRING

R. B. Smith, **An International History of the Vietnam War: The Kennedy Strategy** (New York, 1985).
George McT. Kahin, Intervention: **How America Became Involved in Vietnam** (New York, 1986).
Gabriel Kolko, **Anatomy of a War: Vietnam, the United States, and the Modern Historical Experience** (New York, 1985).

WRITING IN THIS JOURNAL MORE THAN TEN YEARS AGO, Warren F. Kimball identified a pattern in the historiography of wars or diplomatic crises: a first stage in which official or semi-official history written during or soon after the event is challenged by revisionist accounts, often partisan in motivation and hypercritical in tone; a second stage comprised of scholarly responses to revisionism, often incorporating some revisionist arguments, followed in turn by a more scholarly form of revisionism; ultimately, after the dust has settled and passions subsided, a third stage of "eclectic synthesis."[1] The historiography of American involvement in the Vietnam war is following a variation of this pattern with some unusual twists. In the case of a war discredited long before it ended, the orthodox or, at least, generally accepted position was "revisionist" in the sense that it sharply attacked American intervention as unnecessary and even immoral and accused American leaders of deceiving the nation into an unwanted war. Thus, the first wave of revisionism that developed in the late 1970s ironically comprised a spirited and frequently emotional defense of the war and U.S. policy.[2]

The three books reviewed here belong to the second stage. Controversy persists, much as it did during the war, and passions still run high. The issues remain much the same, and positions have been modified only slightly, if at all. But the debate has increasingly moved into the realm of scholarship. These three lengthy

The author gratefully acknowledges the assistance of Professors Richard H. Immerman of the University of Hawaii and Warren F. Kimball of Rutgers University, Newark, who read an earlier version of this essay and offered numerous helpful suggestions.

[1] Warren F. Kimball, "The Cold War Warmed Over," *AHR*, 79 (October 1974): 1119.

[2] Major revisionist works include Guenter Lewy, *America in Vietnam* (New York, 1978); and Norman Podhoretz, *Why We Were in Vietnam* (New York, 1982). For useful critiques of revisionism, see Walter LaFeber, "The Last War, the Next War, and the New Revisionists," *democracy*, 1 (January 1981): 93–103; Paul M. Kattenburg, "Reflections on Vietnam: Of Revisionism and Lessons Yet to Be Learned," *Parameters*, 14 (Autumn 1984): 42–50; and George C. Herring, "The 'Vietnam Syndrome' and American Foreign Policy," *Virginia Quarterly Review*, 57 (Autumn 1981): 594–612.

accounts, totaling more than 1,500 pages, are based on a comprehensive array of sources. Each expands our knowledge of the war in important ways. They represent diverse points of view and, in that sense, continue the debate on the war, but the authors develop their arguments in much greater depth and with much greater sophistication than did earlier commentators.

The issues on which writers are now divided are essentially those that Americans debated during the war. A fundamental concern remains the nature of the war itself. Was it primarily a nationalist struggle, a civil war among Vietnamese, or did it owe as much or more to the cold war conflict between communism and democratic capitalism? How did it begin and who was responsible? Why did the United States make an enormous commitment in an area remote and seemingly insignificant, and can this commitment be defended on grounds of morality or national security? A final and especially controversial issue revolves around the outcome. Did the United States fail because it did not apply sufficient power or because it employed its power improperly, as conservative revisionists now argue? Was domestic dissent in the United States an important or even decisive factor in the outcome? Or was the war decided more by conditions in Vietnam than by what the United States did or did not do? Were these conditions in fact so intractable as to make the war unwinnable as far as the United States was concerned?

RALPH SMITH SEEKS TO PLACE EVENTS IN INDOCHINA in a broad international context. A specialist in Southeast Asia at the University of London, he applies, for the period from December of 1961 to March of 1965, a thesis originally developed in the first volume of a multi-volume series, namely, that the Vietnam war "was the product of a global pattern of conflict which must be analyzed in global terms."[3] Here, in Volume 2, he looks at each side in turn. On the U.S.–South Vietnamese side, he relies primarily on the *Pentagon Papers* and other standard printed sources. He uses Chinese, North Vietnamese, and Soviet radio broadcasts, as well as newspapers, pamphlets, and some captured North Vietnamese documents to analyze the Communist side. U.S. decisions on Vietnam are discussed in the context of world developments, especially events in Southeast Asia and most notably in Indonesia. Decisions the North Vietnamese and National Liberation Front made are discussed in the context of international communism, especially relations with the Soviet Union and China. Smith often discusses U.S. policies and actions in one chapter, Communist in the next.

Smith's arguments place him on the right of the political spectrum. He does not defend U.S. intervention on moral grounds, as conservative revisionists do, and his arguments are complex, in some places sophisticated, but the tone of the book is distinctly revisionist. He blames the war on North Vietnam and its allies, China and the Soviet Union. He defends U.S. escalation, and by implication at least,

[3] R. B. Smith, *An International History of the Vietnam War: The Kennedy Strategy* (New York, 1985), 3. The first volume was published as R. B. Smith, *An International History of the Vietnam War: Revolution versus Containment, 1955–1961* (New York, 1984).

suggests that it was not forceful enough. His handling of controversial issues such as the Tonkin Gulf incident best reveals his political bias.

Smith takes the cold war seriously. He does not attempt to revive the discredited notion of a Communist monolith, and he readily concedes that the Soviet Union and China did not instigate and could not control the war in Vietnam. But he ascribes to Hanoi, Peking, and Moscow greater unity of purpose and action than many scholars have allowed. He accepts at face value the postwar assertions of the Hanoi regime that it controlled and directed the revolution in South Vietnam from the outset. He concedes that Hanoi's decisions were not based on directives from Peking or Moscow, but he insists that North Vietnam could not have succeeded without assistance from its major allies and speculates that "in some cases the decisions of one Party may well have been predicated on those of another."[4] He even suggests that in 1964 there may have been "some kind of tacit understanding" between the Soviet Union and China by which the Russians pursued *détente* with the West while China pushed for revolution in Asia.[5] In any event, he insists, the United States gravely erred in viewing Moscow as indifferent to the struggle in Southeast Asia.

Smith defends U.S. intervention on grounds of *realpolitik*. He flatly rejects the liberal-dove argument that the commitment resulted from blind anticommunism or from a "self-imposed, purely bilateral obligation to defend South Vietnam."[6] Rather, he contends, the Communists posed a real challenge to the global position of the United States in the 1960s, and their intransigence left no way out of Vietnam for either President Kennedy or Johnson except on terms that would have amounted to surrender. He emphasizes the importance of Vietnam to Southeast Asia as a whole. The United States had vital and legitimate economic and strategic interests in the region, especially in Indonesia. South Vietnam was the "key link" in preserving those interests, and the purpose of U.S. policy was to "ensure sufficient stability in Indonesia and Malaysia—in the short as well as the longer term—to allow investment and economic growth to take place."[7]

To meet the threat to these interests, Kennedy began, in December of 1961, to implement a strategy of counterinsurgency. The purpose was to hold the line against Communist expansion in Vietnam while limiting the war to South Vietnam in order to demonstrate that a national liberation movement could be defeated without escalating the conflict into a larger war. The strategy worked well enough for the short run, and, by late 1962, the overall U.S. position in Southeast Asia was much improved. The long-range effect of counterinsurgency was the opposite of what Kennedy had intended, however. Instead of abandoning South Vietnam North Vietnam (with Soviet and Chinese support) escalated the war, forcing Lyndon Johnson to do the same or risk the "loss" of Southeast Asia.

Smith's book stops just at the point where the Second Indochina War begins, and he does not directly address the reasons the United States ultimately failed. He

[4] Smith, *International History: The Kennedy Strategy*, 4.
[5] Smith, *International History: The Kennedy Strategy*, 17.
[6] Smith, *International History: The Kennedy Strategy*, 2.
[7] Smith, *International History: The Kennedy Strategy*, 143.

claims that the major purpose of his book is to determine why Kennedy's strategy of counterinsurgency did not work, but he never really answers the question beyond stating that it failed because the enemy was able to defeat it. In analyzing Johnson's policies, however, he aligns himself with conservative revisionists. Johnson's approach to the war brought the worst of all possible worlds, Smith claims. The bombing was "too big for Communist powers to ignore, yet too small to achieve a major impact on Hanoi."[8] "*Unfortunately,*" he writes elsewhere, "from spring 1964 until the end of his Administration the level of military pressure which Johnson deemed appropriate was never adequate, at any time, to force Hanoi to negotiate on terms he could accept."[9] Smith also minimizes the likelihood that China would have intervened, and so, by implication, he agrees with hawks at the time and revisionists later that a larger and more effective escalation was both necessary and feasible.

Smith's emphasis on the international dimensions of the war is welcome. The conflict is too often discussed in a vacuum, with the focus exclusively on Washington or Hanoi. It is useful to place U.S. decisions in the context of events in Laos, Indonesia, Cuba, and Berlin. Soviet and Chinese support was important to North Vietnamese decisions and success. Smith produces some provocative interpretations. The support of the new Soviet government of Brezhnev and Kosygin in late 1964 was crucial to escalation of the war, he contends, because it made available to North Vietnam the military technology it had to have in a war with the United States. Despite U.S. impressions to the contrary, Smith argues persuasively, China preferred at this stage to keep the war limited to South Vietnam, but it could not restrain its ally without appearing to be less supportive than its Soviet rival. Thus, the Sino-Soviet split was an important factor in the emergence of a larger war.

Smith often strains his limited evidence past the breaking point to prove his thesis of international connections. Without providing documentation, he suggests that Peking may have encouraged the North Vietnamese to mount the attacks that led to the Tonkin Gulf incident. Similarly, he speculates that, in early 1965, Moscow encouraged the North Vietnamese to launch the raids that provoked Johnson to authorize the bombing of North Vietnam on a regular basis, which permitted the Soviets to appear to be responding to U.S. aggression. Again and again, Smith resorts to argument by innuendo. He admits there is no evidence for the second alleged attack in the Tonkin Gulf on 4 August 1964, but he goes on to insist that "it is impossible for the historian to dismiss it out of hand." Arguing on the basis of flimsy evidence that the first incident was deliberately provoked by Hanoi to keep tensions high, he contends that this "makes a second communist initiated incident highly credible."[10]

If Smith demonstrates the importance of studying the Communist side, he also makes clear how frustrating it is. His repeated use of qualification—"it appears,"

[8] Smith, *International History: The Kennedy Strategy*, 378.
[9] Smith, *International History: The Kennedy Strategy*, 272. The emphasis is mine.
[10] Smith, *International History: The Kennedy Strategy*, 297.

"almost certainly," "in all probability," "it may have been"—suggests the enormous problem in drawing firm conclusions about "the other side." The book delivers much less than it promises. Smith is fascinated with time lines, watersheds, and turning points. He finds too much congruity in disparate and unconnected events, and he often imposes order where none exists. In the crucial issues, his modified revisionism is no more convincing than the unqualified variety. He accepts without question the legitimacy of U.S. involvement, and he virtually ignores the existence of widespread non-Communist opposition to the Diem government in South Vietnam. He readily accepts North Vietnamese claims to have directed the revolution in the south, ignoring the differences between northern and southern revolutionaries and between Hanoi and the National Liberation Front.

GEORGE MCT. KAHIN'S *Intervention: How America Became Involved in Vietnam* differs with Smith on virtually every fundamental issue. This book is based on exhaustive research in newly declassified U.S. documents, and those of us who work in the field are deeply indebted to Kahin for securing the declassification of thousands of documents on Vietnam through the Freedom of Information Act in that short period when it was working reasonably well. Kahin has supplemented these documentary sources by interviews with numerous Vietnamese, including Buddhist leaders and former National Liberation Front officials. A distinguished Southeast Asian specialist, Kahin has been intimately involved with Vietnam for three decades, and *Intervention* is richly detailed and profusely documented.

Kahin analyzes in depth the major American decisions between 1945 and 1965, going beyond the *Pentagon Papers* and providing what may well be the authoritative account of U.S. escalation. In contrast to Smith, he plays down the North Vietnamese role in the origins of the Second Indochina War, a stance that makes a significant commentary on his assumptions, but his analysis of the South Vietnamese dimension of the emerging conflict sheds much light on an area that has long remained *terra incognita* to Americans. Kahin's position on the war has not changed substantially. His book *America in Vietnam* (co-authored with John Lewis) was a bible for opponents of the war in the 1970s, and he is now, as he was then, a vigorous and unrelenting exponent of the antiwar position.

In contrast to Smith, Kahin emphasizes the indigenous roots of the war. He minimizes to the point of exclusion the role of the Soviet Union and China. In the face of evidence made available since the end of the war, he retreats somewhat from the position he took in 1969 that the insurgency originated in the south at southern initiative and retained a considerable degree of independence from Hanoi. He concedes that the two "partook of the same nationalism," and that, "in the most fundamental sense," the National Liberation Front was subordinate to the party organization in Hanoi. But he insists that Hanoi's postwar claims to have directed the revolution from the outset have been inflated to meet its present needs—there is thus, he notes, an ironic and "striking convergence" of views between postwar revisionists in the United States and Vietnam. He continues to argue that the revolution erupted spontaneously in the south in the late 1950s and was supported only hesitantly and belatedly by the North Vietnamese. And he contends that differences persisted between the National Liberation Front and North Vietnam and indeed between southerners and northerners on the Central Committee in Hanoi.[11] He appears to believe, although he does not say it outright, that, in the absence of U.S. intervention or with greater U.S. flexibility, there was the possibility for an autonomous and neutralist South Vietnam.

Kahin attacks U.S. intervention on moral and strategic grounds. Vietnam was never of more than peripheral importance to the security of the United States, he contends. Economic interests were significant only to the extent that Vietnam was seen as a barrier to Chinese expansion into areas like Indonesia that, at times, were deemed important. Kahin stresses as the major causes of U.S. intervention the virulent anticommunism that gripped U.S. policymakers in the 1950s and 1960s, swollen estimates of global interests, concern that the "loss" of Vietnam, like China, might have disastrous political consequences domestically, and a pervasive fear among top policymakers of national and personal humiliation. He also persuasively refutes Leslie Gelb's and Daniel Ellsberg's thesis that American presidents acted from a position of weakness and sought only to keep South Vietnam afloat until the next election.[12] An abiding confidence in American power and a blind faith in success dictated major escalations.

Kahin offers a ringing response to those revisionists who have attributed U.S. failure to flawed military strategies or a lack of will. The essential reason the United States failed at each stage of its escalation, he insists, was that its efforts to sustain a client regime in Saigon ran up against the "tidal political force" of Vietnamese nationalism. History bequeathed the United States a flimsy base on which to build a government in South Vietnam, and the United States was able to do little more than construct an artificial society totally dependent on a continued inflow of American dollars. North Vietnam and the National Liberation Front, by contrast, displayed great "courage and stamina" in standing up against what "in the annals of warfare was an unprecedented tonnage of bombs and napalm."[13] Kahin deplores the massive and destructive use of U.S. power in what amounted to "an unprecedented effort to shape and control a country's political power."[14] He is certain that the greater use of force would only have caused more destruction, and he contends that Johnson's fears of Chinese intervention were well founded.

Kahin makes many important contributions. He has presented new evidence on American aid to France during the First Indochina War and makes clear that this aid was much greater than has been previously recognized. In many accounts of U.S. escalation, the Eisenhower administration has escaped censure, and President Eisenhower has been widely praised for not intervening in Vietnam at the time of the Dienbienphu crisis. Kahin argues persuasively that, in making commitments

[11] George McT. Kahin, *Intervention: How America Became Involved in Vietnam* (New York, 1986), 120–21. For comparison, see George McTurnan Kahin and John W. Lewis, *The United States in Vietnam*, rev. edn. (New York, 1969), 110–20.

[12] The Gelb-Ellsberg thesis is in Leslie Gelb and Richard K. Betts, *The Irony of Vietnam: The System Worked* (Washington, D.C., 1978); and in Daniel Ellsberg, *Papers on the War* (New York, 1972), 47–135.

[13] Kahin, *Intervention*, 249, 399.

[14] Kahin, *Intervention*, ix.

to the Diem regime in 1954 and 1955, the Eisenhower administration "moved assertively in a much more fundamental phase of intervention, and in doing so staked American honor and prestige on a policy that, once undertaken, was difficult to reverse."[15] He provides an excellent analysis of the U.S. nation-building program in the late 1950s, especially the Commercial Import Program. He offers a fresh and generally convincing account of the so-called Pentagon Coup, which brought Nguyen Khanh to power in early 1964, demonstrating that U.S. involvement was much deeper than has been thought and may even have been decisive. He is superb on politics in South Vietnam and highly informative on such things as the Buddhist struggle movement. Perhaps surprisingly, he is sympathetic toward Lyndon Johnson, portraying him as a man of great caution, the victim of commitments he had not made, swept along by forces he could not control.

In all respects the best of the three books reviewed here, Kahin's account is in some ways disappointing. The long discussion of U.S. escalation between January, 1964 and August, 1965 constitutes more than half the book but adds remarkably little to what was already known. The emphasis of the book, curiously, is on U.S. policy, which is not the author's primary area of expertise, and one wishes he had devoted more attention to the Vietnamese side, about which he writes with great authority.

In terms of his stated purpose—to explain how the United States intervened—Kahin succeeds admirably, but his restricted focus results in an account as incomplete in its own way as that of Smith. The National Liberation Front and especially the North Vietnamese are virtually invisible in these pages, and, when mentioned, they are normally reacting to moves by the United States. Kahin fails to note steps taken by Hanoi in 1957 and 1959 to gain control of events in the south. He contends that America's initiation of the bombing and introduction of ground troops in early 1965 removed the constraints that had prevented North Vietnam from sending its own troops to the south. There is evidence to indicate, however, that North Vietnam decided to escalate the war as early as the end of 1963, and that it began to send regular units to the south as early as October, 1964.[16] Finally, Kahin makes the Communists seem more amenable to negotiations than they probably were.

By saying little about the Vietnamese and pinning exclusive responsibility on the United States, Kahin weakens an otherwise impressive argument. It is true that U.S. intervention was misguided, and that Hanoi, by virtue of its victory in the First Indochina War, had legitimate claims to national control. Still, to focus almost exclusively on the United States distorts the record. Had the Soviets and Chinese not supported North Vietnam, the war might not have escalated. Had it not escalated, the United States might have acted differently. It could even be argued that, like many other wars, the Second Indochina War began from monumental miscalculations on both sides. William Duiker has suggested that the North

[15] Kahin, *Intervention*, 92.

[16] On this point, see William J. Duiker, *The Communist Road to Power in Vietnam* (Boulder, Colo., 1981), 221–33.

Vietnamese escalated in 1964 on the gamble that, in South Vietnam as earlier in China, the United States would not send its own forces to uphold a client government. Most scholars agree Johnson went to war in 1965 with the expectation that Hanoi would not be able to stand up against American power.[17]

EVEN MORE THAN KAHIN, in *Anatomy of a War: Vietnam, the United States, and the Modern Historical Experience*, Gabriel Kolko still unabashedly articulates the views he developed in the 1960s, the radical critique of U.S. involvement in Vietnam. He has drawn some of his material from visits to Vietnam and discussions with "virtually hundreds of people who played every conceivable role in the war," but his footnotes reveal his reliance on an impressive range of standard historical sources, published and unpublished, American, French, and Vietnamese.[18] Unlike the other two books, Kolko's work is comprehensive, covering the entire war from 1945 to 1975 and evaluating the reasons for its outcome as well as its causes. To Kolko, ideology is more important than methodology and documentation. War, in his view, is at root a "struggle between competing social systems," and his neo-Marxian analysis is heavily weighted on the socioeconomic side.[19] The book is truly sweeping in scope and analyzes in depth the strategies, institutions, and social systems of the three principals: what he calls "the Revolution," comprising North Vietnam and the National Liberation Front, South Vietnam, and the United States. One of the book's major contributions is the detailed examination of the South Vietnamese economy, society, and political structure, matters too often neglected by American scholars but crucial to the outcome of the war.

With regard to the origins of the war, Kolko does not concern himself with the distinctions that Smith and Kahin debate. The various conflicts in Indochina were all part of a single revolutionary process. The Communist party was the instrument of that revolution, sometimes urging the people on, more often than not responding to their wishes. Relations between the revolution and the major Communist powers were "subtle and infinitely complex," he writes. It was often difficult for the Soviet Union and China to resolve the tensions between their national interests and ideological commitments, and the Democratic Republic of Vietnam used "acute analysis" and "brilliant finesse" to maneuver between its two allies and exploit their divisions to secure maximum aid.[20]

In discussing the reasons for U.S. intervention, Kolko agrees with Smith that the raw materials and markets of Southeast Asia were important to the United States, but, he argues, the key to U.S. policy was credibility, the "hypnotic justification which united virtually all those who shaped fundamental policy."[21] Minimizing

[17] Duiker, *Communist Road to Power*, 226.
[18] Gabriel Kolko, *Anatomy of a War: Vietnam, the United States, and the Modern Historical Experience* (New York, 1985), xv.
[19] Kolko, *Anatomy of a War*, 5.
[20] Kolko, *Anatomy of a War*, 401–11.
[21] Kolko, *Anatomy of a War*, 164.

policy differences among the various participants and the importance of personality in shaping policy, he sees U.S. involvement in Vietnam as a "natural outcome of the logic and objectives of its role in the modern era." The "major inheritor of the mantle of imperialism in modern history," the United States acted not to defend a threat to its welfare but because it "sought a controllable responsive order elsewhere, one that would permit the political destinies of distant places to evolve in a manner beneficial to American goals and interests far surpassing the immediate needs of its domestic society."[22] Maintaining credibility in Vietnam was essential to that end. Like Smith, Kolko takes the U.S. rationale for intervention seriously; unlike Smith, he sees it as counterrevolutionary and destructive and questions its legitimacy. Kolko holds the United States exclusively responsible for the war, as does Kahin. "It was for the United States . . . to resolve whether there would be war or peace in Vietnam," Kolko claims.[23]

In contrast to the other two books, *Anatomy of a War* goes through the end of the conflict, and Kolko provides the fullest explanation of the outcome. He agrees with revisionists that U.S. strategy was fundamentally flawed, but there the similarity ends. The basic problem, he contends, was the inability of the United States "to fight a cheap war or to afford a long expensive one."[24] Never comprehending the social forces at work but commanding an abundance of wealth and resources, U.S. leaders persistently relied on technology to compensate for political failure. They "unleashed the greatest flood of firepower against a nation known to history," causing in Vietnam "monumental" human suffering and social and economic dislocation.[25] This strategy proved prohibitively expensive, however, and by 1968 it was taking a heavy toll on the American economy, producing irresistible pressures for withdrawal.

While revisionists have focused on American failure—thereby challenging the view that the war was unwinnable—Kolko properly and persuasively emphasizes the Vietnamese dimension. The contrast he draws between the strength of the revolution and the weakness of the U.S. client state in South Vietnam is, though overstated, basically accurate. Lacking resources, the party had to rely on strategy. Its leaders perceived that people, not technology, made up the "core of the military art," and they acutely analyzed the balance of forces, effectively exploiting their own strengths and the enemy's weaknesses.[26] They retained the strategic and tactical initiative and kept U.S. and South Vietnamese forces dispersed and on the defensive. The North Vietnamese government mobilized the people as the South Vietnamese government never could. The People's Army of Vietnam's (PAVN) great strength was its mobility and flexibility, based, Kolko says, on the popular will.

The U.S. defeat was not, in the final analysis, primarily a defeat of arms but the result of failure to create a viable alternative to the National Liberation Front, and Kolko breaks new ground in analyzing the reasons for this failure. He explores the

[22] Kolko, *Anatomy of a War*, 72.
[23] Kolko, *Anatomy of a War*, 111.
[24] Kolko, *Anatomy of a War*, 291.
[25] Kolko, *Anatomy of a War*, 200.
[26] Kolko, *Anatomy of a War*, 146–49, 182–87.

problem of land tenure, and the social and economic disruptions caused by U.S. military actions. He probes the sources of the endemic corruption that made the system work and limited its effectiveness. He looks at the political machinery that Nguyen Van Thieu created and the chronic problems that afflicted the Army of the Republic of Vietnam. Kolko concludes that South Vietnam's leadership "was just a reflection of the crisis of Vietnamese society in this century and of the absence of a stable foundation for an indigenous ruling class. Dependent entirely on U.S. money and troops, it was now locked into a social transformation of a nation for which the only solution was a continuation of vast American subsidies and the American military presence."[27]

Kolko is saying, of course, that the superior social system won, and he minces no words in assessing the importance of the outcome. He concludes, in a flight of hyperbole, that the Vietnam war was more important for the United States than were World Wars I and II because it "exposed the ultimate constraints on its power in the modern era, its internal tensions, the contradictions between overinvolvement in one nation and its interests and ambitions elsewhere, and its material limits."[28] In contrast, the superior strategy developed by the Communists provides lessons to all those who challenge the United States in its "self-appointed counterrevolutionary mission in the Third World." The war confirmed the "awesome potential of men and women to define their own future against overwhelming opposition."[29] Presumably, similar American efforts elsewhere will meet the same fate.

Kolko's book is fundamentally flawed. It is painfully long, its prose turgid and repetitious. The last half of it, covering the period after the Tet Offensive, adds little that is new, and in general it is not as provocative as Kolko's earlier works, perhaps because the radical position on the war has already been fully articulated.

Kolko *is* forthright about his bias. He concedes his enthusiasm for "autonomous social development in the Third World" and admits that he "fully welcomed" Vietnam's success over the United States. But his claim that his partisanship does not stand in the way of "objective scholarship" is at best naive, at worst disingenuous.[30] He itemizes in great detail the countless "dark deeds" committed by the United States and South Vietnam while glossing over North Vietnamese and Vietcong atrocities. Local party activists sometimes became overzealous and violated orders, he says. In any event, "revolutionary morality did not require sainthood."[31] Throughout the book, he waxes lyrical about the glories of the revolution, while portraying the United States and its South Vietnamese clients as stupid and evil. Sometimes this contrast reaches ludicrous extremes, as when he uses the culinary accomplishments of the PAVN to demonstrate its institutional superiority.[32]

[27] Kolko, *Anatomy of a War*, 296.
[28] Kolko, *Anatomy of a War*, 545–48.
[29] Kolko, *Anatomy of a War*, 557.
[30] Kolko, *Anatomy of a War*, xiv.
[31] Kolko, *Anatomy of a War*, 537.
[32] "Among the captured or deserting revolutionary soldiers," he writes, "praise for the cooking was always high. Preparation of especially delicious meals before offensives was common, and even during combat good food was frequently available"; Kolko, *Anatomy of a War*, 257. This would certainly come as news to those soldiers who survived on such delicacies as jungle moths and dog and monkey meat.

n a number of important points, he is just plain wrong. For example, the Vietminh did not control 60 to 90 percent of the territory of southern Vietnam before the Geneva Conference. And it cannot be unequivocally established that the primary objective of the North Vietnamese Tet Offensive was to influence public opinion in the United States.[33]

Kolko is right in stressing the Vietnamese sources of American failure but wrong in the reasons he gives. North Vietnam's victory was less the product of its social system than of the iron will, fanatical determination, and organizational skills of its leaders, its superior strategy, and the threat to its survival that made possible the extraordinary mobilization of its people.[34] The skeptic, moreover, does not have to accept the central arguments of revisionism to ask, in light of the Kolko thesis, what has happened to the revolution since 1975 to bring about the party's dismal postwar failure and its atrocious human rights record. It is an issue he never raises.

BECAUSE OF THE SPECIFIC EMPHASIS, LIMITATION OF SCOPE OR TOPIC, AND BIAS in each of these books, none of them provides an entirely satisfactory account of a complex and controversial topic. Smith overstates the importance of international factors in the origins of the Second Indochina War and, by virtually ignoring those local forces that were ultimately decisive, leaves a distorted picture of the dynamics of the conflict. Minimizing the role of North Vietnam and the National Liberation Front, Kahin weakens an otherwise excellent analysis of American intervention. Despite his claims to the contrary, Kolko permits ideology and revolutionary enthusiasm to triumph over scholarship.

Taken together, these books move only a step beyond the contemporary debate, a common occurrence, it should be added, in the writing of the history of major conflicts. Twelve years after V-J Day, at a comparable point in the development of World War II historiography, Wayne S. Cole observed that the debate among historians on American entry into that war was to a considerable degree an extension of the pre-war debate on American intervention. "Writers of history have not only dealt with the same basic subject and issues," Cole noted, "but have also used the same arguments, made the same fundamental assumptions, advanced similar hypotheses."[35] Indeed, as Cole pointed out, many of the historians had been participants in the contemporary debate, and that is true in the case of two of the three authors reviewed here. In 1983, Fox Butterfield identified a major characteristic of what he called "the new Vietnam scholarship"—portrayal of the war as "more complex, more morally ambiguous, than either the

[33] For more reliable estimates of Vietminh strength prior to Geneva, see Duiker, *Communist Road to Power*, 164–65; and James Pinckney Harrison, *The Endless War* (New York, 1982), 124–26. Informed speculation about the motives for the Tet Offensive can be found in Robert Shaplen, *Time Out of Hand* (New York, 1970), 395–406; and Duiker, *Communist Road to Power*, 263–65.

[34] Duiker, *Communist Road to Power*, 322–29.

[35] Wayne S. Cole, "American Entry into World War II: A Historiographical Appraisal," *Mississippi Valley Historical Review*, 42 (March 1957): 600–01.

doves or hawks maintained."[36] If moral ambiguity is a touchstone, the books reviewed here obviously belong as much to the debate at the time of the war as to Kimball's second stage of scholarly dialogue.

These books also make clear that scholars are still sharply divided on Vietnam, and their divisions mirror deeper ideological and emotional conflicts among elite groups in the United States and across the world.[37] To a certain extent, of course, historians are never entirely able to shed the intellectual and emotional baggage that develops from the event itself. It is especially difficult to do so when the historical debate is closely linked with current foreign policy debates. It may be many years before Vietnam moves out of the realm of politics and into the realm of history. Kimball's "eclectic synthesis" seems unlikely to emerge until a generation comes along unaffected by Vietnam or until some major event replaces Vietnam as the watershed in American foreign policy. Such a synthesis may mean, as Kimball suggests, an effort to "approach the golden mean by extracting arguments and conclusions from all sides."[38] In the case of Vietnam, it is not likely to mean consensus or the end of debate.

"Ten years after the end of the war," Ronald H. Spector recently observed, "our knowledge of the Vietnam conflict is still incomplete and profoundly confused."[39] Many crucial sources remain unavailable.[40] Many vital topics remain uninvestigated. There is sharp disagreement, Spector noted, even on relatively simple and straightforward questions. It is both noteworthy and disturbing that historians have so far contributed relatively little to the study of the war, leaving the field to journalists, and there does not appear to be a great amount of research underway.[41]

A full agenda awaits those willing to take up the challenge. Recent works by William Duiker, David Marr, Douglas Pike, and Timothy Lomperis make clear what can be done with the Vietnamese sources now available, and there is a crying need for detailed, careful, and dispassionate analysis of the origins and conduct of the war from the side of the North Vietnamese and National Liberation Front.[42] Smith's study suggests the importance of a thorough assessment of North Vietnam's relations with its major allies. We now have a reasonably clear picture of how the United States got into Vietnam. We need more detailed and searching

[36] Fox Butterfield, "The New Vietnam Scholarship," *New York Times Magazine* (13 February 1983): 28.

[37] For an excellent analysis of the divisions among American leadership groups on Vietnam and the ways in which these divisions reflect broader and conflicting "belief systems," see Ole R. Holstri and James N. Rosenau, *American Leadership in World Affairs: Vietnam and the Breakdown of Consensus* (Boston, 1984).

[38] Kimball, "Cold War Warmed Over," 1119.

[39] Ronald H. Spector, "'What Did You Do in the War, Professor?,'" *American Heritage* (December 1986): 101.

[40] Useful introductions to available sources are Ronald H. Spector, *Researching the Vietnam Experience* (Washington, D.C., 1984); and George C. Herring, "Sources for Understanding the Vietnam Conflict," *Society for Historians of American Foreign Relations Newsletter*, 16 (March 1985): 8–30.

[41] On these points, see Spector, "'What Did You Do in the War?,'" 102; and Sandra C. Taylor, "Reporting History: Journalists and the Vietnam War," *Reviews in American History*, 13 (September 1985): 452–53.

[42] Duiker, *Communist Road to Power*; David Marr, *Vietnamese Tradition on Trial* (Berkeley, Calif., 1982); Douglas Pike, *PAVN: People's Army of Vietnam* (Novato, Calif., 1985); and Timothy J. Lomperis, *The War Everyone Lost—and Won* (Baton Rouge, La., 1984).

analysis of why. We need, for the period after 1954, studies comparable to those of Michael Schaller and Andrew Rotter, which place decisions on Vietnam in the context of America's regional and global policies, thus helping to clarify why Vietnam assumed an importance out of all proportion to its intrinsic worth.[43] We need a better understanding of why American leaders have been obsessed with credibility since World War II.[44] In terms of the actual conduct of the war, most of the focus thus far has been on the formulation of strategy and the conduct of military operations. It is to be hoped that Kolko's book will spur closer analysis of the political, social, and economic questions that may be more important. Studies are urgently needed based on the sort of cross-cultural expertise that characterizes the work of Bruce Cumings on the Korean war and Michael Hunt and Akira Iriye on Chinese-American and Japanese-American relations, respectively.[45]

The books reviewed here mark a start in the right direction. If they owe much to the earlier debate, they also depart from it in important ways. They are among the first works to be done by historians using a wide range of sources and historical methods. In terms of the sources used, detail presented, and sophistication of the argument, they meet the tests of Butterfield's "new Vietnam scholarship." All three make major contributions. Kahin provides an authoritative account of the evolution of the American commitment, a convincing explanation of the causes of American involvement, and often profound insight into the way in which U.S. intervention affected South Vietnamese politics. Kolko will be the point of departure for future discussion of Vietnamese politics and society. Smith reminds us, however imperfectly, that decisions made in Hanoi, Moscow, and Peking had important consequences. Perhaps the principal lesson of these books for a frequently insular American reading public is their message that the war cannot be understood apart from its Vietnamese origins and dynamics or its international dimension. It can be hoped these books will stimulate additional work that will take us to a new level of analysis, ultimately producing a clearer and fuller understanding of America's longest and most controversial war.

[43] Michael Schaller, "Securing the Great Crescent: Occupied Japan and the Origins of Containment in Southeast Asia," *Journal of American History*, 69 (September 1982): 392–414; and Andrew Rotter, "The Triangular Route to Vietnam: The United States, Great Britain, and Southeast Asia, 1945–1950," *International History Review*, 6 (August 1984): 404–23.

[44] On this point, see the commentary by John L. Gaddis in *Second Indochina War Symposium: Papers and Commentary*, John Schlight, ed. (Washington, D.C., 1986), 91–96.

[45] Bruce Cumings, *The Origins of the Korean War: Liberation and the Emergence of Separate Regimes, 1945–1947* (Princeton, N.J., 1981); Michael H. Hunt, *The Making of a Special Relationship: The United States and China to 1914* (New York, 1983); and Akira Iriye, *Power and Culture: The Japanese-American War* (Cambridge, Mass., 1981). Lomperis, *War Everyone Lost*, does this as well as anyone writing to date and offers a number of provocative interpretations.

Acknowledgments

Collins, Robert M. "The Economic Crisis of 1968 and the Waning of the 'American Century,'" *American Historical Review* 101 (1996): 396–422. Reprinted with the permission of the author.

Herring, George C. "'Peoples Quite Apart': Americans, South Vietnamese, and the War in Vietnam," *Diplomatic History* 14 (1990): 1–23. Reprinted with the permission of *Diplomatic History.*

Herring, George C. "The 'Vietnam Syndrome' and American Foreign Policy," *Virginia Quarterly Review* 57 (1981): 594–612. Reprinted with the permission of the *Virginia Quarterly Review.*

Paterson, Thomas G. "Historical Memory and Illusive Victories: Vietnam and Central America," *Diplomatic History* 12 (1988): 1–18. Reprinted with the permission of *Diplomatic History.*

LaFeber, Walter. "The Last War, the Next War, and the New Revisionists," *Democracy* 1 (1981): 93–103.

Sharpe, Kenneth E. "The Post-Vietnam Formula Under Seige: The Imperial Presidency and Central America," *Political Science Quarterly* 102 (1987): 549–69. Reprinted with the permission of the author and The Academy of Political Science.

Zagacki, Kenneth S. "Rhetoric, Failure, and the Presidency: The Case of Vietnam," *Communication Studies* 43 (1992): 42–55. Reprinted with the permission of *Communication Studies.*

Kimball, Jeffrey P. "The Stab-in-the-Back Legend and the Vietnam War," *Armed Forces and Society* 14 (1988): 433–58. Reprinted with the permission of Transaction Publishers.

Mohr, Charles. "Once Again — Did the Press Lose Vietnam?" *Columbia Journalism Review* 22 (1983): 51–56. Reprinted with the permission of the *Columbia Journalism Review.*

Patterson, Oscar, III. "An Analysis of Television Coverage of the Vietnam War," *Journal of Broadcasting* 28 (1984): 397–404. Reprinted with the permission of the Broadcasting Education Association.

Wyatt, Clarence R. "'At the Cannon's Mouth': The American Press and the Vietnam War," *Journalism History* 13 (1986): 104–113. Reprinted with the permission of the Greenspun School of Communication.

Franklin, H. Bruce. "The POW/MIA Myth," *Atlantic Monthly* 268 (1991): 45–47, 50, 52–54, 58, 61–62, 65, 68, 71–76, 78–81. Reprinted with the permission of The Atlantic Monthly Company.

Dean, Eric T., Jr. "The Myth of the Troubled and Scorned Vietnam Veteran," *Journal of American Studies* 26 (1992): 59–74. Copyright notice. Reprinted with the permission of Cambridge University Press.

Jacobs, James B., and Dennis McNamara. "Vietnam Veterans and the Agent Orange Controversy," *Armed Forces and Society* 13 (1986): 57–79. Reprinted with the permission of Transaction Publishers.

Foster, Gaines M. "Coming to Terms with Defeat: Post-Vietnam America and the Post-Civil War South," *Virginia Quarterly Review* 66 (1990): 17–35. Reprinted with the permission of the *Virginia Quarterly Review*.

Divine, Robert A. "Vietnam Reconsidered," *Diplomatic History* 12 (1988): 79–93. Reprinted with the permission of *Diplomatic History*.

Hess, Gary R. "The Unending Debate: Historians and the Vietnam War," *Diplomatic History* 18 (1994): 239–64. Reprinted with the permission of *Diplomatic History*.

Herring, George C. "America and Vietnam: The Debate Continues," *American Historical Review* 92 (1987): 350–62. Reprinted with the permission of the author.

ERRATA

The acknowledgment for H. Bruce Franklin's article should read as follows:
"The POW/MIA Myth," excerpted from H. Bruce Franklin, M.I.A. or Mythmaking in America (Rutgers University Press); first published in *Atlantic Monthly*, December 1991. Copyright ©1991 by H. Bruce Franklin. Reprinted by permission of the author.